# Minnesota Symposia on Child Psychology

Volume 36

# Minnesota Symposia on Child Psychology

## The Origins and Organization of Adaptation and Maladaptation

**Volume 36**

Edited by

Dante Cicchetti
and
Glenn I. Roisman

**WILEY**

John Wiley & Sons, Inc.

# Contents

# Preface

DANTE CICCHETTI AND GLENN I. ROISMAN

The chapters in this volume are elaborations of presentations made at the 36th Minnesota Symposium on Child Psychology, October 15–17, 2009. The title of the symposium was "The Origins and Organization of Adaptation and Maladaptation: A Festschrift Honoring the Work of Byron Egeland and Alan Sroufe on the Minnesota Parent-Child Longitudinal Study" (MPCLS). It is no coincidence that the Minnesota Symposium was chosen by the faculty of the Institute of Child Development as the proper forum for this celebratory recognition of the life's work of these two outstanding scholars, who, both individually and collectively, have made groundbreaking contributions to the disciplines of developmental psychology and developmental psychopathology. As co-editors of this volume, we were privileged to be mentored by both Egeland and Sroufe, not only while matriculating in Minnesota's PhD programs in clinical and child psychology, but also throughout our careers to date. Our collaborative work on this Festschrift volume has been a labor of love.

Beginning in 1975, Egeland and his colleague, pediatrician Amos Deinard, recruited a sample of primarily single women who were living in poverty and were in their third trimester of pregnancy. Careful assessments of maternal characteristics, their life circumstances, and prenatal care were conducted. Upon the birth of each of the infants, detailed assessments of child adaptation and life circumstances were completed. This auspicious beginning set the stage for the unfolding of one of the most innovative and influential longitudinal studies in the history of developmental psychology, the MPCLS (see Chapter 1 by Mangelsdorf in this volume).

Shortly thereafter, Egeland and Sroufe joined forces to launch what at present is a 35-year (and counting) investigation of the developmental pathways to adaptive and maladaptive functioning from infancy through adulthood. (See the Sroufe, Egeland, Carlson, & Collins, 2005, APA award-winning volume *The Development of the Person* for an excellent description of the MPCLS.)

Throughout, their research has been characterized by a focus on individual patterns of adaptation with regard to the salient issues of the particular developmental period examined and a measurement approach that is based on multiple sources of information. Long before this approach became more widely advocated, Egeland and Sroufe utilized information gathered from multiple sources (e.g., behavioral observations, experimental tasks, interviews), by multiple informants (i.e., counselors, teachers, parents, children, peers), and in multiple contexts (e.g., home, laboratory, school, camp). They demonstrated that in the prospective investigation of individual patterns of adaptation, it is essential that broadband patterns of competence be assessed (i.e., those that tap the intersection of affect, cognition, social, representational, and behavioral development). The results emanating from the MPCLS have shown that some patterns of adaptation may serve as risk factors for later psychopathology, whereas others may function as protective factors in the face of later risk and/or adversity.

Impressively, for the more than three decades that Egeland and Sroufe have prospectively examined the complex developmental course of individual adaptation, ranging from competence to major disturbance, the methodological and conceptual/theoretical standards set by these investigators has remained at the highest level (see Chapter 4 by Roisman & Haydon in this volume). Parents and children have undergone frequent assessments, and the environment in which the families reside has been measured in a detailed and comprehensive fashion.

Research from the MPCLS has revealed that a system can maintain continuity despite the emergence of new forms that are discontinuous manifestations. Moreover, a broadband assessment approach has helped account for the branching of a disturbance into a variety of disordered manifestations (i.e., known as *multifinality*). In addition, the implementation of their broadband measurement strategy enabled Sroufe and Egeland to discover that there are multiple pathways to the same outcomes: normal, psychopathological, or resilient (i.e., known as *equifinality*).

Through their focus on the interface between normal and abnormal development, Sroufe and Egeland also have made a major contribution to the emergence of the field of developmental psychopathology. According to their organizational perspective, the same principles of differentiation, integration, and self-organization are thought to govern normal and abnormal development, both of the brain and of behavior.

In this regard, the work of Egeland and Sroufe has contributed greatly to the study of risk, psychopathology, and resilience. For example, a subsample of children in the MPCLS were maltreated during their early years of life and followed prospectively. Among their discoveries in the area of maltreatment, Egeland and Sroufe found that a combination of risk and protective factors from different levels of the ecology determined the likelihood of maltreatment occurring. Thus, a combination of high stress and parental psychopathology, not parental pathology per se, was highly predictive of maltreatment. Moreover, the consequences of various subtypes of maltreatment were shown to be devastating, even when controlling for similar salient demographic variables (such as poverty, low socioeconomic status, etc.) that characterized nonmaltreated comparison children. In addition, foster care placement exerted a negative impact on child adaptation, even after controlling for child maltreatment, cognitive ability, social class background, and life stress. Furthermore, research on the MPCLS revealed that the intergenerational transmission of maltreatment was not inevitable. Formerly maltreated individuals who broke the cycle had received long-term psychotherapy, had a supportive spouse, and manifested less dissociative psychopathology than those individuals who perpetuated maltreatment across generations.

In one of the first demonstrations of translational research, based on findings from MPCLS research on the antecedents and quality of attachment, Egeland and Marti Erickson developed project STEEP (Steps to Effective Enjoyable Parenting), a relationship-based preventive intervention program for improving attachment security in high-risk parents and their young children. Such translational research has come to be viewed as critical by federal research granting agencies who stress the importance of reducing the individual, familial, and societal burden of disadvantage and disorder.

Research on the MPCLS also has utilized principles from developmental psychopathology to investigate pathways to antisocial behavior, anxiety, borderline personality, conduct disorder, depression, dissociation, post-traumatic stress disorder (PTSD), and alcohol and substance use and abuse problems. Psychopathology was viewed as developmental deviation and, as such, process questions assumed a central focus in the MPCLS research on the determinants of psychopathology (see Chapter 7 by Yates, Burt, & Troy in this volume). For example, relationship difficulties and negative mental representations often were found to play important roles in the development of the quality of adaptation (see Chapter 5 by Collins, LaFreniere & Simpson; Chapter 8 by Jacobvitz, Hazen, Zaccagnino, Messina, & Beverung; and Chapter 6 by Kobak & Zajac, in this volume). A recurrent finding in the many publications from the MPCLS is that the quality of care a child receives, and the nature of her or his early experience, is very important (see Chapter 2 by Thompson and Chapter 3 by Vaughn and Shin, in this volume).

Although individuals are always affected by their cumulative history of experiences, the work of Alan and Byron has demonstrated that the child's quality of care does not determine a child's outcome. Rather, secure attachments and positive relationships increase the probability that competent adaptation will ensue. Change is possible throughout the course of lifespan development. Transitional turning points offer new challenges and new opportunities for individuals. In fact, these periods of developmental transition may provide special opportunities for change and serve as sensitive periods for intervention.

Because change is constrained by prior development, the longer an individual proceeds along a negative trajectory, the more difficult it becomes to correct the ontogenetic course. Consequently, early interventions are important in order to prevent individuals from becoming entrenched in a maladaptive pathway that leads to diagnosable psychopathology (see Chapter 9 by Toth, Pianta, & Erickson, in this volume).

Egeland and Sroufe have conceptualized resilience—the attainment of positive adaptation in the face of significant adversity—as a dynamic developmental process and not as an inherent inborn characteristic. Their depiction of resilience, undergirded by an organizational developmental perspective, has exerted a prominent influence on the field and has played a critical role in the design and implementation of present-day studies of processes underlying resilience (see Chapter 11 by Cicchetti and Chapter 10 by Belsky & Pluess, in this volume).

We would be greatly remiss if we neglected to note Sroufe and Egeland's incredible history of mentoring graduate students, many of whom have gone on to develop their own productive research careers and all of whom left the Institute of Child Development with the Minnesota stamp of competence through the supportive and caring mentoring of Egeland and Sroufe. On behalf of all the former PhDs mentored by Sroufe and Egeland, we offer our deepest thanks and appreciation. It simply doesn't get any better than working with them.

There is no way that any preface could capture or do justice to the yeoman contributions that Egeland and Sroufe have made to the field. It is extremely rare to have one's scientific work exert such far-ranging impact on two separate fields—developmental psychology and developmental psychopathology. Individually, Egeland and Sroufe have each made signature contributions. Although it is a rare feat in academic circles, two extraordinary psychologists brought their vast individual talents together to create a genuine work of scientific beauty and deep significance.

As editors, we are grateful to the authors for their enthusiastic participation and for providing thoughtful chapters that are illustrative of the far-reaching impact that the work of Egeland and Sroufe has had on the field. Special thanks are due to Betty Carlson, Judy Cook, Michelle Dodds, Michelle Englund, and Brian Peterson for their essential contributions to the work of the MPCLS. Likewise, each of the postdoctoral, graduate, and undergraduate students who have worked on the MPCLS deserve deep gratitude. Current and former faculty and past and present graduate students added much history, spirit, and enthusiasm to the symposium and celebration. In addition, Danielle Bordeleau, Dolly

Britzman, Jeanne Cowan, and Eric Hart provided their invaluable and much-appreciated support and planning abilities.

We also appreciate the support provided by Nicki Crick, Director of the Institute, for her efforts on behalf of this Festschrift, and to Andy Collins and Rich Weinberg for their wonderful help in planning aspects of the gala celebration. Sponsors of this celebration included the Institute of Child Development and the Leon and Marian Yarrow Endowment for Research in Social Relationships.

We owe a debt of gratitude to the late D. O. Hebb, the eminent physiological psychologist, for providing us with an inspirational conclusion to this preface. In 1974, Hebb published a paper in the *American Psychologist* entitled "What Psychology Is All About." In this paper, Hebb lamented how most of the papers published in scientific journals were trivial and devoid of ideas. Hebb felt that, despite being well-done, most of these papers would never be heard from again and would have a transient impact on the field. He went on to state a useful maxim that he had learned from a colleague—namely, "What's not worth doing is not worth doing well." Quite clearly, what Egeland and Sroufe have undertaken *is* worth doing, and they have done it extraordinarily well!

## REFERENCE

Sroufe, L. A., Egeland, B., Carlson, E. A., & Collins, W. A. (2005). *The development of the person: The Minnesota study of risk and adaptation from birth to adulthood.* New York, NY: Guilford Press.

# Contributors

**Jay Belsky, PhD**
Robert M. and Natalie Reid Dorn
    Professor
Department of Human and
    Community Development
University of California, Davis
Director, Institute for the Study of
    Children, Families, and Social
    Issues
Birkbeck University of London
London, UK

**Lauren Beverung**
Doctoral Candidate/Assistant
    Instructor
Department of Human Development
    and Family Sciences
The University of Texas at Austin

**Keith B. Burt, PhD**
Assistant Professor
Psychology Department
University of Vermont

**Dante Cicchetti, PhD**
McKnight Presidential Chair of
    Child Psychology and Psychiatry
    and William Harris Professor
Institute of Child Development
University of Minnesota

**W. Andrew Collins, PhD**
Professor
Institute of Child Development
University of Minnesota

**Martha Farrell Erickson, PhD**
Director Emeritus
Irving B. Harris Training
    Programs
University of Minnesota

**Katherine C. Haydon, PhD**
Post-Doctoral Research Associate
Department of Psychology
University of Illinois at Urbana-
    Champaign

**Nancy Hazen, PhD**
Associate Professor
Department of Human
    Development and Family
    Sciences
The University of Texas at Austin

**Deborah Jacobvitz, PhD**
Chair and Professor
Department of Human
    Development and Family
    Sciences
The University of Texas at Austin

**Roger Kobak, PhD**
Associate Professor
Department of Psychology
University of Delaware

**Peter LaFreniere, PhD**
Professor
Department of Psychology
University of Vermont

**Sarah C. Mangelsdorf, PhD**
Dean and Professor
Weinberg College of Arts and
   Sciences
Northwestern University

**Serena Messina, PhD**
Graduate Student
Department of Educational
   Psychology/Department of
   Human Development and
   Family Science
The University of Texas at
   Austin

**Robert C. Pianta, PhD**
Dean and Professor, Curry School
   of Education
Navartis U.S. Foundation
   Professor of Education
Director, Center for Advanced
   Study of Teaching and Learning
University of Virginia

**Michael Pluess, PhD**
Post-Doctoral Research
   Associate
University of California, Davis

**Glenn I. Roisman, PhD**
Associate Professor
Department of Psychology
University of Illinois at
   Urbana-Champaign

**Nana Shin, PhD**
Post-Doctoral Research Associate
Human Development and Family
   Studies
Auburn University

**Jeffry A. Simpson, PhD**
Professor
Department of Psychology
University of Minnesota

**Ross A. Thompson, PhD**
Professor
Department of Psychology
University of California, Davis

**Sheree L. Toth, PhD**
Director and Associate Professor
Mt. Hope Family Center
University of Rochester

**Michael F. Troy, PhD, LP**
Medical Director, Behavioral
   Health Services
Children's Hospitals and Clinics
   of Minnesota

**Brian E. Vaughn, PhD**
Professor
Human Development and
   Family Studies
Auburn University

**Tuppett M. Yates, PhD**
Assistant Professor
Department of Psychology
University of California, Riverside

**Maria Zaccagnino, PhD**
Institute of Psychology and
    Sociology of Communication
    (IPSC)
University of Lugano, Switzerland

**Kristyn Zajac, PhD**
Assistant Professor
Medical University of
    South Carolina
Department of Psychiatry
    and Behavioral Sciences
National Crime Victims
    Research and Treatment
    Center

CHAPTER

# 1

# The Early History and Legacy of the Minnesota Parent-Child Longitudinal Study

Sarah C. Mangelsdorf

"To raise new questions, new possibilities, to regard old problems from a new angle, requires creative imagination and marks real advance in science."

— Albert Einstein

It is often said that many great acts of creative genius are the result of twists of fate and happenstance. To hear Byron Egeland describe the history of the Minnesota Parent-Child Longitudinal Study (MPCLS), this is the sense you get, that it was all good fortune. However, it was *more* than luck. Egeland tells how, as a new professor at the University of Minnesota in 1973, he was invited by a pediatrician he knew named Amos Deinard to give a talk at the Minneapolis Public Health Department about screening instruments. Deinard was a professor at the University of Minnesota Medical School who worked part-time at the Minneapolis Public Health Clinic. After Egeland gave his talk, he, Deinard, and another pediatrician, Ellen Elkin, got into a discussion about child abuse. Egeland claims, in his offhand way, that he said, "Someone needs to do a prospective study of child abuse." Up to that time all of the research on child abuse had been done retrospectively. That afternoon Dr. Elkin called Egeland on the phone and said, "Why don't we do that prospective study? One of my friends from graduate school is the Director of the Center of Maternal and Child Health, and I ran the idea by him and he likes it." (Egeland, 2010, personal communication).

Egeland, Deinard, and Elkins subsequently wrote a proposal outlining a prospective study of child abuse, which they submitted to the Center of Maternal and Child Health. The grant was initially turned down because the reviewers thought the proposed sample of 250 was too small for them to find many cases of child abuse. However, like any passionate scientists, they revised their proposal and resubmitted it. It was funded in 1975 for three years, and so began the longitudinal study that is known today as the Minnesota Parent-Child Longitudinal Study (MPCLS), which has been ongoing for 35 years!

One of the strongest influences on the theoretical framework for that first grant was the work of Arnold Sameroff. In 1973, Sameroff was a visiting professor at the Institute of Child Development at the University of Minnesota, and he shared a preprint with Egeland of his paper with Michael Chandler (Sameroff & Chandler, 1975) outlining their transactional model of parent-child relationships and child development. This paper proved to be very influential in helping Egeland and Deinard shape their thinking about child abuse.

In 1975, when Egeland and his colleagues first began recruiting subjects, they used prior research on child abuse to inform them of some of the risk factors for child abuse and selected mothers accordingly. Specifically, they recruited mothers who were poor, young (average age at birth of the child was 20.5 years; range was 12–34 years), poorly educated (41% had not completed high school), and the majority (62%) were single parents.

The early findings from the project were quite consistent with the Sameroff and Chandler (1975) model; indeed, there emerged "no simple linear cause of child maltreatment" (Egeland, personal communication, 2010). Rather than finding that parental psychopathology, or parental expectations or beliefs directly predicted child maltreatment, Egeland and his colleagues found that high life stress interacted with maternal characteristics (e.g., anger and hostility) to predict child abuse, but neither factor alone was predictive.

Early on in his longitudinal study, Egeland approached Alan Sroufe at the Institute of Child Development (Egeland was then in the Department of Educational Psychology at Minnesota) about becoming involved with the project because of Sroufe's expertise in early socioemotional development. Sroufe recommended that two of his graduate students, Everett Waters and Brian Vaughn, should begin working with Egeland on the longitudinal study. Waters, as an undergraduate at Johns Hopkins University, had worked as a research assistant with Mary Ainsworth on the study in which she first developed the Strange Situation procedure (Ainsworth, Blehar, Waters, & Wall, 1978). Waters brought his interest in, and training about, attachment with him to Minnesota. Waters and Sroufe had already collaborated on studies of attachment in middle-class samples (e.g., Waters, Wippman, & Sroufe, 1979), so the extension of the study of attachment relationships to Egeland's high-risk sample was a natural one.

In the 36th Minnesota Symposium on Child Psychology in October 2009, leading scholars in developmental psychology presented work that in every case was directly influenced by the scholarship of Egeland, Sroufe, and the tremendous legacy of the MPCLS, or what was referred to for many years as the "mother-child project." However, before discussing how the chapters in this volume are related directly to the theoretical and empirical stage set by Egeland and Sroufe and their longitudinal study, it is important to examine the development courses of these great scholars in order to understand how they came to study what they study. There is, after all, to quote a famous developmental psychologist, "coherence in individual development" (Sroufe, 1979).

Byron Egeland received his PhD in 1966 from the University of Iowa. His dissertation was entitled "The Relationship of Intelligence, Visual-Motor Skills and Psycholinguistic Abilities with Achievement in the First Grade." His first article, published when he was an assistant professor at Syracuse University in 1966, was entitled "Influence of Examiner and Examinee Anxiety on WISC Performance" (Egeland, 1967). Now 44 years later, we may think it strange that one of the world's experts on child maltreatment began his research career studying test performance. In fact, in looking at where he began as a researcher, and where he is today, you might not see any evidence of continuity in his intellectual interests. However, if you read Egeland's first published paper, you discover that he was not *just* looking at test performance. Rather, he was examining how anxiety, of the child and of the examiner, and the interaction, or transaction, between the child's and the examiner's level of anxiety predicted children's test performance (Egeland, 1967).

If you read many of Egeland's other papers published since his first publication, some themes appear repeatedly. For example, Egeland's interest in the study of anxiety remains to this day. In 1997 he and Alan published a paper with child psychiatrist Susan Warren examining child and adolescent anxiety disorders and attachment. In this paper they used attachment insecurity to predict anxiety in 17-year-olds. Remarkably, they found evidence for an association between anxious-resistant attachment and anxiety at age 17 (Warren, Huston, Egeland, & Sroufe, 1997).

Then, almost a decade later, Egeland and his former graduate student Michelle Bosquet published a paper examining the development and stability of anxiety symptoms from infancy through adolescence (Bosquet & Egeland, 2006). Using the MPCLS they were able to document that anxiety is moderately stable from childhood to adolescence. Interestingly, heightened neonatal biobehavioral reactivity and poor regulation predicted emotion regulation difficulties in preschool, which in turn predicted anxiety symptoms in childhood. In addition, insecure attachment relationships in infancy predicted negative peer relationship representations in preadolescence, and these representations predicted anxiety in adolescence.

Thus, it is clear that Egeland's interest in anxiety has been consistent across more than 40 years. Similarly, his belief that outcomes are multiply determined is a theme that runs through much of his research. For example, in one of the first publications to come out of the mother-child project, Everett Waters, Brian Vaughn, and Egeland published a paper entitled "Individual Differences in Infant–Mother Attachment

Relationships at Age One: Antecedents in Neonatal Behavior in an Urban, Economically Disadvantaged Sample." In this paper they concluded that neonatal difficulties must interact with difficult environments to produce anxious attachments (Waters, Vaughn, & Egeland, 1980). So here, just as in his first empirical publication, Egeland was examining how characteristics of the child interacted with characteristics of the environment to predict developmental adaptation. In a way, his focus has *always* been on transactional models of development. This same transactional approach is seen very clearly in one of Egeland's most widely cited papers, written in collaboration with his then-graduate student Ellen Farber, in which they further explored factors associated with both the development of, and stability and change in, the security of attachment relationships (Egeland & Farber, 1984). Consistent with the transactional model that has been the touchstone of much of Egeland's work, they found that characteristics of mothers, infants, and the larger social context were all predictive of attachment security and its stability over time.

Egeland was way ahead of his time, not only in launching a prospective study of child maltreatment, but also because of his multiple risk factors and transactional approach to the study of maltreatment. He was very clear at the outset of the study that he did not believe that any single factor was responsible for abuse and instead examined multiple risk factors (e.g., mother's history of abuse, life stress, neonatal behavior) and protective factors (e.g., social support, loving relationships). Similarly, his approach to the study of the development of parent-child attachment relationships has always been equally nuanced (e.g., Egeland & Sroufe, 1981).

One of the most influential papers based on the MPCLS is an article by Egeland, Deborah Jacobvitz, and Sroufe entitled "Breaking the Cycle of Abuse" (Egeland, Jacobvitz, & Sroufe, 1988). In that paper they identified variables that distinguished mothers who had been abused as children who did not go on to abuse their children from those who did. They found that mothers who had been abused as children, but who did not go on to abuse, were significantly more likely to have had emotional support from a nonparent adult as a child, to have participated in therapy during any period of their lives, and to have had a nonabusive, emotionally supportive relationship with a mate, as compared with mothers who had been abused and *did* go on to abuse their children. This paper does a splendid job of highlighting both why early experience matters and why early experience is not immutable. This theme, that developmental outcomes are multiply determined, is part of the richness of the legacy of the scholarship of Egeland and the MPCLS and is clearly articulated in some of the chapters in this volume, most notably in Cicchetti's chapter on maltreated children (Cicchetti, 2011).

In looking for coherence in Sroufe's intellectual trajectory, similar patterns emerge. Sroufe received his PhD in Clinical Psychology from the University of Wisconsin–Madison in 1967. His first publication in 1967, co-authored with his advisor Peter Lang and entitled "The Effects of Feedback and Instructional Set on the Control of Cardiac-Rate Variability," was not a developmental study, but evidence of his expertise in heart-rate research is echoed again in subsequent papers with Everett Waters, in which they examined how heart rate was related to gaze aversion and avoidance in infants (Sroufe & Waters, 1977), and Brian Vaughn when they studied heart rate and crying in infancy (Vaughn & Sroufe, 1979). However, prior to the publication of those papers, Sroufe's first paper on emotional development was "The Development of Laughter in the First Year of Life" (Sroufe & Wunsch, 1972). This was followed by studies on smiling, stranger anxiety, and almost every other aspect of early emotional development you can imagine, including his work with Dante Cicchetti on affective development in Down's Syndrome children (e.g., Cicchetti & Sroufe, 1976).

Sroufe's fascination and deep understanding of socio-emotional development in childhood is seen throughout his career, from his first sole authored book, *Knowing and Enjoying Your Baby* (Sroufe, 1977), to his more recent book, *Emotional Development: The Organization of Emotional Life in the Early Years* (Sroufe, 1997). The salience of emotion as an organizing principle is clearly echoed across the papers he co-authored based on the MPCLS as well as the book published on the longitudinal study, *The Development of the Person: The Minnesota Study of Risk and Adaptation from Birth to Adulthood* (Sroufe, Egeland, Carlson, & Collins, 2005).

We see this theme of emotion as an organizing construct highlighted in Ross Thompson's chapter in this volume (Thompson, 2011).

To those who know Sroufe as one of the foremost experts in the world on socioemotional development, it may come as a bit of a surprise to know that one of his earliest publications appeared in 1973 in *The New England Journal of Medicine* and was entitled "Treating Problem Children with Stimulant Drugs" (Sroufe & Stewart, 1973). In this paper he questions studies of the effects of stimulants on hyperactive children and ends by suggesting alternative means of managing problem children. Later in the 1980s and 1990s, Sroufe took up this cause again when the World Health Organization issued a report noting that the use of Ritalin to treat children with ADHD had increased in the United States at a rate many times higher than that in other Western industrialized nations. In 1990 Sroufe published a paper with Deborah Jacobvitz, Mark Stewart, and Nancy Leffert about the use, and overuse, of Ritalin and related drugs to treat attentional and hyperactivity problems (Jacobvitz, Sroufe, Stewart, & Leffert, 1990). However, few of us who read the paper in 1990 knew that this issue had been a passionate concern of Sroufe's for almost 20 years by the time the article was published.

A theme that emerges repeatedly in Sroufe's papers is the idea that relationships are carried forward, that our relationship history influences not only how we treat others, but also how others treat us. A good illustration of this theme is a paper Sroufe and Michael Troy published in 1987 that demonstrated that children played differently with other children depending not only on their own attachment history but also on the attachment history of their play partner (Troy & Sroufe, 1987). Similarly, in Frosso Motti's dissertation, she was able to document that teachers in the laboratory preschool at the Institute of Child Development treated children differently depending on their attachment histories. Consistent with Bowlby's (1969/1982) theory that childhood experiences serve as a prototype for subsequent adult love relationships, Glenn Roisman, Andy Collins, Sroufe, and Egeland published a paper (2005) in which they documented that young adults who had experienced a secure relationship with their primary caregiver in infancy were more likely to produce coherent discourse regarding their current romantic relationship and to have a higher-quality interaction when the couple was observed in conflict and collaboration tasks. In the chapters in this volume by Roisman and Haydon, Kobak and Zajac, and Jacobvitz, Hazen, Zaccagnino, Messina, and Beverung, this theme—of how relationships are carried forward—is clearly elaborated.

Another legacy of Egeland and Sroufe's research is the emphasis on the importance of early intervention and prevention. Indeed much of the work that researchers such as Sheree Toth, Martha Erickson, and Robert Pianta have done over their careers has been focused on prevention science and how studies like the MPCLS can inform prevention efforts (e.g., Erickson & Egeland, 2004; Hamre & Pianta, 2005).

In addition to conducting research on prevention, this theme of prevention is reflected every day in the life's work of many of Sroufe and Egeland's former students, who are clinicians working in clinics, schools, hospitals, and private practices. Because of their training in developmental psychopathology, and their relationship-based perspective on emotional development, they are undoubtedly some of the best clinicians working with children and families in the field today. Thus, these clinicians, along with the long history of groundbreaking publications, are an incredible legacy of the MPCLS and of Egeland and Sroufe.

A quote by Esther Thelen perhaps best captures the legacy of the MPCLS: "The premiere developmental question is, of course, the nature of the transition from one developmental stage to another—the emergence of new forms. How does a system retain continuity and yet produce discontinuous manifestations?" (Thelen, 1989). Thanks to the work of Egeland and Sroufe, and their many students, we now have a very good idea about ways in which there is *continuity* from early experience and ways in which there is *lawful change* in social and personality development.

## REFERENCES

Ainsworth, M. D. S., Blehar, M. C., Waters, E., & Wall, S. (1978). *Patterns of attachment: A psychological study of the Strange Situation*. Hillsdale, NJ: Erlbaum.

Bowlby, J. (1968/1982). *Attachment and loss: Vol. 1, Attachment*. New York, NY: Basic Books.

Bosquet, M., & Egeland, B. (2006). The development and maintenance of anxiety symptoms from infancy through adolescence in a longitudinal sample. *Development and Psychopathology, 18*, 517–550.

Cicchetti, D. (2011). Pathways to resilient functioning in maltreated children: From single-level to multilevel investigations. In D. Cicchetti & G. I. Roisman (Eds.), *Minnesota symposia on child psychology: The origins and organization of adaptation and maladaptation, Vol. 36*. Hoboken, NJ: Wiley.

Cicchetti, D., & Sroufe, L. A. (1976). The relationship between affective and cognitive development in Down's syndrome infants. *Child Development, 47*, 920–929.

Egeland, B. (1967). Influence of examiner and examinee anxiety on WISC performance. *Psychological Reports, 21*, 409–414.

Egeland, B., & Farber, E. A. (1984). Infant-mother attachment: Factors related to its development and changes over time. *Child Development, 55*, 753–771.

Egeland, B., Jacobvitz, D., & Sroufe, L.A. (1988). Breaking the cycle of abuse. *Child Development, 59*, 1080–1088.

Egeland, B., & Sroufe, L.A. (1981). Attachment and early maltreatment. *Child Development, 52*, 1080–1088.

Erickson, M. F., & Egeland, B. (2004). Linking theory and research to practice: The Minnesota Longitudinal Study of Parents and Children and the STEEP program. *Clinical Psychologist, 8*, 5–9.

Jacobvitz, D., Hazen, N., Zaccagnino, M., Messina, S., & Beverung, L. (2011). Frightening maternal behavior, infant disorganization, and risks for psychopathology. In D. Cicchetti & G. I. Roisman (Eds.), *Minnesota symposia on child psychology: The origins and organization of adaptation and maladaptation, Vol. 36*. Hoboken, NJ: Wiley.

Jacobvitz, D., Sroufe, L. A., Stewart, M., & Leffert, N. (1990). Treatment of attentional and hyperactivity problems in children with sympathomimetic drugs: A comprehensive review. *Journal of the American Academy of Child Psychiatry, 29*, 677–688.

Hamre, B. K., & Pianta, R. C. (2005). Can instructional and emotional support in the first-grade classroom make a difference for children at risk of school failure? *Child Development, 76*, 949–967.

Kobak, R., & Zajac, K. (2011). Rethinking adolescent states of mind: A relationship/lifespan view of attachment and psychopathology. In D. Cicchetti &

G. I. Roisman (Eds.), *Minnesota symposia on child psychology: The origins and organization of adaptation and maladaptation*, Vol. 36. Hoboken, NJ: Wiley.

Roisman, G. I., Collins, W. A., Sroufe, L. A., & Egeland, B. (2005). Predictors of young adults' representations of and behavior in their current romantic relationship: Prospective tests of the prototype hypothesis. *Attachment and Human Development, 7*, 105–121.

Roisman, G. I., & Haydon, K. C. (2011). Earned-security in retrospect: Emerging insights from longitudinal, experimental, and taxometric investigations. In D. Cicchetti & G. I. Roisman (Eds.), *Minnesota symposia on child psychology: The origins and organization of adaptation and maladaptation*, Vol. 36. Hoboken, NJ: Wiley.

Sameroff, A., & Chandler, M. (1975). Reproductive risk and the continuum of caretaking casualty. In F. D Horowitz, E. M. Hetherington, S. Scarr-Salapatek, & G. M. Siegel (Eds.), *Review of child development research*, Vol. 4. Chicago, IL: University of Chicago Press.

Sroufe, L. A. (1977). *Knowing and enjoying your baby*. New York, NY: Prentice Hall/Spectrum.

Sroufe, L. A. (1979). The coherence of individual development: Early care, attachment, and subsequent developmental issues. *American Psychologist, 34*, 834–841.

Sroufe, L. A., Egeland, B., Carlson, E., & Collins, W. A. (2005). *The development of the person: The Minnesota Study of Risk and Adaptation from Birth to Adulthood*. New York, NY: Guilford Press.

Sroufe, L. A., & Stewart, M. A. (1973). Treating problem children with stimulant drugs. *New England Journal of Medicine, 289*, 407–413.

Sroufe, L. A., & Waters, E. (1977). Heart rate as a convergent measure in clinical and developmental research. *Merrill-Palmer Quarterly, 23*, 3–27.

Sroufe, L. A., & Wunsch, J. P. (1972). The development of laughter in the first year of life. *Child Development, 43*, 1326–1344.

Thelen, E. (1989). Self-organization in developmental processes: Can systems approaches work? In M. R. Gunnar & E. Thelen (Eds.), *Systems and development: The Minnesota Symposia on Child Psychology*, Vol. 22. Hillsdale, NJ: Erlbaum.

Thompson, R. A. (2011). The emotionate child. In D. Cicchetti & G. I. Roisman (Eds.), *Minnesota symposia on child psychology: The origins and organization of adaptation and maladaptation*, Vol. 36. Hoboken, NJ: Wiley.

Troy, M. F., & Sroufe, L. A. (1987). Victimization among preschoolers: Role of attachment relationship history. *Journal of the American Academy of Child and Adolescent Psychiatry 26:* 166–172.

Vaughn, B., & Sroufe, L. A. (1979). The temporal relationship between infant HR acceleration and crying in an aversive situation. *Child Development, 50,* 565–567.

Warren, S. L., Huston, L., Egeland, B., & Sroufe, L. A. (1997). Child and adolescent anxiety disorders and early attachment. *Journal of the American Academy of Child and Adolescent Psychiatry, 36,* 637–644.

Waters, E., Vaughn, B. E., & Egeland, B. R. (1980). Individual differences in mother-infant attachment relationships at age one: Antecedents in neonatal behavior in an urban, economically disadvantaged sample. *Child Development, 51,* 208–216.

Waters, E., Wippman, J., & Sroufe, L. A. (1979) Attachment, positive affect, and competence in the peer group: Two studies in construct validation. *Child Development 50,* pp. 821–829.

# 2

# The Emotionate Child

Ross A. Thompson

How should we understand child development? What is the child like? As long as people have written about young children, emotions have been prominent in their descriptions. Jean Jacques Rousseau described childhood in *Emile* as a time "when laughter was ever on the lips, and when the heart was ever at peace" (2008/1792, p. 63), setting the stage for Victorian and post-Victorian sentimentality concerning children. Freud characterized the id-dominated young child as being utterly consumed by irrational emotionality and the relentless pursuit of gratification until the ego develops. Proponents of the child study movement at the turn of the 20th century were concerned with the growth of moral emotions and emotional self-control as part of character development. The origins of children's emotional adjustment occupied the attention of developmental thinkers at mid-century after the cataclysm of world war. Emotion—often carefree, irrational, disorganizing, or disturbing—has long characterized public perceptions of the nature of the child, with emotional self-control a mark of growing maturity.

In contemporary thinking, however, a very different portrayal of the child has emerged. The "scientist in the crib" is a powerful metaphor for the remarkable cognitive abilities of the young child that have captured scientific and popular attention (see, e.g., Gopnik, Meltzoff, & Kuhl, 2000). Developmental scientists have discovered that young children are, from a surprisingly early age, astute observers and interpreters of the social and nonsocial world. In an era when brain development and a national concern with school readiness have shaped public discourse about childhood, scientific discoveries of early-emerging conceptual skills have focused attention on early learning and cognitive achievement. These discoveries have contributed to a current portrayal of the rational, intuitively insightful young thinker.

Yet the emotional character of the child endures in contemporary studies showing that emotionality is at the heart of early social competence, self-understanding, the growth of conscience, and moral awareness. Emotion is motivationally important to the development of cognitive competence and academic achievement, undermining the traditional distinction between the rational mind and irrational emotion. What is also new about contemporary understanding is an appreciation of the constructive influences of emotion as they are shaped by early relational experience. Whereas emotion in traditional views reflected the primitive, irrational, or egocentric character of immaturity, emotion in contemporary portrayals is seen as an essential contributor to behavioral competence as it is incorporated into and shaped by early relationships. In a sense, the "scientist in the crib" is also an affective and relational explorer, for whom cognition teamed with emotion contributes to developing capability. Attachment theory has made seminal contributions to this contemporary view of the emotionate child, especially in the work of the Minnesota Parent-Child Longitudinal Study (MPCLS) that this volume honors.

This chapter profiles contemporary work on the influence of emotion on developing competence and the significance of early relationships for its influence. In the section that follows, we consider the meaning of the "emotionate child" and the characteristics that distinguish this portrayal of childhood development from others. In the next section, research that has led to this characterization of children is summarized to illustrate the constructive functions of emotion in developing competence and the significance of relationships for this constructive influence. The growth of the emotionate child is considered next, with special emphasis on the development of emotion and emotion regulation through close relationships. In a concluding section, we consider why this matters and how an understanding of the emotionate quality of children has new implications for our thinking about early development.

## THE EMOTIONATE CHILD

What do we mean when we describe the child as "emotionate"? The following definition provides a beginning:

---

**Emotionate** (i-ˈmō-sh(ə-)nət):

1. characterized by emotional apperception, sensitivity, and/or insight (*her sympathetic response showed that she was an emotionate child*)
2. marked by special bearing upon, reference to, or involvement with emotional understanding (*an emotionate side to his nature*)

---

Describing the developing child as "emotionate" describes a child in which emotion is a prominent organizer of behavior and competence. In much the same way that describing someone as "rational" highlights the influence of reason, the term "emotionate" highlights the constructive influences of another internal process—emotion—on action and thought. "Emotionate" carries much different connotational meaning than describing the child as "emotional," which traditionally connotes impulsivity, unthinking, or lack of sophistication. The emotionate child is not a throwback to the thinking of Rousseau, Freud, and their followers. It reflects a new view of the importance of emotion in the development of behavioral competence.

This emergent portrayal of the emotionate child derives from four important conclusions from contemporary research on early development:

First, *Emotional skills predict behavioral competence in multiple developmental domains.* Emotional competence contributes to seminal achievements in early development. In longitudinal analysis, for example, Denham and her colleagues showed that an emotional competence composite (consisting of children's emotion knowledge and emotion regulation skills) at ages 3 to 4 predicted children's social competence in kindergarten (Denham, Blair, Schmidt, & DeMulder, 2002; see also

Denham et al., 2003). The security of attachment also directly predicted later social competence, but its influence was partially mediated by differences in emotional competence. Izard and his colleagues, in a longitudinal study of at-risk young children, reported that differences in emotion knowledge at age 5 predicted positive and negative social behavior and academic competence four years later, controlling for the influence of verbal ability (Izard et al., 2001; see also Trentacosta & Izard, 2007). As discussed later, emotional competence is also associated with conscience development, self-concept, and multiple features of early social cognition. Emotion is predictive of these developmental achievements because of how emotion contributes to the organization of social skills and dispositions, motivation in social and academic settings, and self-awareness.

Second, *Emotion is an entreé into others' internal experience. It also contributes to emergent self-understanding.* Emotion is one of the earliest windows into another's internal experience to develop. Before the first birthday, infants are already aware of the affective meaning of others' emotional expressions and the "aboutness" of these expressions (i.e., their referential quality), which leads to their use in social referencing (Moses, Baldwin, Rosicky, & Tidball, 2001; Thompson & Lagattuta, 2006). Emotion understanding in the second year is a foundation for understanding others' intentions, desires, and goals, and thus contributes to developing theory of mind. Emotions and their causes are prominent in young children's talk about others' internal states, and they are the basis for children's judgments of motives for good or bad behavior (Bartsch & Wellman, 1995; Wright & Bartsch, 2008). Emotions are an early gateway into understanding other mental states in people.

Emotions are also prominent in children's earliest internal self-descriptions, particularly as emotion language is linked to expressions of needs, desires, and concerns (Bretherton, Fritz, Zahn-Waxler, & Ridgeway, 1986). The emergence of self-conscious evaluative emotions (such as pride, shame, and guilt) during the second year further connects emotion with self-understanding (Lagattuta & Thompson, 2007). As discussed later, young children's earliest self-representations are strongly emotional in quality, suggesting that children perceive themselves in large measure by how they respond emotionally to events. Emotion is uniquely influential in the development of social understanding and self-awareness because of the salience of emotions and their centrality to other mental and motivational states. Emotions also constitute an early conceptual bridge between the child's personal experience and the experience of other people.

Third, *Emotion is organized and regulated by relational experience*. As Sroufe (1996) has noted, "[T]he general course of emotional development may be described as movement *from dyadic regulation to self-regulation* of emotion" (p. 151; italics in original). The importance of early relationships to emotion regulation can be observed most clearly in stress management. In a study of the responses of 18-month-olds to moderate stressors, for example, Nachmias, Gunnar, Mangelsdorf, Parritz, and Buss (1996) reported that postsession cortisol elevations were found only for temperamentally inhibited toddlers who were in insecure relationships with their mothers. For inhibited toddlers in secure relationships, the mother's presence helped to buffer the physiological effects of challenging events. In light of what is now known about the plasticity of neurobiological stress circuitry early in development, it is reasonable to conclude that caregiver responsivity contributes to the developing organization of emotion-related reactivity based on recurrent early experiences of stress like this, a conclusion supported by studies of stress reactivity in young children experiencing abuse or neglect (see Gunnar & Vasquez, 2006). Early relational experience is important not only to emotion regulation, but also to the organization of emotional experience and the development of individual emotional dispositions.

Such a conclusion is consistent with attachment theory, which views early secure or insecure relationships as significant for emotional development and emotion regulation (e.g., Cassidy, 1994; Thompson, 1994). Findings from the MPCLS indicate that early mother-child attachment security was associated with greater positive affect in social situations, less petulance and aggression, and greater empathy and socioemotional competence when children were preschoolers, and diminished risk for affective psychopathology at older ages, compared with children with insecure attachment histories (Sroufe, Egeland, Carlson, & Collins, 2005).

As discussed later, better understanding of the influence of secure attachments on emotional development is one of the most important contemporary challenges for attachment research.

Finally, *Emotion is the foundation for early social representations that are the basis for social competence.* Social cognition is emotional in quality. This also begins early, when social expectations in infancy are associated with the positive affectivity of contingent responsiveness and the emotional salience of distress-relief episodes, which also contribute to differential social expectations for mothers and fathers (Lamb & Malkin, 1986; Watson, 2001). Emotions and their regulation are central to differences in attachment security at the end of the first year, reflecting differential representations of parental sensitivity and care. Emotion is encoded into the emergence of desire psychology by which toddlers comprehend differences in goals, desires, and intentions through the emotions associated with their satisfaction or frustration (e.g., Repacholi & Gopnik, 1997). Emotion-related ascriptions are also central to the earliest trait attributions by which young children make judgments about peers as "mean" or "nice" (Giles & Heyman, 2005; Heyman & Gelman, 1999), foreshadowing the emergence of hostile attribution biases. Emotional attributions related to human welfare are foundational to young children's differentiation between moral and social conventional violations (Smetana, 1989). Because emotion is one of the earliest means by which infants and toddlers understand another's internal experience, it may be unsurprising that emotion is prominent in early social-cognitive development. But because social cognition is a bridge between social experience and later social behavior (Dweck & London, 2004), emotion becomes a fundamental organizer of the child as a social being.

The prominence of emotion in early experience has long been recognized, but its constructive influence in the organization of social perception, self-awareness, and emerging behavioral competence reflects a new appreciation of the role of emotion in early development. Although emotion always retains its capacity to disorganize and undermine effective functioning (as do dysfunctional beliefs and thinking), its organizational, representational, and motivational contributions to developing competence contribute to a new view of the emotionate nature of the developing young child.

# THE EMOTIONATE CHILD IN A RELATIONAL CONTEXT

One reason why emotion has these constructive functions is that the meaning of others' emotional expressions is represented from such an early age. Within the first six months, infants can discriminate facial and vocal expressions of emotion in their caregivers, respond affectively to them, and expect these displays to be expressively congruent (see review by Thompson & Lagattuta, 2006). Because of these early-emerging representations of emotion and its basic meaning, others' emotions color person perceptions, social interactions, and social expectations, and through referential communication they alter the infant's appraisals of other people and objects and, later, the self. Emotion has privileged influence because of its salience and because of the inter-subjectivity that is created in recurrent social situations in which infants and adults are sharing common emotional states. This enables shared emotional expression and experience to create a bridge between the baby's internal experience and that of another person as a foundation to psychological understanding of others' affective, evaluative, motivational, and mental states. To the extent that "like me" constitutes an early-emerging conceptual framework for understanding others (Meltzoff, 2007), shared emotional experience contributes to this framework along with action representation. Because these intersubjective experiences begin very early in life, they contribute to emotional appraisals that are a seminal influence on developing social representations, self-understanding, and social competence.

This leads to a second reason why emotion assumes constructive functions in psychological growth: emotional development is embedded in close relational experience. The young child's emoting occurs not just alone but also in a social context—and not just a social context but a responsive, interpretive, regulating, evaluative, and communicative human context that continuously unfolds the meaning of emotional experience for the child. In this context, emotion is observed in another and evoked in the self in ways that contribute to affectively colored representations of people, objects, experiences, and the self. In these contexts, moreover, emotional understanding gradually becomes entrained into cultural, familial, and intergenerational systems of meaning that connect emotion to moral values, social goals, attributional biases, ideal selves, relational schemas, and other conceptual networks. The relational construction of emotion meaning begins nonverbally in infancy, but with the emergence of language it proceeds in earnest as emotions are labeled, discussed, evaluated, and managed. Close relational experience thus contributes, as Sroufe (1996) notes, to the dyadic regulation of emotion, and it also contributes more generally to the social construction of emotion meaning that enlists emotion constructively—or less productively—into the development of behavioral competence.

Individual differences in relational experience thus loom large in emotional development. They contribute to differences in social expectations and emergent self-awareness and to the meaning systems with which emotional experience and understanding have become associated. More fundamentally, how relational experience has organized emotional development contributes to the emotionate nature of the child. In this respect, therefore, it is not only what relational partners *do* and *say* that guides emotional development, but also *who* provides this guidance and the nature of the child's relationship with this person.

In the pages that follow, research on the emotionate child conducted in our lab and elsewhere is summarized to describe the constructive influence of emotion on behavioral competence in a relational context. We consider first the development of conscience and prosocial motivation, then the growth of self-understanding, and finally the early development of social cognition.

## Conscience and Prosocial Motivation

Contemporary research on early conscience development offers a portrayal of the moral qualities of young children that is a stark contrast to traditional portrayals of preconventional moral judgment (Thompson, 2009). As the studies of Kochanska (e.g., Kochanska, Koenig, Barry, Kim, & Yoon, 2010) and others have shown, young children are motivated to cooperate because of relational incentives within the parent-child relationship, their developing representations of behavioral standards, the emergence of a "moral self" that values behaving in a responsible fashion, temperamental qualities (including fear and effortful control) that contribute to self-control, and their self-initiated guilty feelings following misbehavior (see Thompson, Meyer, & McGinley, 2006, for a review). These studies suggest that much more than parents' explicit rewards and punishments are important to the growth of morality in young children.

In Kochanska's research, a "mutually responsive orientation" between mothers and their young children is a crucial relational resource for conscience development (Kochanska, 2002). This describes a relationship of reciprocal cooperation characterized by mutual responsiveness and shared positive emotion. This relationship is important to conscience because it sensitizes young children to the mutual obligations of close relationships and creates in the child a willing, eager receptivity to the adult's socialization initiatives. Many studies with children from a range of ages have confirmed that mother-child relationships characterized by such an orientation predict greater advances in conscience development compared to children in relationships without this orientation (see Kochanska, 2002; Thompson et al., 2006, for reviews).

Attachment theorists recognize a mutually responsive orientation as one of the characteristics of a secure attachment, a conclusion that has been confirmed by findings from the MPCLS and other research (see Sroufe et al., 2005). Attachment security is a relational resource to conscience development that is influential either indirectly (such as when it interacts with the child's temperament) or directly. Several studies report that securely-attached young children are more advanced in conscience development (Kochanska, 1995; Laible & Thompson, 2000). But a secure attachment can also moderate the influence of specific parental socialization practices on cooperative conduct. In a longitudinal study, for example, Kochanska, Aksan, Knaack, and Rhines (2004) found that for securely-attached children, the parent's responsiveness and gentle discipline predicted later conscience, but for insecurely-attached children there was no such association. The moderating influence of security can also buffer negative parenting practices, with parental power assertion leading to children's later resentful opposition and antisocial conduct for insecure dyads, but not for secure ones (see Kochanska, Barry, Stellern, & O'Bleness, 2009). Taken together, these findings suggest that as valuable as are broad indicators of relational quality in the development of conscience, it is important also to understand how specific relational processes function within these relationships to shape young children's moral sensibility.

Our own research has focused on parent-child conversation as an important forum for values transmission and for psychological understanding in young children. The view that parent-child conversation is important to moral socialization has deep roots in developmental theory, particularly in the influence of induction discipline on moral internalization in middle childhood. With new research on conscience development, however, parent-child conversation in early childhood would seem to be especially important to the growth of moral awareness, because this is when preschoolers are developing representations of relational processes and of themselves as moral beings. Our research has focused on parent-child conversations in two contexts. The first is during conflict episodes, the traditional focus of moral socialization research, when parents use verbal arguments to persuade, coerce, negotiate, or otherwise enlist their child's cooperation. The second are conversations outside of the discipline context, in which parents and children reflect on previous episodes of misconduct and good behavior, as a potentially less threatening forum for communicating values in which both partners can discuss the reasons for good or bad conduct. In both circumstances, young children are presented with parental messages concerning responsible behavior and, more importantly, the reasons for acting in that way.

In our initial study, conversations between 4-year-olds and their mothers about past events in which the child either misbehaved or behaved appropriately were recorded and analyzed (Laible & Thompson, 2000). These conversations resemble the everyday discussions shared by mothers and their young children about past behavior, and mothers nominated incidents from the recent past for discussion with the experimenter's help. The conversational transcripts were coded for mothers' references to rules, the consequences of actions, moral evaluative statements (e.g., "that was a nice thing to do"), people's feelings, and other discourse elements. Later, children were observed in an assessment of conscience (from Kochanska & Aksan, 1995) in which their compliance with a maternal prohibition was observed when mothers were absent. Independent measures of the mother-child relationship—their shared positive affect during the laboratory visit and the security of attachment—were also obtained.

The central finding of this study was that mothers who more frequently discussed people's feelings in their conversations, along with providing morally evaluative statements, had children who were more advanced in conscience development. Attachment security and greater positive affect in mother-child interaction were also predictive of children's conscience, and mothers in secure relationships talked more about people's feelings during their conversations with their children. Thus the role of emotion in early moral sensibility revealed in this study is somewhat different than the fear of punishment and anxiety over loss of love commonly emphasized in traditional moral development theory (Thompson, 2009). Maternal comments that heighten young children's sensitivity to the feelings of other people (or the mother's or child's emotions), in the context of an emotionally warm mother-child relationship, are associated with conscience development.

These findings have been replicated in other research. In a follow-up study, measures of mother-child discourse during conflict episodes at home and in the lab when children were 2 1/2 years old were coded in a similar manner, and children were observed at age 3 in a related measure of conscience development (Laible, 2004; Laible & Thompson, 2002). In this prospective longitudinal study, we again found that maternal conversational references to feelings during lab conflict episodes predicted heightened conscience six months later. In both studies, although maternal references to rules and the consequences of behavior were coded, these maternal discourse elements were *never* predictive of conscience development. In another study, 2- to 3-year-old children whose mothers used reasoning and discussed humanistic concerns in resolving conflict with them were more advanced in moral understanding in kindergarten and first grade (Dunn, Brown, & Maguire, 1995). Together, these findings suggest that what is important about parent-child conversation is not the clear and consistent articulation of rules and the consequences of rule violation, but how they sensitize young children to the human dimensions of misbehavior and good behavior and help young children to comprehend the effects of their actions on others' feelings. By putting a human face on early moral socialization, emotions become constructively enlisted into the emergence of conscience through relational experience.

The influence of emotional sensitivity and emotion understanding on *prosocial motivation* may have even earlier origins. Recent research by Warneken and Tomasello (2006, 2007) has reinvigorated interest in the early origins of helping behavior in toddlers. In a series of innovative research procedures, they showed that children as young as 14 months old act prosocially toward unfamiliar adults in the absence of reward or praise for doing so. When an adult was engaged in simple tasks that could not be completed without assistance from the child (e.g., retrieving a marker the adult was drawing with that accidentally fell on the floor), all but two of the 18-month-olds and two-thirds of the 14-month-olds helped readily. By contrast, toddlers were much less likely to assist when the same situations arose from the adult's deliberate action (e.g., tossing the marker on the floor rather than dropping it accidentally), and thus when no help was needed.

Although these responses were (generously) described as "altruistic behavior" by the authors, the study was designed to demonstrate something else. In these and other experimental procedures, toddlers exhibit their capacity for shared intentionality: the ability to participate in the intentional activity of another person (Tomasello & Carpenter, 2007). Shared intentionality is a remarkable social-cognitive achievement in children this young because it requires toddlers to discern the intentions and goals underlying another's behavior, and it is thus a very early manifestation of the "mind reading" skills associated with developing theory of mind. Although the experimenters in these studies exhibited minimal emotional expressiveness throughout, in everyday circumstances the detection of another's goals and intentions is readily enabled by the child's attention to the person's emotional expressions. People look pleased when their goals are achieved, and they respond negatively when their intentions are blocked or thwarted (e.g., Repacholi & Gopnik, 1997).

Emotional understanding may thus be an important early motivator of prosocial behavior.

In our lab, we replicated these findings. Using the procedures devised by Warneken and Tomasello (2006) and several similar assessments of our own design, we also found that 18-month-olds were more likely to assist an unfamiliar adult in experimental conditions in which the adult required assistance to complete the task (e.g., the marker was accidentally dropped on the floor) than in control conditions in which the adult required no help at all (e.g., the marker was deliberately tossed on the floor) (Newton, Goodman, Rogers, Burris, & Thompson, 2010). Interestingly, additional experimental conditions of our design in which the adult looked sad when needing help did not elicit greater amounts of helping than conditions in which the adult looked neutral (as in the original study). However, toddlers who helped in these conditions were higher in their emotion state language, a measure of expressive language that is often used as a proxy for emotion understanding. Toddlers who responded most helpfully when the experimenter looked sad and required assistance showed greater indicators of emotion understanding.

These findings concerning conscience development and early prosocial motivation underscore the importance of the emotion connection that young children can establish with the needs of others as a motivator to cooperative, constructive social behavior. This emotional connection begins in the close relationships that young children share with their caregivers, and it is extended to others through the tutoring in people's feelings and needs that caregivers offer in emotion-focused discourse. This kind of discourse is observed more often when mother-child attachments are secure, consistent with the views of attachment theorists that secure attachments provide a psychological secure base in which feelings can be openly shared and discussed with caring adults. By enlisting emotion constructively into social understanding and sensitivity to the needs of people, early relationships contribute to the development of the emotionate child.

## Self-Understanding

The emergence of self-awareness is an extended process. It begins with experiences of agency in early infancy and is supplemented by physical self-recognition late in the second year. Self-understanding flourishes in the third year with verbal references to feelings, desires, needs, and intentions, assertions of competency and ownership, and categorical identity (such as by gender), together with the young child's sensitivity to behavioral expectations and the emergence of self-conscious evaluative emotions (see review by Thompson, 2006a). It is not surprising, therefore, that researchers have discovered that in addition to describing themselves in terms of physical traits and ability, young children are also capable of characterizing their internal, psychological characteristics. Using carefully designed interview procedures—sometimes involving puppets to aid the young child's self-description—several research groups have found that preschoolers describe themselves using internally consistent, reliable references to internal, personality-like characteristics.

The characteristics that young children choose to describe themselves are emotional in quality. They include self-perceptions of timidity, agreeableness, proneness to negative affect, and positive or negative self-concept for 4- to 5-year-olds (Brown, Mangelsdorf, Agathen, & Ho, 2008; Goodvin, Meyer, Thompson, & Hayes, 2008); depression-anxiety, aggression-hostility, as well as peer acceptance and social and academic competence for 4 1/2- to 7 1/2-year-olds (Measelle, Ablow, Cowan, & Cowan, 1998); positive or negative self-concept in multiple areas of competence for 4- and 5-year-olds (Marsh, Ellis, & Craven, 2002); and self-acceptance and self-control for 5 1/2-year-olds (Eder, 1990). Some evidence shows that these self-descriptions are consistent in year-to-year assessments (Measelle et al., 1998), although this is not always true (Goodvin et al., 2008). The validity of these self-descriptions is suggested by findings that how preschoolers describe themselves is consistent with descriptions provided by their mothers, fathers, or teachers (Brown et al., 2008; Eder & Mangelsdorf, 1997; Measelle et al., 1998). However, the modest associations between children's self-descriptions and the descriptions provided by parents or teachers suggest that considerable additional sources of variance contribute to young children's self-understanding. Early self-awareness is not merely a result of Mead's looking-glass self.

It appears that, in addition to others' attributions, young children have a rich experience of themselves that is emotional in nature. It is not difficult to see why. Young children who are timid and shy carry this emotional quality with them into daily social situations where their anxious reserve is as salient to them as it is to others. Those who are more prone to negative outbursts and tantrums are often as perplexed by their emotional upheavals and the consequences as are the peers and adults around them. Preschoolers who are positive and socially outgoing likewise regularly experience the salient emotional satisfactions of interacting with other people. When young children respond to interview prompts about what they are like, they are drawing on a rich experiential history of living in their own skin that is primarily emotional in quality.

Close relationships are important to developing self-understanding, but perhaps not exclusively because of how young children appropriate the descriptions of them that they overhear or caregivers tell them. In addition, the security of their attachments and the emotional well-being of their caregivers contribute to the emotional experiences from which young children derive a sense of themselves. In our research, young children's self-descriptions were longitudinally elicited from a puppet-assisted interview when they were 4 and 5 years of age, and the security of attachment and maternal perceptions of parenting stress and depressive symptomatology were also measured at each age (Goodvin et al., 2008). We found that positive self-concept at age 5 was predicted by the security of attachment at age 4 (with age 5 attachment security controlled) and by a composite measure of maternal depression/parenting stress at both ages. Children in secure attachments at age 4 had a more positive self-concept one year later, but children whose mothers reported greater stress and depression viewed themselves more negatively.

These findings highlight the importance of emotion to developing self-understanding and the significance of relational experience to early self-awareness. Because of this, young children growing up in contexts of relational and family stress construct their self-concept around experiences of greater challenge, anxiety, and uncertainty compared with preschoolers living in more secure and affirmative family settings. One reason why self-understanding may not be consistent in year-to-year assessments, therefore, is that the emotional climate of the family may change over time in ways that affect developing self-awareness. In each case, however, emotion in the context of close relationships is an organizer of early self-understanding.

## Social Cognition

As noted earlier, emotion is a core feature of early social representations, from infants' expectations for the quality of parental care to the emergence of desire psychology in the second and third years. Considerable research indicates that infants generate expectations for specific caregivers during the first year based on the affective quality of their experiences with those adults (see Thompson, 2006a, for a review). Later, generalized representations of people and relationships emerge from these relationships that are applied to how children approach specific individuals. But how early are person-specific relational expectations generalized to representations for people and relationships in general? Such a question is central to attachment theory, and some evidence shows the importance of emotion to this generalization from specific to global social representations.

In a report by Johnson, Dweck, and Chen (2007), evidence for infants' internal working models of attachment was claimed from the differential looking times of securely-attached and insecurely-attached infants to short video animations of the actions of large and small colored ovals moving on an inclined surface. Twelve- to sixteen-month-old infants were first habituated to the animation of the large, red oval moving away from the small, blue oval as it traversed an incline, at which time the smaller oval pulsed while the sound of a human baby cry was heard. After habituation, infants saw another animation in which either the large oval continued to move away from the smaller one as it traversed another incline (the "unresponsive caregiver") or the large oval backed down the original incline to rejoin the smaller one (the "responsive caregiver"). In each case, the baby cry continued to the end of the animation. Whereas the looking times of insecurely-attached infants did not differ for the two outcome conditions, securely-attached infants looked significantly longer at the "unresponsive caregiver" condition to reflect their greater interest in this (presumably unexpected) outcome. According to the primary author of this study, the baby cry was important for guiding observers' interpretation of the actions as "distressing to the baby circle" (Johnson, personal communication, February 19, 2010). Owing to infants' differential emotional associations with the sound of an infant cry, this may also account for the attachment group differences observed in this study.

In older children, differences in social cognition can be more clearly and finely measured. In the National Institute of Child Health and Human Development Study of Early Child Care and Youth Development (NICHD SECCYD), for example, children ages 4 1/2 and 6 were presented with a series of assessments of their social-cognitive understanding of people and relationships. Negative attribution bias was assessed at each age, for example, based on children's responses to short stories in which the central character acts with ambiguous intent. Social problem-solving skills were evaluated at 54 months as the variety of constructive solutions children could generate to social problems, such as how to make friends with another child. In first grade, there was an assessment of children's aggressive solutions to vignettes about story characters with ambiguous motives, and there was also an index of children's self-reported loneliness.

These are some of the earliest ages at which explicit measures of social-cognitive understanding have been assessed. Consistent with the nature of emergent social representations in the early years, social-cognitive understanding at this age is strongly emotional in quality, focused on themes of loneliness, aggression, hostility, and, more positively, constructive means of solving emotion-laden social dilemmas that are common in peer encounters. Emotion is prominent in young children's interactions with peers, their ways of representing individuals within the peer environment (Heyman & Gelman, 1999), and their general social representations of other children and relational interaction.

Raikes and Thompson (2008a) sought to understand whether children's early relational experiences in the family would contribute to predicting individual differences in their responses to these social-cognitive measures. From the NICHD SECCYD data set, we selected measures of maternal care. These included sensitivity scores obtained from mother-child play sessions at 15, 24, and 36 months (early sensitivity) or 54 months (later sensitivity), and measures of maternal depressive symptomatology at 15, 24, and 36 months (early depression) or later (later depression). Finally, we obtained measures of mother-child relationship—specifically, the security of attachment at 15 months (in the Strange Situation), 24 months (using an observer-report Attachment Q-sort), and 36 months (using a modified Strange Situation procedure). With these measures of early mother-child interaction and their developing relationship to predict the child's later social-cognitive understanding, Table 2.1 summarizes the main effects.

We found that early and later measures of maternal care predicted social cognition at the end of the preschool years, but only weakly.

**Table 2.1    Summary of main results from regressions predicting later social-cognitive understanding from early mother-child relationships**

Note: Summary of main results from Raikes & Thompson (2008); interactions among predictors omitted.

| | Negative Attributions 54 mos | Socially Competent Solutions 54 mos. | Loneliness 1st grade | Aggressive Solutions 1st grade | Negative Attributions 1st grade |
|---|---|---|---|---|---|
| Early Maternal Depression | | | | | + |
| Early Maternal Sensitivity | | + | | − | |
| Later Maternal Depression | | | | | |
| Later Maternal Sensitivity | | | | − | |
| 15 month Attachment | | | | | |
| 24 month Attachment | | + | − | | |
| 36 month Attachment | Avoidant > Secure | Avoidant < Secure | Resistant > Secure | | Resistant > Secure |

*Note*: All associations reported in this chart were significant at or lesser than the p < .05 level.

Children were more likely to provide competent solutions to social problems and fewer aggressive responses when mothers were sensitive in the early years, and the early maternal depression composite was associated with children's negative attribution bias in first grade. Much stronger prediction to later social-cognitive understanding emerged from the security of attachment, a measure of the parent-child relationship, especially at 24 and 36 months. Strange Situation classifications at 15 months were not associated with later measures at all, but children who were securely attached at 24 months were more likely to provide socially competent solutions and less likely to report loneliness at later ages. At 36 months, security was predictive of four of the five social-cognitive measures, with secure children later exhibiting fewer negative attributions, reporting less loneliness, and providing more competent solutions to social problems with peers. Consistent with the expectations of attachment theory and with many findings from the MPCLS (Sroufe et al., 2005), early caregiving relationships were strongly associated with later social-cognitive understanding in ways that may reflect the generalization of expectations and emotions from the attachment relationship to beliefs about people and relationships at later ages.

Why would the security of attachment become a stronger predictor of social cognition at later ages? One straightforward explanation is that later measures of attachment security were simply closer in time to the social-cognitive measures they predicted and this strengthened their association, although this does not seem to have occurred with respect to measures of maternal sensitivity and depressive symptomatology. A more interesting explanation is based on the view that the security of attachment has developmental influences relevant to other emergent achievements in psychological growth at that time (Thompson, 2000). At 36 months, young children are gaining considerable insight into the internal characteristics and motivators of people's behavior. They are at the early stages of developing theory of mind, their emotion understanding is expanding considerably, and they are far more capable of mentally representing the causes and consequences of relational interactions than they are at earlier ages. By contrast, an infant in the Strange Situation has only rudimentary capacities for social understanding. As a consequence, a secure attachment at 36 months is more likely to influence young children's emergent representations of their peers, relational processes, and themselves as social partners than would attachment security at earlier ages.

The studies of social and emotional development discussed thus far highlight two essential features of the emotionate child. First, emotions assume a constructive function in the organization of conscience and prosocial motivation, self-understanding, social representations, and other early achievements because they are prominent in young children's everyday experience and color relationships with others, motivational incentives, evaluations of people and events, and interpretations of others' characteristics. Emotions are organizational in this manner because they constitute a psychological connection between the internal world of the self and another person, and are thus a common referent as a basis for socioemotional understanding. Second, emotions assume these constructive functions because their developmental influences are guided by early relationships. In relational contexts, emotions are interpreted, connected to other human concerns (such as moral values and respect for others), regulated, and incorporated into developing personality and social competence. Relational experience thus colors how emotions influence behavioral competence and self-understanding—whether they contribute to sympathetic or hostile attribution biases, for example, positive or negative self-concept, and cooperative or competitive relations with others. The emotionate qualities of the child develop in the context of relational experience, and one of the fundamental challenges of developmental scientists is to unpack relational experience to better understand its constituent influences.

## DEVELOPMENT OF THE EMOTIONATE CHILD

Many features of early relationships contribute to the constructive incorporation of emotion and emotion understanding into behavioral competence. The emotional climate of the family creates a context of emotional demands, models, evaluations, and coaching that shapes young children's daily emotional experience and the emotion regulatory challenges they face. The quality of parental responsiveness affects how children perceive that their emotional experiences are evaluated and the support they receive in managing their feelings and enlisting them adaptively into social interaction. The emotional expressions of relational partners contribute to the young child's evaluations of people, events, and behavior and their association with broader values, goals, and standards. These and other features of emotional development begin early in life, but with the growth of language and parent-child conversation the socialization of emotion and its incorporation into developing behavioral competence proceeds in earnest.

Language is a significant catalyst for growth in the emotionate child for several reasons (Thompson, 2006b; Thompson, Laible, & Ontai, 2003). First, language provides semantic referents for internal, psychological processes, such as emotions, that are otherwise inchoate, elusive, or confusing to very young children. Language in conversation further embeds these lexical referents into cultural systems of meaning and socially evaluative standards: whether "shy" is good or bad and "needing help" motivates help-giving or judgments of weakness depends on the personal and social context in which these concepts are acquired. Second, conversational discourse directs young children's attention selectively to features of an event that are important to the adult and, in so doing, entrains the child's interpretive focus accordingly. This can occur when conversation occurs *during* a shared experience (Ornstein, Haden, & Hedrick, 2004), in *retrospective* conversation about past events (Nelson & Fivush, 2004), and in *anticipatory* discussions of future events (Hudson, 2002). In each case, the caregiver's conversational prompts guide the child's construal of experience in light of the adult's values, expectations, goals, and sociocultural orientation, such as by talking about what other people were intending rather than the outcomes of their actions alone. As this example illustrates, adults often guide children's interpretations of events by drawing attention to inferences of the internal motivators of people's actions that young children might not attend to or appropriately construe.

A third reason for the importance of language in the development of the emotionate child is how it enables sharing, understanding, and evaluation of internal experience in discourse with another person. Because language lexicalizes psychological processes like emotion, it can objectify the child's internal experience for shared discussion, elaboration, and evaluation. This enables the adult to provide insight into the child's internal experience, but at times it can confront both partners with divergent constructions of the child's experiences, feelings, and motives (see, e.g., Levine, Stein, & Liwag, 1999, and below). In this sense, conversations about the child's internal experience may provide young children with a tutorial in shared and divergent mental states, which is a crucial development in theory of mind. Finally, the growth of language enables the reconstruction of the infant's implicit representations of other people and the self into a more explicit, conscious system of representations that are influenced both by direct experience and by the secondary representations mediated by language. This makes psychological understanding more flexible, accessible, and expansive.

Because of these contributions of language to developing psychological understanding, many contemporary researchers agree with the conclusion of Carpendale and Lewis (2004) that constructing an understanding of others' internal states requires experiences of cooperative social interaction and exposure to talk about mental states (see also Harris, de Rosnay, & Pons, 2005). But the importance of language in conversational discourse means much more. In conversation, an adult's language also conveys evaluations of events and people, moral judgments, causal attributions, trait characterizations of people (including the young child), lessons about socially appropriate conduct, and other messages that are incorporated into discussions of what people are feeling, thinking, and intending. Through parent-child conversation, in other words, the intergenerational transmission of values, expectations, biases, and judgments occurs as young children are learning about the internal world of people.

In this light, the quality of the parent-child relationship is an important part of the conversational context because of how it colors the use of language in parent-child discourse and the psychological understanding it fosters. Relationships influence what is said—whether young children's experience is validated and elaborated or questioned, denied, or criticized—and the evaluations, judgments, and attributions that accompany this communication. Relationship quality influences how it is said, and the nonverbal expressions of warmth, doubt, or rejection that accompany words. Relationships also influence the impact of what is said, because of the child's trust or uncertainty in the source of the message. The influence of parent-child conversation on the development of the emotionate child is thus an interaction of the semantic and pragmatic context of language and the source of the messages the child receives.

## Development of Emotion Understanding

The growth of emotion understanding—a core competence of the emotionate child—illustrates these influences on developing psychological understanding and social competence.

Considerable research indicates that early emotion understanding is enhanced by the amount and quality of emotion-focused conversational discourse between parent and child (see reviews by Dunn, 2002, and Thompson, 2006a). The frequency with which mothers refer to people's emotions and the amount of causal language related to emotion are each associated with preschoolers' emotion understanding. In addition, mothers' elaborative discourse style when discussing emotion-related experiences—in which shared experiences are discussed in depth, with the child prompted by open-ended "wh-" questions to fill in details, and mothers provide evaluations of the child's responses to confirm or correct what the child has said—is also associated with greater emotion understanding.

A study by Ontai and Thompson (2002) helps explain why. We observed 3-year-olds and their mothers as they together read a storybook with emotional themes and also discussed a recent event in which the child had experienced negative emotion. From transcriptions of their conversations, we coded several aspects of the mother's discourse. These included (a) the *frequency* of her references to emotion, (b) her description of the *causes* of emotion, (c) portrayals of the *outcomes* of emotion, (d) *definitions* of emotion (such as explaining an emotion term), (e) *linking events* in the child's life to the situation or story to help the child better understand the emotion, and (f) *requests for information* from the child related to emotion. These elements of maternal emotion-related discourse were highly interrelated, as described by the correlational associations presented in Figure 2.1. When mothers made frequent conversational references to emotion, they also provided their pre-schoolers with considerable additional information about the causes, consequences, and significance of emotional reactions, and solicited from the child additional information about emotion as it related to the child's experience. We also coded the mother's overall elaborative dis-course style and found that each of the discourse features in Figure 2.2 was significantly associated with elaborative discourse.

Early emotion understanding is thus enhanced by conversation with an adult who elaborates and enriches the child's conceptions of the meaning and significance of emotion. The importance of elaborative discourse to the development of autobiographical memory is well-established (Nelson & Fivush, 2004), but these and other studies indicate that elaborative discourse is important to emotional understand-ing as well (see also Laible, 2004; Laible & Song, 2006). Furthermore, experimental studies confirm that mothers can develop the skills to converse in a more elaborative manner with offspring, and the resulting change in maternal conversational style is associated with the predicted effects on young children's representations of experience (see Wareham &

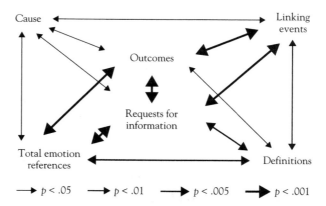

**Figure 2.1**    Correlational associations between maternal discourse elements (from Ontai & Thompson, 2002; reprinted from Thompson et al., 2003)

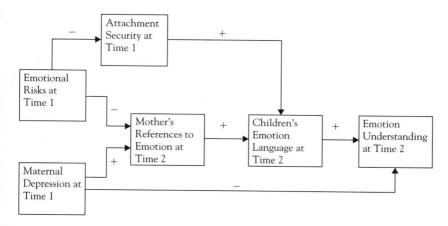

**Figure 2.2**  Relations between family emotional climate, attachment security, mothers' references to emotion, child emotion language, and child emotion understanding in an at-risk sample

(from Raikes & Thompson, 2006, 2008b; reprinted from Thompson, 2010)

Salmon, 2006). Much less is known about other features of maternal discourse that are associated with elaborative style (recall the association of mothers' feeling statements with morally evaluative statements in Laible & Thompson's [2000] study of early conscience) and their consequences for social and emotional understanding.

Conversation is important in a relational context. Mothers in secure attachment relationships converse with their preschoolers in a more elaborative manner than do mothers in insecure relationships (see Reese, 2002, for a review). This may help account for why securely-attached young children are more advanced in emotion understanding, particularly their understanding of negative emotions (Laible, 2004; Laible & Thompson, 1998; Raikes & Thompson, 2006; Steele, Steele, Croft, & Fonagy, 1999). Especially when mothers talk about negative emotional experiences, which are likely to be more confusing and troubling to young children than other events, their elaborative style can validate children's feelings and help them understand and manage these experiences, as well as helping children understand these emotions in other people. This is consistent with Bretherton's (1993) portrayal of the more candid, "open, fluid communication" shared by securely-attached mothers and children that enables greater emotional disclosure, particularly of upsetting or unsettling experiences. When this occurs, security is fostered by the parent's understanding and reassurance conveyed in conversation, and their relationship becomes a psychological secure base for the child (Koren-Karie, Oppenheim, & Getzler-Yosef, 2008).

The importance of this psychological secure base was recently illustrated in a study in our lab in which mothers and their 4 1/2-year-old children were observed while they together recalled two recent experiences in which the child felt sad and angry (Waters et al., 2009). Children varied in how much they sought to avoid these uncomfortable conversational topics by changing the topic to something else, leaving the mother to do something else, or explicitly refusing to talk further. We counted the frequency of these indicators of child avoidance, and found that they were predicted by two characteristics of mother-child conversation. The first was a rating of maternal validation from conversational transcripts based on whether the mother accepted the child's perspective on the recalled event, showed empathy for the child's feelings, and put the child's viewpoint (rather than the mother's) at the center of the conversation. Mothers with high ratings for validation had children with low conversational avoidance. The second was the security of attachment: when mothers and children were in secure relationships, there was less child avoidance. Indeed, mothers in secure attachments were also significantly more validating than were mothers in insecure relationships. These findings provide an empirical elaboration on Bretherton's portrayal of the more "open, fluid communication" shared by securely-attached mothers and children.

Taken together, these studies suggest that the early development of emotion understanding is guided both by the content of mother-child emotion-focused conversation and the emotional support afforded by these conversations. What mothers say contributes to young children's understanding of the causes, consequences, and meaning of emotional experiences in themselves and others. The emotional support mothers provide, such as through validating comments, contributes to the young child's developing confidence that emotions are important and can be comprehended and managed. Mothers in secure relationships are distinctive in each of these conversational qualities, which likely contributes to the greater emotion understanding of their offspring and to the continuing security of the parent-child relationship.

When families are under stress, these conversational elements of developing emotion understanding become especially important, as are the relationships from which they derive. Unfortunately, many young children live in family environments characterized by economic and emotional stress that impairs the development of secure parent-child relationships, and the emotional climate of the family is likely to hinder the growth of emotional competence in these settings. More significantly, emotion may become enlisted for these children into the development of negative attributional biases, impoverished self-concept, and critical (rather than sympathetic) appraisals of the feelings of others. For these reasons, study of the development of the emotionate child in at-risk families is essential to an understanding of how emotional development occurs in contexts of stress and challenge.

Our study recruited a sample of mothers and children from Early Head Start, an early intervention program for families living in poverty (Raikes & Thompson, 2006, 2008b; Thompson, 2010). When children were 2 years old, mothers completed inventories concerning depressive symptomatology and emotional risk factors (e.g., alcohol or drug abuse in the family; domestic violence; a family member with anger management problems), and child-mother attachment security was assessed. One year later, mothers and children were observed discussing recent events when the child felt happy, angry, or sad. From transcriptions of their conversations, the frequency of mothers' references to emotion was counted. We also obtained two measures of the child's emotion language: the child's use of negative emotion words and the child's ability to independently generate labels for emotional states. These measures were highly correlated, so they were combined for analysis. Children also completed a measure of emotion understanding based on Denham's work (see Denham et al., 2002).

The primary findings of the regression analyses to predict emotion understanding are presented in Figure 2.2. Emotion understanding was

associated with children's emotion language and by mothers' conversational references to emotion at age 3 in a now-familiar pattern of discourse
influences. But mothers' emotion-related references were negatively
associated with two antecedent influences from a year earlier: emotional
risks in the family and depressive symptomatology. In this at-risk sample
of families, mothers who reported a greater number of emotional stresses
were less likely to talk about emotions when reminiscing with their
children a year later, perhaps because emotional issues remained troubling matters that restricted mothers' emotion conversational access with
their offspring. By contrast, maternal depression was positively associated
with maternal emotional references a year later, perhaps because of the
ruminative thinking about emotional issues characteristic of depression.
Despite its association with mothers' emotion references in conversation with the child, maternal depression had an independent negative
association with children's emotion understanding at age 3. This may
have derived from other, unmeasured influences of maternal depressive
symptomatology on the family emotional climate, such as the hopeless-
ness, hostility, and self-critical attributions characteristic of depressed
individuals.

Finally, as other studies have found, a secure attachment was predictive of emotion understanding at age 3, but the effects of attachment
were mediated by children's emotion language in conversation with
their mothers. This suggests that one of the benefits of attachment
security is how it enables young children more readily to reflect on, identify, and understand emotions—particularly negative emotions—which
may be one of the benefits of the more "open communication" shared by
securely-attached children with their mothers (Bretherton, 1993).

Taken together, these findings confirm the importance of mother-
child conversation and attachment security to the development of
emotion understanding in young children living in at-risk families as
well as middle-class homes. But conversational discourse is also affected
by broader stresses in family life, particularly for the mother. The
emotional turmoil she experienced as much as a year earlier, and her
own depressive symptomatology at this time, significantly influenced the
frequency of emotion-related references in reminiscing with her young

child. In a sense, her capacity to function as a psychological secure base for her child is contingent on her coping with the emotional demands she encounters, and evidence from this study shows that maternal depression had other, negative consequences for the developing emotion understanding of her child. Other analyses from this study showed that economic stresses had consequences for conversational quality and developing emotion understanding comparable to emotional stresses. The development of the emotionate child is thus affected, directly and indirectly, by the broader family emotional climate as it influences the growth of emotion skills and understanding through conversational discourse in parent-child relationships.

## Development of Emotion Regulation

Emotion regulation is another core competence of the emotionate child because it contributes to enlisting emotions constructively into behavioral competence. It is important not because unregulated emotions inevitably lead to impulsive, disorganized, or incompetent responses, because emotions are regulated from birth and often function adaptively (Thompson, 2011; Thompson, Lewis, & Calkins, 2008). Rather, emotion regulation develops as multiple explicit and implicit capacities for emotional management emerge, become integrated, and contribute to more effective goal-directed behavior. The young child's developing understanding of emotion, and the guidance and support of close relationships, are important influences.

Caregivers provide multifaceted contributions to the growth of emotion regulation early in life (see Thompson & Meyer, 2007, for a review). Their proactive efforts and direct interventions help keep children's emotions within manageable limits, and their emotion coaching contributes to children's self-initiated efforts to regulate their own feelings. The influence of the family emotional climate and parents' supportive or critical responses to children's emotions affect the development of emotion regulation as well as the growth of emotion understanding. Importantly, these socialization efforts occur in the context of young children's developing understanding of emotion regulation processes, about which much less is known. Cole, Dennis, Smith-Simon, and

Cohen (2009) reported that 3- and 4-year-olds could generate strategies for managing sadness and anger, and an increasing proportion of children recognized certain strategies as more appropriate and effective than others (e.g., aggression vs. choosing an alternative activity in response to peer provocation). Davis, Levine, Lench, and Quas (2010) reported that 5- and 6-year-olds could generate metacognitive strategies (involving mental processes to manage feelings, such as changing thoughts or goals) for purposes of emotion management.

In our study with 4 1/2-year-olds described earlier, children responded to an Emotion Regulation Problem Solving interview in which puppets enacted short story vignettes that evoked anger, sadness, or fear in the story character (Waters et al., 2010). Following this, the puppets enacted different emotion regulation strategies (i.e., problem-solving, avoidance, cognitive restructuring, and venting), and children evaluated the effectiveness of each strategy on the basis of the extent to which they thought it would reduce the intensity of the story character's emotions. Young children consistently regarded venting as the least effective strategy, but beyond this, effectiveness ratings were emotion-specific. Avoidance was deemed more effective, for example, than anger or fear in managing sadness. Further analyses revealed that securely-attached children were significantly less likely to endorse venting for emotion regulation than were insecurely-attached children. Perhaps owing to the relational contexts in which venting commonly occurs, children in secure relationships perceived it as being overall a less useful means of managing their emotions.

Recall that mothers and children in this study also together discussed two recent experiences in which the child felt sad and angry. Although they were not explicitly instructed to do so, the large majority (88%) of the mothers in this sample spontaneously talked about different means for managing emotion in these situations, and many commented about the effectiveness of these strategies for making one feel better. Mothers commented most often on the effectiveness of problem-focused coping, emotion-focused coping, attentional redirection, and cognitive reappraisal when discussing emotion-evocative past experiences of the child. By contrast, the effectiveness of venting was much less often endorsed by these mothers. Although young children often vent their negative emotions when they are frustrated or sad, they recognize that this does not help them to feel better, partly because of what they have learned from their mothers.

These are situations, of course, in which emotion and its regulation are discussed in response to imaginary stories. What about actual instances in which parents and children must together manage the child's emotions? In this study, parents and children participated in a task that was designed to frustrate the child (i.e., Stansbury & Sigman's [2000] "denied request task"). Subsequently, mothers and children independently watched a video of their interaction in the task and, at the point when the child's peak negative emotional intensity had been reached on the videotape, each was asked how the child felt at that moment (Waters et al., 2009). Well-trained coders also rated the child's emotional expressions at that moment on the videotape to provide an independent assessment of the child's emotional arousal. When the emotion attributions of mothers and children were compared, we were surprised to find that they agreed only 40% of the time, with mothers especially underidentifying anger in their children when compared with children's self-reports (see Figure 2.3). By contrast, independent observers' ratings agreed with children's self-reports 54% of the time, with high agreement when children self-reported anger and sadness, and less when children reported feeling happy. The low agreement between mothers and their children concerning the child's emotions during an earlier frustration task was surprising in light of the fact that mothers and children each watched a video of this episode before responding. But this is not an unprecedented finding (see Levine et al., 1999), and it reflects the challenges inherent when interpreting a child's emotions in a complex social situation in which the adult is personally participating. This is the challenge facing any parent who seeks to coach a young child's emotion regulation.

Mothers varied in the extent to which their attributions of emotion to their children agreed with the child's self-reports. Two characteristics of mother and child predicted the extent of mother-child concordance. First, mothers who reported believing in the importance of attending to

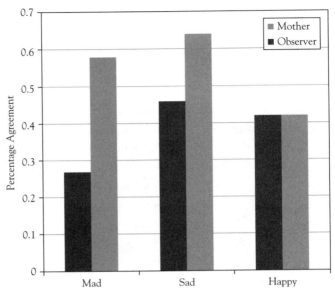

**Figure 2.3**   Concordance of child self-reports of emotion with mother and observer reports
(from Waters et al., 2010)

and accepting their own emotions (based on responses to a subscale of the Trait Meta-Mood Scale by Salovey, Mayer, Goldman, Turvey, & Palfai, 1995) were more likely to provide emotion attributions that agreed with children's self-reports of emotion. Second, mothers in secure attachments with their children were also more concordant in their emotion attributions with the child. In short, sensitivity to the child's emotional experience, which is an essential prerequisite to efforts to help the child manage emotions, was based on the security of attachment and the mother's respect for her own emotional experiences.

In these studies of the development of emotion understanding and emotion regulation, relational experience of various kinds guides the enlistment of emotion into social and behavioral competence. They include the sensitivity with which caregivers perceive and respond to children's emotions, the elaborativeness, support, and coaching provided by parent-child conversations about children's feelings, and the emotional climate of family life that offers models of emotion expression and coping, even in conditions of stress. These and other elements of early relational experience enable young children to better identify, understand, and manage their feelings, to enlist their emotions more constructively into social interactions and motivated action, and to respond more sensitively and appropriately to the feelings of others. Because many of these relational features distinguish secure from insecure parent-child relationships, it is not surprising that securely-attached children are not only more advanced in emotion understanding but are also more competent at emotion regulation (Gilliom, Shaw, Beck, Schonberg, & Lukon, 2002; Kochanska, 2001; Nachmias et al., 1996) and in the enlistment of emotion into social and behavioral competence (see review by Thompson, 2008a).

## CONCLUSION

The developing child is an emotionate child. Despite the cognitivist orientation of contemporary portrayals of the child, such a view has deep roots in developmental theory and everyday thinking about child development. One of the most influential expressions of this view is attachment theory, and especially the organizational perspective on development reflected in the MPCLS that this volume honors. The ideas from this work that emotions are central, especially in the context of primary relationships, to the organization of personality development, and that attachment relationships are emotionally regulatory and are forums for emotion understanding, are well reflected in the research described in this chapter.

Furthermore, the view that the emotional qualities of early experiences, particularly in close relationships, contribute to the development of dynamic representations of self, other people, and social interactions that are affectively colored, relationally guided, and integrative is central to the internal working models construct of attachment theory, and also to the work discussed here. The idea that mental representations of this kind emerge from early relational experience, provide guidance about how to interact with others and expectations for close relationships, and constitute interpretive filters that affect constructions of new relationships and partners is one of Bowlby's most theoretically provocative ideas, even though research directly enlisting the internal working models construct faces formidable conceptual and methodological challenges (Thompson, 2008b; Thompson & Raikes, 2003). Research on the emotionate child provides a means of exploring these provocative formulations using ideas from outside of as well as within attachment theory. In many respects, the generativity of attachment theory is its articulation of several important ideas about early development that motivate research of this kind. The work of Sroufe and Egeland and their colleagues has helped to make these ideas an empirical reality and is thus an inspiration for us all.

In the end, why is it important to recognize developing children as emotionate in nature? One reason is that it underscores the constructive significance of emotion for competence in a range of developmental domains, from sociability to self-regulation to school readiness and academic achievement (see Duncan & Magnuson, 2010). Another reason is that it highlights the centrality of emotion to young children's developing representations of themselves, significant others, and the relationships that color social life. Equally important is a third reason: Recognizing the developing child as emotionate draws our attention to the importance of attending to the development of socioemotional health from early in life and to the conditions in early childhood that create risk to early childhood mental health. In viewing the young child as an emotionate child, we begin to appreciate that a strong and positive sense of self, security in close relationships, and confidence in encounters with other people are essential psychological resources for success in the wider world.

## REFERENCES

Bartsch, K., & Wellman, H. (1995). Children talk about the mind. Oxford, England: Oxford University Press.

Bretherton, I. (1993). From dialogue to internal working models: The co-construction of self in relationships. In C. A. Nelson (Ed.), Minnesota symposia on child psychology: Memory and affect in development, Vol. 26 (pp. 237–263). Hillsdale, NJ: Erlbaum.

Bretherton, I., Fritz, J., Zahn-Waxler, C., & Ridgeway, D. (1986). Learning to talk about emotions: A functionalist perspective. *Child Development, 57,* 529–548.

Brown, G. L., Mangelsdorf, S. C., Agathen, J. M., & Ho, M.-H. (2008). Young children's psychological selves: Convergence with maternal reports of child personality. *Social Development, 17,* 161–182.

Carpendale, J. I. M., & Lewis, C. (2004). Constructing an understanding of mind: The development of children's social understanding within social interaction. *Behavioral and Brain Sciences, 27,* 79–96.

Cassidy, J. (1994). Emotion regulation: Influences of attachment relationships. In N. A. Fox (Ed.), The development of emotion regulation and dysregulation: Biological and behavioral aspects. *Monographs of the Society for Research in Child Development, 59* (2-3), 228–249 (Serial no. 240).

Cole, P. M., Dennis, T. A., Smith-Simon, K. E., & Cohen, L. H. (2009). Preschoolers' emotion regulation strategy understanding: Relations with emotion socialization and child self-regulation. *Social Development, 18,* 324–352.

Davis, E. L., Levine, L. J., Lench, H. C., & Quas, J. A. (2010). Metacognitive emotion regulation: Children's awareness that changing thoughts and goals can alleviate negative emotions. *Emotion. 10,* 498–510.

Denham, S. A., Blair, K. A., DeMulder, E., Levitas, J., Sawyer, K., Auerbach-Major, S., & Queenan, P. (2003). Preschool emotional competence: Pathway to social competence? *Child Development, 74,* 238–256.

Denham, S. A., Blair, K., Schmidt, M., & DeMulder, E. (2002). Compromised emotional competence: Seeds of violence sown early? *American Journal of Orthopsychiatry, 72,* 70–82.

Duncan, G. J., & Magnuson, K. (2010). *The nature and impact of early achievement skills, attention and behavior problems.* Unpublished manuscript, University of California, Irvine.

Dunn, J. (2002). Mindreading, emotion, and relationships. In W. W. Hartup & R. K. Silvereisen (Eds.), *Growing points in developmental science* (pp. 167–176). New York, NY: Psychology Press.

Dunn, J., Brown, J., & Maguire, M. (1995). The development of children's moral sensibility: Individual differences and emotion understanding. *Developmental Psychology, 31,* 649–659.

Dweck, C. S., & London, B. (2004). The role of mental representation in social development. *Merrill-Palmer Quarterly, 50,* 428–444.

Eder, R. A. (1990). Uncovering young children's psychological selves: Individual and developmental differences. *Child Development, 61,* 849–863.

Eder, R. A., & Mangelsdorf, S. C. (1997). The emotional basis of early personality development: Implications for the emergent self-concept. In R. Hogan, J. Johnson, & S. Briggs (Eds.), *Handbook of personality psychology* (pp. 209–240). Orlando, FL: Academic Press.

Giles, J. W., & Heyman, G. D. (2005). Preschoolers use trait-relevant information to evaluate the appropriateness of an aggressive response. *Aggressive Behavior, 31,* 498–509.

Gilliom, M., Shaw, D. S., Beck, J. E., Schonberg, M. A., & Lukon, J. L. (2002). Anger regulation in disadvantaged preschool boys: Strategies, antecedents, and the development of self-control. *Developmental Psychology, 38,* 222–235.

Goodvin, R., Meyer, S., Thompson, R. A., & Hayes, R. (2008). Self-understanding in early childhood: Associations with child attachment security and maternal negative affect. *Attachment & Human Development, 10,* 433–450.

Gopnik, A., Meltzoff, A. N., & Kuhl, P. K. (2000). *The scientist in the crib.* New York, NY: Harper.

Gunnar, M. R., & Vasquez, D. (2006). Stress neurobiology and developmental psychopathology. In D. Cicchetti & D. Cohen (Eds.), *Developmental psychopathology* (2nd ed.), Vol. I. *Developmental neuroscience* (pp. 533–577). Hoboken, NJ: Wiley.

Harris, P. L., de Rosnay, M., & Pons, F. (2005). Language and children's understanding of mental states. *Current Directions in Psychological Science, 14,* 69–73.

Heyman, G. D., & Gelman, S. A. (1999). The use of trait labels in making psychological inferences. *Child Development, 70,* 604–619.

Hudson, J. A. (2002). "Do you know what we're going to do this summer?" Mothers talk to young children about future events. *Journal of Cognition and Development, 3,* 49–71.

Izard, C., Fine, S., Schultz, D., Mostow, A., Ackerman, B., & Youngstrom, E. (2001). Emotion knowledge as a predictor of social behavior and academic competence in children at risk. *Psychological Science, 12,* 18–23.

Johnson, S. C., Dweck, C. S., & Chen, F. S. (2007). Evidence for infants' internal working models of attachment. *Psychological Science, 18,* 501–502.

Kochanska, G. (1995). Children's temperament, mother's discipline, and security of attachment: Multiple pathways to emerging internalization. *Child Development, 66,* 597–615.

Kochanska, G. (2001). Emotional development in children with different attachment histories: The first three years. *Child Development, 72,* 474–490.

Kochanska, G. (2002). Mutually responsive orientation between mothers and their young children: A context for the early development of conscience. *Current Directions in Psychological Science, 11,* 191–195.

Kochanska, G., & Aksan, N. (1995). Mother-child mutually positive affect, the quality of child compliance to requests and prohibitions, and maternal control as correlates of early internalization. *Child Development, 66,* 236–254.

Kochanska, G., Aksan, N., Knaack, A., & Rhines, H. (2004). Maternal parenting and children's conscience: Early security as a moderator. *Child Development, 75,* 1229–1242.

Kochanska, G., Barry, R. A., Stellern, S. A., & O'Bleness, J. J. (2009). Early attachment organization moderates the parent-child mutually coercive pathway to children's antisocial conduct. *Child Development, 80,* 1288–1300.

Kochanska, G., Koenig, J. L., Barry, R. A., Kim, S., & Yoon, J. E. (2010). Children's conscience during toddler and preschool years, moral self, and a competent, adaptive developmental trajectory. *Developmental Psychology, 46,* 1320–1332.

Koren-Karie, N., Oppenheim, D., & Getzler-Yosef, R. (2008). Shaping children's internal working models through mother-child dialogues: The importance of resolving past maternal trauma. *Attachment & Human Development, 10,* 465–483.

Lagattuta, K., & Thompson, R. A. (2007). The development of self-conscious emotions: Cognitive processes and social influences. In R. W. Robins & J. Tracy (Eds.), *Self-conscious emotions* (2nd ed., pp. 91–113). New York, NY: Guilford.

Laible, D. J. (2004). Mother-child discourse surrounding a child's past behavior at 30 months: Links to emotional understanding and early conscience development at 36 months. *Merrill-Palmer Quarterly, 50,* 159–180.

Laible, D., & Song, J. (2006). Constructing emotional and relational understanding: The role of affect and mother-child discourse. *Merrill-Palmer Quarterly, 52,* 44–69.

Laible, D. J., & Thompson, R. A. (1998). Attachment and emotional understanding in preschool children. *Developmental Psychology, 34*(5), 1038–1045.

Laible, D., & Thompson, R. A. (2000). Mother-child discourse, attachment security, shared positive affect, and early conscience development. *Child Development, 71,* 1424–1440.

Laible, D., & Thompson, R. A. (2002). Mother-child conflict in the toddler years: Lessons in emotion, morality, and relationships. *Child Development, 73*, 1187–1203.

Lamb, M. E., & Malkin, C. M. (1986). The development of social expectations in distress-relief sequences: A longitudinal study. *International Journal of Behavioral Development, 9*, 235–249.

Levine, L., Stein, N., & Liwag, M. (1999). Remembering children's emotions: Sources of concordant and discordant accounts between parents and children. *Developmental Psychology, 35*, 790–801.

Marsh, H. W., Ellis, L. A., & Craven, R. G. (2002). How do preschool children feel about themselves? Unraveling measurement and multidimensional self-concept structure. *Developmental Psychology, 38*, 376–393.

Measelle, J. R., Ablow, J. C., Cowan, P. A., & Cowan, C. P. (1998). Assessing young children's views of their academic, social, and emotional lives: An evaluation of the self-perception scales of the Berkeley Puppet Interview. *Child Development, 69*, 1556–1576.

Meltzoff, A. N. (2007). The 'like me' framework for recognizing and becoming an intentional agent. *Acta Psychologica, 124*, 26–43.

Moses, L. J., Baldwin, D. A., Rosicky, J. G., & Tidball, G. (2001). Evidence for referential understanding in the emotions domain at twelve and eighteen months. *Child Development, 72*, 718–735.

Nachmias, M., Gunnar, M., Mangelsdorf, S., Parritz, R. H., & Buss, K. (1996). Behavioral inhibition and stress reactivity: The moderating role of attachment security. *Child Development, 67*, 508–522.

Nelson, K., & Fivush, R. (2004). The emergence of autobiographical memory: A social-cultural developmental theory. *Psychological Review, 111*, 486–511.

Newton, E. K., Goodman, M., Rogers, C. R., Burris, J., & Thompson, R. A. (2010, April). *Individual differences in toddlers' prosocial behavior.* Paper presented at the biennial meeting of the Conference on Human Development, New York.

Ontai, L. L., & Thompson, R. A. (2002). Patterns of attachment and maternal discourse effects on children's emotion understanding from 3- to 5-years of age. *Social Development, 11*(4), 433–450.

Ornstein, P. A., Haden, C. A., & Hedrick, A. M. (2004). Learning to remember: Social-communicative exchanges and the development of children's memory skills. *Developmental Review, 24*, 374–395.

Raikes, H. A., & Thompson, R. A. (2006). Family emotional climate, attachment security, and young children's emotion understanding in a high-risk sample. *British Journal of Developmental Psychology, 24*(1), 89–104.

Raikes, H. A., & Thompson, R. A. (2008a). Attachment security and parenting quality predict children's problem-solving, attributions, and loneliness with peers. *Attachment & Human Development, 10,* 1–26.

Raikes, H. A., & Thompson, R. A. (2008b). Conversations about emotion in high-risk dyads. *Attachment & Human Development, 10*(4), 359–377.

Reese, E. (2002). Social factors in the development of autobiographical memory: The state of the art. *Social Development, 11,* 124–142.

Repacholi, B. M., & Gopnik, A. (1997). Early reasoning about desires: Evidence from 14- and 18-month-olds. *Developmental Psychology, 33,* 12–21.

Rousseau, J. J. (2008). *Emile* (B. Foxley, Trans.). New York, NY: Biblio Life (originally published 1792).

Salovey, P., Mayer, J. D., Goldman, S. L., Turvey, C., & Palfai, T. P. (1995). Emotional attention, clarity, and repair: Exploring emotional intelligence using the Trait Meta-Mood Scale. In J. Pennebaker (Ed.), *Emotion, disclosure, & health* (pp. 125–154). Washington, DC: American Psychological Association.

Smetana, J. G. (1989). Toddlers' social interactions in the context of moral and conventional transgressions in the home. *Developmental Psychology, 25,* 499–508.

Sroufe, L. A. (1996). *Emotional development.* New York, NY: Cambridge University Press.

Sroufe, L. A., Egeland, B., Carlson, E. A., & Collins, W. A. (2005). *The development of the person: The Minnesota Study of Risk and Adaptation from Birth to Adulthood.* New York, NY: Guilford.

Stansbury, K., & Sigman, M. (2000). Responses of preschoolers in two frustrating episodes: Emergence of complex strategies for emotion regulation. *Journal of Genetic Psychology, 161,* 182–202.

Steele, H., Steele, M., Croft, C., & Fonagy, P. (1999). Infant-mother attachment at one year predicts children's understanding of mixed emotions at six years. *Social Development, 8,* 161–178.

Thompson, R. A. (1994). Emotion regulation: A theme in search of definition. In N. A. Fox (Ed.), The development of emotion regulation and dysregulation: Biological and behavioral aspects. *Monographs of the Society for Research in Child Development, 59* (2-3), 25–52 (Serial no. 240).

Thompson, R. A. (2000). The legacy of early attachments. *Child Development, 71*(1), 145–152.

Thompson, R. A. (2006a). The development of the person: Social understanding, relationships, self, conscience. In W. Damon & R. M. Lerner (Eds.), *Handbook of child psychology* (6th ed.), Vol. 3. *Social, emotional, and personality development* (N. Eisenberg, Vol. Ed.) (pp. 24–98). Hoboken, NJ: Wiley.

Thompson, R. A. (2006b). Conversation and developing understanding: Introduction to the special issue. *Merrill-Palmer Quarterly, 52*(1), 1–16.

Thompson, R. A. (2008a). Early attachment and later development: Familiar questions, new answers. In J. Cassidy & P. R. Shaver (Eds.), *Handbook of attachment* (2nd ed., pp. 348–365). New York, NY: Guilford.

Thompson, R. A. (2008b). Attachment-related mental representations: Introduction to the special issue. *Attachment & Human Development, 10*(4), 1–12.

Thompson, R. A. (2009). Early foundations: Conscience and the development of moral character. In D. Narvaez & D. Lapsley (Eds.), *Personality, identity, and character: Explorations in moral psychology* (pp. 159–184) New York, NY: Cambridge University Press.

Thompson, R. A. (2010). Feeling and understanding through the prism of relationships. In S. D. Calkins & M. A. Bell (Eds.), *Child development at the intersection of emotion and cognition* (pp. 79–95). Washington, DC: American Psychological Association.

Thompson, R. A. (2011). Emotion and emotion regulation: Two sides of the developing coin. *Emotion Review. 3*, 53–61.

Thompson, R. A., & Lagattuta, K. (2006). Feeling and understanding: Early emotional development. In K. McCartney & D. Phillips (Ed.), *The Blackwell handbook of early childhood development* (pp. 317–337). Oxford, England: Blackwell.

Thompson, R. A., Laible, D. J., & Ontai, L. L. (2003). Early understanding of emotion, morality, and the self: Developing a working model. In R. V. Kail (Ed.), *Advances in child development and behavior,* Vol. 31 (pp. 137–171). San Diego, CA: Academic.

Thompson, R. A., Lewis, M., & Calkins, S. D. (2008). Reassessing emotion regulation. *Child Development Perspectives, 2*(3), 124–131.

Thompson, R. A., & Meyer, S. (2007). The socialization of emotion regulation in the family. In J. Gross (Ed.), *Handbook of emotion regulation* (pp. 249–268). New York, NY: Guilford.

Thompson, R. A., Meyer, S., & McGinley, M. (2006). Understanding values in relationship: The development of conscience. In M. Killen & J. Smetana (Eds.), *Handbook of moral development* (pp. 267–297). Mahwah, NJ: Erlbaum.

Thompson, R. A., & Raikes, H. A. (2003). Toward the next quarter-century: Conceptual and methodological challenges for attachment theory. *Development and Psychopathology, 15*(4), 691–718.

Tomasello, M., & Carpenter, M. (2007). Shared intentionality. *Developmental Science, 10,* 121–125.

Trentacosta, C. J., & Izard, C. E. (2007). Kindergarten children's emotion competence as a predictor of their academic competence in first grade. *Emotion, 7,* 77–88.

Wareham, P., & Salmon, K. (2006). Mother-child reminiscing about everyday experiences: Implications for psychological interventions in the preschool years. *Clinical Psychology Review, 26,* 535–554.

Warneken, F., & Tomasello, M. (2006). Altruistic helping in human infants and young chimpanzees. *Science, 311,* 1301–1303.

Warneken, F., & Tomasello, M. (2007). Helping and cooperation at 14 months of age. *Infancy, 11,* 271–294.

Waters, S. F., Raikes, H. A., Virmani, E. A., Meyer, S. C., Jochem, R., & Thompson, R. A. (2010, April). *What do children know about emotion regulation?* Poster presented at the biennial meeting of the Conference on Human Development, New York, NY.

Waters, S. F., Virmani, E. A., Thompson, R. A., Meyer, S., Raikes, H. A., & Jochem, R. (2009). Emotion regulation and attachment: Unpacking two constructs and their association. *Journal of Psychopathology and Behavioral Assessment, 32,* 37–47.

Watson, J. S. (2001). Contingency perception and misperception in infancy: Some potential implications for attachment. *Bulletin of the Menninger Clinic, 65,* 296–320.

Wright, J. C., & Bartsch, K. (2008). Portraits of early moral sensibility in two children's everyday conversations. *Merrill-Palmer Quarterly, 54,* 56–85.

# 3

# Attachment, Temperament, and Adaptation

## One Long Argument

BRIAN E. VAUGHN AND NANA SHIN

In this chapter, we consider the current status of attachment and temperament interpretations of adaptive functioning across infancy and childhood in light of the findings and conceptual advances arising from the Minnesota Parent-Child Longitudinal Study (MPCLS; Sroufe, Egeland, Carlson, & Collins, 2005). Achieving this goal requires an historical consideration of the interactions between both the theories grounding attachment and temperament and the science associated with those theories over the past 40 years. This is complicated for several reasons, not the least of which is because the temperament domain lacked a unifying *paradigm* (in the sense that Thomas Kuhn used this term) until the late 1990s and, instead, was divided into incompletely

Work on this chapter has been supported in part by NSF grants: BCS0623019 and BCS0843919. Our thinking about relations between the domains of attachment and temperament has been influenced by collaborations with Kelly K. Bost and Marinus van IJzendoorn (Vaughn & Bost, 1999; Vaughn, Bost, & van IJzendoorn, 2008), and the present chapter both synthesizes and extends insights from past work. We acknowledge here their contributions to the present chapter.

overlapping schools rather than a single accepted theory and, in no small part, because the principals from the MPCLS (i.e., Alan Sroufe, Byron Egeland, and their collaborators) have repeatedly found conceptual and empirical means of obstructing any encroachment on the attachment domain by temperamental theorists. Interestingly, even though it is no longer appropriate to consider temperament theory as "pre-paradigm," the general answer(s) to questions of how attachment and temperament are related has not changed much.

Accordingly, in the first section of the chapter, we identify some broad similarities and differences between attachment and temperament theories, the kinds of questions arising from each, and the kinds of data to which the two theories gave rise. This background introduces the first major contest between attachment and temperament; namely, do the individual differences in infant behavior relevant to attachment security depend on lived experiences encountered by infants with their caregivers over the course of the first year, or do these differences arise from endogenously organized temperamental traits (e.g., Chess & Thomas, 1982; Kagan, 1982)? Early on, Alan Sroufe (1985; Sroufe & Waters, 1982) settled this argument on conceptual grounds, but it has continued to fester empirically for nearly 30 years, even though reviews of the empirical literature (e.g., Mangelsdorf & Frosch, 1999; Vaughn & Bost, 1999) failed to sustain temperament interpretations of the organization of infant secure-base behavior in the Strange Situation (although, when other measures of attachment security such as the Attachment Q-sort are used, some overlap in content is occasionally seen).

The second major theme in attachment/temperament research is less contentious and is focused on (potential) interactions between attachment quality and aspects of temperament that may both uniquely and jointly forecast adaptive (or maladaptive) functioning in social, emotional, and/or cognitive domains during childhood and beyond. This theme offers a *rapprochement* of sorts between attachment and temperament and suggests a way in which the first question might be reconsidered. The third major section of the chapter reviews this literature. The fourth section of the chapter returns to the goals and accomplishments of the MPCLS, as they intersect with the research tradition(s) relating attachment and temperament domains. Finally, we conclude the chapter with some speculations about the most promising new directions that may be taken by researchers investigating the intersection of attachment and temperament domains.

# THE THEORY OF ATTACHMENT AND SCHOOLS OF TEMPERAMENT

The Bowlby-Ainsworth theory of attachment explains how and why infant-parent bonds are assembled over the first years of life and how interpersonal experiences in the context of attachment relationships set developmental trajectories with regard to the assembly of subsequent close relationships. Although implications for personality development and the regulation of affect, cognition, and behavior in the service of adaptive functioning are implicit in attachment theory and central to Bowlby's agenda (e.g., Bowlby, 1988), attachment *relationships* are explicitly social, and the primary emphases of the theory are on the construction, maintenance, and subjective meaning of attachment bonds. In contrast, most models of temperament were proposed as explanations of organized individual differences in styles of action or in the actions themselves. Temperament dimensions often are linked explicitly to personality functioning. For most temperament theorists, temperamental attributes carry implications for social functioning, but interpersonal exchanges and relationships are not the source(s) of temperament (see Goldsmith et al., 1987). Characterized in these ways, it is clear that discourse between conceptual domains involves the classic contrast between interactionist and essentialist worldviews. This contrast is a rhetorical device, because conceptual frameworks for both domains have bits of both views embedded in them that will (we hope) become clearer as our narrative unfolds.

## The Bowlby-Ainsworth Theory of Attachment

Bowlby (1982) acknowledged four broad intellectual influences on his thinking about the nature of the child's tie to the mother: psychoanalytic theory, especially its object relations variants; ethology and animal behavior; general systems theory; and cognitive psychology. To this mix of influences, Ainsworth added security theory, as it had been described by Blatz and elaborated in her own thinking and research (see Ainsworth & Marvin, 1995), before she joined in the attachment enterprise with Bowlby. Bowlby borrowed insights concerning the nature of the early child-caregiver bond from psychoanalytic theory (e.g., the infant-caregiver relationship is a love relationship, and therefore the dissolution of the child-caregiver bond through prolonged separations results in a real grief experience for the child; the early child-caregiver bond serves as a model for subsequent intimate relationships). To the extent that the early love relationship constructed in the context of caregiver-infant interactions constitutes the foundation for learning to "love well," the child-caregiver attachment can be construed as one cornerstone of both inter- and intrapersonal adjustment across the lifespan.

Ethology and animal behavior provided Bowlby with the motivational tools and empirical data he needed to explain the child's tendency to seek and maintain proximity to caregivers once he discarded Freud's hydraulic motivational model. He appropriated the ethological concept of a "behavioral system," organized to maintain proximity to the caregiver, as the mechanism governing attachment behavior, and he explained the presence of this system in terms of evolution by natural selection. Locating the infant's motivation for proximity seeking and contact maintenance in evolutionary deep time rather than in developmental time made possible the decoupling of attachment behavior from other motivational systems (e.g., hunger, sex) that both psychoanalysts and behaviorists used to explain the child's tie to the caregiver. Control systems theory provided him with key features of the behavioral system, including its "set goal," and operational processes like "goal-correction" and "feedback."

Finally, cognitive psychology and Piaget's genetic epistemology provided Bowlby with key insights (e.g., the infant's active participation in the co-construction of attachment relationships as a consequence of intrinsic motivations to exercise existing skills; mental models based on the social transactions resulting from the infant's active participation) he needed to extend the scope of attachment beyond the behavioral system.

Bowlby had in mind a distinctively human component of attachment that would organize, abstract, and internally represent early social transactions as models for imposing meaning on future transactions with others in close relationships. These models made the early attachment relationship portable and allowed the young child to tolerate conditions such as daily separations from the attachment figure without succumbing to distress and disorganization of affect, thought, and behavior. As the child matured, these models could also become objects of conscious reflection. Thus, while the roots of attachment are buried in our phylogeny, the products and outcomes resulting from attachment processes in the human lineage transcend the products and outcomes experienced by our primate cousins.

At its core, Bowlby's theory is normative and explanatory. That is, the domain of attachment is an essential human adaptation that is common across all members of our species. The theory explains why infants come to organize behavior with reference to major caregivers and how this phenomenon unfolds over the early years, but Bowlby had more in mind. He also believed that experiences with attachment figures were critical in shaping individual differences in the expression and control of affect, behavior, and cognition; however, Bowlby did not actually invest much of his career observing or analyzing the minutiae of these experiences. This was the contribution of Mary Ainsworth, who organized and conducted the two landmark studies that grounded Bowlby's ideas in observational data (Ainsworth, 1967; Ainsworth, Blehar, Waters, & Wall, 1978). These data provided the secure base from which attachment researchers have explored the myriad implications about individual differences contained in Bowlby's volumes. Importantly, Ainsworth's data demonstrated that individual differences in the organization of attachment behavior at the end of the first year were predictable from qualities of the history of interactions characterizing the infant-caregiver pair throughout that year.

## Temperament Schools

Whereas attachment theory's roots and major claims are relatively easy to specify, finding the core concepts and enumerating the major claims of temperament theories was difficult to impossible until the late 1990s. This was because at least four different (and moderately distinct) schools of thought identified only partially overlapping dimensions of temperament (see Goldsmith et al., 1987). The schools differed in terms of their characterization of the dimensional domain of temperament, the relation of temperament to biological substrates (e.g., genes, physiological processes, accidents of birth, early experience), and whether (or how) temperament developed over the life course. For our purposes, these perspectives are grouped into four broad categories: (1) behavioral style; (2) emergent personality; (3) emotion/physiological regulation models; and (4) social construction. This grouping is ad hoc insofar as all perspectives imply some form of biologically based, endogenously organized traits that appear early in life and tend to show at least moderate ordering consistency over time. Furthermore, some approaches do not fall neatly into a single category, and many of the empirical studies designed to connect temperament dimensions with attachment constructs employed methods derived from multiple schools. Nevertheless, this helps us organize the assumptions and claims of the several schools, especially with reference to domains of action and behavioral style that overlap the domains of action, affect, and cognition claimed by attachment theory.

### Behavioral Style

The notion that temperament refers to the style with which behaviors are exhibited rather than to the content of behavior or its motivational underpinnings is associated with Alexander Thomas and Stella Chess (e.g., Thomas & Chess, 1977; Thomas, Chess, Birch, Hertzig, & Korn, 1963). They argued that temperament is a property of persons that is not derivative of any other attribute or motivational source and that the expression of temperament is dynamically tuned to the constraints imposed by external stimuli, opportunities, expectations, and demands. They further argued that temperament should be assessed in social contexts, in part because the constraints of specific social contexts will lead to variations in the expression of the underlying temperamental attribute. Ordering consistency is expected across time, but this approach to temperament is sufficiently elastic as to accommodate marked changes in the rank orderings of individuals on temperament dimensions, because the dimensions are malleable under constraints (which they did not clearly specify) imposed by the social environment. Finally, Thomas and Chess saw no necessary connection between personality and temperament.

Behavioral style theory explains *why* infants and children differ with respect to *how* they behave in everyday life. These differences are believed to reflect variations in constitutionally grounded temperamental attributes. Thomas and Chess (in Goldsmith et al., 1987) claimed that these attributes are present and can be assessed from early infancy and that they are at least moderately stable from infancy to childhood. Although the profile of temperament for a given child may change as a consequence of instruction in a specific and constraining social environment, most intra-individual variations in the expression of temperament do not reflect lability in the underlying temperamental attribute (see Thomas & Chess in Goldsmith et al., 1987, p. 509). Thus, while change with respect to the salience of a temperamental attribute may be observed and can be explained in a specific case, the behavioral style perspective does not specify a normative developmental trajectory for temperament.

## Emergent Personality Theory

Buss and Plomin (1984) characterized temperament as basic personality primitives that are genetically grounded and highly heritable, can be detected early in life, and demonstrate relatively high rank-order stability across developmental periods. Buss and Plomin (1984) identified three traits that meet these criteria: emotionality, activity, and sociability. From this perspective, temperament is indistinguishable from personality during infancy. However, with increasing age these personality primitives differentiate; for example, primordial distress, the indicator of emotionality for infants, is assumed to split into fear and anger after the first year (Buss and Plomin in Goldsmith et al., 1987, p. 518). Furthermore, they suggest that normative changes in the level of expression of temperament traits are expectable (e.g., the expression of emotionality declines past infancy in response to pressures from the social environment and in response to central nervous system [CNS] maturation and associated regulatory mechanisms).

## Emotional/Physiological Regulation

This grouping of conceptual frameworks is somewhat messy. Two approaches (i.e., Goldsmith & Campos and Rothbart & Derryberry) and two related empirical positions (temperamental "proneness to distress" [e.g., Gunnar and associates] and "proneness to behavioral inhibition" [Kagan and associates; Fox and associates]) are included.

Goldsmith and Campos (e.g., Goldsmith in Goldsmith et al., 1987; Goldsmith & Campos, 1986, 1990) proposed a temperament model grounded in the functionalist perspective on the emotions and their development articulated by Campos and associates (e.g., Campos, Mumme, Kermoian, & Campos, 1994; Goldsmith & Campos, 1990). This model of emotional development differs in several ways from other approaches to understanding the development of the emotions (e.g., Izard & Malatesta, 1987). The functionalist perspective assumes that primary emotions (e.g., joy/pleasure, anger, fear) regulate internal psychological processes as well as social/interpersonal activity, are specifiable in terms of unique and measurable behavioral patterns, and require no instruction from the social environment for their expression (Goldsmith et al., 1987). Temperament is defined in terms of individual differences in tendencies to experience and express the primary emotions. Relations between temperament and personality are straightforward insofar as traits such as aggressiveness are expected to be affected by individual differences in the experience and expression of the primary emotion anger (see Goldsmith in Goldsmith et al., 1987, p. 511). This model allows for other influences on the assembly of personality traits but assumes a strong relation between individual differences on those traits and individual differences on temperament dimensions.

Goldsmith and Campos distinguish their position from the others by including motivational components and by deemphasizing heritability. They noted that many emotional expressions imply motivational states, and they also noted that species-specific traits are canalized and so are not heritable in the behavioral genetics sense. In this model, primary emotions and their inborn communication system(s) have the same status as the attachment behavioral system in attachment theory. They are biological primitives or givens that support goals of individual and inclusive fitness and provide a foundation for the construction of individual differences in patterns of behavior over the life course. Developmentally, each emotion retains its set goal, but the means by which that goal is maintained, both in expressive and in receptive aspects, changes as a child matures. For most primary emotions, integration should be complete by the end of the first year of life. This suggests that stability with respect to rank orderings of individuals is not likely to be attained from early infancy. Because the inputs into temperament integrations will almost certainly come both from within and from outside the infant, it should be important to identify the social experiences that aid in the achievement and consolidation of such integrations.

The Rothbart and Derryberry (e.g., Rothbart & Derryberry, 1981) temperament model incorporated the behavioral phenomena discussed by Goldsmith and Campos (although they did not fully endorse the functionalist approach), but it did not limit the domain of temperament to emotional experience and expression. Rothbart (1989a, 1989b, 1989c) indicated that the scope of this theory extends to physiological and cognitive mechanisms underlying reactivity and regulation more generally. She defined temperament as constitutionally based individual differences in self-regulation and reactivity, with *constitutional* referring to the person's relatively enduring biological makeup, influenced over time by heredity, maturation, and experience (Rothbart, 1989a). *Reactivity* refers to arousal in motor, affective, autonomic, or endocrine domains, whereas *self-regulation* refers to processes that modulate the characteristic level of reactivity in response to endogenous and exogenous parameters. Although the reactivity and self-regulation constructs are distinct, they are not orthogonal at the level of measurement. Thus, a single observed behavior may be motivated by both reactive and self-regulative processes. In this model, temperament-relevant behavior may be observed in emotional, attentional, or motor activities. Defined in this manner, the domain of temperament covers much that might otherwise be considered cognitive development (e.g., Ruff & Rothbart, 1996) and interpersonal/social development (Rothbart, 1989c).

Rothbart suggested that temperament undergoes normative developmental change in conjunction with the maturational timetable governing shifts in the organization of physiological and cognitive processes that, in turn, underlie reactivity and self-regulation. Furthermore, because the underlying maturational timetables are not necessarily synchronized, some temperamental attributes may show normative and/or individual rank-order changes while other attributes remain stable (Rothbart, in Goldsmith et al., 1987, p. 516). Finally, some temperamental attributes are emergent rather than being specified in the earliest months of life. For example, in her model (Rothbart, 1989c), "behavioral inhibition" is not clearly defined until the second half of the first year and is dependent on CNS maturation and achievements in both motor and cognitive domains. She also suggests that most temperamental traits show significant, albeit modest, degrees of rank-order stability during infancy.

In addition to standing as an independent framework for describing and explaining normative and individual-difference aspects of temperament, the Rothbart-Derryberry approach grounds two important (and related) empirical approaches to temperament that have been explicitly directed at explaining the behavioral phenomena addressed by attachment theory; namely: "proneness to distress" and "behavioral inhibition." Kagan and associates (e.g., Garcia-Coll, Kagan, & Reznick, 1984; Kagan, Reznick, & Snidman, 1988) argued that the extremes of the behavioral inhibition dimension (either "inhibited" or "bold") are associated with characteristic patterns of autonomic nervous system and neuroendocrine responses (e.g., Fox, 1994; Kagan, Resnick, & Snidman, 1987) that broadly reflect CNS integrity and are stable after the toddler period. They (e.g., Kagan, Resnick, & Snidman, 1989) differed from other theorists in that their view of temperament does not *require* continuous dimensions. Rather, the salience of the behavioral inhibition construct is appreciated primarily at the extremes (the top or bottom 10% to 15% of cases) and is expected to show continuity only for the extreme cases.

Fox and associates (e.g., Calkins & Fox, 1992; Calkins, Fox, & Marshall, 1996; Fox, 1994) reported findings consistent with Kagan's notion that individual differences along the behavioral inhibition dimension have antecedents in both autonomic and CNS functioning. Their general findings were, however, more consistent with a "continuous dimension" than with a "discrete type" interpretation. Fox and associates argued that behavioral inhibition arises as an individual-difference dimension later in development than does reactivity. Calkins (1994) also suggested that socialization influences interact with endogenously organized trajectories of reactivity to produce inhibited or bold types in early childhood.

Gunnar and associates were more concerned with Rothbart and Derrryberry's construct of negative reactivity (usually operationalized as "proneness to distress" in their research) and its concomitant relations with the functioning of the hypothalamic-pituitary-adrenocortical (HPA) axis (e.g., Gunnar, 1994; Stansbury & Gunnar, 1994). Their data suggested that individual differences in HPA functioning could be assessed reliably very early in life and that those differences have expectable correlates in behavioral outcomes assessed some months later (e.g., Gunnar, Porter, Wolf, & Rigatuso, 1995). These findings tended to support the notion from Rothbart and Derryberry's theory concerning the primacy of reactivity and regulation as sources of temperament-relevant behaviors. Gunnar does not posit a necessarily causal relation between HPA indicators and temperament; rather, these systems may interact and be mutually regulating (e.g., Gunnar, Larson, Hertsgaard, Harris, & Broderson, 1992).

## Temperament as Social Construction

Bates (e.g., Bates, 1980; Bates & Bayles, 1984; Bates, Freeland, & Lounsbury, 1979) proposed an approach to conceptualizing temperament in terms of observable behaviors, but without making a strong interpretation regarding the underlying sources of individual differences along the several temperamental dimensions. The most salient temperamental attribute from this perspective is "difficultness," a construct first introduced by Thomas et al. (1963). Bates's difficultness construct differs from the behavioral style construct in that individual differences arise as much from the observer's (usually a parent's) perception that the behavior of the child is difficult for that observer as they may from some endogenously organized attribute of the child. Bates and Bayles (1984) documented diverse subjective and objective correlates of difficultness in children across the infancy period, using measures designed within this perspective. Although the problem of observer subjectivity with regard to temperament ratings behavior had been noted repeatedly (e.g., Sameroff, Seifer, & Elias, 1982; Vaughn, Bradley, Joffe, Seifer, & Barglow, 1987; Vaughn, Deinard, & Egeland, 1980), Bates was the first major temperament theorist to face the issue directly.

The behavioral territory claimed by Bates's theory resembles that of behavioral style theory and the theories of emotional expression/ regulation. However, unlike other approaches, Bates's construal of temperament comes close to being a social co-construction. In this aspect, his temperament dimensions share qualities with attachment relationships. That is, both difficult temperaments and attachments require the contributions of interacting partners, and both domains are seen as instrumental in setting a trajectory for later positive or negative adaptations in intra- and interpersonal realms of activity (see Bates, Maslin, & Frankel, 1985).

### Temperament Theory

That was then. By the mid-1990s the schools of temperament were unified under the psychobiological paradigm of Mary Rothbart, Hill Goldsmith, and their associates (Kagan, 2003, offers a similar appraisal). Derryberry and Rothbart (1997) defined *temperament* as affective, motivational, and cognitive (attentional) adaptations that are constitutional (i.e., grounded in neuroanatomical and physiological structures that are inherited) but also are shaped by experience. Constitutionally based differences in *reactivity* and *self-regulation* in the domains of attention, emotionality, and motor activity are the phenotypic expressions of temperament. Rothbart and Bates (2006) have recently presented an exhaustive review of this formulation of temperament theory and its implications for development; the interested reader is referred to their chapter for details.

## CONCEPTUAL RELATIONS BETWEEN ATTACHMENT AND TEMPERAMENT

### Potential and Realized Points of Conceptual Contact

On the surface, it seems that biological temperament constructs should converge with the normative understandings of attachment (Bowlby, 1982), because both Bowlby's explanation for the presence of the attachment behavioral system and temperament constructs depend to a greater or lesser extent on evolved, genetically inherited information. Surprisingly, the normative aspects of attachment did not excite the interest of temperament researchers. For example, Bowlby's notion that a species-specific, neurally based behavioral system regulates proximity and contact between children and adult caregivers retains its uniqueness and specificity under the modern temperament theory. Likewise, the notion that the child-caregiver relationship, from its earliest expression, is a love relationship (and, that loss in a love relationship leads to grieving) has no alternative temperament interpretation.

Although the biologically grounded aspects of attachment theory were not contested (or even considered) in temperament research, two distinct research programs have addressed the intersection of temperament and the socially constructed aspects of attachment (i.e., individual differences in attachment security). The first of these programs considered potential redundancies between the construct domains of temperament and attachment, whereas the second examined potential interactions between temperament and attachment security as predictors of salient life outcomes (for reviews and commentary, see Goldsmith & Alansky, 1987; Goldsmith & Harman, 1994; Kagan, 1984; Seifer & Schiller, 1995; Vaughn, Bost, & van IJzendoorn, 2008). Of these two broad research aims, the second would seem to be the most generative and implicative. Nevertheless, the first research aim captured the attention of temperament researchers during the "pre-paradigm" stage of temperament research, and the issue has surfaced again in some more recent studies. The literature generated by the redundancy question is voluminous, the results are somewhat chaotic, and the studies have been critically reviewed elsewhere (e.g., Mangelsdorf & Frosch, 1999; Vaughn & Bost, 1999; Vaughn et al., 2008). Rather than provide an extensive review, we present the general results of more than 70 such studies in Table 3.1.

## Testing Conceptual Redundancy

The most fundamental test of whether temperament and attachment constructs are redundant concerns possible differences between children enjoying secure attachments versus all others. When Strange Situation

Table 3.1 Empirical associations between attachment and temperament

| Temperament Perspective | Attachment Measure | Temperament Measure | Security | B vs. A and/or C and/or D | A vs. C | SS Behavior | Maternal Sensitivity-Responsivity |
|---|---|---|---|---|---|---|---|
| *Temperament as Behavioral Style* | | | | | | | |
| Bohlin, Hagekull, & Anderson (2005)* | SS[a] | TBQ[3] | – | N/A | N/A | N/A | N/A |
| Bohlin, Hagekull, Germer, Anderson, & Lindberg (1989) | Separation-reunion[a] | BBQ[2] | N/A | N/A | N/A | – | N/A |
| Booth-LaForce & Oxford (2008)* | AQS(O)[c] | ITQ-R[2] | + | N/A | N/A | N/A | + |
| Egeland & Farber (1984) | SS[a,b] | ITQ[1,3] | N/A | – | – | N/A | N/A |
| Fagot & Leve (1998)* | SS[b] | TTS[4] | – | N/A | N/A | N/A | N/A |
| Frodi, Bridges, & Shonk (1989) | SS[a] | ITQ-R[2] | N/A | + | – | N/A | N/A |
| Hagekull & Bohlin (2004)* | SS[a] | TBQ[3,4] | – | N/A | N/A | N/A | N/A |
| Kemp (1987) | SS[a] | ITQ[3] | N/A | + | + | – | N/A |
| Mangelsdorf, Gunnar, Kestenbaum, Lang, & Andreas (1990)* | SS[a] | TTA[3] | N/A | – | – | – | + |
| Nair & Murray (2005) | AQS(M)[d] | BSQ[5-6] | + | N/A | N/A | N/A | N/A |
| Pierrehumbert, Miljkovitch, Plancherel, Halfon, & Ansermet (2000) | SS[c] | PTQ[6] | N/A | – | – | – | N/A |
| Rieser-Danner, Roggman, & Langlois (1987) | SS[a] | TTS[3] | N/A | + | + | N/A | N/A |
| Seifer, Schiller, Sameroff, Resnick, & Riordan (1996)* | SS[a] | ITQ-R[3] | N/A | – | – | N/A | – |
| | AQS(O) | | + | N/A | N/A | N/A | – |

| Study | Attachment measure | Temperament measure | | | | | | |
|---|---|---|---|---|---|---|---|---|
| Stevenson-Hinde, & Shouldice (reported in Vaughn et al., 1992) | AQS(M)[d] | BSQ[5] | + | N/A | N/A | N/A | N/A | N/A |
| Trudel (reported in Vaughn et al., 1992) | AQS(M)[b] | TTS modified[4] | + | – | – | – | N/A | N/A |
| Vaughn, Lefever, Seifer, & Barglow (1989) | SS[a] | ITQ-R[3] | N/A | – | N/A | N/A | N/A | N/A |
| Hron-Stewart (reported in Vaughn et al., 1992) | AQS(O)[c] | TTS[4] | – | N/A | N/A | N/A | N/A | N/A |
| Joffe (reported in Vaughn et al., 1992) | AQS(O)[a] | ITQ-R[3] | – | N/A | N/A | N/A | N/A | N/A |
| Wachs & Desai (1993) | AQS(M)[c] | TTS[4] | + | N/A | N/A | N/A | N/A | + |
| Weber, Levitt, & Clark (1986) | SS[a] | DOTS[3] | N/A | – | – | – | + | NA |
| *Temperament as Emerging Personality* | | | | | | | | |
| Belsky, Fish, & Isabella (1991) | SS[a] | ICQ + observations[2,3] | N/A | – | – | N/A | N/A | – |
| Bohlin, Hagekull, & Anderson (2005)* | SS[a] | EAS[6] | – | N/A | N/A | N/A | N/A | N/A |
| Bretherton, Biringen, Ridgeway, & Maslin (1989) | PI[b], AQS(M)[c,d] | CCTI[4,5] | N/A | N/A | N/A | N/A | N/A | + |
| Crockenberg (1981) | SS[a] | NBAS[1] | N/A | – | – | – | – | + |
| Crockenberg & McCluskey (1986) | SS[a] | NBAS[1] | N/A | – | + | + | + | + |
| Hagekull & Bohlin (2003) | SS[a] | CCTI[4] | N/A | – | – | N/A | N/A | N/A |
| Hagekull & Bohlin (2004)* | SS[a] | CCTI[3,5] | + | N/A | N/A | N/A | N/A | N/A |
| Lewis & Feiring (1989) | Other separation-reunion[a] | Observed sociability[2] | N/A | + | + | + | + | N/A |

(Continued)

69

**Table 3.1 (Continued)**

| Temperament Perspective | Attachment Measure | Temperament Measure | Security | B vs. A and/or C and/or D | A vs. C | SS Behavior | Maternal Sensitivity-Responsivity |
|---|---|---|---|---|---|---|---|
| Rydell, Bohlin, & Thorell (2005) | Doll play[d] | EAS[6] (Shyness) | N/A | – | – | N/A | N/A |
| Seifer et al. (1996)* | SS[a] | EAS[3] | N/A | – | – | N/A | – |
| | AQS(O) | | + | N/A | N/A | N/A | – |
| Susman-Stillman, Kalkoske, Egeland & Waldman (1996) | SS[a] | Observation[1] ITQ[2,3] | N/A | – | + | N/A | + |
| van den Boom (1989) | SS[a] | NBAS[1] ICQ[3] | N/A | + | N/A | N/A | + |
| van den Boom (1994) | SS[a] | NBAS[1] | N/A | + | + | N/A | + |
| Waters, Vaughn & Egeland (1980) | SS[a] | NBAS[1] | N/A | + | + | N/A | N/A |
| *Temperament as Biologically Founded Substrates: Physiological Regulation, Reactivity, Proneness to Distress, and Behavioral Inhibition* | | | | | | | |
| Balleyguier (1991) | SS[a] | Neonatal Irritability[1] | N/A | + | – | N/A | + |
| Bohlin, Hagekull, & Anderson (2005)* | SS[a] | Inhibition[3,6] | – | N/A | N/A | N/A | N/A |
| Booth-LaForce & Oxford (2008)* | AQS(O)[c] | CBQ[6] | + | N/A | N/A | N/A | + |
| Bradshaw, Goldsmith, & Campos (1987) | SS[a] | IBQ[3] | N/A | – | – | + | N/A |
| Braungart-Rieker, Garwood, Powers, & Wang (2001) | SS[a] | Affect[2] Regulation[2] | N/A | + | + | N/A | + |

70

| | | | | | | | | |
|---|---|---|---|---|---|---|---|---|
| Braungart & Stiffer (1991) | SS[a] | Reactivity[3] | N/A | + | - | + | + | N/A |
| | | Regulation[3] | | + | - | + | + | N/A |
| Burgess, Marshall, Rubin, & Fox (2003) | SS[a] | Inhibition[4] | N/A | + | - | + | N/A | N/A |
| | | CCTI[6] | | - | - | - | | |
| Calkins & Fox (1992) | SS[a] | Neonatal reactivity[1] | N/A | + | - | + | + | N/A |
| | | 5 month Reactivity[2] | | - | - | - | | |
| | | IBQ[2] | | + | - | + | - | N/A |
| | | TBAQ[3,4] | | - | - | - | N/A | N/A |
| Denham & Moser (1994) | P[1] | IBQ[3] | N/A | N/A | N/A | N/A | N/A | + |
| Del Carmen, Pedersen, Huffman, & Bryan (1993) | SS[a] | BRP[2] | N/A | - | - | - | N/A | N/A |
| Fagot & Leve (1998)* | SS[b] | Observation[4] | - | N/A | N/A | N/A | N/A | N/A |
| Gunnar, Mangelsdorf, Larson, & Hertsgaard (1989) | SS[a] | LTA[3] | N/A | - | - | + | + | N/A |
| Hertsgaard, Gunnar, Erickson, & Nachmias (1995) | SS[b] | Cortisol Levels[4] | N/A | - | - | - | N/A | N/A |
| Ispa, Fine, & Thornburg (2002) | AQS(M)[a] | IBQ[3] | + | N/A | N/A | N/A | N/A | N/A |
| Izard, Haynes, Chisholm, & Baak (1991) | SS[a] | IBQ[3] | + | N/A | N/A | N/A | N/A | N/A |
| | | Emotional Expressiveness[2,3] | | | | | | |

*(Continued)*

Table 3.1   (Continued)

| Temperament Perspective | Attachment Measure | Temperament Measure | Security | B vs. A and/or C and/or D | A vs. C | SS Behavior | Maternal Sensitivity-Responsivity |
|---|---|---|---|---|---|---|---|
| Kanaya (1986) | Other separation-reunion[a] | | | | | | |
| Karrass & Braungart-Rieker (2004) | SS[a] | IBQ[2,3] | N/A | + | N/A | N/A | N/A |
| Kochanska (1995) | AQS(M)[c,d] | Observed Fearfulness[5] CBQ Composite[5] | + | N/A | N/A | N/A | N/A |
| Kochanska, Aksan, & Carlson (2005) | SS[a] | Proneness to anger[3] | N/A | - | - | N/A | N/A |
| Kotsaftis (reported in Vaughn et al., 1992) | AQS(M)[d] | CBQ[5] | + | N/A | N/A | N/A | N/A |
| Laible (2004) | AQS (M)[d] | CBQ[5-6] | + | N/A | N/A | N/A | N/A |
| Laible, Panfile, & Makariev (2008) | AQS (M)[c] | TBAQ[5] | + | N/A | N/A | N/A | N/A |
| Mangelsdorf et al. (1990)* | SS[a] | LTA[3] | N/A | - | - | - | + |
| Mangelsdorf et al. (2000) | SS[a] | IBQ[3] LAB-TAB[3] | N/A | + / - | - / + | N/A | - |
| Marshall & Fox (2005) | SS[a] | Motor Activity/ Reactivity[2] | N/A | - | - | N/A | N/A |

72

| Study | Code | Measure | | | | | |
|---|---|---|---|---|---|---|---|
| Miyake & Chen (1984) | SS[a] | Irritability/Proneness to distress[1,2] | N/A | + | N/A | N/A | N/A |
| Miyake, Chen, & Campos (1985) | SS[a] | Irritability/Proneness to distress[1,2] | N/A | + | N/A | N/A | N/A |
| Nachmias, Gunnar, Mangelsdorf, Parritz, & Buss (1996) | SS[b] | TBAQ[4] | N/A | - | - | N/A | N/A |
| | | Inhibition[3] | N/A | - | - | N/A | N/A |
| Pauli-Pott, Friedl, Hinney, & Hebebrand (2009) | SS[b] | Emotionality (Observation + IBQ)[2,3] | N/A | - | - | N/A | N/A |
| | | Fear (Observation + IBQ)[2,3] | | - | | | |
| Pauli-Pott, Haverkock, Pott, and Beckmann (2007) | SS[b] | Negative emotionality[2,3] | N/A | - | - | N/A | N/A |
| Rubin, Hastings, Stewart, Henderson, & Chen (1997) | Separation-reunion[c] | TBAQ[5] | + | N/A | N/A | N/A | N/A |
| | | Inhibition | + | N/A | N/A | N/A | N/A |
| Seifer et al. (1996)* | SS[a] | IBQ[3] | N/A | - | - | N/A | + |
| | AQS(O) | | + | N/A | N/A | N/A | N/A |
| Shamir-Essakow, Ungerer, & Rapee (2005) | SS[d] | STSC[6] | N/A | - | + | N/A | N/A |
| | | Inhibition[6] | N/A | - | + | N/A | N/A |
| Stevenson-Hinde & Marshall (1999) | SS[d] | Inhibition[6] | N/A | - | + | N/A | N/A |

(Continued)

**Table 3.1  (Continued)**

| Temperament Perspective | Attachment Measure | Temperament Measure | Security | B vs. A and/or C and/or D | A vs. C | SS Behavior | Maternal Sensitivity-Responsivity |
|---|---|---|---|---|---|---|---|
| Thompson, Connell, & Bridges (1988) | SS[a,b] | Temperamental fear[3,4] | N/A | N/A | N/A | + | N/A |
| Thompson & Lamb (1984) | SS[a] | Observed emotional responsiveness[3,4] | N/A | + | + | + | N/A |
| van Bakel & Riksen-Walraven (2004a) | SS[a] | TBAQ[3] | - | - | - | N/A | N/A |
| | AQS (M)[a] | | + | N/A | N/A | N/A | N/A |
| van Bakel & Riksen-Walraven (2004b) | SS[a] | TBAQ[3] | - | N/A | N/A | N/A | N/A |
| | AQS (M)[a] | | + | N/A | N/A | N/A | N/A |
| *Temperament as Social Construction* | | | | | | | |
| Bates, Maslin, & Frankel (1985) | SS[a] | ICQ[2,3] | N/A | - | - | + | N/A |
| Belsky & Rovine (1987) | SS[a] | NBAS[1] | N/A | + | + | N/A | N/A |
| | | ICQ[2] | N/A | - | - | N/A | N/A |
| Diener, Nievar, & Wright (2003) | AQS(M)[a-d] | PSI[3-6] | + | N/A | N/A | N/A | – |
| Emery, Paquette, & Bigras (2008) | SS[a] | ICQ[2] | N/A | - | N/A | N/A | – |
| Moran & Pederson (1998) | Home visit[a] | PSI[3] | N/A | + | + | N/A | N/A |
| | | AQS(M)[3] | | + | + | | |
| | | ICQ[4] | | + | + | | |
| | SS[b] | PSI/AQS/ICQ | | - | - | | |

74

| Study | Attachment measure | Temperament measure | | | | | |
|---|---|---|---|---|---|---|---|
| Scher & Mayseless (2000) | SS[a] | ICQ[3] | | – | | N/A | N/A |
| Seifer et al. (1996)* | SS[a] | ICQ[3] | | – | – | N/A | – |
| | AQS(O) | | + | | | N/A | N/A |
| Stams, Juffer, & van IJzendoorn (2002) | SS[a] | ICQ[3,4,5] | – | | N/A | N/A | N/A |
| Szewczyk-Sokolowski, Bost, & Wainwright (2005) | AQS(O)[d] | ICQ[5-6] | + | | N/A | N/A | N/A |
| Tarabulsy et al. (2008) | AQS(M)[a] | ICQ[2] | + | | N/A | N/A | N/A |
| | AQS(O)[a] | | – | | | | |
| Volling & Belsky (1992) | SS (Father)[a] | ICQ (Mother)[2] | N/A | + | N/A | N/A | N/A |

*Note:* More articles are represented in Table 3.1 than are cited in the text. +, effect tested and significant; –, effect tested and not significant; N/A, effect not tested.

*Multiple category placements

*Attachment measures:* AQS-M (Attachment Q-sort-mother); AQS-O (Attachment Q-sort-Observer); PI (parent interview); SS (Strange Situation); other separation-reunion. [a]Attachment assessed between 11 and 15 months; [b]Attachment assessed between 16 and 20 months; [c]Attachment assessed between 21 and 36 months; [d]Attachment assessed after 36 months.

*Temperament measures:* BBQ (Baby Behavior Questionnaire); BRP (Behavioral Responsiveness Paradigm); BSQ (Behavioral Style Questionnaire); CBQ (Children's Behavior Questionnaire); CCTI (Colorado Child Temperament Inventory); DOTS (Dimensions of Temperament Survey); EAS (Emotionality, Activity, Sociability); IBQ (Infant Behavior Questionnaire); ICQ (Infant Characteristics Questionnaire); ITQ (Infant Temperament Questionnaire); ITQ-R (Infant Temperament Questionnaire-Revised); LAB-TAB (Laboratory Temperament Assessment Battery); LTA (Louisville Temperament Assessment); NBAS (Neonatal Behavioral Assessment Scale); PSI (Parent Stress Index); PTQ (Parent Temperament Questionnaire); TBAQ (Toddler Behavior Assessment Questionnaire); TBQ (Toddler Behavior Questionnaire); TTS (Toddler Temperament Scale). [1]Temperament assessment during neonatal period; [2]Temperament assessment in first half of first year; [3]temperament assessment between 6 and 15 months; [4]temperament assessment between 16 and 24 months; [5]temperament assessment between 25 and 42 months; [6]temperament assessment after 42 months.

classifications are the criterion of attachment security, only 2 of 11 tests (see Table 3.1) were significant. On the other hand, when the Attachment Q-sort "Security" criterion (AQS, Waters, 1995) was the indicator of attachment security, 22 of 25 correlation tests reported in these studies were significant. In general, temperamental reactivity scores were negatively associated with the AQS Security score.

This difference in the patterning of results for the two gold standard measures for infant attachment (see van IJzendoorn, Vereijken, Bakermans-Kranenburg, & Riksen-Walraven, 2004) seems curious but may be interpreted in at least two ways. First, some investigators have suggested that the securely attached (i.e., Group B) cases are diverse with respect to reactivity and/or regulation domains (e.g., Belsky & Rovine, 1987; Braungart-Rieker, Garwood, Powers, & Wang, 2001; Thompson & Lamb, 1984) and that secure subgroups B1 and B2 may share the reactivity pattern of Group A (insecure-avoidant) infants, whereas subgroups B3 and B4 may share the reactivity pattern of Group C (insecure-resistant) infants. Although this conjecture remains controversial and has frequently failed to replicate (e.g., Vaughn et al., 1989), it could account for the failure to find significant differences when children classified as secure in the Strange Situation are contrasted against the combination of all others.

Second, there are several reasons why reactivity, perhaps especially negative reactivity, should be negatively associated with attachment security when security is assessed in "ordinary" contexts using the AQS (as opposed to "emergency" contexts, such as separations from the caregiver in unfamiliar places). Bowlby (1969/1982) recognized that affect expression and regulation were central features of attachment relationships. He believed that the presence of the attachment figure was an occasion for joy and pleasure, whereas the loss or threat of loss of the attachment figure would be associated with sadness and anger or fear in the attached child. Consistent with this argument, securely attached children are often described as expressing more positive affect in the context of interactions with their attachment figures than are insecurely attached children (e.g., Waters, Wippman, & Sroufe, 1979). The AQS includes items descriptive of the child's expression of positive and negative affect in the context of interaction and in the context of impending or realized separations, which reflect Bowlby's emphasis on the attachment figure's regulation of the child's affect experience. Consequently, the AQS security score and reports on reactivity and/or regulation completed by the attachment figure might be expected to overlap, especially if the same informant (the parent) completes both the temperament and the AQS measures. This is true for studies listed in Table 3.1. Of 13 associations between the AQS security score and measures of temperament, all were significant when mothers completed both instruments, and 7 of 10 associations proved significant when observers provided the AQS scores. Interestingly, the magnitudes of associations tended to be substantially larger in samples for which mothers provided data for both measures than for samples in which observer's AQS scores were correlated with temperament scores from maternal reports. Several reviewers have identified a range of concerns about maternal AQS scores (see Moss, Bureau, Cyr, & Dubois-Comtois, 2006; van IJzendoorn et al., 2004), and it seems likely that the elevated correlations found when mothers completed both measures arose because the attachment and temperament data came from a common source.

Many of the studies listed in Table 3.1 tested for specific group differences (e.g., B vs. A; B vs. C; A vs. C; total of 117 statistical tests). Of 62 tests using separate contrasts involving the secure (Group B) cases, 23 reached significance, but results of many studies are difficult to interpret. The only result showing any consistency across studies suggests that insecure-resistant (Group C) infants tend to be more negatively reactive than do secure (Group B) infants. For the A vs. C contrast, only 15 of 55 tests were significant, and some of these studies contradict each other. For example, in some studies, avoidant children were described as temperamentally easier (Kemp, 1987), more sociable (Susman-Stillman, Kalkoske, Egeland, & Waldman, 1996), or less behaviorally inhibited (Burgess, Marshall, Rubin, & Fox, 2003) than were children classified as insecure-resistant. But, other studies suggested that insecure-avoidant children are more temperamentally difficult (Frodi, Bridges, & Shonk, 1989), highly irritable (van den Boom, 1994), less sociable (Lewis and Feiring, 1989), or higher on fearfulness (Mangelsdorf, McHale, Diener, Goldstein, & Lehn, 2000) than secure and/or insecure-resistant children. In other studies, insecure-resistant children were found to be the most negatively reactive and/or inhibited (e.g., Miyake, Chen, & Campos, 1985; Moran & Pederson, 1998; Stevenson-Hinde & Marshall, 1999; Waters, Vaughn, & Egeland, 1980). Yet other studies (e.g., Belsky & Rovine, 1987; Braungart-Rieker et al., 2001; Susman-Stillman et al., 1996) combined the insecure-avoidant with the B1 and B2 (securely attached) subgroups and also combined the insecure-resistant cases with the B3 and B4 (securely attached) subgroups for analyses. Results suggested that children in the A+B1+B2 group were less negatively reactive and better regulated than the C+B3+B4 group.

In a few studies, temperament scores were tested as predictors of child behaviors in the Strange Situation and/or in relation to rated maternal sensitivity to child communicative signals. Again, results are inconsistent (e.g., 11 of 20 associations with child behavior significant; 15 of 26 correlations with maternal sensitivity significant) and difficult to interpret. For example, Vaughn et al. (1989) found that negative reactivity was associated with infant crying during the separation episodes of the Strange Situation but was not associated significantly with crying during the reunion episodes (which are critical for determining the infant's attachment classification). So, although crying at the threat of loss of the attachment figure (i.e., at separation) is an attachment behavior in Bowlby's sense, it is not an indicator of attachment security. The general results of analyses examining relations between temperament ratings and maternal sensitivity measures are more consistent (infants who are more reactive or less able to regulate affect and behavior tend to have mothers rated as less sensitive), but in most studies the assessments of temperament and maternal sensitivity are concurrent and the direction of effects cannot be determined. Furthermore, the indicators for maternal sensitivity vary widely across studies, and the specific dimensions of reactive or regulatory temperament that show significant associations with maternal sensitivity also differ from study to study.

Taken together, the results of studies testing the redundancy of temperament and attachment security constructs provide scant support for the notion that individual differences along temperamental reactivity or regulation dimensions are causally related to individual differences in attachment security. Even when measures from both construct domains show moderately consistent correlations across studies (as with negative reactivity dimensions and the AQS security score or maternal sensitivity scores), the results cannot be decisive because both theories offer plausible (and opposed) explanations for those correlations.

## Testing Interactions Between Attachment and Temperament Domains

Although we have characterized the two broad research programs as though they were sequentially organized, several studies reported in Table 3.1 also tested potential interactions between attachment and temperament as predictors to a variety of outcomes. For example, Gunnar and associates (e.g., Gunnar, Broderen, Nachmias, Buss, & Rigatuso, 1996) systematically examined relations among attachment security, fearful temperament, and cortisol reactivity. In their study, attachment security was related to *baseline* cortisol levels (taken during medical checkups and inoculations at 2, 4, and 6 months of age) and to maternal responsiveness. Neither cortisol *reactivity* nor behavioral *reactivity* at the clinic visits predicted attachment classifications, but attachment security moderated relations between temperamental fearfulness and cortisol reactivity. A positive relation between fear and cortisol reactivity was observed *only* for insecure cases. This suggests that attachment security was a protective factor buffering the effects of high fearfulness on cortisol reactivity. Schieche and Spangler (2005) reached a similar conclusion concerning protective effects of attachment security (albeit using a different assessment context and different indices of reactivity). Schieche and Spangler also noted that security moderated relations between behavioral inhibition and task behavior in a problem-solving task. Whereas insecure-inhibited children decreased task involvement and sought proximity to the mother as the tasks became more difficult, secure-inhibited children increased task-related help-seeking in the difficult tasks. For the insecure-inhibited cases, proximity seeking was associated with increasing cortisol reactivity, but for secure-inhibited cases, seeking task-relevant instrumental assistance had a negative relation with cortisol reactivity.

Some more recent examples of a moderating role for attachment security in buffering the influences of temperamental reactivity are reported by Gilissen et al. (2007, 2008), who studied physiological stress responses to fear-inducing film clips. Skin conductance and heart rate variability were measured during the film clips. Children responded to the fear-inducing film clip with increases in skin conductance and decreases in heart rate variability. Attachment security affected the physiological reactivity to fearful clips in temperamentally reactive children but not in less-reactive children, irrespective of age. Temperamentally reactive children who *also* had a less secure relationship had the highest skin conductance responses to the film clip, whereas reactive children with a more secure relationship showed the lowest skin conductance responses. Consistent with the differential susceptibility hypothesis (Belsky, 2005), these findings suggest that attachment security may play a more salient role for temperamentally reactive children, both for better and for worse.

These kinds of findings suggest that a systematic investigation of whether and how attachment and temperament interact would be useful. Accordingly, in the next section of this chapter, we consider the kinds of claims made about specific aspects of behavior, cognition, and affect made by modern attachment and temperament theories and review studies that have used constructs and measures from both attachment and temperament that may support those claims.

## Attachment and Temperamental Reactivity or Regulation as Predictors of Adaptive Functioning

In the Bowlby/Ainsworth theory, the attachment *system* regulates proximity and contact with the caregiver, whereas the secure-base *relationship* supports the child's exploration of the immediate and far environments by regulating his or her feeling of security in the context of novelty and challenge (Sroufe, 1996; Sroufe et al., 2005). The secure-base relationship also supports construction of mental representations of the self and others, especially others with whom a close relationship has been co-constructed. Thus, although the attachment system functions autonomously most of the time, attachment working models are at least potentially accessible to conscious contemplation (although preverbal children's representations are sensorimotor rather than internal or mental).

They are also susceptible to instruction from the social environment. This leads us to suggest that consequences of attachment in adaptive functioning domains should be most apparent when *interpersonal* outcomes are considered. This may be especially true when personality and adjustment outcomes are contingent on socializing transactions between the child and attachment figure. Conversely, we would expect to find that influences of attachment security or type of insecurity would be less evident (although not absent) in broad aspects of personality (e.g., extraversion or conscientiousness), cognitive functioning (e.g., IQ), and other outcomes that are thought to be highly heritable. Likewise, it seems likely that attachment-related variables would less strongly predict aspects of adjustment (e.g., measures of problem behaviors or criminality or achievement in academic and work settings), which, although often explicit targets of parental and other socialization efforts, may be more directly associated with demographic or contextual factors (e.g., SES, ethnicity/race, immigrant status, neighborhood quality, behavioral profiles of peers) and with heritable attributes identified above than with attachment relationships per se.

In contrast, the emphasis in modern temperament theory is on constitutionally based reactivity and regulation in relation to activity, attention, and affect (e.g., Buss, Davidson, Kalin, & Goldsmith, 2004; Gunnar et al., 1995; Kagan, 1994; Rothbart, 2004). This implies significant associations with heritable dimensions of personality (e.g., Halverson, Kohnstamm, & Martin, 1994; McCrae et al., 2000). Furthermore, to the extent that temperament is defined as *regulation* of motor activity, attention, and affect, individual differences in regulatory capacity and motivation should be causal antecedents to a range of outcomes such as externalizing problem behaviors, including attention deficit-hyperactive and conduct disorders (e.g., Nigg, Goldsmith, & Sachek, 2004; Rettew, Copeland, Stanger, & Hudziak, 2004), anxiety disorders (e.g., Prior, Smart, Sanson, & Oberklaid, 2000), and adjustment in settings such as schools (e.g., Eisenberg et al., 2004; Nelson, Martin, Hodge, Havill, & Kamphaus, 1999).

Thus, we would expect that associations between temperament and relational outcomes (e.g., friendships, teacher-child relationships) would be less prominent (but not necessarily absent) than associations between aspects of temperament and heritable aspects of personality and cognitive functioning. Of course, these broad dimensions of adjustment, personality, and cognition overlap to an extent with the kinds of outcomes we suggest are consequences of attachment, so interactions across these domains should be expected, even though the nature of those interactions (e.g., mediating, moderating) has not (yet) been derived from either attachment or temperament theories.

## Interpersonal Outcomes Predicted From Attachment and Temperament Constructs

That attachment security predicts parent-child interaction and relationship quality and aspects of peer interaction throughout the childhood years has been well documented (e.g., Arend, Gove, & Sroufe, 1979; Matas, Arend, & Sroufe, 1978; Waters et al., 1979). Secure attachments in infancy predict smoother and more harmonious parent-child interactions during the toddler period, perhaps especially in the context of developmentally challenging tasks (Matas et al., 1978) and specific patterns of positive peer interactions in preschoolers (e.g., LaFreniere & Sroufe, 1985). However, these studies did not consider the possibility that temperamental characteristics of the child might also contribute to these interactions and the relationships they support (see Chess & Thomas, 1983, for a discussion). Kochanska's studies (e.g., Kochanska, 1995) are exemplars of this approach to parent-child interactions and relationships, and we review representative studies from her research program (and qualifications on her conclusions suggested by others) as follows.

Kochanska has tested several temperament dimensions, especially fearfulness/anxiety proneness, as mediators of relations between attachment security, maternal discipline, and behavioral and cognitive indicators of children's developing conscience from toddlerhood through early childhood (e.g., Kochanska, 1995, 1997, 2001). In early studies, she (e.g., Fowles & Kochanska, 2000) reported that different aspects of parent-child interactions and relationships contributed to conscience development in children with lower versus higher levels of temperamental fearfulness. Attachment security was the primary predictor of internalization (of maternal directives/prohibitions) for fearless children, but for more fearful children maternal gentle discipline was the primary predictor. Subsequently, Kochanska, Aksan, and Carlson (2005) studied temperamental proneness to anger and attachment security as predictors of receptive cooperation with mothers and fathers. Security, but not anger proneness, significantly predicted later receptive cooperation. Anger proneness did not interact with attachment security in predicting later receptive cooperation in mother-child interactions. For the father-child data, however, a significant interaction was obtained; the association between anger proneness and receptive cooperation was significant only when the child was insecure with the father.

Schieche and Spangler (2005) tested the predictive utility of behavioral inhibition (a presumed component of fearfulness/anxiety proneness), adrenal-cortical reactivity (assessed in a problem-solving task context), and attachment security for toddlers' behavior in the problem-solving task. Attachment security in infancy predicted toddler task orientation, help seeking, and the balance of attachment and exploratory behaviors in the problem-solving tasks, whereas behavioral inhibition predicted aspects of the child's approach to the task. For insecure children, high behavioral inhibition predicted elevated adrenal-cortical reactivity, but this relation was not found in the group of secure children. Furthermore, physiological reactivity showed different patterns of relations with toddler behavior in the problem-solving tasks for secure and insecure children (with significant relations found only for insecure cases). Thus, in contrast with Kochanska's (1995, 1998) findings, attachment security moderated the potential influences of behavioral inhibition and physiological reactivity on child behavior.

Van der Mark, Bakermans-Kranenburg, and van IJzendoorn (2002) also examined relations between fearfulness, attachment security, and compliance with maternal directives and prohibitions ("do x" vs. "don't do x") in a longitudinal study from 16 to 22 months of age. Neither attachment security nor fearfulness, nor their interaction, had consistent significant relations with children's committed compliance; rather, compliance was related to the quality of maternal behavior (as sensitive or intrusive). These findings are consistent with Kochanska's more recent findings (e.g., Kochanska, Forman, Aksan, & Dunbar, 2005; Kochanska & Murray, 2000) suggesting that qualities of parental behavior (which are antecedents of child attachment security), rather than security per se, affect aspects of conscience development. Even so, Kochanska, Aksan, Knaack, and Rhines (2004) suggested that the efficacy of parental socialization is contingent on attachment security. That is, securely attached toddlers were more readily influenced by parental socialization attempts than were insecurely attached children.

Both attachment security and temperamental reactivity and/or regulation have been identified as critical antecedents to peer social competence and to relationships with peers and teachers (e.g., Eisenberg, Fabes, Guthrie, & Reiser, 2000; Park & Waters, 1989; Suess, Grossmann, & Sroufe, 1992). There are, however, fewer reports concerning joint relations between attachment and temperament as predictors of aspects of teacher and peer relationships or peer social competence that have been published.

Szewczyk-Sokolowski, Bost, and Wainright (2005) assessed attachment security (i.e., AQS security score), difficult temperament, and children's sociometric acceptance concurrently for a sample of preschool children and reported that both attachment security and difficult temperament were significant correlates (positive for attachment, negative for temperamental difficulty) of peer sociometric acceptance, whereas only difficult temperament was significantly (positively) associated with peer rejection. The interaction of attachment security and difficult temperament was not significant. Rydell, Bohlin, and Thorell (2005) tested joint relations of attachment representation (assessed using a story completion task), shyness, and peer competence as well as teacher-child relationships in a preschool sample. As in the Szewczyk-Sokolowski et al. (2005) report, there were main effects of both attachment and shyness, but the interaction of these dimensions was not significant. Attachment security positively predicted peer competence outcomes and teacher-child relationship patterns. Shy children tended to have fewer conflicts with peers (as compared to more bold children), but also had less optimal relationships with teachers (again, in comparison to more bold peers).

Bohlin, Hagekull, and Andersson (2005) tested relations between attachment, temperament, and peer social competence at early school age. Attachment at 15 months was a significant positive correlate of social competence at age 8. Behavioral inhibition assessed during infancy (at 13 and 15 months) did not predict social competence measures; however, behavioral inhibition assessed at age 4 was a significant negative predictor of social competence at age 8. These latter results were qualified by an interaction with attachment. For securely attached cases, high behavioral inhibition showed a significant positive association with social competence at age 8, whereas for insecure participants high behavioral inhibition was significantly negatively associated with social competence.

In a longitudinal study of children adopted as infants, Juffer and associates (e.g., Jaffari-Bimmel, Juffer, van IJzendoorn, Bakermans-Kranenburg, & Mooijaart, 2006; Stams, Juffer, & van IJzendoorn, 2002) examined relations among attachment, temperament, and social adaptation from infancy to adolescence. Attachment security assessed during infancy, as well as easy temperament, predicted prosocial development at age 7 (Stams et al., 2002). Effects of attachment during infancy on positive social development at age 14 were mediated by childhood (age 7) positive social development and by a social development (age 7) to maternal sensitivity (age 14) pathway. Effects of infant and childhood temperament were also mediated (by positive social development at age 7, temperament at age 14, and maternal sensitivity at age 14). Temperament explained a substantially larger part of the variance in social development than attachment security or parental sensitivity. The interaction of attachment and temperament in infancy did not have a significant pathway in the overall model (Jaffari-Bimmel et al., 2006). The results suggest that both attachment and temperament constructs contribute to subsequent positive social development, albeit through different and noninteracting pathways.

Considered together, the results from both parent-child interaction and peer competence studies are consistent with our suggestion that attachment security should be a significant predictor of outcomes in interpersonal domains. Measures of both temperamental reactivity and regulation also show significant relations with social outcomes measured later in childhood. However, Kochanska's research program suggests that socialization practices are the proximal causal factors leading to variations in social outcomes (at least for compliance and conscience) and that these may be moderated by attachment quality, such that securely attached children are more easily socialized by parents than are insecure children. Social outcomes assessed outside the family are predictable from both attachment and temperament constructs. Only modest evidence suggests that attachment security and temperament domains interact in the prediction(s) to outcomes in the peer group, and the available data suggest that attachment security moderates relations between temperament and peer competence outcomes rather than the reverse.

## Intrapersonal Outcomes Predicted From Attachment and Temperament Constructs

Although Bowlby argued that attachment, or attachment-related phenomena, should be causal antecedents to aspects of personality and psychopathology (e.g., Bowlby, 1980), and temperament has been linked explicitly with somatic reactivity and regulation as well as with personality and psychopathology, only a handful of studies have considered both attachment and temperament constructs as predictors of outcomes in these domains, and older or nonstandard temperament measures were used in some studies. We review representative studies for three domains (physiological reactivity and regulation, personality, and problem behaviors), but none of these offer the breadth of programmatic research available for the outcome domains previously discussed.

Both attachment theory and modern temperament theories posit associations between their constitutive construct domains and adaptive responses to stress/distress. Whereas temperament approaches tend to treat reactivity and regulation of affect and behavior as broad trait-like aspects of the person, attachment theory assumes that arousal and regulation of affect, cognition, and behavior in the context of the threat of loss or separation from an attachment figure are governed by the attachment behavioral system and that, with the assembly of internal working models, these adaptive processes may generalize to other social contexts (see Sroufe et al., 2005). Furthermore, attachment theory suggests that the attachment figure plays an important role in regulating arousal throughout childhood; this is not solely the responsibility of the child (e.g., Spangler, Schieche, Ilg, Maier, & Ackermann, 1994; Sroufe, 1996). Given the relevance of arousal and regulation in both attachment and temperament domains, it is not surprising that studies have related temperament and/or attachment to the physiological systems governing the production and breakdown of cortisol (a major stress hormone), especially the HPA axis (e.g., Gunnar et al., 1992; Spangler, Fremmer-Bombik, & Grossmann, 1996). Several of these studies included measures of both attachment and temperament as correlates of cortisol reactivity in response to stress (e.g., Gunnar et al., 1996; Schieche & Spangler, 2005).

Van Bakel and Riksen-Walraven (2004a, 2004b) used both the Strange Situation classifications and the AQS as attachment security indicators in a study of temperament, parent-child interaction in the context of a teaching task, and cortisol reactivity in a task testing both social (stranger) and nonsocial (toy robot) fearfulness. Strange Situation classifications were unrelated to the temperament measures and the measure of cortisol reactivity, but the AQS security score had significant associations with anger proneness (negative) and pleasure (positive) from the temperament assessment, task orientation in the parent-child teaching task, and social fear (in the stranger interaction task). Interactions of the attachment and temperament measures did not yield significant effects. Thus, in contrast to studies reviewed earlier, no special protective effect of attachment security (assessed by either the Strange Situation or the AQS) was observed in the relation between cortisol reactivity and fearfulness/inhibition.

In addition to cortisol activation, researchers have also examined cardiac reactivity in relation to child temperament and attachment security. In general, these studies are based on the theoretical notion that individual differences in autonomic nervous system responses related to arousal may influence social engagement behaviors. In particular, the vagal system is proposed to regulate vagal input to the heart and facilitate changes in heart rate required to promote social communication when there are challenges to homeostasis, and when this regulatory mechanism is not applied, the sympathetic nervous system is recruited and more defensive behavior may be exhibited (e.g., Porges, Doussard-Roosevelt, Portales, & Greenspan, 1996).

Stevenson-Hinde and Marshall (1999) examined heart period (HP, the interval between heartbeats) and respiratory sinus arrhythmia (RSA) during a modified Strange Situation in relation to children's attachment security and behavioral inhibition in a sample of preschool children. They found that for secure and for low inhibited children, HP significantly increased at reunion with the caregiver, but this increase was not evident for highly inhibited or insecure children. RSA also increased at reunion except for the highly inhibited children. Thus, in general, separation from caregivers was associated with increases in heart rate, whereas reunion tended to be associated with decreasing heart rate (with the exceptions noted), and these physiological changes were affected by both attachment quality and temperament.

Although these results are not consistent, procedural differences between them (e.g., age ranges, measures of behavioral inhibition, length of separation from mother) make reconciliation difficult. Additional studies will be needed to clarify relations between these sympathetic and parasympathetic nervous system indicators and both attachment and temperament domains.

Hagekull and Bohlin (2003) studied both attachment security and temperament during toddlerhood as predictors of the "big five" personality traits at 8 to 9 years old. The temperament variables were not associated with attachment security. Attachment security predicted Extraversion, Openness (both positively), and Neuroticism (negatively) (3 of 5 correlations significant). The temperament dimensions yielded two (of 15) significant associations, both with Extraversion. One (of 15 tested) interaction between attachment security and the temperament scores was significant. Secure children had lower scores on Neuroticism than insecure children at high and low levels of emotionality, but secure children with high emotionality scores had higher Neuroticism scores than did secure children with low emotionality scores.

Although both attachment and temperament frameworks have been invoked by investigators studying problem behaviors (e.g., Erickson,

Egeland, & Sroufe, 1985), only a few reports include measures from both domains. McCartney et al. (2004) used data from the NICHD Study of Early Child Care and Youth Development data set to examine attachment (Strange Situation at 15 and 36 months, AQS at 24 months) as a predictor to externalizing problems. A temperament measure was completed by the mother at the 6-month home visit and was used to index reactivity/difficultness. Problem behaviors were rated by mothers and by teachers at 36 months. Small but significant associations between attachment security and maternal ratings of both internalizing and externalizing behavior problems were found. Difficult temperament also predicted maternal ratings of behavior problems. The interaction of temperament and attachment was not significant. Attachment security also had modest but significant predictive associations to (nonparental) caregiver-rated internalizing and externalizing behaviors; however, there was no significant predictive association between teacher-rated behavior problems and mother-rated temperamental difficulty. Adding the attachment x difficulty interaction did not add significant variance to the regression equation. Burgess et al. (2003) also reported direct effects of infant behavioral inhibition (vs. uninhibited temperament) and attachment on maternal reported externalizing behaviors at 4 years of age. In this study, however, only the insecure-avoidant infants had elevated externalizing scores, and the interaction of avoidance and uninhibited temperament produced the highest externalizing scores.

A few studies examined the role of both attachment and temperament in the development of anxiety disorders. Manassis, Bradley, Goldberg, Hood, and Swinson (1995) examined these relations in a sample of preschool children with anxious mothers. Insecure attachment predicted internalizing problems and indicators of childhood anxiety, whereas behavioral inhibition was associated with somatic difficulties. Additionally, Warren, Huston, Egeland, and Sroufe (1997) followed up 172 adolescents who had been seen in the Strange Situation during infancy and found that insecure-resistant attachment predicted anxiety disorders in adolescence over and beyond maternal anxiety and maternal reports of child temperament. More recently, Shamir-Essakow, Ungerer, and Rapee (2005) tested relations between insecure attachment, behavioral inhibition (maternal report and lab procedure), and anxiety disorders (DSM-IV criteria) in an at-risk sample of preschool children. Both behavioral inhibition and insecure attachment were unique and significant predictors of child anxiety, even after controlling for maternal anxiety. Children who were inhibited, insecure, and whose mothers were anxious had the highest anxiety levels.

The results reviewed in this section are mixed and difficult to reconcile. In most of the studies, findings run contrary to our expectations that temperament rather than attachment should be the primary predictor of outcomes from developmental domains with high heritability (e.g., physiological reactivity, personality). When interactions were significant, typically the attachment variable moderated effects of temperament on a given outcome rather than the reverse, and this holds across all areas reviewed.

## TEMPERAMENT, ATTACHMENT, AND THE MINNESOTA PARENT-CHILD LONGITUDINAL STUDY

From its inception, the MPCLS was intended as a study of adaptive development and adjustment for children in risky environments. It was expected that both developmental and adjustment outcomes would depend on the nature of the external and internal resources available to the child. External resources included (but were not limited to) a supportive family environment committed to the support of the child's growth. Internal resources included physical integrity (e.g., motor/physical systems, regulatory systems, CNS) and temperamental attributes (e.g., activity level, emotional reactivity). When the project was launched, the dominant approach to temperament was the Thomas and Chess behavioral style school, and behavioral style questionnaires were selected as temperament measures. However, it became clear that these measures were flawed (e.g., Vaughn et al., 1980) insofar as temperament dimensions from the questionnaires proved to be associated as much with domains that could not be construed as infant temperament (e.g., maternal personality) as they were with observed infant behavior. Although a few early studies from the MPCLS did suggest that physical and CNS integrity was an important antecedent to interactions contributing to attachment (e.g., Waters et al., 1980), behavioral style temperament during infancy did not prove to be a very useful predictor to attachment or to other social outcomes assessed on the course of the project (see Sroufe et al., 2005). Although it would not be fair to claim that the MPCLS data led directly to the undermining of the behavioral style school, these findings were consistent with the growing concerns among temperament researchers that did result in a reformulation of temperament theory in the 1990s.

With respect to the two large research programs reviewed, the MPCLS has contributed to both, although in different ways. We noted that Sroufe (e.g., 1985; Sroufe & Waters, 1982) addressed the construct redundancy issue early on. He argued that infants co-construct unique, independent attachments with each parent, but their temperaments should not differ as a function of the parent with whom they happen to be interacting. If temperament accounted for attachment, then attachments with mothers and fathers should be considerably more concordant than they actually are. Belsky and Rovine (1987) proposed that negative emotionality could be used to group children in the Strange Situation in a manner that was orthogonal to the security/insecurity dimension and that cross-parent differences would occur at the same end of the emotionality dimension (e.g., a child classified as avoidant with one parent would be classified as B1 or B2 with the other parent, if there was a secure vs. insecure difference). However, this framework produced mixed results, and Belsky later modified his proposal (e.g., Belsky, Rosenberger, & Crnic, 1995). Sroufe (e.g., 1996) also was critical of the modern temperament theory's construal of temperamental regulatory mechanisms and dimensions. He argued that the social regulation of arousal/tension is observable throughout infancy and toddlerhood, and the child's experience of being regulated forms the foundation of later self-control and self-regulation of affect, thought, and behavior after the toddler period. Indeed, much of what felt security entails is both the down- and up-regulating of psychological tension. Consequently, Sroufe argued that attachment relationships are the primary structures regulating the expression and experience of emotional reactivity during infancy. This position is reflected in many of the studies examining interactions between attachment and temperament domains.

As with the first question, the MPCLS data set produced one of the first empirical studies of the interactive effects of temperamental negative reactivity and sociability and attachment-relevant (i.e., maternal sensitivity) variables as they jointly predicted Strange Situation classifications (i.e., Susman-Stillman et al., 1996). Importantly, they attempted to develop theoretically relevant hypotheses for the kinds of interactions they examined. Two types of interaction models were tested for temperament and sensitivity data collected at both 0 to 3 months and 6 months: (1) moderator models in which the relation between maternal sensitivity and attachment security (secure vs. nonsecure in the Strange Situation) was contingent on the level of infant temperament, and (2) mediator models in which effects of infant temperament were transmitted via maternal sensitivity. Consistent with the majority of studies, no significant direct effects of temperament on attachment security were observed. However, for the 0- to 3-month data, a moderating effect of temperament proved significant. The relation between sensitivity and attachment security was significant only for less-reactive infants. They also reported a significant mediation model for the 6-month data, but this is difficult to interpret because the main effect of temperamental reactivity on attachment was not, itself, significant. Subsequent tests found no evidence for significant interaction effects in the prediction of insecure classifications (i.e., avoidant vs. resistant). Although the yield from the temperament x sensitivity interaction analyses in this study was not large, we believe that the study design was significant and grounded many of the studies of attachment x temperament interactions published over the last 15 years.

## CONCLUSION: WHERE CAN WE GO FROM HERE?

The conceptual frameworks of both temperament and attachment have progressed substantially over the last 30 years. Studies focused on temperament now have a single, grounded theory to guide hypotheses and data collection, rather than the handful of frameworks that were competing for intellectual space in the 1980s. Attachment theory and research has become a juggernaut accumulating and assimilating facts and theoretical concepts from cognitive, social, clinical, and developmental psychology, as well as from psychoanalytic theory. From the current vantage point of both theoretical perspectives, the question of redundancies in explanatory constructs now seems quaint, historical, and somewhat misguided. Rather, it appears that advances in understandings of adaptation and development will come from posing theoretically informed questions about how the unique and joint effects of temperament and attachment may lead to a better understanding of both normative and individual growth. We had this sort of approach in mind when we suggested that attachment constructs should be relatively more informative than temperament constructs when examining interpersonal relationship outcomes and that temperament constructs should be relatively more informative when examining intrapersonal outcomes. Although this conjecture did not receive strong support from the studies available for review (both domains were useful in predicting outcomes in both inter- and intrapersonal domains), we did find that attachment security was more likely to moderate effects of temperament on outcomes than the reverse. There is also a hint in some of the studies of physiological reactivity and regulation that parenting quality and practices may modulate or tune the development of physiological and/or neurological structures that underlie both temperament and attachment security. Should new studies confirm this tantalizing hint, researchers from both theoretical frameworks gain an additional layer of complexity to integrate and then to leverage into broader and more implicative studies of growth and change. We anticipate that data from the MPCLS will be relevant and available to address such questions.

# REFERENCES

Ainsworth, M. D. S. (1967). *Infancy in Uganda: Infant care and the growth of love.* Baltimore, MD: Johns Hopkins University Press.

Ainsworth, M. D. S., Blehar, M. C., Waters, E., & Wall, S. (1978). *Patterns of attachment: A psychological study of the Strange Situation.* Hillsdale, NJ: Erlbaum.

Ainsworth, M. D. S., & Marvin, R. S. (1995). On the shaping of attachment theory and research: An interview with Mary D. S. Ainsworth (Fall, 1994). In E. Waters, B. E. Vaughn, G. Posada, & K. Kondo-Ikemura (Eds.), Caregiving, cultural, and cognitive perspectives on secure-base behavior and working models: New growing points of attachment theory and research. *Monographs of the Society for Research in Child Development, 60* (2–3, Serial No. 244), 3–21.

Arend, R., Gove, F. L., & Sroufe, L. A. (1979). Continuity of individual adaptation from infancy to kindergarten: A predictive study of ego resiliency and curiosity in preschoolers. *Child Development, 50,* 950–959.

Balleyguier, G. (1991). The development of attachment according to the temperament of the newborn. *Psychiatrie de l'Enfant, 34,* 641–657.

Bates, J. E. (1980). The concept of difficult temperament. *Merrill-Palmer Quarterly, 26,* 299–319.

Bates, J. E., & Bayles, K. (1984). Objective and subjective components in mothers' perceptions of their children from age 6 months to 3 years. *Merrill-Palmer Quarterly, 30,* 111–130.

Bates, J. E., Freeland, C. A. B., & Lounsbury, M. L. (1979). Measurement of infant difficultness. *Child Development, 50,* 794–803.

Bates, J., Maslin, C., & Frankel, K. (1985). Attachment security, mother-child interaction, and temperament as predictors of behavior problem ratings at age three years. In I. Bretherton & E. Waters (Eds.), Growing points of attachment theory and research. *Monographs of the Society for Research in Child Development, 50* (1–2, Serial No. 209), 167–193.

Belsky, J. (2005). Differential susceptibility to rearing influence: An evolutionary hypothesis and some evidence. In B. Ellis & D. Bjorklund (Eds.), *Origins of the social mind: Evolutionary psychology and child development* (pp. 139–163). New York, NY: Guilford Press.

Belsky, J., Fish, M., & Isabella, R. (1991). Continuity and discontinuity in infant negative and positive emotionality: Family antecedents and attachment consequences. *Developmental Psychology, 27,* 421–431.

Belsky, J., Rosenberger, K., & Crnic, K. (1995). The origins of attachment security: "classical" and "contextual" determinants. In S. Goldberg, R. Muir, & J. Kerr (Eds.), *Attachment theory: Social, developmental, and clinical perspectives* (pp. 153–184). Hillsdale, NJ: The Analytic Press.

Belsky, J., & Rovine, M. (1987). Temperament and attachment security in the strange situation: An empirical rapprochement. *Child Development, 58,* 787–795.

Bohlin, G., Hagekull, B., & Andersson, K. (2005). Behavioral inhibition as a precursor of peer social competence in early school age: The interplay with attachment and nonparental care. *Merrill-Palmer Quarterly, 51*, 1–19.

Bohlin, G., Hagekull, B., Germer, M., & Anderson, K., & Lindberg, L. (1989). Avoidant and resistant reunion behaviors as predicted by maternal interactive behavior and infant temperament. *Infant Behavior and Development, 12*, 105–117.

Booth-LaForce, C., & Oxford, M. L. (2008). Trajectories of social withdrawal from grades 1 to 6: Prediction from early parenting, attachment, and temperament. *Developmental Psychology, 44*, 1298–1313.

Bowlby, J. (1980). *Attachment and loss. Vol. 3: Loss: Sadness and depression.* New York, NY: Basic Books.

Bowlby, J. (1982). *Attachment and loss. Vol. 1: Attachment* (originally published in 1969). New York, NY: Basic Books.

Bowlby, J. (1988). *A secure base: Clinical applications of attachment theory.* London, England: Tavistock.

Bradshaw, D., Goldsmith, H., & Campos, J. (1987). Attachment, temperament, and social referencing: Interrelationships among three domains of infant affective behavior. *Infant Behavior and Development, 10*, 223–231.

Braungart, J., & Stifter, C. (1991). Regulation of negative reactivity during the SS: Temperament and attachment in 12-month-old infants. *Infant Behavior and Development, 14*, 349–364.

Braungart-Rieker, J. M., Garwood, M. M., Powers, B. P., & Wang, X. (2001). Parental sensitivity, infant affect, and affect regulation: Predictors of later attachment. *Child Development, 72*, 252–270.

Bretherton, I., Biringen, Z., Ridgeway, D., & Maslin, C. (1989). Attachment: The parental perspective. Special Issue: Internal representations and parent-infant relationships. *Infant Mental Health Journal, 10*, 203–221.

Burgess, K. B., Marshall, P. J., Rubin, K. H., & Fox, N. A. (2003). Infant attachment and temperament as predictors of subsequent externalizing problems and cardiac physiology. *Journal of Child Psychology and Psychiatry, 44*, 819–831.

Buss, K. A., Davidson, R. J., Kalin, N. H., & Goldsmith, H. H. (2004). Context-specific freezing and associated physiological reactivity as dysregulated fear response. *Developmental Psychology, 40*, 583–594.

Buss, A., & Plomin, R. (1984). *Temperament: Early developing personality traits.* Hillsdale, NJ: Erlbaum.

Calkins, S. D. (1994). Origins and outcomes of individual differences in emotion regulation. In N. A. Fox (Ed.), The development of emotion regulation: Biological and biobehavioral considerations. *Monograph of the Society for Research in Child Development, 59*, 53–72 (2–3, Serial No. 240).

Calkins, S., & Fox, N. A. (1992). The relations among infant temperament, security of attachment, and behavioral inhibition at twenty-four months. *Child Development, 63*, 1456–1472.

Calkins, S. D., Fox, N. A., & Marshall, T. R. (1996). Behavioral and psychological antecedents of inhibition in infancy. *Child Development, 67*, 523–540.

Campos, J. J., Mumme, D. L., Kermoian, R., & Campos, R. G. (1994). A functionalist perspective on the nature of emotion. In N. A. Fox (Ed.), The development of emotion regulation: Biological and behavioral considerations. *Monographs of the Society for Research in Child Development, 59*, 284–303.

Chess, S., & Thomas, A. (1982). Infant bonding: Mystique and reality. *American Journal of Orthopsychiatry, 52*, 213–222.

Chess, S., & Thomas, A. (1983). *Origins and evolution of behavior disorders: From infancy to adult life.* New York, NY: Brunner Mazel.

Crockenberg, S. B. (1981). Infant irritability, mother responsiveness, and social support influences on the security of infant-mother attachment. *Child Development, 52*, 857–865.

Crockenberg, S., & McCluskey, K. (1986). Change in maternal behavior during the baby's first year of life. *Child Development, 57*, 746–753.

Del Carmen, R., Pedersen, F. A., Huffman, L. C., & Bryan, Y. E. (1993). Dyadic distress management predicts subsequent security of attachment. *Infant Behavior and Development, 16*, 131–147.

Denham, S., & Moser, M. (1994). Mother's attachment to infants: Relations with infant temperament, stress, and responsive maternal behavior. *Early Child Development and Care, 98*, 1–6.

Derryberry, D., & Rothbart, M. K. (1997). Reactive and effortful processes in the organization of temperament. *Development and Psychopathology, 9*, 633–652.

Diener, M. L., Nievar, M. A., & Wright, C. (2003). Attachment security among mothers and their young children living in poverty: Associations with maternal, child, and contextual characteristics. *Merrill-Palmer Quarterly, 49*, 154–182.

Egeland, B., & Farber, E. (1984). Infant-mother attachment: Factors related to its development and changes over time. *Child Development, 55*, 753–771.

Eisenberg, N., Fabes, R. A., Guthrie, I. K., & Reiser, M. (2000). Dispositional emotionality and regulation: Their role in predicting quality of social functioning. *Journal of Personality and Social Psychology, 78*, 136–157.

Eisenberg, N., Spinrad, T. L., Fabes, R. A., Reiser, M., Cumberland, A., Shepard, S. A., . . . et al. (2004). The relations of effortful control and impulsivity to children's resiliency and adjustment. *Child Development, 75*, 25–46.

Emery, J., Paquette, D., & Bigras, M. (2008). Factors predicting attachment patterns in infants of adolescent mothers. *Journal of Family Studies, 14*, 65–90.

Erickson, M., Egeland, B., & Sroufe, L.A. (1985). The relationship between quality of attachment and behavior problems in preschool in a high risk sample. In I. Bretherton & E. Waters (Eds.), Growing points in attachment theory and research. *Mongraphs of the Society for Research in Child Development, 50* (Nos. 1–2, Serial No. 209), 147–186.

Fagot, B. I., & Leve, L. D. (1998). Teacher ratings of externalizing behavior at school entry for boys and girls: Similar early predictors and different correlates. *Journal of Child Psychology and Psychiatry, 39*, 555–566.

Fox, N. A. (1994). Dynamic cerebral processes underlying emotion regulation. In N. A. Fox (Ed.), The development of emotion regulation: Biological and biobehavioral considerations. *Monographs of the Society for Research in Child Development, 59* (2–3, Serial No. 240), 152–166.

Fowles, D. C., & Kochanska, G. (2000). Temperament as a moderator of pathways to conscience in children: The contribution of electrodermal activity. *Psychophysiology, 37*, 788–795.

Frodi, A., Bridges, L., & Shonk, S. (1989). Maternal correlates of infant temperament ratings and of infant-mother attachment: A longitudinal study. *Infant Mental Health Journal, 10*, 273–289.

Garcia-Coll, C., Kagan, J., & Reznick, J. S. (1984). Behavioral inhibition in young children. *Child Development, 55*, 1005–1019.

Gilissen, R., Koolstra, C. M., van IJzendoorn, M. H., Bakermans-Kranenburg, M. J., & van der Veer, R. (2007). Physiological reactions of preschoolers to fear-inducing film clips: Effects of temperamental fearfulness and quality of the parent–child relationship. *Developmental Psychobiology, 49*, 187–195.

Gilissen, R., Bakermans-Kranenburg, M. J., van IJzendoorn, M. H., & van der Veer, R (2008). Parent–child relationship, temperament, and physiological reactions to fear-inducing film clips: Further evidence for differential susceptibility. *Journal of Experimental Child Psychology, 99*, 182–195.

Goldsmith, H. H., & Alansky, J. A. (1987). Maternal and infant temperamental predictors of attachment: A meta-analytic review. *Journal of Consulting and Clinical Psychology, 55*, 805–816.

Goldsmith, H. H., Buss, A. H., Plomin, R., Rothbart, M. K., Thomas, A., Chess, S., Hinde, R. A., & McCall, R. R. (1987). Roundtable: What is temperament? Four approaches. *Child Development, 58,* 505–529.

Goldsmith, H. H., & Campos, J. J. (1986). Fundamental issues in the study of early temperament: The Denver Twin Temperament Study. In M. Lamb, A. Brown, & B. Rogoff (Eds.), *Advances in developmental psychology:* Vol. 4 (pp. 7–37). Hillsdale, NJ: Erlbaum.

Goldsmith, H. H., & Campos, J. J. (1990). The structure of temperamental fear and pleasure in infants. *Child Development, 61,* 1944–1964.

Goldsmith, H. H., & Harman, C. (1994). Temperament and attachment: Individuals and relationships. *Current Directions in Psychological Science, 3,* 53–57.

Gunnar, M. R. (1994). Psychoneuroendocrine studies of temperament and stress in early childhood: Expanding current models. In J. E. Bates & T. D. Wachs (Eds.), *Temperament: Individual differences at the interface of biology and behavior* (pp. 175–198). Washington, DC: APA Press.

Gunnar, M. R., Broderen, L., Nachmias, M., Buss, K., & Rigatuso, J. (1996). Stress reactivity and attachment security. *Developmental Psychobiology, 29,* 191–204.

Gunnar, M., Larson, M., Hertsgaard, L., Harris, M., & Broderson, L. (1992). The stressfulness of separation among 9-month-old infants: Effects of social context variables and infant temperament. *Child Development, 63,* 290–303.

Gunnar, M., Mangelsdorf, S., Larson, M., & Hertsgaard, L. (1989). Attachment, temperament, and adrenocortical activity in infancy: A study of psychoendocrine regulation. *Developmental Psychology, 25,* 355–363.

Gunnar, M. R., Porter, F. L., Wolf, C. M., & Rigatuso, J. (1995). Neonatal stress reactivity: Predictions to later emotional temperament. *Child Development, 66,* 1–13.

Hagekull, B., & Bohlin, G. (2003). Early temperament and attachment as predictors of the five factor model of personality. *Attachment and Human Development, 5,* 2–18.

Hagekull, B., & Bohlin, G. (2004). Predictors of middle childhood psychosomatic problems: An emotion regulation approach. *Infant and Child Development, 13,* 389–405.

Halverson, C. F., Kohnstamm, G. A., & Martin, R. (1994). *The developing structure of temperament and personality from infancy to adulthood.* Hillsdale, NJ: Erlbaum.

Hertsgaard, L., Gunnar, M., Erickson, M. F., & Nachmias, M. (1995). Adrenocortical responses to the SS in infants with disorganized/disoriented attachment relationships. *Child Development, 66,* 1100–1106.

Ispa, J. M., Fine, M. A., & Thornburg, K. R. (2002). Maternal personality as a moderator of relations between difficult infant temperament and attachment security in low-income families. *Infant Mental Health Journal, 23,* 130–144.

Izard, C. E., Haynes, O. M., Chisholm, G., & Baak, K. (1991). Emotional determinants of infant-mother attachment. *Child Development, 62,* 906–917.

Izard, C. E., & Malatesta, C. (1987). Perspectives on emotional development: I. Differential emotions: Theory of early emotional development. In J. D. Osofsky (Ed.), *Handbook of infant development* (2nd ed., pp. 355–379). New York, NY: Wiley.

Jaffari-Bimmel, N., Juffer, F., van IJzendoorn, M. H., Bakermans-Kranenburg, M. J., & Mooijaart, A. (2006). Social development from infancy to adolescence: Longitudinal and concurrent factors in an adoption sample. *Developmental Psychology, 42,* 1143–1153.

Kagan, J. (1982). *Psychological research on the human infant: An evaluative summary.* New York, NY: W. T. Grant Foundation.

Kagan, J. (1984). *The nature of the child.* New York, NY: Basic.

Kagan, J. (1994). *Galen's prophecy: Temperament and human nature.* New York, NY: Basic Books.

Kagan, J. (2003). Biology, context, and developmental inquiry. *Annual Review of Psychology, 54,* 1–23.

Kagan, J., Reznick, J. S., & Snidman, N. (1987). The physiology and psychology of behavioral inhibition in children. *Child Development, 58,* 1459–1473.

Kagan, J., Reznick, J. S., & Snidman, N. (1988). Biological bases of childhood shyness. *Science, 240,* 167–171.

Kagan, J. J., Reznick, S., & Snidman, N. (1989). Issues in the study of temperament. In G. A. Kohnstamm, J. E. Bates, & M. K. Rothbart (Eds.), *Temperament in childhood* (pp. 133–144). New York, NY: Wiley.

Kanaya, Y. (1986). Are maternal emotions associated with infant temperament and attachment? *Research and Clinical Center for Child Development, 9,* 51–58.

Karrass, J., & Braungart-Reiker, J. M. (2004). Infant negative emotionality and attachment: Implications for preschool intelligence. *International Journal of Behavioral Development, 28,* 221–229.

Kemp, V. (1987). Mother's perceptions of children's temperament and mother-child attachment. *Scholarly Inquiry for Nursing Practice, 1,* 51–68.

Kochanska, G. (1995). Children's temperament, mothers' discipline, and security of attachment: Multiple pathways to emerging internalization. *Child Development, 66,* 597–615.

Kochanska, G. (1997). Multiple pathways to conscience for children with different temperaments: From toddlerhood to age 5. *Developmental Psychology, 33*, 228–240.

Kochanska, G. (1998). Mother-child relationship, child fearfulness, and emerging attachment: A short-term longitudinal study. *Developmental Psychology, 34*, 480–490.

Kochanska, G. (2001). Emotional development in children with different attachment histories: The first three years. *Child Development, 72*, 474–490.

Kochanska, G., Aksan, N., & Carlson, J. J. (2005). Temperament, relationships, and young children's receptive cooperation with their parents. *Developmental Psychology, 41*, 648–660.

Kochanska, G., Askan, N., Knaack, A., & Rhines, H. M. (2004). Maternal parenting and children's conscience: Early security as a moderator. *Child Development, 75*, 1229–1242.

Kochanska, G., Forman, D. R., Aksan, N., & Dunbar, S. B. (2005). Pathways to conscience: Early mother-child mutually responsive orientation and children's moral emotion, conduct, and cognition. *Journal of Child Psychology and Psychiatry, 46*, 19–34.

Kochanska, G., & Murray, K. T. (2000). Mother-child mutually responsive orientation and conscience development: From toddler to school age. *Child Development, 71*, 417–431.

LaFreniere, P. J., & Sroufe, L. A. (1985). Profiles of peer competence in the preschool: Interrelations among measures, influence of social ecology, and relation to attachment history. *Developmental Psychology, 21*, 56–66.

Laible, D. (2004). Mother-child discourse in two contexts: Links with child temperament, attachment security, and socioemotional competence. *Developmental Psychology, 40*, 979–992.

Laible, D., Panfile, T., & Makariev, D. (2008). The quality and frequency of mother-toddler conflict: Links with attachment and temperament. *Child Development, 79*, 426–443.

Lewis, M., & Feiring, C. (1989). Infant, mother, and mother-infant interaction behavior and subsequent attachment. *Child Development, 60*, 831–837.

Manassis, K., Bradley, S., Goldberg, S., Hood, J., & Swinson, R. (1995). Behavioral inhibition, attachment, and anxiety in children of mothers with anxiety disorders. *Canadian Journal of Psychiatry, 40*, 87–92.

Mangelsdorf, S. C., & Frosch, C. A. (1999). Temperament and attachment: One construct or two? *Advances in Child Development and Behavior, 27*, 181–220.

Mangelsdorf, S. C, Gunnar, M., Kestenbaum, R., Lang, S, & Andreas, D. (1990). Infant proneness to distress, temperament, maternal personality and mother-infant attachment. *Child Development, 61*, 820–831.

Mangelsdorf, S. C., McHale, J. L., Diener, M., Goldstein, L. H., & Lehn, L. (2000). Infant attachment: Contributions of infant temperament and maternal characteristics. *Infant Behavior and Development, 23*, 175–196.

Marshall, P. J., & Fox, N. A. (2005). Relations between behavioral reactivity at 4 months and attachment classification at 14 months in a selected sample. *Infant Behavior and Development, 28*, 492–502.

Matas, L., Arend, R. A., & Sroufe, L. A. (1978). Continuity of adaptation in the second year: The relationship between quality of attachment and later competence. *Child Development, 49*, 547–556.

McCartney, K., Tresch Owen, M., Booth, C. L., Clarke-Stewart, A., & Vandell, D. L. (2004). Testing a maternal attachment model of behavior problems in early childhood. *Journal of Child Psychology and Psychiatry, 45*, 765–778.

McCrae, R. R., Costa, P. T., Jr., Ostendorf, F., Angleitner, A., Hrebickova, M., . . . et al. (2000). Nature over nurture: temperament, personality, and life span development. *Journal of Personality and Social Psychology, 78*, 173–186.

Miyake, K., & Chen, S. (1984). Relation of temperamental disposition to classification of attachment: A progress report. *Research and Clinical Center for Child Development (Annual Report)*, 17–25.

Miyake, K., Chen, S., & Campos, J. (1985). Infant temperament, mother's mode of interaction, and attachment in Japan: An interim report. *Monographs of the Society for Research in Child Development, 50*, 276–297.

Moran, G., & Pederson, D. R. (1998). Proneness to distress and ambivalent relationships. *Infant Behavior and Development, 21*, 493–503.

Moss, E., Bureau, J-F., Cyr, C., & Dubois-Comtois, K. (2006). Is the maternal Q-set a valid measure of preschool child attachment behavior? *International Journal of Behavioral Development, 30*, 488–497.

Nachmias, M., Gunnar, M. R., Mangelsdorf, S., Parritz, R. H., & Buss, K. (1996). Behavioral inhibition and stress reactivity: The moderating role of attachment security. *Child Development, 67*, 508–522.

Nair, H., & Murray, D. (2005). Predictors of attachment security in preschool children from intact and divorced families. *The Journal of Genetic Psychology, 166*, 245–263.

Nelson, B., Martin, R. P., Hodge, S., Havill, V., & Kamphaus, R. (1999). Modeling the prediction of elementary school adjustment from preschool temperament. *Personality and Individual Difference, 26*, 687–700.

Nigg, J. T., Goldsmith, H. H., & Sachek, J. (2004). Temperament and attention deficit hyperactivity disorder: The development of a multiple pathway model. *Journal of Clinical Child & Adolescent Psychology, 33,* 42–53.

Park, K. A., & Waters, E. (1989). Security of attachment and preschool friendships. *Child Development, 60,* 1076–1081.

Pauli-Pott, U., Friedl, S., Hinney, A., & Hebebrand, J. (2009). Serotonin transporter gene polymorphism (5-HTTLPR) environmental conditions, and developing negative emotionality and fear in early childhood. *Journal of Neural Transmission, 116,* 503–512.

Pauli-Pott, U., Haverkock, A., Pott, W., & Beckmann, D. (2007). Negative emotionality, attachment quality, and behavior problems in early childhood. *Infant Mental Health Journal, 28,* 39–53.

Pierrehumbert, B., Miljkovitch, R., Plancherel, B., Halfon, D., & Ansermet, F. (2000). Attachment and temperament in early childhood: Implications for later behavior problems. *Infant and Child Development, 9,* 17–32.

Porges, S. W., Doussard-Roosevelt, J. A., Portales, A. L., & Greenspan, S. I. (1996). Infant regulation of the vagal "brake" predicts child behavior problems: A psychological model of social behavior. *Developmental Psychobiology, 29,* 697–712.

Prior, M., Smart, D., Sanson, A., & Oberklaid, F. (2000). Does shy-inhibited temperament in childhood lead to anxiety problems in adolescence? *Journal of the American Academy of Child and Adolescent Psychiatry, 39,* 461–468.

Rieser-Danner, L. A., Roggman, L., & Langlois, J. H. (1987). Infant attractiveness and perceived temperament in the prediction of attachment classifications. *Infant Mental Health Journal, 8,* 144–155.

Rettew, D. C., Copeland, W., Stanger, C., & Hudziak, J. J. (2004). Associations between temperament and DSM-IV externalizing disorders in children and adolescents. *Journal of Developmental and Behavioral Pediatrics, 25,* 383–391.

Rothbart, M. K. (1989a). Temperament in childhood: A framework. In G. A. Kohnstamm, J. E. Bates, & M. K. Rothbart (Eds.), *Temperament in childhood* (pp. 59–73). New York, NY: Wiley.

Rothbart, M. K. (1989b). Biological processes in temperament. In G. A. Kohnstamm, J. E. Bates, & M. K. Rothbart (Eds.), *Temperament in childhood* (pp. 77–110). New York, NY: Wiley.

Rothbart, M. K. (1989c). Temperament and development. In G. A. Kohnstamm, J. E. Bates, & M. K. Rothbart (Eds.), *Temperament in childhood* (pp. 187–247). New York, NY: Wiley.

Rothbart, M. K. (2004). Temperament and the pursuit of an integrated developmental psychology. *Merrill-Palmer Quarterly, 50*, 492–405.

Rothbart, M. K., & Bates, J. E. (2006). Temperament. In N. Eisenberg (Volume Ed.), *Social, emotional, and personality development* (Vol. 3, pp. 99–166) of W. Damon & R.M. Lerner (Eds.-in-Chief), *Handbook of child psychology.* Hoboken, NJ: Wiley.

Rothbart, M. K., & Derryberry, D. (1981). Development of individual differences in temperament. In M. E. Lamb & A. L. Brown (Eds.), *Advances in developmental psychology* (Vol. 1, pp. 37–86). Hillsdale, NJ: Erlbaum.

Rubin, K. H., Hastings, P. D., Stewart, S. L., Henderson, H. A., & Chen, X. (1997). The consistency and concomitants of inhibition: Some of the children, all of the time. *Child Development, 68*, 467–483.

Ruff, H. A., & Rothbart, M. K. (1996). *Attention in early development: Themes and variations.* New York, NY: Oxford University Press.

Rydell, A-M., Bohlin, B., & Thorell, L. B. (2005). Representations of attachment to parents and shyness as predictors of children's relationships with teachers and peer competence in preschool. *Attachment and Human Development, 7*, 187–204.

Sameroff, A. J., Seifer, R., & Elias, P. K. (1982). Sociocultural variability in infant temperament ratings. *Child Development, 53*, 164–171.

Scher, A., & Mayseless, O. (2000). Mothers of anxious/ambivalent infants: Maternal characteristics and child-care contexts. *Child Development, 71*, 1629–1639.

Schieche, M., & Spangler, G. (2005). Individual differences in biobehavioral organization during problem-solving in toddlers: The influence of maternal behavior, infant-mother attachment and behavioral inhibition on the attachment-exploration balance. *Developmental Psychobiology, 46*, 293–306.

Seifer, R., & Schiller, M. (1995). The role of parenting sensitivity, infant temperament, and dyadic interaction in attachment theory and assessment. In E. Waters, B. E. Vaughn, G. Posada, & K. Kondo-Ikemura (Eds.), *Constructs, cultures, and caregiving: New growing points of attachment theory and research. Monographs of the Society for Research in Child Development.* 60 (2–3, Serial No. 244), 146–174.

Seifer, R., Schiller, M., Sameroff, A. J., Resnick, S., & Riordan, K. (1996). Attachment, maternal sensitivity, and infant temperament during the first year of life. *Developmental Psychology, 32*, 12–25.

Shamir-Essakow, G., Ungerer, J. A., & Rapee, R. M. (2005). Attachment, behavioral inhibition, and anxiety in preschool children. *Journal of Abnormal Child Psychology, 33*, 131–143.

Spangler, G., Fremmer-Bombik, E., & Grossmann, K. (1996). Social and individual determinants of attachment security and disorganization during the first year. *Infant Mental Health Journal, 17,* 127–139.

Spangler, G., Schieche, M., Ilg, U., Maier, U., & Ackermann, C. (1994). Maternal sensitivity as an external organizer for biobehavioral regulation in infancy. *Developmental Psychobiology, 27,* 425–437.

Sroufe, L. A. (1985). Attachment classification from the perspective of infant-caregiver relationships and infant temperament. *Child Development, 56,* 1–14.

Sroufe, L. A. (1996). *Emotional development: The organization of emotional life in the early years.* New York, NY: Cambridge.

Sroufe, L. A., Egeland, B., Carlson, E. A., & Collins, W. A. (2005). *The development of the person: The Minnesota study of risk and adaptation from birth to adulthood.* New York, NY: Guilford.

Sroufe, L. A., & Waters, E. (1982). Temperament and attachment: A response to Chess and Thomas. *American Journal of Orthopsychiatry, 52,* 743–746.

Stams, G-J. J. M., Juffer, F., & van IJzendoorn, M. H. (2002). Maternal sensitivity, infant attachment, and temperament in early childhood predict adjustment in middle childhood: The case of adopted children and their biologically unrelated parents. *Developmental Psychology, 38,* 806–821.

Stansbury, K., & Gunnar, M. R. (1994). Adrenocortical activity and emotion regulation. In N. A. Fox (Ed.), The development of emotion regulation: Biological and biobehavioral considerations. *Monographs of the Society for Research in Child Development, 59* (2–3, Serial No. 240), 108–134.

Stevenson-Hinde, J., & Marshall, P. J. (1999). Behavioral inhibition, heart period, and respiratory sinus arrhythmia: An attachment perspective. *Child Development, 70,* 805–816.

Suess, G. J., Grossmann, K., & Sroufe, L. A. (1992). Effects of infant attachment to mother and father on quality of adaptation in preschool: From dyadic to individual organization of self. *International Journal of Behavioral Development, 15,* 43–65.

Susman-Stillman, A., Kalkoske, M., Egeland, B., & Waldman, I. (1996). Infant temperament and maternal sensitivity as predictors of attachment security. *Infant Behavior and Development, 19,* 33–47.

Szewczyk-Sokolowski, M., & Bost, K. K., & Wainright, A.B. (2005). Attachment, temperament, and preschool children's peer acceptance. *Social Development, 14,* 379–397.

Tarabulsy, G. M., Provost, M. A., Larose, S., Moss, E., Lemelin, J-P., Moran, G., Forbes, L., & Pederson, D. R. (2008). Similarities and differences in mothers' and observers' ratings of infant security on the Attachment Q-Sort. *Infant Behavior and Development, 31*, 10–22.

Thomas, A., & Chess, S. (1977). *Temperament and development.* New York, NY: Brunner/Mazel.

Thomas, A., Chess, S., Birch, H. G., Hertzig, M. E., & Korn, S. (1963). *Behavioral individuality in early childhood.* New York, NY: New York University Press.

Thompson, R., Connell, J. & Bridges, L. (1988). Temperament, emotion, and social interactive behavior in the SS: A component process analysis of attachment system functioning. *Child Development, 59*, 1102–1110.

Thompson, R. A., & Lamb, M. (1984). Assessing qualitative dimensions of emotional responsiveness in infants: Separation reactions in the SS. *Infant Behavior and Development, 7*, 423–445.

van Bakel, H. J. A., & Riksen-Walraven, J. M. (2004a). AQS security scores: What do they represent? A study in construct validation. *Infant Mental Health Journal, 25*, 175–193.

van Bakel, H. J. A., & Riksen-Walraven, J. M. (2004b). Stress reactivity in 15-month-old infants: Links with infant temperament, cognitive competence, and attachment security. *Developmental Psychobiology, 44*, 157–167.

van den Boom, D. C. (1989). Neonatal irritability and the development of attachment. In G. Kohnstamm, J. Bates, & M. Rothbart (Eds.), *Temperament in childhood* (pp. 299–318). Chichester, England: Wiley.

van den Boom, D. (1994). The influence of temperament and mothering on attachment and exploration: An experimental manipulation of sensitive responsiveness among lower-class mothers with irritable infants. *Child Development, 65*, 1457–1477.

van der Mark, I. L., Bakermans-Kranenburg, M. J., & van IJzendoorn, M. H. (2002). The role of parenting, attachment, and temperamental fearfulness in the prediction of compliance in toddler girls. *British Journal of Developmental Psychology, 20*, 361–378.

van IJzendoorn, M. H., Vereijken, C. M. J. L., Bakermans-Kranenburg, M. J., & Riksen-Walraven, J. M. (2004). Assessing attachment security with the Attachment Q Sort: Meta-analytic evidence for the validity of the observer AQS. *Child Development, 75*, 1188–1213.

Vaughn, B. E., & Bost, K. K. (1999). Attachment and temperament: Redundant, independent, or interacting influences on interpersonal adaptation and personality development? In J. Cassidy & P. R. Shaver (Eds.), *Handbook of attachment: Theory, research, and clinical applications* (pp. 198–225). New York, NY: Guilford Press.

Vaughn, B. E., Bost, K. K., & van IJzendoorn, M. H. (2008). Attachment and temperament: Additive and interactive influences on behavior, affect, and cognition during infancy and childhood. In J. Cassidy & P. R. Shaver (Eds.), *Handbook of attachment: Theory, research, and clinical applications* (pp. 192–216). New York, NY: Guilford Press.

Vaughn, B. E., Bradley, C. B., Joffe, L. S., Seifer, R., & Barglow, P. (1987). Maternal characteristics measured prenatally predict ratings of temperamental """"difficulty"""" on the Carey Infant Temperament Questionnaire. *Developmental Psychology, 23*, 160–170.

Vaughn, B. E., Deinard, A., & Egeland, B. (1980). Measuring temperament in pediatric practice. *Journal of Pediatrics, 96*, 510–514.

Vaughn, B. E., Lefever, G., Seifer, R., & Barglow, P. (1989). Attachment behavior, attachment security, and temperament during infancy. *Child Development, 60*, 728–737.

Vaughn, B. E., Stevenson-Hinde, J., Waters, E., Kotsaftis, A., Lefever, G. B., Shouldice, A., Trudel, M., & Belsky, J. (1992). Attachment security and temperament in infancy and early childhood: Some conceptual clarifications. *Developmental Psychology, 28*, 463–473.

Volling, B., & Belsky, J. (1992). Infant, father, and marital antecedents of infant-father attachment security in dual-earner and single-earner families. *International Journal of Behavioral Development, 15*, 83–100.

Wachs, T., & Desai, S. (1993). Parent reports of toddler temperament and attachment: Their relation to each other and to the social microenvironment. *Infant Behavior and Development, 16*, 391–396.

Waters, E. (1995). The Attachment Q-set (Version 3.0). In E. Waters, B. E. Vaughn, G. Posada, & K. Kondo-Ikemura (Eds.), Caregiving, cultural, and cognitive perspectives on secure-base behavior and working models: New growing points of attachment theory and research. *Monographs of the Society for Research in Child Development, 60* (2–3, Serial No. 244), 234–246.

Warren, S., Huston, L., Egeland, B., & Sroufe, L. A. (1997). Child and adolescent anxiety disorders and early attachment. *Journal of the American Academy of Child and Adolescent Psychiatry, 36*, 637–644.

Waters, E., Vaughn, B. E., & Egeland, B. (1980). Individual differences in infant-mother attachment relationships at age one: Antecedents in neonatal behavior in an economically disadvantaged sample. *Child Development, 51,* 208–216.

Waters, E., Wippman, J., & Sroufe, L. A. (1979). Attachment, positive affect, and competence in the peer group: two studies in construct validation. *Child Development, 50,* 821–829.

Weber, R., Levitt, M., & Clark, C. (1986). Individual variation in attachment security and Strange Situation behavior: The role of maternal and infant temperament. *Child Development, 57,* 56–65.

# 4

# Earned-Security in Retrospect

## Emerging Insights from Longitudinal, Experimental, and Taxometric Investigations

GLENN I. ROISMAN AND KATHERINE C. HAYDON

The Minnesota Parent-Child Longitudinal Study (MPCLS; Sroufe, Egeland, Carlson, & Collins, 2005) has provided an historically significant and generative template for longitudinal research in the field of developmental psychology, serving notably as a methodological and conceptual foundation for the current generation of large-scale studies focused on normative and atypical social development (e.g., The NICHD Study of Early Child Care and Youth Development [SECCYD]). The uncommon success of the MPCLS is no doubt attributable to many factors, preeminent among them the tireless efforts and incredible genius of the two individuals whom this Festschrift volume honors.

This chapter highlights one especially innovative aspect of the MPCLS that has for more than 30 years supported its generativity— the way in which Byron Egeland, Alan Sroufe, Andy Collins, and their many student and faculty colleagues have thoughtfully and repeatedly leveraged the prospective, multi-method, and multi-informant nature of their data set to reinterpret findings emerging from other developmental studies relying either on cross-sectional comparisons or longitudinal analyses that were not fully prospective (for just a few excellent examples based on the MPCLS, see Aguilar, Sroufe, Egeland, & Carlson, 2000; Egeland, Jacobvitz, & Sroufe, 1988; Sroufe, Egeland, & Kreutzer, 1990). We do so here primarily via the extended example of a line of research attempting to identify and explore the strengths and vulnerabilities of individuals who have successfully overcome difficult early interpersonal experiences with primary caregivers.

More specifically, the principal goal of this chapter is to detail—and, as necessary, clarify—some emerging insights into the developmental significance of earned-security drawn from its first longitudinal investigation based on the MPCLS and additional, programmatic extensions of this work that we, together with our colleagues, have conducted in the Relationships Research Laboratory at the University of Illinois at Urbana-Champaign. Using George, Kaplan, and Main's (1985) Adult Attachment Interview (AAI), individuals have been traditionally classified as earned-secure based on their ability to coherently describe below-average childhood experiences with one or more primary caregivers in childhood (Pearson, Cohn, Cowan, & Cowan, 1994). Early research using this inherently *retrospective* operationalization of attachment-related resilience offered robust evidence that such individuals—like secure adults generally—provide sensitive caregiving to their young children (Pearson et al., 1994; Phelps, Belsky, & Crnic, 1998) and share high-quality relationships with their romantic partners (Paley, Cox, Burchinal, & Payne, 1999).

However, consistent with the notion that there nevertheless may be a price paid for having struggled through early interpersonal challenges, there is also evidence in studies in this area that earned-secures self-report relatively high levels of internalizing distress—in many cases at rates comparable to or in excess of those typical of insecure adults (Pearson et al., 1994; Roisman, Padrón, Sroufe, & Egeland, 2002; Roisman, Fortuna, & Holland, 2006). Part 1 of this chapter offers some preliminary discussion of the AAI (the methodological foundation of the earned-security literature), and Part 2 explores the development of retrospective definitions of earned-security, evaluating in particular the importance and impact of empirical work based on the Pearson definition of earned- and continuous-security (Pearson et al., 1994).

The meaning of the earned-secure classification (articulated above) began to be reconsidered with the publication of Roisman et al.'s (2002) examination of the early histories of such adults within the MPCLS—the focus of Part 3 of this chapter. Roisman et al. (2002) were able to replicate evidence that earned-secures, retrospectively defined, resolve conflict effectively with their romantic partners despite simultaneously reporting relatively high levels of internalizing symptomatology as young adults. However, this provocative study was also, more importantly, able to provide what no prior investigation could—the very first and crucial test of the validity of the earned-secure subclassification by way of observational data on young adult participants' actual (i.e., observed) experiences with maternal caregivers in infancy, childhood, and adolescence. Interestingly—and inconsistent with the view that earned-secures experience pervasively negative childhood experiences—such adults were shown in Roisman et al. (2002) to have experienced rather high-quality maternal caregiving experiences in the Minnesota elevated-risk cohort in the years before maturity, raising questions about the validity of Pearson and colleagues' (1994) retrospective diagnosis of earned-security.

Although the prospective nature of the data drawn from the MPCLS went a long way in shining light on the nature of earned-security, retrospectively assessed, Roisman et al.'s (2002) work presented something of a paradox: If earned-secures actually benefit from supportive early experiences, why, then, do such individuals recall relatively negative childhood experiences as adults? In Part 4, we discuss the results of a mood induction study designed to address this important question. Specifically, in an experiment that the first author conducted with Keren Fortuna and Ashley Holland, we followed up on the possibility (presciently suggested by Phelps et al., 1998) that the internalizing distress reported by earned-secures—rather than being a consequence of having overcome negative early attachment-related experiences—might instead play a role in biasing participants' recall of early life events as adults. Consistent with this hypothesis—and as will be discussed in detail later—Roisman, Fortuna, and Holland (2006) discovered that rates of earned- versus continuous-security could actually be experimentally manipulated among secure adults using a brief mood induction procedure.

Part 5 of this chapter reflects on and offers a taxometric rejoinder to some more recent critiques of the Roisman et al. (2002) and Roisman et al. (2006) studies. Specifically, some have questioned the implications of the fact that early findings in the literature have been built on a fairly liberal definition of earned-security, advocating instead for more conservative criteria by which adults can be retrospectively identified as having overcome harsh early life experiences (Hesse, 2008). No response to this important critique can be definitive without (additional, forthcoming) prospective data based on large longitudinal cohorts. Nonetheless, we review the scant data that do exist relevant to evaluating newer definitions of earned-security, tentatively concluding that any retrospective definition of earned-security is likely to be problematic, particularly in terms of serving as a rough proxy for *prospective* assessments of attachment-related change (what we will for convenience refer to as "prospectively defined earned-security" in this chapter, but with reservations clarified in the final section). In this context, we will also present additional data on the latent structure of adult attachment based on the published literature on earned-security (Roisman, Fraley, & Belsky, 2007) that speak directly to the assumption that—as Main and Goldwyn (e.g., 1998) have suggested—earned-security should be conceptualized and operationalized as a low-base-rate category.

After noting some of the implications of the earned-security literature for the validity of the AAI more generally, we conclude in Part 6 with a description of ongoing work that has the goal of refining our understanding of the (a) antecedents (e.g., paternal), (b) biological correlates (i.e., electrophysiological and genetic), and (c) developmental outcomes associated with earned-security, retrospectively defined, and discuss some complications that arise from recent discoveries regarding the latent structure and taxonicity of adult attachment-related individual differences as assessed with the AAI (Haydon, Roisman, & Burt, in press; Roisman, Fraley, & Belsky, 2007). We believe that each of these issues is especially important in relation to more fully addressing a remaining paradox about earned-secures, who—despite experiencing a good deal of internalizing distress in their adult lives—nonetheless manage to serve as effective parents and romantic partners. In this section we finally detail some of the challenges associated with, and offer some suggestions regarding the use of, *prospective* definitions of earned-security in future research.

# PART 1: THE ADULT ATTACHMENT INTERVIEW: AN OVERVIEW

The development of the AAI (George, Kaplan, & Main, 1985; Main, Kaplan, & Cassidy, 1985), the most widely used and well-validated instrument in developmental research for studying attachment in adults, was based on a concerted effort to understand how adults organize their discourse when reflecting on their early childhood experiences (Hesse, 2008). Through careful analysis—eventually informed by the insights of the linguistic philosopher Paul Grice (Grice, 1975) about the nature of collaborative discourse—Mary Main and her colleagues were able to discover which aspects of parents' narratives regarding their childhood experiences predict whether their children will be classified as secure or insecure in the Strange Situation Procedure (van IJzendoorn, 1995). This knowledge is used to classify adults into one of several categories (e.g., secure-autonomous, preoccupied, dismissing) that reflect the interviewee's *state of mind* with respect to attachment.

More specifically, the AAI is an hour-long interview in which adults are asked a set of questions regarding their childhood experiences, providing memories relevant to loss, separation, rejection, and trauma. Based exclusively on adults' verbal responses (AAIs are transcribed verbatim), individuals are typically classified by trained coders into one of three primary categories that reflect the coherence of the discourse they produce. The majority of adults, described as *secure-autonomous*, freely and flexibly evaluate their childhood experiences, whether described as supportive or more challenging in nature. In contrast, a large minority of adults are described as *dismissing*. Dismissing individuals defensively distance themselves from the emotional content of the interview by normalizing harsh early memories, for example, or by idealizing their caregivers. Least common are *preoccupied* adults, who are unable to discuss their childhood without becoming overwhelmed by their prior relationship experiences (see Hesse, 1999, for more details). In addition to classifying adults into one of these three mutually exclusive groups, coders also categorize individuals as *unresolved* if their discourse becomes confused while talking about loss or abuse experiences.

The scientific yield of research exploring developmental questions using the AAI categories has been substantial (for comprehensive reviews, see Bakermans-Kranenburg & van IJzendoorn, 2009; Hesse, 1999, 2008). For example, the AAI has been crucial in providing evidence that (a) relationship experiences with primary caregivers in childhood are internalized and carried forward into adulthood (Roisman, Madsen, Hennighausen, Sroufe, & Collins, 2001); (b) adults' discourse can provide researchers with leverage in terms of understanding childhood experiences with malevolence and support (Allen & Hauser, 1996; Fraley, 2002; Waters, Hamilton, & Weinfield, 2000); and (c) the way that parents talk about their early experiences with caregivers reliably predicts the quality of their adult relationships (Cohn, Silver, Cowan, Cowan, & Pearson, 1992; van IJzendoorn, 1995).

Nonetheless, because of the resource-intensive nature of AAI administration and coding, the samples that typify work of this kind are often too small to examine differences among insecure adults (Roisman, 2007). In addition, some AAI transcripts paradoxically appear to combine elements of secure and insecure categories (i.e., unresolved-secures) or different, putatively incompatible forms of insecurity (i.e., "cannot classify" transcripts that showed mixed evidence of dismissing and preoccupied states of mind), facts that present conceptual challenges for the Main and Goldwyn (1998) categorical coding system (see Haydon et al., in press; Roisman, Fraley, & Belsky, 2007; and below for an alternative, empirically derived perspective on the latent structure of the AAI).

Although the categories described earlier are often the focus of empirical reports published in the developmental literature, it is important to note that AAI coders actually use a set of continuous rating scales to inductively sort participants into attachment groups. Two kinds of variables are quantified by coders. The first set, known as the *inferred experience* scales, reflects AAI coders' impressions of participants' experiences with caregivers during childhood, including assessments of maternal and paternal love, rejection, neglect, pressure to achieve, and role reversal. Although such information is conceptually orthogonal to the assessment of security in the AAI (for empirical evidence related to this claim, see Haydon et al., in press), several investigators have used a subset of these scales to distinguish between secure individuals with putatively negative early relationship experiences with at least one parent (i.e., earned-secures) and secure adults with largely positive experiences with their caregivers (i.e., continuous-secures; see Pearson et al., 1994). It is important to point out that these subcategories carry with them two key assumptions, which we explore, respectively, in Parts 3 and 5 of this chapter: (1) they accurately reflect the (observable) reality of secure adults' childhood experiences; and (2) secure adults' early experiences can reasonably be characterized as qualitatively positive or negative in nature. (Note that we refer here to *secure* adults specifically, because the Main and Goldwyn [1998] system intentionally conflates insecure states of mind with negative inferred experiences, though it allows secure adults to vary freely with respect to inferred experience across the range of possible values.)

The second set of ratings made by AAI coders reflects the coherence of participants' discourse regarding their childhood attachment experiences (i.e., their *state of mind*). For example, per Main and Goldwyn's (1998) coding system, nine-point scales are used to rate the participant's tendency to idealize and/or normalize childhood experiences with caregivers (*mother idealization* and *father idealization*), the inability to recall events from childhood (*lack of memory*), the extent to which one or both caregivers are derogated (*derogation*), the expression of unreasonable fears that their child may die (*fear of loss*), current active resentment toward parents (*mother anger* and *father anger*), and passive or rambling attachment-related discourse (*passivity*).

These state-of-mind scales are used to assist the coder in classifying participants into one of the two major insecure categories. Main and Goldwyn (1998) contend that a dismissing state of mind is reflected in any combination of high scores on scales that tap a participant's tendency to idealize parents, derogate them, or show failures of memory (according to the categorical coding system, dismissing adults also occasionally fear the loss of their own child). Preoccupation is identified through signs of anger and/or passivity. Security, in contrast, is defined not only by the relative absence of high scores on these indicators, but also by evidence that an adult is able to explore his or her thoughts and feelings about childhood experiences without becoming angrily or passively overwhelmed while discussing them. By definition, such an ability to "freely evaluate" one's experiences without becoming emotionally overwrought in the recounting of one's autobiography is reflected in the overall *coherence of mind* and *coherence of transcript* scales.

Adults who are able to modify their outlook on their childhood experiences during the AAI as a function of spontaneous reflection are given high scores on *metacognitive monitoring*, another indicator of security. As mentioned earlier, participants receive a primary unresolved classification (irrespective of whether they are otherwise classified as secure, dismissing, or preoccupied) when they score at or above the midpoint on either the *unresolved loss* or *unresolved abuse* scales, which reflect the degree to which individuals' discourse becomes disorganized while discussing loss or abuse experiences, respectively.

## PART 2: THE IMPACT OF THE PEARSON DEFINITION OF EARNED-SECURITY

The observation that a substantial subset of adults coherently describe their childhood experiences as relatively difficult—and that the reported experiences of such adults might be expected to be veridical with their actual experiences in childhood—is as old as the literature on the AAI. In their now-classic introduction of the AAI to the field, Main, Kaplan, and Cassidy (1985) suggest as much by noting: "Many of these [secure] parents recalled favorable early experiences (Main & Goldwyn, in press [1998]). Many, however, had had unfavorable attachment-related experiences in childhood, particularly in the form of loss or rejection" (p. 91). However, it would not be until almost 10 years later that Pearson, Cohn, Cowan, and Cowan (1994) would formalize and empirically evaluate a means for distinguishing individuals who coherently described relatively negative childhood experiences (retrospectively defined "earned-secures") from adults who coherently described relatively supportive childhood experiences with their caregivers (retrospective "continuous-secures") in their study of forty 42-month-old children and their primary caregivers (both maternal and paternal caregivers were included in this initial study of earned-security).

There were two major consequences of the introduction of the Pearson definition of earned- and continuous-security to the field. First, Pearson et al. (1994) quickly established a clear pattern of evidence that earned-secures, retrospectively defined (a) are interpersonally effective (in the Pearson study indistinguishable from their continuous-secure counterparts in terms of their provision of warmth and structure in interaction with their preschoolers) despite (b) reporting relatively high levels of depressive symptomatology as assessed via self-report with the Center for Epidemiological Studies-Depression Scale (CES-D; Radloff, 1977)—comparable to insecure adults in this latter regard. These results were predictably (and quite reasonably) interpreted at the time to suggest that the ability to coherently talk about one's childhood experiences—irrespective of whether such adults described their experiences as generally supportive or more difficult—confers advantages in terms of parenting one's own children. Nonetheless, the earned-secure classification also carried developmental risks, as the adult lives of such individuals were marked (i.e., presumably by their early adversity) by way of significant internalizing distress.

A second consequence of Pearson's initial study, though more subtle, has perhaps ultimately had farther-reaching consequences with respect to the development of this area of research. Specifically, the Pearson definition of earned-security requires only that secure participants' loving scores are below the scale midpoint (less than five on a nine-point scale), and their neglect and/or rejecting scores are above the scale midpoint in relation to one primary caregiver, a fact that has subsequently led to some justifiable concern that the definition might be overly liberal. There are three interrelated issues here. First, some have concluded that defining individuals as earned-secure might be unwise merely given evidence of below-average caregiving (Hesse, 2008). Second, the Pearson definition leaves open the possibility that earned-secures might describe compensatory experiences with another primary caregiver (i.e., individuals labeled as earned-secure by the Pearson definition in some cases do not recall *pervasively* negative childhood experiences, even as can be clearly demonstrated within their AAI narratives).

Finally—and closely related to this second point—given that there are reliable mean-level differences in maternal versus paternal inferred experience scales of the AAI, suggesting that mother figures on average score as having provided significantly more positive caregiving along the crucial dimensions rated by coders (higher levels of love, less rejection and neglect), it is not surprising that earned-secures are defined as such somewhat disproportionately because of paternal versus maternal caregiving experiences. (Note that these maternal versus paternal differences on the inferred experiences scales of the AAI are presently of unknown origin: they may be a methodological artifact of the AAI protocol or coding system or a result of cultural norms regarding the nature of maternal and paternal roles in caregiving.)

Despite these issues—the implications of which we will address in detail later—the earned-security literature flourished post-Pearson with two follow-up studies by Phelps, Belsky, and Crnic (1998) and Paley, Cox, Burchinal, and Payne (1999). Both of these reports offered two important contributions to advancing the narrative in this area. First, they solidified the evidentiary basis that retrospectively defined earned-secures (again, by the Pearson definition) are interpersonally effective. Phelps et al. (1998), for example, studying ninety-seven 27-month-olds and their mothers, showed that earned-secures parent as proficiently as did continuous-secures under conditions of high life stress, suggesting key evidence that earned-secures had actually broken the intergenerational cycle in that low life stress was not masking or buffering latent vulnerabilities. Likewise, Paley et al. (1999), in their study of 138 married couples, demonstrated that such effects were not specific to parenting, in that female (but not male) earned-secure participants in their sample showed more positive affect and less withdrawal than did insecure participants during a standard marital conflict resolution task.

Second, and even more crucial to progress in this area, was that both of these studies (and Phelps et al., 1998, in particular) offered some significant caveats about the use of Pearson's retrospective approach to recovering prospective pathways associated with attachment-related change. It is worth reminding readers in this context that coding of the AAI focuses primarily on how adults talk about their childhood experiences (i.e., narrative coherence), not how individuals characterize their early experiences (i.e., narrative content). Phelps et al. (1998) went further, however, in noting:

> Researchers have questioned the accuracy of self-reports, suggesting they are vulnerable to . . . defensive processes or distortions in memory. . . . The field still awaits the results of a longitudinal study that can determine whether subjects' actual experiences match their probable experiences gathered with the AAI. (p. 34)

Nor were those who made empirical contributions to this literature the only individuals to publicly express such concerns. For example, in his first review of the AAI literature in the *Handbook of Attachment* (Cassidy & Shaver, 1999), Hesse (1999) noted: "We do not know whether those who appear to be [retrospectively-defined] earned-secure have in fact substantially positive experiences that are now, ironically, coherently misrepresented" (p. 426; see also Sroufe, Carlson, Levy, & Egeland, 1999).

# PART 3: A FIRST LOOK AT THE EARLY HISTORIES OF RETROSPECTIVELY DEFINED EARNED-SECURES

It was against this backdrop that the first author, together with Elena Padrón—and ultimately in close collaboration with Alan Sroufe and Byron Egeland—set out to use the MPCLS data set to address the range of open questions related to the earned-secure classification. It would be historically convenient if our initial analyses were intended to address what is now clear was the looming question in this area— that of whether earned-security, as measured retrospectively, in fact reflects life trajectories characterized by attachment-related resilience in prospect. Instead, however, the work that culminated in Roisman et al. (2002) actually began as a more straightforward effort to replicate the findings that had accumulated in the earned-security literature using a prospective assessment of earned-security. We (Roisman & Padrón, 2000) attempted to do so by cross-classifying attachment categories in infancy (available at 12 and 18 months as assessed with the Strange Situation Procedure; Ainsworth, Blehar, Waters, & Wall, 1978) with AAI classifications, then only available at age 19 on the MPCLS cohort (26-year AAIs have been subsequently collected and coded). Having defined earned-secures prospectively as individuals with documented insecure relationships with their maternal caregivers in infancy (paternal attachment data were not available on this cohort) who nonetheless coherently described their childhood experiences as young adults (i.e., they were classified as non-unresolved secure on the AAI at age 19), we examined this group in contrast to prospectively defined continuous-secures (i.e., secure in infancy and young adulthood) and an insecure comparison group (i.e., insecure in adulthood irrespective of their early attachment histories) on an observational assessment of their romantic interaction behavior at age 20 to 21 and in terms of their self-reported depressive symptomatology acquired at age 23 (assessed with the Young Adult Self-Report, YASR; Achenbach, 1997).

Consistent with our expectations—as well as prior studies of earned-security using Pearson's retrospective criterion—prospectively defined earned-secures in the MPCLS were interpersonally effective in the context of their interactions with romantic partners. However, such individuals managed to be so *without manifesting any apparent depressive liabilities*, as had previously been documented by Pearson using her retrospective definition of earned-security (for details, see Roisman et al., 2002). Although it might reasonably appear naïve now, this latter finding came as something of a surprise for us at the time and led to what would become a critical reframing of our effort—to use the MPCLS to examine the key question suggested most explicitly by Phelps and her colleagues (1998) of whether retrospectively defined earned-secures in fact overcome insecure attachments in infancy and/or difficult experiences with primary caregivers in childhood.

Nonetheless, we wanted to pursue this question strategically and with what seems, in retrospect, to be an almost extreme degree of care (this being one of Alan Sroufe's major contributions to the resulting paper, and a general strategy that has powerfully shaped how the first author engages new research problems to this day). Most important, we needed to be sure—perhaps especially given the high-risk nature of the sample—that earned-secures in the MPCLS, retrospectively defined using the Pearson definition, shared the same psychological profile with individuals so identified in prior studies of lower-risk cohorts (Pearson et al., 1994; Phelps et al., 1998; Paley et al., 1999). Specifically, we believed it crucial to demonstrate, first, that such individuals were interpersonally effective and, second, that they succeeded in being so despite reporting relatively high levels of depressive symptomatology.

In short, the evidence that emerged when the Pearson definition was employed with the age 19 AAI data from the MPCLS cohort was entirely in line with previous reports by Pearson, Phelps, Paley, and their colleagues—though diverged notably from our initial analyses based on prospectively defined attachment change groups identified in the MPCLS. Specifically, retrospectively defined earned-secures were rated as engaged in romantic relationships in adulthood of comparable quality to continuous-secures, and higher quality than insecures at age 20 to 21. Nonetheless—but as predicted—retrospective earned-secures also described themselves as more depressed in comparison to continuous-secures at age 23, as assessed by the Young Adult Self-Report (Achenbach, 1997) and, moreover, were consistently described (both by their maternal caregivers and by themselves) as being the most depressed group in Kindergarten/ grade 1 and at age 16, as measured by the Child Behavior Checklist and Youth Self-Report, respectively (Achenbach, 1991a, 1991b).

Now confident that the earned-secures we had identified retrospectively in the MPCLS were comparable to those previously identified in studies using the Pearson definition, we then moved to the more central question at hand of whether retrospectively defined earned-secures were more likely than continuous-secures to have experienced insecure attachments to primary caregivers that were subsequently overcome. We felt this question could be addressed most straightforwardly by examining whether there was significant convergence between our prospectively and retrospectively defined attachment groups. Strikingly, however, we found no evidence that the Pearson definition converged with the prospective attachment change groups (see Table 2 from Roisman et al., 2002).

Retrospectively assessed earned-secures were no more likely than continuous-secures to have had anxious infant attachment histories with their maternal caregivers in Roisman et al. (2002). Nonetheless, we did wonder whether this was really a fair test of the validity of the earned-secure classification. Of some relevance, the AAI probes memories between approximately 5 and 12 years of age—as such, the expectation that the valence of secure adults' life narratives can retrodict their security in infancy might well be unreasonable. Given this, we next compared the retrospectively defined earned-secure, continuous-secure, and insecure groups on observationally assessed ratings of the maternal parenting they encountered in childhood and adolescence (i.e., 24 months, 42 months, and 13 years). If retrospective earned-secures overcame pervasively malevolent parenting experiences, they should be more likely than continuous-secures to have mothers who received significantly poorer ratings in the task-centered observations of developmentally appropriate maternal caregiving that were conducted in the MPCLS participants' earlier lives.

To be sure, participants coded as earned-secure on the basis of Pearson et al.'s (1994) retrospective system *report* as adults having experienced greater childhood parenting-specific adversity than other secure/autonomous participants. Nevertheless, the data presented in Roisman et al. (2002) called into question the assumption that retrospectively defined earned-secures actually *encountered* greater parental adversity in childhood than continuous-secures. Using the Pearson et al. (1994) system of operationalizing earned-security, the longitudinal, prospective data presented in our paper paradoxically revealed instead that earned-secures were the beneficiaries of among the most *supportive* maternal care in the MPCLS sample during childhood and adolescence (see Table 5 from Roisman et al., 2002).

As we noted at the time, lacking father-child observational data on the majority of the MPCLS participants (again, a large percentage of the MPCLS participants did not have a stable male figure in the home), we could not know with confidence whether the supportive maternal care we observed among earned-secures took place within the context of a more generally supportive family dynamic in childhood or if it was compensatory, leaving open the possibility that retrospectively defined earned-secures actually do experience poorer relationships with male figures in childhood relative to their continuous-secure counterparts. Moreover, no observations of parent-child interactions were conducted between the ages of 5 and 12 in the MPCLS data set, a period, as afore-mentioned, that is emphasized in the AAI assessment of childhood memories. As a counterpoint, however, given the family and personal history of depressive symptomatology in the lives of the retrospectively defined earned-secures uncovered in this and the Pearson et al. (1994) study, we could also not rule out the possibility that self-described differences in early experience between retrospectively defined earned- and continuous-secures are primarily a function of positive and/or negative reporting biases.

Although the possibility remains that the retrospectively defined earned-secures featured in the Roisman et al. (2002) study actually struggled with unmeasured forms of adversity in childhood—a point to which we will return later in this chapter—the results of this first longitudinal study using Pearson's definition of earned-security squarely emphasized that it should not be assumed that they experience either insecure attachments in infancy or pervasively malevolent experiences with parents in childhood and suggested further that the term earned-secure may well be a misnomer, at least as applied to such individuals. To be sure, we have no reason to believe Pearson and her colleagues (1994) presupposed that their system for operationalizing earned- versus continuous-security would provide a veridical window on any adult's infant attachment history. However, it is fair to say that the Pearson system *is* meant to provide an overall and generally applicable depiction of participants' actual encounters with harsh parenting in childhood. Moreover, viewed through the lens of the findings of Roisman et al. (2002), the fact that retrospectively defined earned-secures had been shown in prior research to parent as effectively as do continuous-secures (and more capably than insecures) proved not to be necessarily remarkable; results based on the MPCLS suggested that their parenting skill may simply be a natural extension of the supportive care from which they benefited in their own childhood (Pearson et al., 1994; Phelps et al., 1997).

Alternatively stated, even if it turns out that the early supportive maternal experiences we identified in Roisman et al. (2002) (should this pattern of results replicate in other samples) are compensatory to other forms of adversity—unmeasured or unexamined in this initial study based on the MPCLS and thus far undiscovered in other data sets— the term earned-security would still be problematic in that it implies that such adults' security was acquired primarily via their own efforts. Roisman et al. (2002) suggests instead that earned-secures appear able to talk about early distressing events coherently because of either consistent or ameliorative support in childhood—they do not rise above difficult parenting through sheer will; rather, earned-secures' success is scaffolded by caring adults, their ability to freely evaluate their childhood experiences is a natural extension of a supportive past, though perhaps not exclusively so.

This initial work with the MPCLS cohort nonetheless left behind a rather striking paradox in its wake: Why do earned-secures, who have supportive early experiences with their primary caregivers, report negative early memories—and why are they so unhappy? Of note, one possibility we considered before the publication of Roisman et al. (2002) was that perhaps there was no real discrepancy to be explained. As we discussed earlier, earned-secures are somewhat disproportionately identified on the basis of their retrospective reports about *paternal* rather than maternal childhood experiences, but Roisman et al. (2002) focused exclusively on prospective data on *maternal* caregiving. Hesse (2008) recently offered this observation as a possible explanation for the results obtained in Roisman et al. (2002).

There are at least two reasons why this reasoning is flawed, although (absent additional data) admittedly not fatally. First, this observation does not explain why the retrospective earned-secure group in Roisman et al. (2002) had positive (i.e., above average) maternal experiences—as observed prospectively in childhood and adolescence—given that the maternal experience scores of the earned-secure group (as measured retrospectively via the AAI) suggested that such individuals in general had more problematic maternal experiences than did continuous-secures and inferred experiences roughly comparable to insecure adults (see Table 1 in Roisman et al., 2002). Said another way, the contrast between the retrospective versus prospective data on maternal experiences in Roisman et al. (2002) offers a *prima facie* case for a discrepancy between retrospective reports about and prospective evidence regarding earned-secures' maternal experiences. Second, in follow-up analyses in Roisman et al. (2002) we explicitly excluded earned-secures with above-average maternal inferred experience scores (see p. 1217) and reexamined whether the retrospectively defined earned-secure group, once purged of individuals identified as such exclusively because of harsh inferred experiences with paternal (but not maternal) caregivers, converged with our prospective assessment of earned-security. It did not.

## PART 4: EXPLAINING THE PARADOX: A FIRST APPROXIMATION

Although the relevant empirical corpus is admittedly thin, we believe the evidence, taken together, supports the view that the data in Roisman et al. (2002) present a genuine paradox: If earned-secures have relatively supportive early histories—at least with their maternal caregivers—what, then, accounts for their depressive symptomatology? Interestingly, one explanation for this paradox emerged rather early in the earned-security literature. As emphasized by Phelps et al. (1998) in their follow-up to the seminal paper on earned-security (Pearson et al., 1994), recollection is clearly a reconstructive process that can be strongly influenced and even distorted by subsequent experiences (Henry, Moffitt, Caspi, Langley, & Silva, 1994; Yarrow, Campbell, & Burton, 1970). As such, Phelps et al. (1998) were particularly concerned that the AAI's inferred experience scales might pick up potential depression-related biases toward selectively remembering negative childhood memories, an observation that was especially astute in that an empirical link had already been demonstrated between earned-security and self-reported depressive symptomatology

(Pearson et al., 1994). Although Pearson et al. (1994) reasonably conceptualized such depressive symptomatology to be a consequence of successfully overcoming negative life events, Phelps et al. (1998) were the first to suggest that, alternatively, meeting criteria for retrospectively defined earned-security might be a consequence of depression-related biases in recall. They noted at the time:

> It is . . . conceivable that . . . [retrospectively defined] earned secures have childhoods as positive as continuous secures but because of a depressogenic style they focus on and remember negative experiences in their pasts more readily than do continuous secures. (Phelps et al., 1998, p. 34)

This intriguing hypothesis—that depressive symptomatology might not be a consequence but a cause of earned-security, retrospectively assessed—initially struck us as empirically intractable. Clearly, additional evidence drawn from nonexperimental studies that earned-secures report more internalizing distress than do continuous-secures—and comparable levels to insecures—could be just as reasonably interpreted as consistent with the hypothesis that earned-secures report elevated levels of internalizing problems resulting from (unmeasured) early attachment-related adversity as it would the alternative that symptoms of depression color adults' retrospective reports about their early experiences, with implications for how such experiences are later characterized by AAI coders. Without input from Sarah Schoppe-Sullivan, then an advanced graduate student in Sarah Mangelsdorf's laboratory (then) at the University of Illinois at Urbana-Champaign, our work on earned-security would likely have been stymied. Nonetheless, good fortune placed the first author in one of Mangelsdorf's lab meetings devoted to the then-controversial results of Roisman et al. (2002). When the first author noted that it would be impossible and unethical to, say, depress undergraduate students in order to attempt to experimentally manipulate the valence of secure adults' life narratives (and test the hypothesis suggested in Phelps et al.,1998), Schoppe-Sullivan fatefully remarked: "Why not?"

What Schoppe-Sullivan was alluding to was all too clear to a developmental psychologist with the kind of broad methodological training that typifies departments of psychology: That clinical and social psychologists often use mood induction procedures to simulate affective states (e.g., Gomez, Cooper, & Gomez, 2000), and that such experimental procedures routinely provide crucial tests of causal hypotheses that would be unethical or impossible to conduct otherwise. With this borrowed flash of insight, we (Roisman et al., 2006) soon after began the development of an experiment designed to manipulate the valence of secure adults' AAI narratives ($N = 100$; 57 secure) via mood induction.

The logic of our experiment was straightforward: Following up on speculation that earned-security might result from depressogenic biases in the recall of early experiences, this work—published eventually as Roisman et al. (2006)—examined the hypothesis that both trait depressive affect (i.e., reports of internalizing distress) as well as state sadness (i.e., an experimentally induced sad mood) would be associated with earned-versus continuous-security. Furthermore, we expected that such effects of the mood induction would largely be a consequence of differences observed on secure adults' inferred life experience ratings across experimental conditions (participants were administered either a Sad or Happy mood induction). We did not expect, however, that the mood induction would manipulate the base rates of security/insecurity observed in this study (e.g., the *coherence* of young adults' life narratives).

The mood induction we used involved three components: (a) instrumental music delivered through headphones, (b) mental focus on an autobiographical memory relevant to achieving a happy or sad mood state, and (c) explicit instruction to achieve the desired emotional state (Hernandez, Vander Wal, & Spring, 2003). In an attempt to further enhance the efficacy of the mood induction via "bogus pipeline" procedures (Roese & Jamieson, 1993), noninvasive sensors used to measure electrodermal and cardiovascular response were adhered to participants' fingers and torsos. (Bogus pipeline procedures are designed to reduce self-presentation biases by falsely convincing participants that physiological measures provide a direct window into their cognitive and affective experience. In contrast to most studies using this technique, however, we did not use deception by explicitly making this claim to the participants in our experiment.) After the mood induction, participants were informed by a research assistant that they were about to complete a second study focused on their memories about their childhood experiences with caregivers. At this point, a second research assistant unaware of the experimental condition participants experienced entered the room to conduct the AAI.

Although a meta-analytic estimate suggests that about 43% of secure adults can be further subclassified as earned-secure (using the definition originally given by Pearson et al., 2004; see Roisman et al., 2006), 62% of the secure young adults who underwent a mood manipulation procedure designed to induce sadness just before the administration of the AAI were subsequently classified as earned-secure in our study, whereas only 18% of secure adults who received a mood induction that induced happiness were so classified. Furthermore, the mood induction procedure, as expected (a) did not manipulate the coherence of adults' narratives (i.e., rates of [in]security were comparable across conditions and typical of young adults generally); (b) results could not be attributable to participants' or interviewers' expectations (i.e., debriefing suggested that participants rarely guessed the hypothesis of the study and interviewers remained unaware of the experimental condition); and (c) effects obtained were large in magnitude (i.e., participants' self-reports of internalizing problems measured premanipulation, in addition to the effects of the mood induction, in aggregate explained 45% of the variance in earned- versus continuous-security—equivalent to a multiple $r = .67$). Also as expected, among secure adults the mood induction procedure consistently manipulated trained coders' impressions of the inferred life experiences of the young adult participants of this study across experimental conditions. (As an aside, we also found some evidence of ironic effects of the mood induction on the inferred experiences of *insecure* adults, with such individuals actually tending to describe their early experiences more positively in the Sad and more negatively in the Happy condition.)

Given that virtually all adults have the capacity to recall both relatively positive and negative experiences with parents, we speculated in Roisman et al. (2006) that the mood induction procedure facilitated secure adults' recollection of either sad or happy memories, with implications for objective coders' overall judgments about the quality of their early experiences. This point warrants emphasis, particularly given that Hesse (1999, p. 426) had previously indicated, as noted earlier, that "we do not know whether those who appear to be [retrospectively defined] 'earned secure' have in fact had substantially positive early experiences that are now, ironically, coherently misrepresented." Although earlier data from Roisman et al. (2002) support the view that retrospective 'earned-secures' childhood experiences with maternal caregivers are generally supportive in nature, it does not necessarily follow directly that such life events are being *distorted* in the context of earned-secures' AAI narratives. The AAI merely requires adults to provide specific memories that characterize their relationships with caregivers in childhood. As such, it seems unlikely that this information *exhaustively* describes a given adult's childhood experiences with his or her caregivers. The bottom line here is that our intuition is that secure adults' reported experiences in Roisman et al. (2006) were likely not fabricated, although they may well have been nonrepresentative—that is, most secure individuals can recall both substantially supportive and negative early memories, but current and long-standing mood-states have powerful influences on memory retrieval.

## PART 5: AN OPERATIONAL CRITIQUE AND A TAXOMETRIC REJOINDER

We have attempted to be clear in this chapter and elsewhere that the results of Roisman et al. (2002) and Roisman et al. (2006) speak most directly to the validity of the *Pearson* definition of earned-security. Nonetheless, the results of our work are discussed as if the problems of the Pearson system may well generalize beyond the data at hand; that is, in both studies—and Roisman et al., 2006, in particular—we speculate as to whether the problems endemic to the Pearson system (i.e., its failure to retrodict early experiences in Roisman et al., 2002, and its susceptibility to mood induction in Roisman et al., 2006) are caused more generally by the *retrospective* nature of the assessment of earned-security in Pearson.

However, an alternative hypothesis must be entertained: Given the relatively lax criteria originally proffered by Pearson and her colleagues (i.e., evidence of merely *below-average* parenting *by a single caregiver*), perhaps earned-security, retrospectively assessed, is being overestimated and thus mismeasured. Said another way, perhaps the issue is not so much the use of a retrospective definition of earned-security, but the fact that we are currently using the wrong one. Clearly, this argument has been implicit for some time now in Main and Goldwyn's (1998) suggestions for identifying earned-secures retrospectively in their AAI coding manual—and was made explicit more recently by Hesse (2008).

To be sure, the Pearson definition results in a relatively large percentage of secure adults being classified as earned-secure. As we noted earlier, in Roisman et al. (2006) we estimated via meta-analysis of the published data then available in the earned-security literature that a full 43% of secure adults meet the Pearson definition (aggregate $N = 290$), which, depending on one's assumptions about the base rates of non-unresolved but otherwise secure participants in the population, maps onto about 23% of all adults. (For this estimate, we drew on the average of the base rates for male and female nonclinical participants that contributed data to Bakermans-Kranenburg & van IJzendoorn, 2009.)

Is it reasonable for 43% of all secure participants to meet criteria for earned-security (and, given the mutually exclusive and exhaustive nature of the Pearson system, that 57% of all secure adults can be accurately labeled continuous-secure)? On the one hand, such a large percentage strikes us, albeit on the basis of intuition alone, as high. Moreover, such a high rate would seem difficult to square with one of the primary tenets of attachment theory. Specifically, how could adult security be built on the foundation of supportive early experiences if about half of all secure adults (assuming that their retrospective reports are veridical) actually have difficult early experiences? On the other hand, perhaps attachment-related change is more common than we suppose; Bowlby was certainly never as precise about making these kinds of point predictions as would be ideal. Given such ambiguity, the question of how many earned-secures is too much strikes us as one perhaps best left as an empirical question that can be addressed most straightforwardly via descriptive analyses of relevant prospective data.

That said, given the relatively high rates of earned-security identified in the initial Pearson et al. (1994) study (the investigators of this small sample study actually found that a full two-thirds of their secure adults met criteria for earned-security), it seems quite reasonable that Main and Goldwyn (1998) shortly afterward began developing more conservative (yet still retrospective) criteria for identifying earned-secures in their coding manual for the AAI. Specifically, they suggest (1) that earned-security should reflect negative experience with both primary caregivers, and (2) that such experiences should be highly aversive (AAI loving scores ≤ ~3 for both caregivers; Main & Goldwyn, 1998). Main and Goldwyn (1998) similarly advocate for conservative criteria for identifying continuous-secures, suggesting that their mean inferred loving score = 6.5 or greater for primary caregivers discussed during the AAI.

Main's conservative definition provides a clear challenge to the interpretation of the prior studies on earned-security. Could many of the problems with the Pearson system be attributable to it using an overly liberal threshold for the identification of earned-secure adults? Or perhaps instead is it the case that retrospective systems for identifying earned-security are more generally vulnerable to the kinds of problems documented in the Roisman et al. studies? Unfortunately, one major practical impediment to adjudicating between these two possibilities is the very low base rate of earned- (and continuous-) security using Main and Goldwyn's (1998) definitions. For example, we previously estimated based on data from Roisman et al. (2006) and Roisman et al. (2002) that the base rate of earned-security by Main's new definition runs at approximately 2% of the total population, which would require a normative-risk sample on the order of about 1,000 participants to identify a group of earned-secures large enough to conduct proper statistical analyses. (As an aside, given this low base rate it might in the future be advantageous to look to studies of higher-risk cohorts to identify earned-secures in sufficient numbers by Main's definition for systematic examination.)

It is of note that the Main definition results in a relatively small percentage of participants reaching criteria for being identified as continuous-secure as well. In Roisman et al. (2006), 40% of secure participants met their criterion; a mere 22% met Main's stringent criteria in

Roisman et al. (2002). Furthermore, as might be surmised, in both data sets a *majority* of secure participants did not meet Main's criteria *either* for earned- or continuous-secure status (54% in Roisman et al., 2006, and 72% in Roisman et al., 2002). Why should this be?

First and most substantively, one important fact overlooked in the published literature on earned-security is that measures of maternal and paternal inferred experience actually tend to factor separately by caregiver (Haydon, Roisman, & Burt, in press). In other words, the assumption that adults' reports about the valence of their caregiving experiences during the AAI depict their childhood experiences as homogeneously negative or positive across caregivers is not supported by the data. As such, relatively few individuals' AAI narratives would be expected to reveal evidence of pervasively negative experiences with both maternal and paternal caregivers. Second, although it may be tempting to conclude that one of the virtues of the Main and Goldwyn (1998) definition of earned-security is that it would seem to point to the great difficulty individuals have in maintaining coherent discourse while discussing extremely negative early experiences with both maternal and paternal caregivers, this conclusion overlooks an important methodological explanation for this observation.

Specifically, it is not only the case that few secure participants receive extreme scores on the inferred experience dimensions; this is true of *insecure* adults as well. One of the unintended gifts of the earned-security literature is that it has become convention (based on the template established in Pearson et al., 1994) to report and compare the mean inferred experience (and coherence) scale scores for earned-secures, continuous-secures, and insecures. What is rather striking when one looks at these data across relevant studies (see Pearson, et al., 1994; Phelps et al., 1998; Paley et al., 1999; Roisman et al., 2002; Roisman et al., 2006) is that insecure participants on average tend to receive maternal and paternal (inferred experience) love scores in the range of 2.8 to 5.3 on a nine-point scale ($M = 4.4$ for maternal [meta $N = 298$] and 3.6 for paternal caregivers [meta $N = 297$]), values generally *above* the threshold that defines the Main criterion for earned-security (the $SDs$ for the means reported above were approximately 1.5).

Despite these very serious challenges (perhaps most problematic the fact that a majority of participants cannot be unambiguously classified as having clearly problematic or clearly supportive childhood experiences based on the Main criteria), we can draw on some (limited) data to adjudicate the Main system, to which we now turn. From our perspective, determining whether any criterion for recovering prospective pathways from retrospective data is valid boils down to just two issues, that of (1) *sensitivity* (i.e., Does the definition reliably identify those it should?) and (2) *specificity* (i.e., Does the definition reliably exclude those it should?).

First, does the relatively small group of earned-secures based on Main and Goldwyn (1998; again, approximately 2% of the population as estimated in Roisman et al., 2006) actually identify a good portion of secure adults who had insecure attachment relationships in infancy? In theory, one way to address this would be to examine what the available prospective, longitudinal data reveals about how common it is for secure adults to have had insecure relationships in infancy with both mothers and fathers. Unfortunately, we simply do not know the answer to this question, given that so few longitudinal investigators have collected maternal and paternal attachment data from infancy forward (for two important exceptions see Main, Hesse, & Kaplan, 2006, and Steele & Steele, 2006). Nonetheless, for this chapter we *were* able to roughly estimate from relevant longitudinal investigations that approximately 14% (meta $N = 313$) of participants in the literature to date have had insecure *maternal* attachments in infancy but were nonetheless classified as secure on the AAI in adulthood (see Table 4.1). Thus, by at least one valid operationalization of prospectively assessed earned-security, the Main definition clearly underestimates its prevalence—indirect evidence that Main and Goldwyn's criterion for earned-security has poor sensitivity.

Similar concerns emerge in examining the specificity of Main and Goldwyn's retrospective definition of earned-security. First, as reported in Roisman et al. (2006), in the MPCLS sample Roisman et al. (2002) found that three out of 153 participants met Main's restrictive definition. However, two of these participants actually had a *secure* attachment to their mothers in infancy, suggesting that the Main definition misclassified these participants (assuming the goal of Main's criteria is to identify

**Table 4.1  Key longitudinal studies of the adult attachment interview with prospective data from infancy**

| Study and Key Reference | Source | # of AAIs Administered | Age(s) AAI Administered | % Prospective Earned-Secure | Notes |
|---|---|---|---|---|---|
| *AAI Studies With Strange Situation Procedure Data in Infancy* | | | | | |
| E. Waters' Dissertation Sample Waters et al. (2000) | Journal | 50 | 20–21 | 10% (5/50) | • Disorganization not coded<br>• Used Main and Goldwyn's (1998) AAI classification system<br>• Percentage earned-secure based on 12-month Strange Situation (18-month data also available). |
| Family Lifestyles Project Hamilton (2000) | Journal | 30 | 17.5 (Mean) | 7% (2/30) | • No reference to disorganization<br>• Used Main and Goldwyn (1998) |
| Minnesota Parent-Child Longitudinal Study Weinfield, Whaley, & Egeland (2004) | Journal | 169 (164 that could be coded; 125 in key analysis) | 19 and 26 | 15% (19/125) | • Disorganized infants coded as insecure in determination of percentage prospective earned-secure<br>• 12- and 18-month Strange Situation data composited in relevant analyses<br>• Used Main and Goldwyn (1998)<br>• Data reported are for age 19 (age 26 data currently unpublished) |
| M. Lewis Longitudinal Sample Lewis, Feiring, & Rosenthal (2000) | Journal | 84 | Senior year of high school | Not applicable | • Administered nonstandard Strange Situation (one separation and reunion)<br>• Two individuals with no training in Main and Goldwyn (1998) rated participants using Kobak's (1993) AAI Q-Sort |

| Study | | Sample | Age | Disorganized | Notes |
|---|---|---|---|---|---|
| Bielefeld Longitudinal Study Grossmann, Grossmann, & Kindler (2006) | Chapter | By age 21–22, 38 of 49 original participants still enrolled | 16 and 22 | Not reported | • Used Kobak's (1993) AAI Q-Sort and Main and Goldwyn (1998) system at both AAI assessments |
| Regensburg Longitudinal Study Grossmann, Grossmann, & Kindler (2006) | Chapter | By age 21–22, 38 of 51 original participants still enrolled | 16, 18, and 21 | Not reported | • Used Kobak's (1993) AAI Q-Sort at all time periods<br>• Also used Main and Goldwyn (1998) at least at 21 |
| London Parent-Child Project Steele & Steele (2006) | Chapter | 66 | 16 | 26% (17/66) | • Disorganized infants included with insecures<br>• Used Main and Goldwyn (1998) |
| Haifa Longitudinal Study Sagi-Schwartz & Aviezer (2006) | Chapter | 71 | 17–18 | Not reported | • Used Main and Goldwyn (1998)<br>• Kibbutzim Study |
| Berkeley Longitudinal Study Main, Hesse, & Kaplan (2006) | Chapter | 42 | 19 | 2% (1/42) | • Disorganized infants included with insecures<br>• Used Main and Goldwyn(1998) |

(Continued)

**Table 4.1** (Continued)

| Study and Key Reference | Source | # of AAIs Administered | Age(s) AAI Administered | % Prospective Earned-Secure | Notes |
| --- | --- | --- | --- | --- | --- |
| *AAI Studies Without Strange Situation Procedure Data in Infancy* | | | | | |
| Brody and Massie Longitudinal Study Bahadur (1998) | Dissertation | 76 | 30 | Not applicable | • Applied Waters & Deane (1985) Attachment Q-Set to footage of an infant-caregiver interaction available on cohort<br>• Used Main and Goldwyn (1998) |
| UCLA Longitudinal Study Beckwith, Cohen, & Hamilton (1999) | Journal | 89 (86 in key analyses) | 18 | Not applicable | • Used Main and Goldwyn (1998)<br>• 3 participants lacked early maternal sensitivity data<br>• Study of premature infants |
| Total across studies | | ~750 | | 14% (44/313) | |

*Note:* % Prospective Earned-Secure = Percentage of individuals in each sample that had an insecure attachment to their maternal caregiver in infancy—as assessed by the Strange Situation Procedure—who nonetheless coherently described their early childhood experiences during the AAI in adolescence or young adulthood. Data presented were primarily drawn from published journal articles cited, Grossmann, Grossmann, and Waters (2006), and Mudita Bahadur's (1998) dissertation. Additionally, the first author acquired some unpublished data pertinent to the percentage of prospective earned-secures for the London Parent-Child Project and Berkeley Longitudinal Study via e-mail correspondence with Howard Steele and Erik Hesse, respectively. For meta-analysis of this literature in relation to stability see Fraley (2002). Note finally that we intentionally excluded longitudinal studies of the AAI that did not acquire prospective data from infancy (e.g., Allen & Hauser, 1996).

secure adults who experienced an insecure infant-caregiver relationship). Second, in our earned-security experiment (Roisman et al., 2006), two of 98 participants met Main and Goldwyn's (1998) criteria for earned-security, and both were in the Sad condition, leading to questions about whether the clearly difficult experiences discussed by these two participants were representative of their early experiences generally or were instead at least in part a product of mood-related distortions in memory retrieval.

All of this said, the data that do exist with respect to the Main definition of earned-security are clearly limited, which provides a clear upper limit on their generalizability. Furthermore, the only direct examination of the validity of any definition of earned-security requires additional prospective data based on large longitudinal investigations in which (a) sufficient numbers of earned-secures can be identified by both conservative and more lax retrospective criteria and then (b) examined against the observed experiences of such individuals in infancy, childhood, and adolescence. However, one remaining empirical question can now be addressed, at least preliminary. Specifically, implicit in the Main and Goldwyn (1998) definition of earned-security is a taxometric assertion: that earned-security reflects a low-base-rate category.

In our experience, developmental psychologists tend not to think about the issue of taxonicity (e.g., whether categories or continua best reflect the underlying variation in attachment-related individual differences) as an empirical question at all, but rather one of convenience, preference, or inherited theoretical orientation. Although taxonicity of one's data was once regarded as being at the researcher's discretion, this is no longer tenable given developments in the area of taxometrics. Indeed, it was Paul Meehl and his colleagues (Meehl, 1973, 1995; Meehl & Yonce, 1996)—working in the Department of Psychology at the University of Minnesota in parallel with the great strides made in developmental science a building away at the Institute of Child Development—who developed a suite of methods designed precisely to address questions about the distributional properties of individual differences (i.e., their taxonicity). Meehl and colleagues' contributions thus highlight both the fact that the assumption that earned-security is a low-base-rate taxon is a testable one, as well as that alternative hypotheses must be considered. In this case, (a) the earned-security distinction might be a categorical one, but not particularly low base rate (e.g., Pearson et al., 1994) or (b) the inferred life experiences of secure adults might in fact be distributed *continuously*.

All of Meehl's taxometric work rests on his covariance mixture theorem, which states that if a true categorical distinction exists, then relevant indicators should be weakly correlated within categories and more strongly correlated around taxonic boundaries. As an example, if one posits that the distinction between dismissing and secure states of mind regarding attachment is categorical, then it follows that the individual indicators of this (taxonic) distinction (e.g., idealization of caregivers, inability to produce memories that support one's general characterization of early caregiving experiences) should be essentially uncorrelated within each of the categories. This is because all members of a taxon should have similarly high (or low) ratings on these scales, and the lack of variation should produce essentially nil associations among the various indicators. In contrast, at the taxonic boundary (i.e., the point on the various scales at which the categorical threshold is met and participants are qualitatively dismissing versus secure on one or the other side of the boundary), indicators of the categorical distinction are expected to be nontrivially correlated, because it is around such boundaries that the categories are most likely to be "mixed."

Although Meehl developed several independent taxometric tools that adjudicate between categorical and dimensional structure, in this context, we will introduce just one of these, known as MAXCOV-HITMAX (MAXCOV; Meehl, 1973; Meehl & Yonce, 1996). MAXCOV serves as one of the most widely used methods for addressing questions about taxonicity (for a detailed overview of MAXCOV, see Meehl, 1973, or Waller & Meehl, 1998). In MAXCOV—per the covariance mixture theorem—one examines the covariance between (every set of) two indicators of a latent construct as a function of a third indicator, or, more often, the mean of the rest of the indicators of the taxon or dimension. The function characterizing these conditional covariances (roughly correlations when based on standardized indicators) across $x$ ($x$ is often called the "cut-variable" and is typically the standardized average of all of the indicator variables or a composite of all indicator pairs) is called a MAXCOV function, and its shape depends on the taxonic status of the latent variable under investigation.

For example, if the latent variable is categorical with a base rate of 50% of the population, the MAXCOV curve tends to have a mountain-like peak centered on the midpoint of $x$. In samples in which the base rate is less than 50%, the peak will be shifted to the right; in samples in which the base rate is larger than 50%, the peak will be shifted to the left. If the latent variable is continuous, however, the MAXCOV curve will tend to resemble a flat line (see Fraley & Spieker, 2003, for graphical illustrations). Moreover, if a true taxon exists, the covariance function provides an estimate of the base rate of the category (this is because, as just mentioned, if high levels of $x$ are rare, then the MAXCOV curve's peak is shifted right; if high levels of $x$ are common, then the peak is shifted left).

Using this logic, Chris Fraley, Jay Belsky, and the first author acquired raw data from all published studies of earned-security, resulting in the aggregation of three data sets with complete AAI scale data (Paley et al., 1999; Phelps et al., 1998; Roisman et al., 2006; aggregate $N = 504$). Although our study focused on the latent structure and taxonicity of AAI state-of-mind dimensions more generally (see following discussion), most pertinent to the issue of the taxonicity of earned-security, we submitted the inferred experience scales of the AAI among secure participants only ($n = 278$; maternal and paternal inferred love, rejection, and neglect—relevant variables were reverse coded) to MAXCOV. We did so with the foreknowledge that, if earned-security is a low-base-rate taxon, the mean correlation among the inferred experience scales should be highest for secure individuals who were rated by coders as having experienced relatively more difficult caregiving experiences (that is, we could expect a peak at the right-hand side of the MAXCOV function). What we found instead was that the resultant function was flat (see Figure 3 from Roisman et al., 2007), suggesting that—at least among secure adults—the inferred life experiences of such individuals appear to be distributed continuously. (Note that we also examined inferred life experience indicators separately by parental caregiver, and the results were essentially identical.)

## PART 6: CONCLUSIONS AND FUTURE DIRECTIONS

### The AAI Is Valid

We are occasionally asked if our investigations of earned-security suggest that the AAI might not be valid. The answer is straightforward: *Clearly not.* All of the studies we have discussed in this chapter strongly support two crucial aspects of the validity of the AAI—its predictive and retrodictive properties. First, all of the published work in the earned-security literature, including our own, is entirely compatible with other evidence that adult security is intimately tied to interpersonal functioning (e.g., Hesse, 2008; Haydon et al., in press; van IJzendoorn, 1995). Second, findings from Roisman et al. (2002) in particular fit well with evidence that adult security appears to emerge from supportive childhood experiences with primary caregivers (Beckwith et al., 1999; Fraley, 2002; Hamilton, 2000; Waters et al., 2000; Roisman et al., 2001). We regard Roisman et al. (2002) as providing among the strongest support for the claim that states of mind regarding early experiences, as inferred from the coherence of AAI discourse, can provide a window on childhood experiences with parents. This is because the earned-secure group, whether defined conservatively or more liberally, provides a risky test of the hypothesis that secure adults tend to have supportive early histories. Roisman et al. (2002) demonstrated that this appears to be true (in terms of maternal caregiving at least) *both* for secure individuals who retrospectively describe their experiences as more (i.e., continuous-secures) or less (i.e., earned-secures) supportive. At the most general level of abstraction, we view the Roisman et al. (2002) study based on the MPCLS as underscoring the major premise of the AAI—that it is not the events of childhood that are described but the coherence with which they are described that is an important indicator of developmental history.

That said, studies critical of retrospective assessments of earned-security do also underscore the invaluable nature of longitudinal studies like the MPCLS and, conversely, the difficulty in recovering prospectively valid developmental pathways from retrospective data. In short, there is presently no published prospective evidence that the valence of secure participants' narratives about their early lives provides a basis for a veridical understanding of their early experience (Roisman et al., 2002). Instead, the phenomenon of earned-security may well best be explained, at least tentatively, by memory-related retrieval biases that lead some secure adults to discuss relatively negative and others to discuss relatively positive childhood experiences (Roisman et al., 2006).

## Earned-Security in Retrospect

We used the phrase "emerging insights" in the title of this chapter to reference the dynamic and admittedly incomplete nature of what we can with confidence conclude about the nature of retrospectively defined earned-security. The literature on earned-security presently leaves unanswered several questions about such adults, including uncertainties about the roots of their security in adulthood, their (inferred) depressogenic biases, and how such individuals—who report high levels of internalizing distress—nonetheless manage to produce coherent discourse about their childhood experiences while demonstrating that they are highly effective parents (Pearson et al., 1994; Phelps et al., 1998) and romantic partners (Paley et al., 1999; Roisman et al., 2002). These questions make the phenomenon of retrospectively defined earned-security a fascinating puzzle for developmental psychology, and, as such, we offer some specific suggestions for future research.

First, we regard it as absolutely essential to determine whether the results of Roisman et al. (2002) will replicate in a straightforward sense (i.e., for maternal caregivers) and more broadly (i.e., for paternal caregivers), irrespective of one's definition of earned-security (liberal and more restrictive), in more normative and other higher-risk samples. Toward that end, together with collaborators in the NICHD Early Child Care Research Network, we in the Relationships Research Laboratory at the University of Illinois at Urbana-Champaign are currently coding approximately 850 AAIs gathered at age 17.5 years from the NICHD Study of Early Child Care and Youth Development cohort for just this purpose. One major strength of the NICHD SECCYD data set is its inclusion of observational assessments of maternal *and* paternal caregiving from childhood through midadolescence that can potentially provide some clarity about the childhood caregiving antecedents of retrospectively defined earned-security.

However, even clear evidence that retrospectively defined earned-secures have relatively supportive experiences with maternal and paternal caregivers in infancy, childhood, and adolescence would merely scratch the surface on the developmental foundations of the phenomenon. Of high importance are (a) the examination of additional, complementary hypotheses regarding the origins of variation in secure adults' inferred life experiences (in this volume, for example, Kobak and Zajac [2011] advance the novel hypothesis that retrospectively defined earned-secures' negative evaluations of their childhood experiences result from the biasing filter of more recent difficulties with primary caregivers—an intriguing prediction in that it suggests that earned-secures might actually have *increasingly* problematic experiences with parents over time) and (b) the examination of earned-secures' putative depressogenic biases as *part of an unfolding developmental process* (Sroufe, 1997) rather than giving in to the Cartesian temptation to treat such biases as somehow operating as a totally exogenous influence in the development of retrospectively defined earned-security. Said another way, earned-secures' depressogenic biases are also a product of developmental history, albeit one that has yet to be articulated.

Conducting relevant future work, however, will require meeting a serious challenge: We must begin to measure such biases directly. Instead, investigators studying earned-secures have been too comfortable regarding reports of depressive symptomatology documented in Pearson et al. (1994) and Roisman et al. (2002), as well as the mood induction procedure used in Roisman et al. (2006), as crude proxies for either trait-like or more temporary biases in cognition and affect that influence the valence of the early memories that are recalled during the AAI. Although many approaches to characterizing earned-secures' depressogenic biases are possible, given their empirical links to depressive symptomatology, we are currently leveraging tools from neuroscience (i.e., frontal activation asymmetries in electrophysiology) and molecular genetics (i.e., variable number tandem repeats [VNTRs] and single nucleotide polymorphisms [SNPs] implicated in serotonergic functioning) to examine potential endophenotypic and genetic correlates of earned-security, retrospectively defined.

Questions also still remain regarding the finding in Roisman et al. (2002) that, at roughly the same time, mothers of retrospectively defined earned-secures were rated as highly capable caregivers yet self-reported both high levels of distress themselves and, a few years later, in their children. This finding continues to be intriguing but is clearly not anomalous. Pearson et al. (1994) were the first to show evidence that retrospectively defined earned-secures were effective caregivers despite reporting relatively high levels of depressive symptomatology.

Reflecting on Pearson et al. (1994) and our own findings, we speculated in Roisman et al. (2002) that secure states of mind regarding earlier attachment experiences function as relational buffers, moderating (i.e., attenuating) the very reliable associations typically observed between maternal depression and suboptimal parenting. Recently, the first direct test of this hypothesis was published (McMahon, Barnett, Kowalenko, & Tennant, 2006), in which it was demonstrated that the association between maternal depression and child insecurity, as assessed by the Strange Situation Procedure, was moderated by maternal states of mind regarding attachment measured by the AAI. As expected, the infants of depressed but secure mothers were at attenuated risk for insecurity as compared to the children of depressed mothers with insecure states of mind. Nonetheless, it remains to future work to determine precisely what it is about being secure that allows some depressed mothers to so reliably function as effective caregivers (Pearson et al., 1994; Phelps et al., 1998) and romantic partners (Paley et al., 1999; Roisman et al., 2002).

One final caveat is in order in relation to future research examining retrospective definitions of earned-security: All such work is complicated, we believe, by recent findings with respect to the latent structure of individual differences in adult attachment, as assessed with the AAI. For example, building on Roisman, Fraley, and Belsky (2007; $N = 504$)—which produced evidence for two modestly correlated dimensions (i.e., dismissing and preoccupied states of mind) underlying individual differences in attachment as assessed by the Adult Attachment Interview (AAI) using the Main and Goldwyn (1998) classification system—we recently replicated and extended relevant evidence in a large sample of adults ($N = 842$) who completed AAIs coded using Kobak's (1993) AAI Q-set (Haydon et al., in press). Principal components analysis of item-level Q-sort data yielded two relatively orthogonal states of mind (dismissing and preoccupied) and two inferred experience (maternal and paternal) components.

There are two consequences of these recent findings. First, what the field now refers to as "security" in fact might more accurately reflect the co-occurrence of two empirically distinct patterns of adult attachment-related variation: (1) the freedom to evaluate one's early childhood experiences and (2) preoccupation. Rank-order change on either of these dimensions is possible but has not yet been explored in the earned-security literature. Second, it might be unwise to use definitions of earned-security that summarize over empirically distinctive aspects of inferred experiences with maternal and paternal caregivers given that the relevant variation appears to be caregiver-specific. One possible solution in future research on earned-security is to study the phenomenon as two-, three-, and four-way interactions among various configurations of the state of mind and inferred experience dimensions that reflect the empirically derived latent structure of the AAI.

## Earned-Security in Prospect

Given the clear challenges that confront investigators hoping to use retrospective data to make inferences about positive attachment-related change, the reader might wonder why retrospective studies of earned-security were ever conducted. The answer almost certainly boils down to one of pragmatics. Although the most straightforward approach to characterizing earned-security is to use data drawn from long-term, longitudinal studies, it is of some significance that before the year 1999 (which marked the publication of Beckwith, Cohen, & Hamilton, 1999), no relevant data were available in the literature. Even today we estimate that—the ongoing effort related to the NICHD SECCYD aside—only approximately 750 AAIs have been administered to participants followed prospectively from infancy, and that less than half of those data are currently published in peer-reviewed journals (half of the AAIs in the peer-reviewed literature derive from the MPCLS; see Table 4.1).

Nonetheless, even if such data were not in short supply, it should be appreciated that operationalizing earned-security using *prospective* definitions is not necessarily a straightforward undertaking. One historical impediment, perhaps, is the term *earned security*, which as discussed earlier connotes having developed a coherent narrative about childhood experiences by overcoming early adversity through sheer force of will (i.e., "pulling oneself up by one's bootstraps"), rather than via a range of dynamic factors operating both within and outside of the attachment system. There are two problems here. First, the term *earned-secure* has the potential to short-circuit a developmental analysis by conflating the *measurement* of positive attachment-related change with a testable *hypothesis* about its foundations. This issue is compounded by the fact that the evidence thus far suggests little support for the claim that individuals with insecure infant attachments to primary caregivers who nonetheless tell coherent AAI narratives as young adults manage to do so because they are simply "resilient" individuals—rather, multiple levels of support for such change appear to be operative (Weinfield, Sroufe, & Egeland, 2000; Weinfield, Whaley, & Egeland, 2004).

Second, the term *earned-secure* also implies that a single operational definition is adequate to capture the myriad ways that individuals rise above difficult interpersonal experiences. This seems to us unlikely. For example, it could be that some kinds of positive attachment-related trajectories (perhaps particularly change documented in the years of maturity) are best accounted for by actions of the individual (e.g., seeking therapy)—to the extent that these are not predictable from prior developmental experiences. In contrast, other forms of attachment-related resilience are, as has already been documented, scaffolded by compensatory supports in early and later caregiving environments (Sroufe et al., 2005).

As such, for progress to be made, we think it useful to reframe questions about earned-security as embedded within a family of interrelated proposals about positive attachment-related trajectories across the life course (Roisman et al., 2005). Positive attachment-related change—as a subset of life trajectories characterized by resilience more generally— always reflects two judgments: (1) Has the individual experienced early attachment-related adversity or risk? and (2) Has the individual achieved security in adulthood? (Masten, 2001) Thus far, however, both of these questions have been addressed using a fairly narrow prospective definition of early challenge and later security. Specifically, in the few prospective studies that exist, earned-secures have been identified almost exclusively as adults secure on the AAI who had an insecure relationship with a primary caregiver in infancy (Roisman et al., 2002).

The debate within the earned-security literature has already outlined several alternative operationalizations of early attachment-related *adversity* that warrant prospective analysis. First, at a minimum, we need systematic analyses in which early adversity is operationalized as the impact of insecurity and/or difficult early experience with maternal versus paternal caregivers. Second, we will also need to attend to the developmental timing of such interpersonal challenges as well as potential intermediary compensatory experiences (i.e., in infancy versus childhood versus adolescence). For example, almost all prospective work on positive attachment-related trajectories has been constrained by research designs that focus on change during the relatively early life course (i.e., infancy to young adulthood). There is likely much to learn about adult-onset attachment-related change (both for better and worse) from studies tracking individuals through the early years of adulthood and beyond.

Conversely, we believe it would be to the field's advantage to consider the many ways in which adults might be judged to be secure. The earned-security literature has relied to date on only one manifestation of adult security (i.e., as assessed by the AAI). However, adulthood involves the ongoing revision of existing attachment representations in concert with the formation of new attachment relationships, as well as the elaboration and co-organization of *multiple* attachment representations (Bretherton, 1995; Overall, Fletcher, & Friesen, 2003; Owens et al., 1995). Thus, security variously reflects representations of early caregiving experiences (as is measured by the AAI), representations of specific current relationships (as assessed by the Current Relationship Interview; Treboux, Crowell, & Waters, 2004), and even self-reports of low levels of anxiety and avoidance in the close relationships of adulthood generally (i.e., attachment style; Roisman et al., 2007).

In addition to our expectation that many kinds of attachment-related deflections are supported by changes in the caregiving environment post-infancy, we hypothesize that opportunities for security (variously defined) are also likely to emerge from (at least) three sources in adulthood. First, romantic attachment relationships might offer compensatory (i.e., corrective) experience for those with insecure histories (Sroufe et al., 2005), which may be reflected in positive change toward security. Becoming a parent might also, perhaps through priming the salience of early experience with one's own parents, prompt a reexamination of one's attachment history (Simpson, Winterheld, Rholes, & Oriña, 2007). Third, it is possible that positive attachment-related change might emerge through continued relationships with caregivers in adulthood. Depending on the content and quality of those interactions, continued experience with caregivers may revise representations of early history toward (or away from) a coherent state of mind regarding attachment (but see Kobak & Zajac, 2011, this volume).

Of note, each of these attachment experiences in adulthood may serve as a turning process in which the existing representation of early experience is altered or, alternatively, could be viewed themselves as forms of prospective attachment-related resilience (e.g., irrespective of whether corrective experiences with romantic partners promote life course deflections toward a secure state of mind as assessed by the AAI, experiencing a secure relationship with a romantic partner in adulthood despite early attachment-related adversity is a bona fide form of positive attachment-related change).

Prospective tests of this kind thus challenge us to broaden the earned-security literature beyond the measurement context in which it began (i.e., the AAI). Multiple operationalizations of early attachment-related adversity similarly require us to marshal measures of attachment security and caregiving experiences across childhood and adolescence rather than only in infancy and early childhood. Finally, incorporating assessments of experience and representation with multiple representational targets (i.e., caregivers, romantic partners, and children) will likely yield a richer view of security in adulthood. Taking such a developmental perspective thus reframes earned-security in terms of *the processes by which different forms of positive attachment-related change predictably emerge* (Egeland, Sroufe, & Carlson, 1993). As we have already suggested, prospective approaches also have the potential to help address unresolved issues about the developmental origins of two phenomena robustly associated with earned security assessed retrospectively in adulthood, including open questions about the origins of such individuals' (a) interpersonal effectiveness and (b) depressogenic biases in their retrieval of childhood memories.

In sum, largely because of insights from a series of studies of the MPCLS cohort, it has become clear that associations between earlier attachment-related experience and attachment security in adulthood are rather complex and multifaceted (e.g., Haydon, Collins, Simpson, & Salvatore, revised and resubmitted; Roisman et al., 2002; Roisman et al., 2005; Weinfield et al., 2004). Earned-security, prospectively defined, is likely to be no exception to this rule when viewed in the broader developmental context of the elaborated attachment system as it operates in adulthood. Nonetheless, we expect that adopting a broader view of earned-security will result in a clearer set of testable hypotheses regarding the source(s) of and process(es) underlying distinctive forms of positive attachment-related change. Such future work is almost certainly to become one (of so very many) aspect of the enduring intellectual legacy of the MPCLS and its longtime principal investigators, Byron Egeland and Alan Sroufe.

## REFERENCES

Achenbach, T.M. (1991a). *Manual for the Child Behavior Checklist/4-18 and 1991 profile*. Burlington, VT: University of Vermont Department of Psychiatry.

Achenbach, T.M. (1991b). *Integrative guide for the 1991 CBCL/4-18, YSR, and TRF profiles*. Burlington, VT: University of Vermont Department of Psychiatry.

Achenbach, T.M. (1997). *Manual for the Young Adult Self-Report and Young Adult Behavior Checklist*. Burlington, VT: University of Vermont Department of Psychiatry.

Aguilar, B., Sroufe, L. A., Egeland, B., & Carlson, E. (2000). Distinguishing the early-onset/persistent and adolescence-limited antisocial behavior types: From birth to 16 years. *Development and Psychopathology, 12,* 109–132.

Ainsworth, M. D. S., Blehar, M. C., Waters, E., & Wall, S. (1978). *Patterns of attachment: A psychological study of the Strange Situation*. New York, NY: Erlbaum.

Allen, J. P., & Hauser, S. T. (1996). Autonomy and relatedness in adolescent-family interactions as predictors of young adults' states of mind regarding attachment. *Development and Psychopathology, 8,* 793–809.

Bahadur, M. A. (1998). The continuity and discontinuity of attachment: A longitudinal study from infancy to adulthood. Unpublished doctoral dissertation, New York University.

Bakermans-Kranenburg, M. J., & van IJzendoorn, M. H. (2009). The first 10,000 Adult Attachment Interviews: Distributions of adult attachment representations in clinical and non-clinical groups, *Attachment & Human Development, 11,* 223–263.

Beckwith, L., Cohen, S. E., & Hamilton, C. E. (1999). Maternal sensitivity during infancy and subsequent life events relate to attachment representation at early adulthood. *Developmental Psychology, 35,* 693–700.

Bretherton, I. (1995). A communication perspective on attachment relationships and internal working models. In E. Waters, B. E. Vaughn, G. Posada, & K. Kondo-Ikemura (Eds.), *Caregiving, cultural, and cognitive perspectives on secure-base behavior and working models: New growing points of attachment theory and research* (Vol. 60, pp. 216–233). Chicago, IL: University of Chicago Press.

Cassidy, J., & Shaver, P. R. (Eds.). (1999). *Handbook of attachment: Theory, research, and clinical applications*. New York, NY: Guilford Press.

Cohn, D. A., Silver, D. H., Cowan, C. P., Cowan, P. A., & Pearson, J. L. (1992). Working models of childhood attachment and couple relationships. *Journal of Family Issues, 13,* 432–449.

Egeland, B., Jacobvitz, D., & Sroufe, L. A. (1988). Breaking the cycle of abuse. *Child Development, 59,* 1080–1088.

Egeland, B., Sroufe, L. A., & Carlson, E. A. (1993). Resilience as process. *Development and Psychopathology, 5,* 517–528.

Fraley, R. C. (2002). Attachment stability from infancy to adulthood: Meta-analysis and dynamic modeling of developmental mechanisms. *Personality and Social Psychology Review, 6,* 123–151.

Fraley, R. C., & Spieker, S. J. (2003). Are infant attachment patterns continuously or categorically distributed? A taxometric analysis of Strange Situation behavior. *Developmental Psychology, 39,* 387–404.

George, C., Kaplan, N., & Main, M. (1985). Adult Attachment Interview. Unpublished manuscript, University of California, Berkeley.

Gomez, R., Cooper, A., & Gomez, A. (2000). Susceptibility to positive and negative mood states: Test of Eysenck's, Gray's and Newman's theories. *Personality and Individual Differences, 29,* 351–366.

Grossmann, K., Grossmann, K. E., & Kindler, H. (2006). Early care and the roots of attachment and partnership representations: The Bielefeld and Regensburg Longitudinal Studies. In K. E. Grossmann, K. Grossmann, & E. Waters (Eds.), *Attachment from infancy to adulthood: The Major Longitudinal Studies* (pp. 98–136). New York, NY: Guilford Press.

Grossmann, K. E., Grossmann, K., & Waters, E. (Eds.) (2006). *Attachment from infancy to adulthood: The Major Longitudinal Studies.* New York, NY: Guilford Press.

Grice, H. P. (1975). Logic and conversation. In P. Cole & J. L. Moran (Eds.), *Syntax and semantics III: Speech acts.* (pp. 41–58). New York, NY: Academic Press.

Hamilton, C. E. (2000). Continuity and discontinuity of attachment from infancy through adolescence. *Child Development, 71,* 690–694.

Haydon, K. C., Collins, W. A., Simpson, J. A., & Salvatore, J. E. (revised and resubmitted). Antecedents of discordance between generalized and partner-specific attachment representations in adulthood: A developmental perspective on the organization of romantic functioning. *Child Development.*

Haydon, K. C., Roisman, G. I., & Burt, K. B. (in press). In search of security: The latent structure of the Adult Attachment Interview revisited. *Development and Psychopathology.*

Henry, B., Moffitt, T., Caspi, A., Lanley, J., & Silva, P. (1994). On the "remembrance of things past": A longitudinal evaluation of the retrospective method. *Psychological Assessment, 6,* 92–101.

Hernandez, H., Vander Wal, J. S., & Spring, B. (2003). A negative mood induction procedure with efficacy across repeated administrations in women. *Journal of Psychopathology and Behavioral Assessment, 25,* 49–55.

Hesse, E. (1999). The Adult Attachment Interview: Historical and current perspectives. In J. Cassidy & P. R. Shaver (Eds.), *Handbook of attachment: Theory, research, and clinical applications.* (pp. 395–433). New York, NY: The Guilford Press.

Hesse, E. (2008). The Adult Attachment Interview: Protocol, method of analysis, and empirical studies. In J. Cassidy & P. R. Shaver (Eds.), *Handbook of attachment: Theory, research, and clinical applications* (2nd ed., pp. 366–382). New York, NY: The Guilford Press.

Kobak, R.R. (1993). *The Adult Attachment Interview Q-set.* Unpublished document, University of Delaware.

Kobak, R. R., & Zajac, K. (2011). Rethinking adolescent states of mind: A relationship/lifespan view of attachment and psychopathology. In D. Cicchetti & G. I. Roisman (Eds.), *Minnesota symposia on child psychology: The origins and organization of adaptation and maladaptation* (Vol. 36). Hoboken, NJ: Wiley.

Lewis, M., Feiring, C., & Rosenthal, S. (2000). Attachment over time. *Child Development, 71,* 707–720.

Main, M., & Goldwyn, R. (1998). Adult attachment rating and classification systems, Version 6.0. Unpublished manuscript, University of California at Berkeley.

Main, M., Hesse, E., & Kaplan, N. (2006). Predictability of attachment behavior and representational processes at 1, 6, and 19 years of age: The Berkeley longitudinal study. In K. E. Grossmann, K. Grossmann, & E. Waters (Eds.), *Attachment from infancy to adulthood: The Major Longitudinal Studies* (pp. 245–304). New York, NY: Guilford Press.

Main, M., Kaplan, N., & Cassidy, J. (1985). Security in infancy, childhood, and adulthood: A move to the level of representation. In I. Bretherton & E. Waters (Eds.), Growing points of attachment theory and research. *Monographs of the Society for Research in Child Development, 50* (1 & 2), 66–104.

Masten, A. S. (2001). Ordinary magic: Resilience processes in development. *American Psychologist, 56,* 227–238.

McMahon, C. A., Barnett, B., Kowalenko, N. M., & Tennant, C. C. (2006). Maternal attachment state of mind moderates the impact of postnatal depression on infant attachment. *Journal of Child Psychology and Psychiatry, 47,* 660–669.

Meehl, P. E. (1973). MAXCOV-HITMAX: A taxonomic search method for loose genetic syndromes. *Psychodiagnosis: Selected papers* (pp. 200–224). Minneapolis: University of Minnesota Press.

Meehl, P. E. (1995). Bootstraps taxometrics: Solving the classification problem in psychopathology. *American Psychologist, 50,* 266–275.

Meehl, P. E., & Yonce, L. J. (1996). Taxometric analysis; II. Detecting taxonicity using covariance of two quantitative indicators in successive intervals of a third indicator (MAXCOV procedure). *Psychological Reports, 78,* 1091–1227.

Overall, N. C., Fletcher, G. J. O., & Friesen, M. D. (2003). Mapping the intimate relationship mind: Comparisons between three models of attachment representations. *Personality and Social Psychology Bulletin, 29,* 1479–1493.

Owens, G., Crowell, J., Pan, H., Treboux, D., O'Connor, E., & Waters, E. (1995). The prototype hypothesis and the origins of attachment working models: Adult relationships with parents and romantic partners. In E. Waters, B. E. Vaughn, G. Posada, & K. Kondo-Ikemura (Eds.), *Caregiving, cultural, and cognitive perspectives on secure-base behavior and working models: New growing points of attachment theory and research* (Vol. 60, pp. 216–233). Chicago, IL: University of Chicago Press.

Paley, B., Cox, M. J., Burchinal, M. R., & Payne, C. C. (1999). Attachment and marital functioning: Comparison of spouses with continuous-secure, earned-secure, dismissing, and preoccupied attachment stances. *Journal of Family Psychology, 13*, 580–597.

Pearson, J. L., Cohn, D. A., Cowan, P. A., & Cowan, C. P. (1994). Earned- and continuous-security in adult attachment: Relation to depressive symptomatology and parenting style. *Development and Psychopathology, 6*, 359–373.

Phelps, J. L., Belsky, J., & Crnic, K. (1998). Earned security, daily stress, and parenting: A comparison of five alternative models. *Development and Psychopathology, 10*, 21–38.

Radloff, L. S. (1977). The CES-D scale. A self-report depression scale for research in the general population. *Applied Psychological Measurement, 1*, 385–401.

Roese, N. J., & Jamieson, D. W. (1993). Twenty years of bogus pipeline research: A critical review and meta-analysis. *Psychological Bulletin, 114*, 363–375.

Roisman, G. I. (2007). The psychophysiology of adult attachment relationships: Autonomic reactivity in marital and premarital interactions. *Developmental Psychology, 43*, 39–53.

Roisman, G. I., Collins, W. A., Sroufe, L. A., & Egeland, B. (2005). Predictors of young adults' representations of and behavior in their current romantic relationship: Prospective tests of the prototype hypothesis. *Attachment & Human Development, 7*(2), 105–121.

Roisman, G. I., Fortuna, K., & Holland, A. (2006). An experimental manipulation of retrospectively defined earned and continuous attachment security. *Child Development, 77*, 59–71.

Roisman, G. I., Fraley, R. C., & Belsky, J. (2007). A taxometric study of the Adult Attachment Interview. *Developmental Psychology, 43*, 675–686.

Roisman, G. I., Holland, A., Fortuna, K., Fraley, R. C., Clausell, E., & Clarke, A. (2007). The Adult Attachment Interview and self-reports of attachment style: An empirical rapprochement. *Journal of Personality and Social Psychology, 92*, 678–697.

Roisman, G. I., Madsen, S. D., Hennighausen, K. H., Sroufe, L. A., & Collins, W. A. (2001). The coherence of dyadic behavior across parent-child and romantic relationships as mediated by the internalized representation of experience. *Attachment & Human Development, 3*, 156–172.

Roisman, G. I., & Padrón, E. (2000, June). A prospective study of earned attachment security: Romantic relationship quality, global adjustment, and internalizing distress. Poster-presentation to the American Psychological Society, Miami Beach, FL.

Roisman, G. I., Padrón, E., Sroufe, L. A., & Egeland, B. (2002). Earned-secure attachment status in retrospect and prospect. *Child Development, 73*, 1204–1219.

Sagi-Schwartz, A., & Aviezer, O. (2006). Correlates of attachment to multiple caregivers in kibbutz children from birth to emerging adulthood: The Haifa Longitudinal Study. In K. E. Grossmann, K. Grossmann, & E. Waters (Eds.), *Attachment from infancy to adulthood: The major longitudinal studies* (pp. 165–197). New York, NY: Guilford Press.

Simpson, J. A., Winterheld, H. A., Rholes, W. S., & Oriña, M. M. (2007). Working models of attachment and reactions to different forms of caregiving from romantic partners. *Journal of Personality and Social Psychology, 93*, 466–477.

Sroufe, L. A. (1997). Psychopathology as an outcome of development. *Development and Psychopathology, 9*, 251–268.

Sroufe, L. A., Carlson, E. A., Levy, A. K., & Egeland, B. (1999). Implications of attachment theory for developmental psychopathology. *Development and Psychopathology, 11*, 1–13.

Sroufe, L. A., Egeland, B., Carlson, E. A., & Collins, W. A. (2005). *The development of the person: The Minnesota study of risk and adaptation from birth to adulthood.* New York, NY: Guilford Press.

Sroufe, L. A., Egeland, B., & Kreutzer, T. (1990). The fate of early experience following developmental change: Longitudinal approaches to individual adaptation in childhood. *Child Development, 61*, 1363–1373.

Steele, H., & Steele, M. (2006). Understanding and resolving emotional conflict: The London Parent-Child Project. In K. E. Grossmann, K. Grossmann, & E. Waters (Eds.), *Attachment from infancy to adulthood: The major longitudinal studies* (pp. 137–164). New York, NY: Guilford Press.

Treboux, D., Crowell, J. A., & Waters, E. (2004). When "new" meets "old": Configurations of adult attachment representations and their implications for marital functioning. *Developmental Psychology, 40*(2), 295–314.

van IJzendoorn, M. (1995). Adult attachment representations, parental responsiveness, and infant attachment: A meta-analysis on the predictive validity of the adult attachment interview. *Psychological Bulletin, 117*, 387–403.

Waller, N. G., & Meehl, P. E. (1998). *Multivariate taxometric procedures: Distinguishing types from continua. Advanced quantitative techniques in the social sciences* (Vol. 9). Thousand Oaks, CA: Sage.

Waters, E., & Deane, K. E. (1985). Defining and assessing individual differences in attachment relationships: Q-methodology and the organization of behavior in infancy and early childhood. In I. Bretherton & E. Waters (Eds.), Growing points of attachment theory and research. *Monographs of the Society for Research in Child Development, 50* (1–2, Serial No. 209), 41–65.

Waters, E., Hamilton, C. E., & Weinfield, N. S. (2000). Stability of attachment security from infancy to adolescence and early adulthood: General introduction. *Child Development, 71,* 678–683.

Waters, E., Merrick, S., Treboux, D., Crowell, J., & Albersheim, L. (2000). Attachment security in infancy and early adulthood: A 20-year longitudinal study. *Child Development, 71,* 684–689.

Weinfield, N. S., Sroufe, L. A., & Egeland, B. (2000). Attachment from infancy to early adulthood in a high-risk sample: Continuity, discontinuity, and their correlates. *Child Development, 71,* 695–702.

Weinfield, N. S., Whaley, G. J. L., & Egeland, B. (2004). Continuity, discontinuity and coherence in attachment from infancy to late adolescence: Sequelae of organization and disorganization. *Attachment & Human Development, 6*(1), 73–97.

Yarrow, M. R., Campbell, J. D., & Burton, R. V. (1970). Recollections of childhood: A study of the retrospective method. *Monographs of the Society for Research in Child Development, 35,* 1–83.

—❧◆☙—

# Relationships Across the Lifespan

## The Benefits of a Theoretically Based Longitudinal-Developmental Perspective

W. Andrew Collins, Peter LaFreniere, and Jeffry A. Simpson

Asking *how* a developmental perspective influences the study of relationships requires one to look historically at significant points of connection between typical social development research conducted before the 1960s in relation to social development research conducted today. In this chapter, we present a retrospective review of the issues and findings that dominated the field of social development before the rich conceptual and methodological innovations introduced by attachment theory and the programs of research it generated, many of which were launched in the late 1960s and early 1970s. While doing so, we also highlight the remarkable impact of the three decades of research conducted by Alan Sroufe, Byron Egeland, and their collaborators at the University of Minnesota. As will become apparent, the long-standing program of research conducted by the Sroufe/Egeland research group did more to

___

The authors contributed equally to this chapter.

reveal the many benefits of adopting a theoretically based longitudinal-development perspective than perhaps any other research group in the history of developmental psychology.

We begin by reviewing important points of connection between social development research conducted before 1965 and social development research being conducted today. While doing so, we address questions such as: *What* did attachment theory and research offer the emerging field of social development research? *Why* and *how* did the lifespan developmental perspective inherent in attachment theory provide such fertile ground for this nascent field?

## ATTACHMENT THEORY AND SOCIAL DEVELOPMENT RESEARCH

Attachment theory (Bowlby, 1973, 1980) provided many new opportunities for research on change and adaptation across the lifespan. Before 1965, social development researchers focused on distinct and isolated social behaviors (e.g., the frequency of certain acts), often independent of the social context in which they occurred. The developmental/attachment perspective, in contrast, examined the behavior of individuals *within* relationships, focusing primarily on the pattern, organization, and functional meaning of certain clusters of behaviors. The majority of research conducted before 1965 also emphasized experimental manipulations of proximal environments (or, more often, analogs of environments). Attachment theory, by comparison, focused on the sampling of different social contexts and tasks that typified the specific developmental challenges of a given developmental period. As a result, the attachment perspective generated new questions about *process*—the *how*, rather than merely the what and how much, of developmental change. Another closely related historical shift was an emerging interest in the ability of individuals to understand the significance of other people and relationships based on their own interpersonal histories and salient social experiences.

In the late 1970s and 1980s, research on the boundary between the relationships of parents and children and childhood friendships and adult relationships began to flourish, eventually resulting in the wider field of close relationships. Among social psychologists, the typical focus has been on nonfamilial close relationships (e.g., romantic relationships). Among developmental psychologists, the emphasis has centered on familial relationships and close friendships. In recent years, these two major research traditions have both begun to investigate other types of relationships (e.g., with co-workers, members of one's wider social network).

## THE ATTACHMENT ERA

The study of mother-infant attachment came of age during the 1970s. Bowlby's (1973, 1980) tremendous theoretical synthesis was complemented by important methodological and empirical advances made by luminaries such as Mary Ainsworth, Alan Sroufe, Byron Egeland, Mary Main, Everett Waters, and several others. In this section, we briefly review research based on Ainsworth's Strange Situation paradigm and describe longitudinal studies that have examined the developmental significance of early attachment across the lifespan.

### The First Attachment Relationship

Bowlby theorized that the interactive history between infants and their caregivers largely determines the quality of the attachment bond that exists during infancy and early childhood. According to Bowlby (1973), infants develop stable expectations about the availability and responsiveness of their caregivers based on how the caregivers respond when the infants are distressed. Bowlby called the cognitive representations that infants construct from such interactions *internal working models*. Mary Ainsworth, who was the first investigator to marshal strong empirical support for some of Bowlby's fundamental attachment hypotheses, created the Strange Situation to study these transactional patterns within a stressful setting when infants were typically 9 to 12 months old. She reasoned that infants who avoid their caregivers when distressed, or who display a mixture of approach and resistant behaviors when distressed, should not be able to benefit from the contact comfort that most effective caregivers provide. These ultimately dysfunctional behaviors were presumed to reflect a history of either rejecting or inconsistent/chaotic care provided by caregivers. Indeed, one central premise of attachment theory is that the history and quality of a relationship can be discerned from a careful analysis of infants' behavior in relation to changes in the current social context, particularly during separation and reunion episodes with their caregivers.

Home ratings of maternal sensitivity conveyed by mothers to their infants during the first year of life indicated that, when caregivers were rated as higher on sensitivity, their attachment relationships with their infants were more likely to be secure in the Strange Situation. In contrast, caregivers who rejected their infants' bids for contact and comfort were more likely to have insecurely attached infants in the Strange Situation (Ainsworth, Blehar, Waters, & Wall, 1978; Blehar, Lieberman, & Ainsworth, 1977). These seminal findings were first replicated in early studies that emanated from the Minnesota Parent-Child Longitudinal Study (MPCLS; Egeland & Farber, 1984), and then by other research teams (e.g., Bates, Maslin, & Frankel, 1985; Belsky & Isabella, 1988; Isabella & Belsky, 1991). The specific link between caregiver rejection and avoidant attachment has also been replicated in several studies (e.g., K. Grossman, E. E. Grossman, Spranger, Suess, & Unzer, 1985; Isabella, 1993).

Other research from the MPCLS confirmed that the emotional availability and quality of communication displayed by caregivers is meaningfully related to attachment security in the Strange Situation. Egeland and Sroufe (1981), for example, found that infants whose mothers were depressed tended to be insecurely attached. Not all infants of depressed parents, however, developed insecure attachments. Egeland and Sroufe (1981) documented that the *quality* of caregiving, not depression per se, best predicts attachment classification. For example, when caregiving is very insensitive, as in the case of child abuse or severe neglect, disruptions of infant-caregiver security occur at disproportionately higher rates. Moreover, among maltreated infants, higher rates of all insecure attachment classifications are witnessed, with nearly 90% of maltreated infants developing insecure attachments (Crittenden, 1992), especially the disorganized pattern (Carlson, Cicchetti, Barnett, & Braunwald, 1989).

## Temperament and Attachment

Attachment researchers generally agree that an infant's temperamental traits are also visible in the Strange Situation. For example, babies who have more difficult temperaments are more upset by repeated separations from their caregivers. However, using parental reports and measures of cortisol reactivity to stress, research has found that temperament predicts the amount of crying during separation, but not during reunion, episodes (Gunnar, Mangelsdorf, Larson, & Herstgaard, 1989; Vaughn, Lefebvre, Seifer, & Barglow, 1989). Temperament appears to dictate what infants "require" from their caregivers when they reunite with them (Thompson, 1990), similar to infants who recently have been ill or stressed requiring more contact upon reunion before they can fully settle down. However, being upset by separations from caregivers is not the same as being insecurely attached.

Attachment scholars believe that attachment status and temperament are largely independent constructs (see also Vaughn & Shin, 2011, this volume). Sroufe (1996) suggests two main reasons for this. First, attachment status and temperament represent different levels of analysis. Assessments of attachment focus on the overall organization of behavior. Thus, it is not how much an infant cries and squirms that counts but the *context and sequencing* with specific behaviors that is critical. Infants who cry a great deal during separations and who squirm mightily with a stranger are still classified as securely attached if they are comforted by their caregivers during reunions and then quickly return to play. Second, securely attached infants tend to show considerable differences of behavioral style, from being slow to arouse and noncuddly (B1) to being slow to warm-up and easily aroused (B4).

These conceptual distinctions are also supported by recent behavioral genetics findings, which show considerable heritability for temperament traits but negligible heritability for attachment classifications (e.g., Bokhorst et al., 2000; O'Connor & Croft, 2001; Roisman & Fraley, 2008). Although temperament traits are related to certain behaviors observed in the Strange Situation, they are not systematically related to attachment quality unless difficult temperament is combined with unresponsive caregiving. Longitudinal studies that have included repeated measurements of infant temperament, maternal caregiving, and infant attachment status across time are perhaps most relevant to this debate. This research has confirmed that the quality of maternal caregiving, not the infant's inborn temperament, best predicts the quality of infant-mother attachment (e.g., Ainsworth et al., 1978; Bates et al., 1985; Blehar et al., 1977; Egeland & Farber, 1984; Vaughn et al., 1989).

Although temperament is not directly related to attachment security, infant characteristics can have an indirect impact if they affect the quality of caregiving the infant receives. For example, newborns who have neurological problems are *not* more likely to be insecurely attached, except when they experience lower levels of social and emotional support from their caregivers (Crockenberg, 1981). Similarly, infant proneness to distress does not forecast anxious attachment, except in combination with higher levels of maternal controllingness (Mangelsdorf, Gunnar, Kestenbaum, Lang, & Andreas, 1990).

In their longitudinal study, van den Boom (1991, 1994) investigated the emotional development of infants at risk for developing insecure attachments (i.e., highly irritable infants who are born to low socioeconomic status [SES] mothers; see van den Boom & Hoeksma, 1994). Newborns classified as highly irritable at 10 and 15 days using Brazelton's Neonatal Behavioral Assessment Scale were more likely to be insecurely attached (especially avoidant) at one year compared to nonirritable infants from the same low-SES sample. These irritable infants were also judged by their mothers to be more difficult at 6 and 12 months according to parental ratings of temperament, and these mothers were minimally responsive to the relatively few positive expressions of their irritable infants. Mothers of future anxious-resistant children were inconsistent in their responses to them, displaying a mixture of effective soothing and ineffective attempts at distraction, which often increased their infants' distress. Mothers of future avoidant children tended to ignore their child's crying for longer periods, and they were more distant in their soothing attempts. These findings, which are consistent with Ainsworth and colleagues' earlier work, can be viewed in terms of child effects on maternal behavior (e.g., prolonged infant irritability suppresses maternal sensitivity) and maternal caregiving effects on attachment classification.

Consistent with the general view that attachment security is not fixed by biology but rather is shaped by the caregiving environment, research by Egeland/Sroufe and others has also confirmed that (1) attachment security can change during infancy, with changes being meaningfully related to corresponding changes in the caregiving environment (Vaughn, Waters, Egeland, & Sroufe, 1979); (2) interventions that improve caregiver sensitivity and responsiveness also increase infant-caregiver attachment security (van IJzendoorn, Juffer, & Duyvesteyn, 1995); (3) quality of attachment can vary, depending on whether the infant is assessed with his or her mother or father (Fox, Kimmerly, & Shafer, 1991; Main & Weston, 1982); and (4) infants who have identical attachment classifications can have different temperaments (Sroufe, 1996).

## Attachment and Social Competence

As we have seen, attachment theorists propose that patterns of co-regulation established in earlier attachment relationships generate internal working models that guide thoughts, feelings, and behavior in later relationships (Bowlby, 1980; Sroufe, 1983, 1996). Most developmental psychologists view an infant's early attachment relationship(s) as laying the foundation for subsequent relationships, because the attitudes, expectations, and interpersonal skills that a child acquires are carried forward and reintegrated into new social and developmental contexts. Accordingly, competence during one developmental period promotes adaptation within that period, but it also paves the way for the formation of competence during the *next* developmental period (see Sroufe & Rutter, 1984).

According to attachment theory, children's representational models are closely interwoven with their emerging self-concept and broader representation of relationships. If children perceive their attachment figures as trustworthy, loving, and sensitive, then they are likely to view themselves as lovable and worthy of comfort and support from others. On the other hand, if attachment figures reject or rebuff children's bids for comfort, particularly when they are distressed, then the children should not only view attachment figures as rejecting, but the children should also view themselves as not worthy of comfort or support (Bretherton, 1985). Once formed, these representations ought to guide the processing of social information, especially the child's beliefs, attitudes, and feelings about the self in the context of future close relationships. Although internal working models usually remain open to new input as children meet new people, they tend to be relatively stable, because children actively select partners and form new relationships that fit with their existing working models. According to Bowlby (1973, 1980), working models should be fairly resistant to change once they develop, partly because they tend to operate outside of conscious awareness and partly because new information tends to be assimilated into them.

## Toddler Period

Developmental theorists such as Ainsworth (Ainsworth, Bell, & Slayton, 1974), Erikson (1963), Kopp (1989), and Sroufe (1996) view the toddler period as critical for the development of an autonomous self-system, one capable of achieving independence and initiative as well as responsiveness and conformity to the rules and expectations of others. Human evolution is rooted in the basic primate patterns of group living, which involve elements of both cooperation and competition. In all known cultures, the socialization of children changes dramatically during toddlerhood, in that they are exposed to a wider variety of social partners than they were during infancy. Fathers also become more central to the socialization of toddlers, and they typically provide a different mode of interaction, often engaging children in vigorous physical play while providing emotional support. In many societies, siblings take on added responsibilities in caring for their younger brothers or sisters and serving as challenging playmates. Rudimentary peer interaction also begins to occur during this period, with most interaction centering on interesting objects that attract the attention of toddlers. In addition, other adults besides parents become more involved with the children, especially grandparents, relatives, and other members of the community. Despite this increased diversity of social partners, the central developmental tasks of the toddler period still revolve around changes in the ongoing relationship with the primary caregivers (usually parents).

Attachment theorists believe that children's capacity for emotion regulation is shaped in their closest relationships. Sroufe (1996) used the term *guided self-regulation* to reflect the intermediate position of toddlers. Guided self-regulation falls between an earlier stage when *dyadic-regulation* is provided mostly by the caregivers and a later stage when the pre-schoolers achieve *true self-regulation*. During the guided self-regulation stage, toddlers learn how to regulate their own emotions and behavior within the limits and guidelines provided by their caregivers. Two major influences on this learning process have been identified: (1) the *overall quality* of the parents' approach to disciplining their toddlers during this period is more important than any specific child-rearing practices; and (2) *attachment history* affects the transition toward autonomous functioning. In this research, variables are created to index qualitative dimensions of parenting that operate across different social contexts.

Sroufe and colleagues claim that emotional support and quality of assistance are central features of parental competence (Matas, Arend, & Sroufe, 1978). In their approach, which has now been widely adopted within the field of developmental psychology, toddlers and their parents are presented with a series of problem-solving situations, each of which presents the parent-toddler dyad with a novel challenge. The first situation (free play) is minimally challenging, particularly with respect to the issue of autonomy. The next situation, in which the parent is instructed to interrupt the child's play at a prearranged signal and then to get the child to put away the toys, tests how smoothly the dyad can accommodate a potential conflict of wills. The third situation involves a graded series of physical problems that start simple and become more difficult, assuring that the child will be taxed beyond his or her capabilities when trying to solve the latter problems. This procedure assesses the flexibility of the parent-child dyad, including parental support and guidance, along with the child's emotion regulation and motivation capacities.

Toddlers who are securely attached to their mothers tend to be more enthusiastic when performing these tasks, expressing greater positive affect and less frustration. They also are more successful by virtue of their greater persistence, flexibility, and cooperation. Toddlers who have an anxious attachment history with their mothers display different behavioral patterns. Early anxious-resistant attachment is associated with poorer emotional regulation during the tasks. These toddlers tend to be clingy and prone to emotional dysregulation, becoming frustrated or oppositional during cleanup and problem-solving situations. Toddlers who have an anxious-avoidant history tend to be more disengaged during the tasks, showing less pleasure and little enthusiasm while doing them. Moreover, they typically ignore their mothers' attempts to involve them more in the tasks. This research was important because it demonstrates continuity in the pattern of the child's emotional competence and maternal sensitivity across different developmental phases, at a time when some researchers questioned whether such continuities even existed.

Several other studies provide convergent evidence for these results plus further connections between attachment in infancy and the quality of the later parent-toddler relationship. Maslin and Bates (1983), for example, documented that securely attached infants have less conflict with their mothers at age two than do toddlers with a history of insecure attachment. Specifically, toddlers assessed as anxious-avoidant earlier in life are more likely to engage in conflicts with their mothers. Reciprocally, their mothers are also more restrictive and controlling. Similar to attachment assessment research, these studies reveal disturbances in the parent-child relationship rather than problems that reside exclusively within the child. During the toddler years, however, the tensions and problems experienced with primary attachment figures may be carried forward into other adult-child relationships (e.g., Londerville & Main, 1981). In sum, the capacity for regulating arousing stimulation is critical to positive adaptation in both the family system and the peer system.

### The Preschool Period

During the preschool years, attachment behaviors are transformed, reflecting advances in language, cognition, and shifting issues in psychosocial adjustment. For most children, a new partnership with the primary caregivers (i.e., parents) emerges, one that reflects these advances and allows for increased autonomy and initiative within and beyond the dyad (Erikson, 1963; Sroufe, 1983). Within the parent-child relationship, secure children incorporate more perspective-taking, mutual communication of affect and desires, and joint planning. However, several deviations from this pattern are possible (Crittenden, 1992; Sroufe, 1989). According to transactional models, the child becomes a more active agent rather than a passive recipient of environmental input. New social milieus, such as preschool, may be constructed very differently by different children based on their attachment history. Children seek out or avoid various resources and opportunities within these new niches based on expectations associated with genetic propensities, past experiences, and former relationships.

Considerable research has established a clear link between infants' primary attachment relationships and the quality of their later peer relations. Compared to insecurely attached preschoolers, securely attached preschoolers tend to behave more positively toward their peers and receive more positive behavior from peers, they are better liked by peers, they enjoy more positive and synchronous friendships, and they are more highly regarded by their teachers as being helpful, cooperative, empathic, and socially competent (e.g., Erickson, Egeland, & Sroufe, 1985; Jacobson & Willie,1986; LaFreniere & Sroufe, 1985; Sroufe, 1983; Sroufe, Schork, Motti, Lawroski, & LaFreniere, 1984; Youngblade & Belsky, 1992).

A recent paper based on the NICHD Study of Early Child Care and Youth Development (SECCYD; NICHD Early Child Care Research Network, 2006) suggests that there are continuing positive effects of early attachment security, even after parental conditions change. For example, declining parenting quality does not predict increased classroom externalizing problems among children who have early secure attachments with their mothers, whereas it does for children who were insecurely attached at 15 months. Securely attached children seem to be protected against declining maternal parenting, suggesting that early attachment could be a protective factor by enabling securely attached children to approach social situations with more confidence and more positive expectations of others.

Attachment history is also related to behavioral problems in pre-schoolers. In the MPCLS, for example, attachment assessments at 12 and 18 months predicted behavior in the preschool classroom (Erickson et al., 1985). In this high-risk, inner-city sample, behavioral problems (assessed by teacher ratings) were evident in 85% of infants who had stable insecure attachments, 60% who had unstable attachments (being secure at one time but insecure at the other), and 29% who had stable secure attachments. Other risk factors within the home indicate why some securely attached infants display later behavioral problems in preschool whereas some insecurely attached infants do not. Compared to securely attached infants who did not display later problems, those that did had mothers who were less emotionally supportive and not as clear or consistent in their guidance and limit-setting during the toddler and early preschool years. These mothers also experienced more confusion and disorganized mood states during this period, and they were less involved with their children than mothers of secure infants who did not experience later behavior problems.

Comparisons between insecure infants with and without behavior problems also indicates that those without problems had mothers who were warmer, more supportive, and more appropriate in their limit-setting when children were 42 months old. Reciprocally, these children were also more affectionate and compliant with their mothers during this later assessment. These findings are important because they demonstrate continuity of child adaptation in stable environments and coherence in child adaptation in unstable ones. That is, when children with an earlier history of secure attachment are subsequently exposed to less-than-adequate maternal care, they are more likely to exhibit behavior problems than are secure infants in stable caregiving environments. Similarly, anxiously attached infants can become well-functioning preschoolers if their caregivers respond adequately to their needs during later developmental stages (see Sroufe, Egeland, Carlson, & Collins, 2005).

Anxious-resistant attachment during infancy is also a risk factor for internalizing behavior problems, including anxiety, excessive dependency on adults, social withdrawal, passivity, and submissiveness with peers (e.g., Erikson et al., 1985; LaFreniere & Sroufe, 1985; Sroufe, Fox, & Pancake, 1983). As infants and toddlers, these children tend to be wary, easily upset, and difficult to soothe. They also engage in less exploration and occasionally display angry, tantrum-like behavior, all presumably in response to having received inconsistent or chaotic care in the past (Ainsworth et al., 1978). In the MPCLS, infants classified as anxious-resistant at

12 and 18 months tended to become lower-status, peripheral members of their preschool peer groups three years later (LaFreniere & Sroufe, 1985; Sroufe, 1983). Some of these children also exhibited passivity and an infantile dependence on adults, whereas others were more forward with their peers but became easily overaroused and disorganized when faced with minor frustrations.

Children who have anxious-avoidant attachments have a different set of strengths and liabilities in their social adaptation and emotional adjustment to the preschool classroom in the MPCLS. Their adoption of an avoidant behavioral style to cope with chronic insensitivity and rejection from their past caregivers lays the foundation for a defensive personality characterized by hostility and negative expectations of others. In a naturalistic observational study that compared the emotional expressions of preschoolers who had different attachment histories, anxious-avoidant children expressed greater hostility and negative affect toward their peers, and they were more rejected by their peers than were securely attached children (LaFreniere & Sroufe, 1985).

Recent studies have replicated and extended these findings. For example, McElwain, Cox, Burchinal, and Macfie (2003) found that a history of avoidant attachment predicted greater instrumental aggression during child-friend interactions; a history of anxious-resistant attachment, on the other hand, predicted less self-assertion among friends. Following children of adolescent mothers from 12 months to 9 years of age, Munson, McMahon, and Spieker (2001) found that children who had histories of avoidant or disorganized attachment showed higher levels of externalizing problems at age 9 compared to children who had secure attachment histories. Lyons-Ruth, Easterbrooks, and Cibelli (1997) found that infants who had avoidant or disorganized histories were rated higher on both internalizing and externalizing symptoms at age 7 compared to children who had secure attachment histories.

Finally, in the NICHD SECCYD, involving more than 1,000 U.S. children, infants who had avoidant classifications were most vulnerable to parenting risks, demographic risks, and problematic outcomes several years later (NICHD Early Child Care Research Network, 2006). Relations between early attachment and child outcomes during the first three years of life have also been examined in the NICHD SECCYD data, often replicating results originally found in the MPCLS. For example, McElwain et al. (2003) found that an avoidant attachment history is associated with more instrumental aggression during child-friend inter-actions, whereas an anxious-resistant attachment history is associated with less self-control and less assertion among friends, even when maternal sensitivity and current attachment status are statistically controlled.

One consistent finding across many studies is that avoidantly attached preschoolers are at risk for externalizing problems expressed via relational aggression. Troy and Sroufe (1987), for instance, observed pairs of preschoolers during a series of dyadic play sessions across time. They found that a higher percentage of children who had avoidant histories took advantage of and mistreated their play partners. In all cases of victimization, the "exploiter" had an avoidant history, whereas the "victim" tended to be a child who had an anxious-resistant history. Preschool teachers also had distinct emotional reactions to children who had different attachment histories. They often nurtured and protected children who have anxious-resistant histories, but sometimes reacted with anger to the open defiance and bullying of children who have avoidant histories. These emotional responses from new caregivers (i.e., preschool teachers) underscore the transactional nature of these different developmental trajectories.

Finally, infants who are disorganized show no coherent attachment strategy during infancy and respond to their mothers in the Strange Situation with a variety of contradictory behaviors, odd or mistimed movements, and disoriented responses. Some research has linked the disorganized attachment pattern to specific forms of behavioral and emo-tional problems in preschoolers. Main and Solomon (1990), for instance, believe that these children respond to internal conflict by displaying con-tradictory or incomplete behavior patterns that were originally formed in response to chronic abusive or frightening parental behaviors. As preschoolers, these children are inflexible and controlling, possibly to bring some order to an otherwise chaotic network of close relationships. The disorganized pattern may also entail some degree of role reversal between the parent and the child with regard to caregiving or punishment.

In fact, such behaviors are mediated by deviant patterns of emotional regulation and communication in the parent-child relationship (Lyons-Ruth, Repacholi, McLeod, & Silva, 1991). Consistent with their poor emotion-regulation skills, there is a greater incidence of aggression, externalizing disorders, and oppositional defiant disorder among most disorganized children (see Lyons-Ruth & Jacobvitz, 1999; van IJzendoorn, Schuengel, & Bakermans-Kranenburg, 1999).

# ATTACHMENT AND RELATIONSHIPS OUTSIDE THE FAMILY

Despite the significance of parent-child relationships in predicting individual competence for initiating, maintaining, and managing relationships outside of the family (Collins & Van Dulmen, 2006), other relationships and social influences are also important. For example, early peer-group competence is a critical forerunner of affiliating well with peers in social groups, in forming and maintaining friendships, and in the emergence and maintenance of romantic relationships. Measures of peer competence collected as part of the MPCLS show impressive continuity between early childhood and late adolescence, with correlations ranging from .40 to .89. Moreover, these measures are reliably related to composite measures of the quality of early caregiving experience (Sroufe et al., 2005). These relations reflect important interpersonal and intrapersonal processes in social development.

One striking example is the discovery that adhering to the normative expectation of gender segregation in middle-childhood peer groups strongly predicts successful functioning in mixed-gender adolescent peer groups and in romantic relationships in early adulthood (Englund, Levy, Hyson, & Sroufe, 2000; Simon, Aikins, & Prinstein, 2008). This connection is likely to be a transactional one. Many adolescents believe that being involved in a romantic relationship is central to belonging and status within their peer groups, and the extensiveness of peer networks further facilitates involvement in dating. Participation in mixed-gender peer groups may particularly encourage and support involvement in romantic relationships. More specifically, the timing and extent of *involvement* in romantic relationships may be further facilitated by opportunities and social support for romantic experiences in established mixed-gender peer groups. Indeed, the selection of dating partners during early adolescence is influenced by group norms and values regarding the importance of social status and physical appearance.

There is little direct evidence, however, that peer group contexts contribute substantially to the actual *quality* of romantic relationships or to their cognitive and emotional features (see Collins & Van Dulmen, 2006). These findings are important because they suggest that these indicators of peer competence—relationship involvement and relationship quality—are differentially related to distinct features of romantic relationships in the same individuals. Specifying the contributions of each indicator to adult relationship competence is an especially promising direction for future research (Haydon, Collins, & Van Dulmen, 2005).

Although an attachment perspective is frequently presumed to imply a strong emphasis on early life experience, we do not view development as principally a product of early caregiver-child relationships. Rather, current behavior reflects the continuous interplay of early experience *in combination with* current experiences. This hypothesis was recently tested by Carlson, Sroufe, and Egeland (2004), who demonstrated that early experiences with primary caregivers are carried forward in mental representations (i.e., working models), but they also impact social behavior directly. Across time, representations of prior relationship experiences and current relationship experiences interact to produce adaptations in later relationships. Late-adolescent social functioning, including functioning in relationships, is the outcome of this dynamic, interactive process.

## EXTENSIONS TO ADULT RELATIONSHIPS

The impact and legacy of Egeland and Sroufe's research extends far beyond developmental psychology. Indeed, their work has influenced thinking and research in several areas of psychology, including social, personality, and clinical psychology. Within each of these areas, their research and perspective have advanced our understanding of adult relationship functioning. There are several reasons for this pervasive legacy. For example, Sroufe and Egeland's collaboration brought the full implications of attachment theory directly into mainstream thought and debate in psychology during the late 1970s and 1980s. Bowlby (1973, 1980) claimed that attachment theory was a lifespan theory of personality and social development, but Sroufe and Egeland confirmed how different attachment patterns assessed early in life predict distinct types of social behavior in early and middle childhood.

Their groundbreaking research also accentuated the importance of studying *dyadic behavior*, rather than the frequency with which each partner displayed certain behaviors, in *attachment-relevant situations*. Their persistent focus on how dyads—especially parent-child dyads early in life—respond to situations that activate the attachment system of one or both dyad members ushered in diathesis-stress predictions that, at the time, were unique to attachment theory. These findings helped establish attachment theory as a major and novel theoretical perspective in the 1980s. Their research also introduced new theory-centered methods of coding behavior in dyadic interactions. Before Egeland/Sroufe, most coding systems focused on counts or ratings of isolated behaviors rather than clusters of *functionally related* behaviors presumed to tap higher-level constructs central to a theory (e.g., secure-base behavior). The novel approaches to behavioral coding that Sroufe and Egeland pioneered influenced many scholars outside of developmental psychology, particularly those who studied romantic relationship dynamics (e.g., Simpson, Rholes, & Nelligan, 1992; Simpson, Rholes, & Phillips, 1996).

Of even greater importance, their research brought to the fore the pivotal role that *early life stressors* assume in social development from infancy into middle adulthood (Sroufe et al., 2005). While conducting this pioneering work, Egeland and Sroufe also developed several new and important constructs that now figure prominently in psychology. These constructs include heterotypic continuity, lawful discontinuity, resilience as a developmental process, developmental coherence, and felt security. It is difficult to imagine what the field of social development would look like today without these seminal contributions.

Sroufe and Egeland's primary program of research was guided by two fundamental questions: (1) "What are the primary *sources* of significant influences on personal and relational functioning?" and (2) "What are the specific *processes* through which these influences occur?" Answers to these questions are essential if one wants to predict and really understand social development across the lifespan. Several studies conducted by Sroufe, Egeland, and their colleagues are shining exemplars of this unique approach to understanding social development. We now highlight how the Egeland/Sroufe perspective of social development has influenced our own research on the antecedents of emotion in adult romantic relationships.

## A Longitudinal-Developmental Perspective on Emotion in Relationships

Bowlby (1980) believed that emotional reactions to relationship events are rooted in earlier relationship experiences, initially with early caregivers and then with other significant relationship partners during adolescence and adulthood (see also Ainsworth, 1989; Waters & Cummings, 2000). This core tenet of attachment theory has inspired several longitudinal studies in which the same individuals have been studied continuously from infancy onward. One of the most famous and influential studies has been the MPCLS (see Sroufe et al., 2005). This seminal project has focused on how early attachment experiences prospectively predict the quality and functioning of close relationships in adolescence and early-to-middle adulthood.

Although Bowlby (1973, 1980) hypothesized that working models guide how individuals think, feel, and behave in later relationships, he also believed that representations of early relationship experiences should not necessarily predict later relationship outcomes in a direct or straightforward manner. Rather, representations should be continuously modified and updated as individuals enter and leave different attachment relationships across successive phases of development (Carlson et al., 2004). Relationship experiences with early peers in childhood, for instance, should (and do) predict the quality of close friendships in adolescence. Moreover, the quality of experiences with caregivers in infancy and early childhood should (and typically do) forecast the quality of adolescent friendships, above and beyond the contributions of more concurrent experiences with same-age peers (Sroufe, Egeland, & Carlson, 1999).

In adult relationships, individuals' patterns of attachment during infancy (assessed by the Strange Situation) also predict certain features of their behavior with their romantic partners in early adulthood (Collins & Van Dulmen, 2006; Roisman, Collins, Sroufe, & Egeland, 2005). For example, if individuals had a disorganized attachment pattern in infancy, their observer-rated conflict resolution interactions with current romantic partners in early adulthood reveal fewer secure-base behaviors, less balance between couple functioning and each partner's personal interests and needs, less caring, less trust, less emotional closeness, less sensitivity to each other's needs and wishes, and poorer general outcomes. In addition, if individuals were disorganized during infancy, both they and their romantic partners display greater hostility during conflict resolution interactions, as rated by observers.

As Sroufe, Egeland, and their colleagues have shown, attachment insecurity in infancy and early childhood also forecasts other important relationship outcomes across time, such as peer competence rated by classroom teachers between the ages of 6 and 8 (Sroufe et al., 1999) and ratings of parent-child interactions at age 13 (Sroufe et al., 2005). There also are clear links between these chronologically later measures of family interaction and subsequent romantic relationship behaviors and perceptions assessed early in adulthood (Roisman, Madsen, Hennighausen, Sroufe, & Collins, 2001). Until 2007, however, no research had investigated whether or how the nature of early parent-child relationships (before age 13) were related to the experience of positive and negative emotions in adult romantic relationships.

## A Longitudinal Study of Emotion in Relationships

To fill this gap in our knowledge, we (Simpson, Collins, Tran, & Haydon, 2007; see also Roisman, Collins, Sroufe, & Egeland, 2005) conducted a study that focused on 78 target participants in the MPCLS. Between the ages of 20 to 23, each target participant and his or her current romantic partner completed self-report relationship measures.

Each couple was also videotaped while trying to resolve a major conflict in their relationship. The primary goal of our investigation was to test whether and how attachment experiences and relationships during critical stages of development—during infancy, middle childhood, and adolescence—are systematically related to the self-reported experience and the observer-rated expression of emotions with romantic partners in early adulthood. We tested our predictions by comparing participants who had secure versus insecure attachment histories at age 1.

We hypothesized that the emotional qualities of romantic relationships in early adulthood should be predicted by a set of sequential links from attachment security status at age 1, to the quality of peer relationships in childhood at ages 6 to 8, to the quality of relationships with close friends in adolescence at age 16. We anticipated that the quality of childhood peer relationships and the quality of close friendships in adolescence would mediate the link between early attachment status (assessed in the Strange Situation at age 1) and the emotional tenor of adult romantic relationships (assessed at ages 20 to 23). Specifically, we conjectured that individuals classified as secure in infancy would be rated as more socially competent by their grade-school teachers. Early social competence, in turn, would predict stronger-rated secure-base friendships during adolescence. And friendship security during adolescence would then predict both the experience and expression of less negative relative to positive emotion in adult romantic relationships.

This developmental model is anchored on the principle that relationships at any stage of development can be influenced by both familial and extrafamilial relationships at earlier stages (Sroufe et al., 2005). As a result, attachment relationships with caregivers early in life should have an impact not only on later relationships with caregivers, but also on other important relationships with peers, close friends, and romantic partners across time. This developmental process should involve dynamic interactions between experiences in one's successive relationships and the mental representations of those experiences, which often are constructed and revised across relationships from each successive earlier period (Carlson et al., 2004).

Measures were collected at three critical stages of social development: (1) during early childhood (at age 1), (2) during early elementary school (grades 1 to 3; ages 6 to 8), and (3) during adolescence (at age 16). Assessments were made at these specific periods of social development, because each one represents a stage at which new and different kinds of relationships are being formed and developed. This measurement approach is consistent not only with the current conceptualization of social development, but also with the principle of heterotypic continuity (Rutter & Sroufe, 2000). According to this principle, the infancy measures obtained from target participants at age 1 assessed their attachment and exploratory behaviors with their caregivers in the Strange Situation. The middle childhood measures at ages 6 to 8 assessed target participants' competence at engaging peers in social interactions and their attunement to interpersonal dynamics in organized peer groups across grades 1 to 3. The adolescence measure at age 16 assessed the nature and quality of target participants' behaviors indicative of having secure attachment representations of close same-sex friends (e.g., greater disclosure, more trust, and more authenticity). And the early adulthood measures at ages 20 to 23 indexed the experience and expression of emotions evident in target participants' current romantic relationships. Although target participants' behaviors, relationships, and relationship representations were assessed by different measures in different relationships at different points of social development, the underlying *meaning and function* of those behaviors and representations should be consistent across time, because the measures tap the general coherence of attachment representations and behaviors at each developmental stage (Sroufe & Waters, 1977).

As predicted, we found that the experience and expression of emotions in adult romantic relationships were meaningfully tied to attachment-relevant experiences earlier in social development. As shown in Figure 5.1, target participants' early attachment security at age 1 predicted their competence with peers (rated by teachers) during early elementary school. Elementary school peer competence, in turn, predicted the degree of security evident in target participants' representations of their close friendships at age 16. This measure in turn predicted daily reports of emotions experienced in romantic relationships (reported by target participants *and* their partners), as well as the expression of emotions (rated by observers) during a videotaped conflict-resolution task. Thus, corroborating Bowlby's conjectures and fundamental principles originally

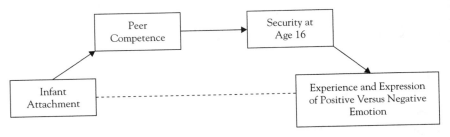

**Figure 5.1**   Links between infant attachment and later relationship outcomes

articulated by Sroufe/Egeland, the experience and expression of emotion in romantic relationships is connected in predictable and meaningful ways to experiences in earlier relationships and phases of social development. However, earlier developmental stages have the strongest and most direct impact on the stages immediately following them (Carlson et al., 2004).

## THE BROADER LEGACY

Even today, many nondevelopmental psychologists disregard how the *past*—a person's unique developmental history—situates, frames, and influences the *present*—what is currently happening in a person's life and how he or she interprets current events. As Egeland and Sroufe have repeatedly demonstrated in their long-standing programs of research, a complete understanding of interpersonal outcomes in adulthood requires that one consider how processes associated with different levels of analysis—especially ontogeny—have operated to shape current relationship outcomes (Tinbergen, 1963). This viewpoint is just beginning to be appreciated in the wider field of close relationship.

Understanding an individual's complete developmental history may also clarify whether and why current relationship outcomes are likely to be stable versus variable across time, along with the variables that are likely to change certain outcomes. Consider, for example, two adults who have the same level of marital satisfaction at a given point of their lives but have very different developmental histories. A person who starts and continues across the life course on an insecure trajectory is likely to have less stable levels of marital satisfaction that may be changed by different events than someone who starts and continues life on a secure trajectory. Someone who has an insecure history, for instance, may react in a more extreme manner to positive and especially negative daily events in their relationship than an individual who has a secure history (Campbell, Simpson, Boldry, & Kashy, 2005). Given the benevolent and forgiving nature of their internal working models, secure people should be more inclined to ignore, discount, or dismiss minor partner transgressions, opting to remain focused on the long-term goals they want to achieve for their partners and their relationships.

In conclusion, supporting several core principles originally articulated by Sroufe, Egeland, and their colleagues, our work shows that the relationship past is meaningfully tied to the present for many people, but primarily through what occurs in different relationships at intervening stages of social development. One must understand the trajectory of an individual's relationship history to fully appreciate, situate, and comprehend his or her adult relationships. This view of how development and relationships continually intersect across the lifespan is one of the major and lasting legacies of Sroufe and Egeland's work on the entire field of psychology.

## REFERENCES

Ainsworth, M. D. S. (1989). Attachments beyond infancy. *American Psychologist, 44,* 709–716.

Ainsworth, M. D. S., Bell, S., & Slayton, D. (1974). Infant-mother attachment and social development: Socialization as a product of reciprocal responsiveness to signals. In M. Richards (Ed.), *The integration of the child into the social world.* New York, NY: Cambridge University Press.

Ainsworth, M. B. S., Blehar, M., Waters, E., & Wall, S. (1978). *Patterns of attachment.* Hillsdale, NJ: Erlbaum.

Bates, J., Maslin, C., & Frankel, K. (1985). Attachment security, mother-child interaction, and temperament as predictors of behavior problem ratings at age three years. In I. Bretherton & E. Waters (Eds.), Growing points in attachment theory and research. *Monographs of the Society for Research in Child Development, 50* (No. 209), 167–193.

Belsky, J., & Isabella, R. (1988). Maternal, infant and social-contextual determinants of attachment security: A process analysis. In J. Belsky &

T. Nezworski (Eds.), *Clinical implications of attachment* (pp. 41–94). Hillsdale, NJ: Erlbaum.

Blehar, M., Lieberman, A., & Ainsworth, M. (1977). Early face to face interaction and its relation to later infant-mother attachment. *Child Development, 48,* 182–194.

Bokhorst, C. L., Bakermans-Kranenburg, M. J., Pasco Fearon, R. M., van IJzendoorn, M. H., Fonagy, P., & Schuengel, C. (2000). The importance of shared environment in mother-infant attachment security: A behavioral genetic study. *Child Development, 74,* 1769–1782.

Bowlby, J. (1973). *Attachment and loss: Vol. II. Separation, anxiety, and anger.* New York, NY: Basic Books.

Bowlby, J. (1980). *Attachment and loss: Loss (Vol. 3).* New York, NY: Basic Books.

Bretherton, I. (1985). Attachment theory: Retrospect and prospect. In I. Bretherton & E. Waters (Eds.), Growing points of attachment theory and research. *Monographs of the Society of Research in Child Development, 50* (1–2, Serial No. 209), 3–35.

Campbell, L., Simpson, J. A., Boldry, J., & Kashy, D. A. (2005). Perceptions of conflict and support in romantic relationships: The role of attachment anxiety. *Journal of Personality and Social Psychology, 88,* 510–531.

Carlson, E. A., Sroufe, L. A., & Egeland, B. (2004). The construction of experience: A longitudinal study of representation and behavior. *Child Development, 75,* 66–83.

Carlson, V., Cicchetti, D., Barnett, D., & Braunwald, K.G. (1989). Disorganized/ disoriented attachment relationships in maltreated children. *Developmental Psychology, 25,* 525–531.

Collins, W. A., & Van Dulmen, M. (2006). "The course of true love(s) . . .": Origins and pathways in the development of romantic relationships. In A. Booth & A. Crouter (Eds.), *Romance and sex in adolescence and emerging adulthood: Risks and opportunities* (pp. 63–86). Mahwah, NJ: Erlbaum.

Crittenden, P. M. (1992). Treatment of anxious attachment in infancy and early childhood. *Development and Psychopathology, 4,* 575–602.

Crockenberg, S. (1981). Infant irritability, mother responsiveness, and social support influences on the security of infant-mother attachment. *Child Development, 52,* 857–865.

Egeland, B., & Farber, E. (1984). Infant-mother attachment: Factors related to its development and changes over time. *Child Development, 55,* 753–771.

Egeland, B., & Sroufe, L. A. (1981). Developmental sequelae of maltreatment in infancy. In D. Cicchetti & R. Rizley (Eds.), *Development approaches to child maltreatment: New directions for child development* (pp. 77–91). San Francisco, CA: Jossey-Bass.

Englund, M., Levy, A., Hyson, D., & Sroufe, L. A. (2000). Adolescent social competence: Effectiveness in a group setting. *Child Development, 71,* 1049–1060.

Erickson, M., Egeland, B., & Sroufe, L. A. (1985). The relationship between quality of attachment and behavior problems in preschool in a high risk sample. In I. Bretherton & E. Waters (Eds.), Growing points in attachment theory and research. *Monographs of the Society for Research in Child Development* (No. 209), 147–186.

Erikson, E. H. (1963). *Childhood and society* (2nd ed.). New York, NY: Norton.

Fox, N. A., Kimmerly, N. L., & Schafer, W. D. (1991). Attachment to mother/ attachment to father: A meta-analysis. *Developmental Psychology, 62,* 210–225.

Grossmann, K., Grossman, E. E., Spranger, G., Suess, G., & Unzer, L. (1985). Maternal sensitivity and newborn orienting responses as related to quality of attachment in northern Germany. In I. Bretherton & E. Waters (Eds.), Growing point in attachment theory and research. *Monographs of the Society for Research in Child Development* (No. 209), 233–356.

Gunnar, M., Mangelsdorf, S., Larson, M., & Herstgaard, L. (1989). Attachment, temperament, and adrenocortical activity in infancy: A study of psychoendocrine regulation. *Developmental Psychology, 25,* 355–363.

Haydon, K. C., Collins, W. A., & van Dulmen, M. (2005). Peer competence and friendship quality: Distinct or overlapping precursors of adult romantic relationships? In C. Booth-LaForce (Chair), Friendship and social adaptation: Longitudinal studies and new approaches. Symposium at the meeting of the Society for Research in Child Development, Atlanta, GA.

Isabella, R. (1993). Origins of attachment: Maternal interactive behavior across the first year. *Child Development, 64,* 605–621.

Isabella, R. A., & Belsky, J. (1991). Interactional synchrony and the origins of infant-mother attachment: A replication study. *Child Development, 62,* 373–384.

Jacobson, J. L., & Willie, D. E. (1986). The influence of attachment pattern on developmental changes in peer interaction from the toddler to the preschool period. *Child Development, 57,* 338–347.

Kopp, C. (1989). Regulation of distress and negative emotions: A developmental view. *Developmental Psychology, 25,* 343–354.

LaFreniere, P., & Sroufe, A. L. (1985). Profiles of peer competence in the preschool: Interrelations between measures influence of social etiology, and relation to attachment history. *Developmental Psychology, 21,* 56–69.

Londerville, S., & Main, M. (1981). Security of attachment, compliance, and maternal training methods in the second year of life. *Developmental Psychology, 17*, 289–299.

Lyons-Ruth, K., Easterbrooks, M. A., & Cibelli, C. D. (1997). Infant attachment strategies, infant mental lag, and maternal depressive symptoms: Predictors of internalizing and externalizing problems at age 7. *Developmental Psychology, 33*, 681–692.

Lyons-Ruth, K., & Jacobvitz, D. (1999). Attachment disorganization: Unresolved loss, relational violence, and lapses in behavioral and attentional strategies. In J. Cassidy & P. R. Shaver (Eds.), *Handbook of attachment: Theory, research, and clinical applications* (pp. 520–554). New York, NY: Guilford Press.

Lyons-Ruth, K., Repacholi, B., McLeod, S., & Silva, E. (1991). Disorganized attachment behavior in infancy: Short-term stability, maternal and infant correlates, and risk-related subtypes. *Development and Psychopathology, 3*, 377–396.

Main, M., & Solomon, J. (1990). Procedures for identifying infants as disorganized/disoriented during the Ainsworth Strange Situation. In M. T. Greenberg, D. Cicchetti, & E. M. Cummings (Eds.), *Attachment in the preschool years* (pp. 121–160). Chicago, IL: University of Chicago Press.

Main, M., & Weston, D. R. (1982). Avoidance of the attachment figure in infancy: Descriptions and interpretations. In C. M. Parkes & J. Stevenson-Hinde (Eds.), *The place of attachment in human behavior* (pp. 31–59). New York, NY: Basic Books.

Mangelsdorf, S., Gunnar, M., Kestenbaum, R., Lang, S., & Andreas, D. (1990). Infant proneness-to-distress temperament, maternal personality, and mother-infant attachment: Associations and goodness of fit. *Child Development, 61*, 820–831.

Maslin, C., & Bates, J. (1983, April). Precursors of anxious and secure attachments: A multivariate model at age 6 months. Paper presented at the meeting of the Society for Research in Child Development, Detroit, MI.

Matas, L., Arend, R., & Sroufe, L. (1978). Continuity of adaptation in the second year: The relationship between quality of attachment and later competence. *Child Development, 49*, 547–556.

McElwain, N. L., Cox, M. J., Burchinal, M. R., & Macfie, J. (2003). Differentiating among insecure mother-infant attachment classifications: A focus on child-friend interaction and exploration during solitary play at 36 months. *Attachment and Human Development, 5*, 136–164.

Munson, J. A., McMahon, R. J., & Spieker, S. J. (2001). Structure and variability in the developmental trajectory of children's externalizing problems: Impact of infant attachment, maternal depressive symptomatology, and child sex. *Development and Psychopathology, 13,* 277–296.

NICHD Early Child Care Research Network. (2006). Infant–mother attachment classification: Risk and protection in relation to changing maternal caregiving quality. *Developmental Psychology, 42,* 38–58.

O'Connor, T. G., & Croft, C. M. (2001). A twin study of attachment in preschool children. *Child Development, 72,* 1501–1511.

Roisman, G., Collins, W. A., Sroufe, L. A., & Egeland, B. (2005). Predictors of young adults' security in their current romantic relationships: A prospective test of the prototype hypothesis. *Attachment and Human Development, 7,* 105–121.

Roisman, G. I., & Fraley, R. C. (2008). A behavior-genetic study of parenting quality, infant attachment security, and their covariation in a nationally representative sample. *Developmental Psychology, 44,* 831–839.

Roisman, G. I., Madsen, S. D., Hennighausen, K. H., Sroufe, L. A., & Collins, W. A. (2001). The coherence of dyadic behavior across parent-child and romantic relationships as mediated by the internalized representation of experience. *Attachment and Human Development, 3,* 156–172.

Rutter, M., & Sroufe, L. A. (2000). Developmental psychopathology: Concepts and challenges. *Development and Psychopathology, 12,* 265–296.

Simon, V., Aikins, J., & Prinstein, M. (2008). Romantic partner selection and socialization during early adolescence. *Child Development, 79,* 1676–1692.

Simpson, J. A., Collins, W. A., Tran, S., & Haydon, K. C. (2007). Attachment and the experience and expression of emotions in adult romantic relationships: A developmental perspective. *Journal of Personality and Social Psychology, 92,* 355–367.

Simpson, J. A., Rholes, W. S., & Nelligan, J. A. (1992). Support-seeking and support-giving within couples in an anxiety-provoking situation: The role of attachment styles. *Journal of Personality and Social Psychology, 62,* 434–446.

Simpson, J. A., Rholes, W. S., & Phillips, D. (1996). Conflict in close relationships: An attachment perspective. *Journal of Personality and Social Psychology, 71,* 899–914.

Sroufe, L. A. (1983). Infant-caregiver attachment and patterns of adaptation in preschool. In M. Perlmutter (Ed.), *Minnesota symposia on child psychology: The roots of maladaptation and competence* (Vol. 16, pp. 129–135). Hillsdale, NJ: Lawrence Erlbaum.

Sroufe, L. A. (1989). Relationship, self, and individual adaptation. In A. J. Sameroff & R. N. Emde (Eds.), *Relationship disturbances in early childhood* (pp. 70–94). New York, NY: Basic Books.

Sroufe, L. A. (1996). *Emotional development: the organization of emotional life in the early years.* New York, NY: Cambridge University Press.

Sroufe, L. A., Egeland, B., & Carlson, E. A. (1999). One social world: The intergrated development of parent-child and peer relationships. In W. A. Collins & B. Laursen (Eds.), *Relationships as developmental context: The 30th Minnesota symposium on child psychology* (pp. 241–262). Hillsdale, NJ: Erlbaum.

Sroufe, L. A., Egeland, B. Carlson, E. A., & Collins, W.A. (2005). *The development of the person: The Minnesota Study of risk and adaptation from birth to adulthood.* New York, NY: Guilford Press.

Sroufe, L. A., Fox, N. E., & Pancake, V. R. (1983). Attachment and dependency in developmental perspective. *Child Development, 54,* 1615–1627.

Sroufe, L. A., & Rutter, M. (1984). The domain of developmental psychopathology. *Child Development, 55,* 17–29.

Sroufe, L. A., Schork, E., Motti, F., Lawroski, N., & LaFreniere, P. (1984). The role of affect in social competence. In C. E. Izard, J. Kagan, & R. B. Zajonc (Eds.), *Emotions, cognition, and behavior* (pp. 289–319). Cambridge, England: Cambridge University Press.

Sroufe, L. A., & Waters, E. (1977). Attachment as an organizational construct. *Child Development, 48,* 1184–1199.

Thompson, R. A. (1990). Emotion and self-regulation. *Nebraska Symposium on Motivation* (pp. 367–467). Lincoln: University of Nebraska Press.

Tinbergen, N. (1963). On the aims and methods of ethology. *Zietschrift fur Tierpsychologie (Journal of Comparative Ethology), 20,* 410–433.

Troy, M. & Sroufe, L.A. (1987). Victimization among preschoolers: The role of attachment relationship history. *Journal of the American Academy of Child and Adolescent Psychiatry, 26,* 166–172.

van den Boom, D. C. (1991). The influence of infant irritability on the development of the mother-infant relationship in the first six months of life. In J. K. Nugent, B. M. Lester, & T. B. Brazelton (Eds.), *The cultural context of infancy* (Vol. 2, pp. 63–89). Norwood, NJ: Ablex.

van den Boom, D. C. (1994). The influence of temperament and mothering on attachment and exploration: An experimental manipulation of sensitive responsiveness among lower-class mothers with irritable infants. *Child Development, 65,* 1457–1477.

van den Boom, D. C., & Hoeksma, J. B. (1994). The effect of infant irritability on mother-infant interaction: A growth-curve analysis. *Developmental Psychology, 30,* 581–590.

van IJzendoorn, M. H., Juffer, F., & Duyvesteyn, M. G. C. (1995). Breaking the intergenerational cycle of insecure attachment: A review of the effects of attachment-based interventions on maternal sensitivity and infant security. *Journal of Child Psychology and Psychiatry, 36,* 225–248.

van IJzendoorn, M. H., Schuengel, C., & Bakermans-Kranenburg, M. J. (1999). Disorganized attachment in early childhood: Meta-analysis of precursors, concomitants, and sequelae. *Development and Psychopathology, 11,* 225–249.

Vaughn, B. E., Lefebvre, G. B., Seifer, R., & Barglow, P. (1989). Attachment behavior, attachment security, and temperament during infancy. *Child Development, 60,* 728–737.

Vaughn, B. E., & Shin, N. (2011). Attachment, temperament, and adaptation: One long argument. In D. Cicchetti & G. I. Roisman (Eds.), *Minnesota symposia on child psychology: The origins and organization of adaptation and maladaptation* (Vol. 36). Hoboken, NJ: Wiley.

Vaughn, B., Waters, E., Egeland, B., & Sroufe, L. A. (1979). Individual differences in infant-mother attachment at 12 and 18 months: Stability and change in families under stress. *Child Development, 50,* 971–975.

Waters, E., & Cummings, E. M. (2000). A secure base from which to explore close relationships. *Child Development, 71,* 164–172.

Youngblade, L. M., & Belsky, J. (1992). Parent-child antecedents of five-year-olds' close friendships: A longitudinal analysis. *Developmental Psychology, 28*(4), 700–713.

# Rethinking Adolescent States of Mind

## A Relationship/Lifespan View of Attachment and Psychopathology

ROGER KOBAK AND KRISTYN ZAJAC

The Minnesota Parent–Child Longitudinal Study (MPCLS) illustrates both the strengths and possibilities inherent in a developmental model of psychopathology. In this approach, psychopathology is understood not simply as a cluster of phenotypic symptoms but rather as the outcome of "developmental deviations" or failures to achieve stage-salient adaptive outcomes (Sroufe, 1997). Some of these difficulties originate early in development, whereas other problems may be limited to later developmental stages (Sroufe, Carlson, Levy, & Egeland, 1999). In adolescence, problems in adaptation may occur in school, family, and peer contexts and impaired functioning in these domains has been implicated in DSM-IV conduct, mood, anxiety, and dissociative disorders. Attachment processes continue to operate during adolescence both as an aspect of personality and in relationships with adult caregivers and romantic partners. As such, individual differences in self-regulatory strategies and in the quality of attachment relationships are often implicated in the development and maintenance of adolescent psychopathology.

Most studies of adolescent attachment have relied on the assessment of personality or "states of mind" during the Adult Attachment Interview (AAI; George, Kaplan, & Main, 1996). The interview provides semi-structured protocol that tests the adolescents' ability to access, reflect upon, and integrate memories of their relationships with mothers and fathers. AAI transcripts are classified into autonomous, dismissing, preoccupied, and unresolved "states of mind" (Main & Goldwyn, 1998) based on a close analysis of interview discourse (Hesse, 2008). These states of mind have been referenced as the gold standard for studies of attachment and psychopathology in both adolescence and adulthood (Allen, 2008; Bakermans-Kranenburg & van IJzendoorn, 2009; Kobak, Cassidy, Lyons-Ruth, & Ziv, 2006).

Yet, after two decades of AAI research, the MPCLS findings point to the need to take a fresh look at adolescent states of mind. More specifically, the findings suggest that: (a) states of mind are still developing between late adolescence and adulthood (Sroufe, Carlson, Egeland, & Collins, 2005); (b) measures of the early caregiving environment provide a very limited account of later-developing states of mind (Weinfield, Sroufe, & Egeland, 2000); and (c) the relationship between states of mind and inferred experiences with parents is substantially more complicated than originally thought (Roisman & Haydon, 2011, this volume). Together, these studies highlight the need to understand adolescent states of mind in the broader context of Bowlby (1979) and Ainsworth's (1989) lifespan model of attachment relationships. This relationship/lifespan model needs to address: (a) the continuing interplay between the adolescents' inner organization of attachment expectations and the quality of care available from an adult caregiver; (b) how this dynamic interplay changes between childhood and adolescence; (c) how the adolescent organizes bonds with multiple attachment figures; and (d) how caregiver-adolescent attachments support the eventual formation of attachments with romantic partners and caregiving bonds with offspring.

In the first part of this chapter, we describe and compare two models for studying attachment over the lifespan. The *personality/early experience* framework has been the predominant approach to attachment studies for the past two decades. It has focused extensively on how children internalize their experiences in the infant-caregiver relationship as an enduring feature of their developing personalities. This approach relies on the constructs of working models and attachment strategies to describe aspects of personality that maintain continuity in an individual's developmental pathway. What we call the *relationship/lifespan* framework draws on aspects of attachment theory that have received less attention. This framework defines security as a continuing feature of attachment relationships from infancy through adulthood (Bowlby, 1979; Ainsworth, 1989) and points to a broader network of attachment constructs that can be tested as proximal antecedents and sequelae of adolescent personality or states of mind. The relationship model directs attention to how the current quality of caregiver-adolescent attachment bonds may influence trajectories of maladaptation and psychopathology during late adolescence and emerging adulthood. Key developmental tasks during adolescence include managing risky behavior with peers, forming an affectional bond with a sexual partner, and preparing for childbearing and childcare. A secure attachment bond with an adult caregiver can facilitate adaptive management of these tasks, whereas the lack of such a relationship puts the adolescent at risk for maladaptive outcomes and psychological disorders.

## TWO VIEWS OF DEVELOPMENTAL PATHWAYS

At the heart of Bowlby's attachment theory is the dynamic transaction between the child's developing personality and the caregiving environment (Bowlby, 1979, p. 104). The "internal" or organismic contributions result from the activity of the attachment system in developing and maintaining a bond with the caregiver. The set goal of the attachment system is the "availability of the attachment figure" (Ainsworth, 1990), but how the child maintains this set goal within tolerable limits is guided by expectancies based on prior experience with the caregiver, the child's ability to signal his or her needs, and the caregiver's ability to read and respond to those signals. Throughout childhood and adolescence, the environment provided by the caregiver continues to transact with and shape the child's expectancies and strategies for maintaining the attachment bond. This dynamic transaction is subject to developmental transformations as the child moves from infancy to adulthood.

The complexity of Bowlby's transactional model has presented a challenge to attachment researchers. In the face of this challenge, researchers used a heuristic that we term the personality/early experience model. This model views individual differences in infant attachment security as a prototype for subsequent personality development and explains continuity between infancy and later developmental periods as the product of working models or internal expectancies for caregiver availability. These internalized expectancies are thought to be formed early in development, are presumed to be carried forward into later developmental periods, and are thought to be relatively resistant to change. The Strange Situation classifications provided a typology of these early developing aspects of personality in infancy. However, in later developmental periods, assessment of these expectancies or working models has relied primarily on representational measures that include narratives, interviews, or self-reports with children, adolescents, and adults.

The second view that we term the relationship/lifespan model draws from Bowlby's postulate that attachment bonds play a continuing role in individual adaptation from the cradle to the grave. This model conceives of attachment security as relationship specific and as a product of the ongoing transaction between the individual's expectancies and the caregiver's ability to serve as a source of safety and base for exploration. Communication is a central marker of attachment security in this model. Secure relationships are characterized by direct and open signaling of concerns, sensitive and contingent response to signals, and cooperative negotiation of goal conflicts. A challenge for this model is to account for how attachment bonds change in childhood, adolescence, and adulthood. The personality/early experience and relationship/lifespan models have different implications for: (a) the relative scope of claims for the predictive validity of attachment measures; (b) whether to assess attachment as an aspect of the individual or of a relationship; and (c) the degree to which early experiences predict later outcomes (see Table 6.1).

Table 6.1   Two views of developmental pathways

| | Personality/Early Experience | Relationship/Lifespan |
|---|---|---|
| Early vs. Later Experience | Infant adaptations in relationship with primary caregiver form prototype | Developmental change<br><br>(a) In caregiver-child relationships—goal-corrected partnership<br>(b) In organized preferences for multiple attachment figures |
| Continuity in Developmental Pathways | Primarily maintained by internal organization established in infancy | Initially maintained by caregiver sensitivity and subsequently by the caregiver-child dyad |
| Contextual Influences | Conceptualized as stress and adversity | Conceptualized in terms of:<br><br>(a) The effects on caregiver availability<br>(b) The effects of multiple attachment bonds<br>(c) The effect of family context on relationships |
| Personality | Aspect of an individual—Attachment strategies—rules for processing attachment information | Aspect of a relationship Expectancies or forecasts for caregiver availability |
| Attachment Security | Adaptive self-regulation—flexible deployment of attention | Confident expectancies for caregiver availability and trustworthiness |
| Attachment System set goal | Maintaining felt security | Monitoring the attachment figure's availability |
| AAI | Emphasis on states of mind as unitary aspect of personality | Emphasis on inferred expectancies for mother and father availability |
| Prediction | General—Adaptive self-regulation leads to resilience in adverse circumstances | Domain specific—Most evident in continuity within attachment relationships. |
| Assessment | Narrative or self-report measures | Observations of dyadic interactions |
| | Focus on self-regulatory processes | Focus on relationships as regulatory systems |
| | | Preference paradigms for identifying hierarchy of attachment figures |

## The Personality/Early Experience Model—Attachment Security as Flexible and Adaptive Self-Regulation

Ainsworth viewed the patterns of infant behavior in the Strange Situation as reflecting expectancies for the attachment figure's availability (Ainsworth, Blehar, Waters, & Wall, 1978). This underlying expectancy, or working model, built from interactions with the caregiver during the first year of life, guided and organized the patterns of behavior observed in the Strange Situation. These patterns (secure, avoidant, and resistant) have been understood as the child's conditional strategies for maintaining the attachment bond (Main, 1990). When a child has confident expectations in a caregiver's availability, he or she adopts a primary strategy of open communication of attachment needs and reliance on the caregiver as a source of comfort and is classified as secure. Conversely, when the child lacks confidence in the caregiver, he or she adopts a secondary strategy of either minimizing or deactivating attachment signals that characterize avoidant infants or of maximizing or hyperactivating the attachment system characteristic of ambivalent/resistant infants (see Cassidy & Kobak, 1988; Kobak, Cole, Fleming, Ferenz-Gillies, & Gamble, 1993; Main, 1990; Shaver & Mikulincer, 2007).

The attachment strategies that Ainsworth observed and classified in the Strange Situation have also served as prototypes for assessing individual differences in adults' attachment security (Hazan & Shaver; 1987). Caregivers' AAI classifications were also specifically developed to parallel their infants' classifications in the Strange Situation (Main, Kaplan, & Cassidy, 1985). In the personality/early experience model, attachment security becomes largely synonymous with adaptive self-regulation. These regulatory strategies are presumed to develop during infancy, operate largely outside of awareness, and carry forward into later developmental periods. Hesse (2008) notes that "deeply internalized strategies for regulating emotion and attention" can be understood to organize participant's discourse in response to interview questions in the AAI (p. 555).

These self-regulatory strategies are thought to generalize to how an individual thinks and behaves in challenging or stressful situations, and they have been associated with a broad range of outcomes (Belsky &

Cassidy, 1994; Belsky & Fearon, 2002a). Evidence for associations between infant attachment classifications and adaptation comes from both the Minnesota Parent-Child Longitudinal Study (MPCLS; Sroufe, Carlson, Egeland, & Collins, 2005) and the NICHD study, with attachment predicting not only a range of psychosocial outcomes but also the development of early language and school readiness competencies (Belsky & Fearon, 2002a). Similarly, studies using the AAI with adolescent samples suggest that attachment strategies influence a broad range of adaptive and maladaptive outcomes (Allen, 2008).

The personality/early experience model has relied on the child's inner organization or "working models" as a way of accounting for continuity between infancy and later developmental stages. This working models construct has guided most of the efforts to measure individual differences in attachment at later developmental periods (see Solomon & George, 2008, for review), based primarily on coding systems designed to infer children's expectancies for caregiver availability from children's narratives. Whereas some methods elicit narratives with indirect or projective techniques, such as doll play or word prompts, other methods rely on autobiographical narratives of memories in which attachment-related needs are likely to be activated. These methods were based on the "move to the level of representation," which coincides with children's emerging linguistic competence (Main, Kaplan, & Cassidy, 1985).

The narrative assessments of internal working models face several stringent tests of their validity. First, if infant attachment is a prototype for subsequent attachment organization, there should be enduring effects of infant attachment on later attachment measures. Using sophisticated modeling techniques, Fraley (2002) examined the studies of stability in attachment measures across the lifespan. This produced some limited support for the prototype hypotheses, insofar as the relations between infant and adult attachment measures did not asymptote toward zero in the initial studies linking infant attachment to adult AAIs. However, this early meta-analysis noted striking gaps in the literature available to fully test the prototype hypothesis. Notably, there were no studies of stability in working models between middle childhood and early adolescence and very few studies of short-term test-retest stability in post-infant assessments. In addition to lack of support for stability in narrative attachment measures, there is little available evidence linking internal working models to concurrent assessments of caregiver availability.

## The Relationship/Lifespan Model—Attachment Security as Expectancies for a Caregiver's Availability

In contrast to the view that internal working models are the primary mechanism that carries infant attachment security forward into later developmental periods, the relationship/lifespan model views security as a quality of a current relationship. In this view, the child's attachment security is the product of the continuing interplay between the child's expectancies and the quality of the caregiving environment. Although infancy is a formative period for the child's initial expectancies for caregiver availability, the relationship/lifespan model stresses the developing child's continuing need to monitor the caregiver's availability. As a result, perceived threats to the caregiver's availability can elicit negative emotional reactions that are similar to infants' responses to physical separations (Kobak & Madsen, 2008). Not only do older children and adolescents continue to monitor their caregiver's availability, but caregivers continue to facilitate the child's mastery of new developmental challenges. The interplay between the child's expectancies and the caregiver's availability determines the security of the attachment bond from the cradle to the grave.

The relative contributions of the caregiver and child to the security of an attachment bond changes with development. Bowlby's "environmental sensitivity" hypothesis posits that the child's expectancies or working models are more malleable early in development and gradually become more resistant to change over the course of childhood and adolescence (Bowlby, 1973, p. 367). As a result, the caregiver's contribution to infant and toddler's experience has a unique and important role in starting the child on an adaptive or maladaptive pathway. Because the infant's expectancies are very malleable, the caregiving environment initially plays a larger role in maintaining the child's trajectory than do internalized aspects of the child's personality. Gradually, over the course of childhood and adolescence, the child's inner organization or expectancies for caregiver availability take on an increasingly significant role in maintaining the quality of an attachment bond.

The greater plasticity in early development suggests that the Strange Situation is best understood as a measure of the emerging *relationship* between the child and their caregiver (Sroufe et al., 2005). The child's behavior in the Strange Situation is organized by expectations for the caregiver's availability that has been built from interactions with the caregiver over the course of infancy (Ainsworth et al., 1978). As a result, infant classifications reflect *both* the quality of early care and the emerging aspects of the child's expectations and strategies for maintaining access to the caregiver. The continuing contribution of the caregiving environment to the toddler's adaptation was clearly noted in coding of both the child's persistence and the caregiver's supportive presence in the tool problem-solving task (Matas, Arend, & Sroufe, 1978). Because the child's expectancies remain malleable and highly sensitive to changes in the caregiving environment, much of the predictive value of the Strange Situation can be attributed to continuities in the caregiving environment rather than from the child's internalized expectancies (Belsky & Fearon, 2002b). A major implication of the relationship model is that measures of the infant's early attachment organization in the Strange Situation are likely to have greater predictive validity if they incorporate multiple assessments of child expectancies (Sroufe et al., 2005) and measures of the caregiving environment over the course of infancy and early childhood (Belsky & Fearon, 2002a).

A major challenge for the relationship/lifespan model is conceptualizing and assessing the security of attachment bonds in childhood and adolescence. Although infancy is a sensitive period for forming an attachment bond, the caregiver-child relationship is transformed by the emergence of later cognitive and linguistic capacities. Beginning in early childhood, the child's ability to take the caregiver's goals into account and to negotiate joint plans verbally provides a means of reassuring the child of the caregiver's availability when faced with conflicts. As a result, the ability to negotiate goal conflicts cooperatively becomes a critical test of security in the attachment relationships of older children and adults (Kobak & Duemmler, 1994; Moretti & Obsuth, 2009).

Caregiver-child goal conflicts change with stage-salient development tasks (Sroufe & Fleeson, 1986; Wynne, 1984). In early childhood, the child must remain assured of caregiver availability as the caregiver establishes rules and consequences for the child's behavior. Cooperative negotiation of these goal conflicts creates a context for the child to develop a greater capacity for impulse regulation (Sroufe, 1996). During adolescence, the autonomy-related conflicts about curfew, household responsibilities, allowances, or schoolwork must be negotiated in order to reassure the adolescent of continued access to the caregiver. As adolescents and adults form new reciprocal attachment bonds with a close friend or sexual partner, they must also negotiate with their partners about living arrangements, finances, and eventually childcare. The security of the attachment bond and the child's expectancies for caregiver availability are maintained through cooperative discussion, although not necessarily resolution of goal conflicts.

Attachment processes play a less prominent role in childhood and adolescence than during infancy. During these later periods, the child's attachment system operates with less intensity and frequency than during infancy, and the caregiver's protective role becomes more nuanced and subtle. Compared to the infancy period, less is known about the caregiver's role in maintaining a secure attachment bond or about the bond's influence on the developing child's capacities for impulse regulation and empathy. The goal-corrected partnership phase continues through adolescence, as the caregiver continues to monitor the child's safety and intervene judiciously if the child engages in dangerous behaviors. Adolescents for their part will rely on the caregivers in emergency situations or as a source of guidance in situations that are novel or risky. Furthermore, threats to the availability of the caregivers will continue to activate the attachment system. Thus, most adolescents will maintain a bond with their caregivers through low-intensity activation of the attachment system and guide their attachment behavior with expectancies for the caregivers' availability and responsiveness built from prior interactions.

By defining security as a quality of an attachment bond, the relationship/lifespan model leaves open the possibility that security differs considerably across relationships. This possibility has been most extensively investigated in studies of attachment classifications with mothers and fathers. The initial studies that compared children's security with mothers and fathers in the Strange Situation indicated that security in one relationship was relatively independent of security in the other relationship (Main & Weston, 1981; Sroufe, 1985). A meta-analysis of 11 studies of infants' classifications with mothers and fathers did yield a small to modest degree of concordance (Fox, Kimmerly, & Schafer, 1991). Efforts to test attachment security in multiple relationships in older children and adults have also demonstrated that substantial variability exists in the security of specific attachment relationships (Cowan & Cowan, 2007; Furman & Simon, 2004). The relative independence of attachment security in relationships with mothers, fathers, and romantic partners illustrates the need for assessing security as a relationship construct and points to more nuanced explanations of how attachment is associated with adaptation across developmental periods.

Viewing attachment security as a relationship construct leads to new questions about how contextual factors may account for concordance in attachment security across different relationships. The most obvious source of concordance in the child's relationships with mothers and fathers is their clustering within the family context (Cowan, Cowan, & Mehta, 2009). A variety of mechanisms operating within families may affect caregivers' availability and account for modest levels of convergence. For instance, studies of attachment security with mothers and fathers usually require intact two-parent families. As a result, the quality of the marital relationship is likely to affect both mothers' and fathers' ability to provide sensitive care and increase concordance in their child's attachment (Cowan & Cowan, 2009). Unfortunately, these studies fail to represent growing numbers of children who grow up in single-parent or unmarried families with cohabiting partners (Bumpass & Lu, 2000; Cherlin, 2004). Relatively little is known about secondary attachment figures in single-parent families or the concordance of attachment security between primary and secondary caregivers in nonmarried households.

## The Lifespan Model of Attachment Bonds

The relationship/lifespan model must also address the formation of new attachment bonds with friends and sexual partners that emerge over the course of adolescence and adulthood. In her later writing, Ainsworth (1989) described a lifespan model of affectional bonds that accounted for the continuing role that attachment processes play in adolescent and adult relationships. Her model expanded upon the attachment, fear, and exploration behavioral systems identified during infancy to include the role that affiliation, sexual, and caregiving systems play in forming affectional bonds during adolescence and adulthood. This perspective provides a model of how motivational systems account for the formation of affectional bonds at different developmental stages (see Table 6.2).

Ainsworth (1989) defined affectional bonds as "relatively long-enduring ties in which there is a desire to maintain closeness with a partner" (p. 711). The presence of an affectional bond is signaled by predictable emotional reactions to appraisals of the partner's availability. These include pleasure or joy upon reunion, distress as a result of inexplicable separation, and grief at the loss of the partner. Different behavioral systems motivate the formation of different types of affectional bonds. Bonds with friends are initially motivated by the affiliative system, whereas adult pair bonds are initially motivated by the sexual system and may be maintained by caring for offspring. Bonds with children are motivated by a caregiving system designed to monitor and protect offspring. Bonds with kin clearly meet criteria for long-enduring ties, and some individuals often rely on kin for support, affiliation, and possibly attachment.

Only a select few of the affectional bonds that adolescents and adults form with close friends or sexual partners are likely to become attachments. The degree to which an affectional bond with a friend or sexual partner can be considered an attachment depends on whether an individual seeks security or relies on his or her partner for protection and support. Ainsworth pointed out that not all attachment bonds are secure and, thus, extended her definition of an attachment bond to one in which the individual seeks security with a partner, rather than necessarily deriving security from the relationship. In other words, to count as an attachment figure, a partner should meet general criteria for an affectional

**Table 6.2    A lifespan model of affectional bonds**

| Developmental Phases | Tasks | Assessments |
|---|---|---|
| Infant-Toddler | Formation of bonds with primary caregiver | Home observations |
| | Formation of bonds with secondary caregivers | Caregiver sensitivity |
| | | SS as relationship specific |
| | Attachment hierarchy—Selective preferences for caregivers | |
| Early Childhood | Attachment bonds become goal-corrected partnership | (a) Multiple attachment bonds |
| | | (b) Attachment hierarchy |
| | | (c) Cooperative—Goal-corrected partnership |
| Middle Childhood | Expansion of social network to include peers and friends | Security with mother/father |
| | | Marital relationship as moderator |
| Adolescence | Maintenance of bonds with adult caregivers | Communication during goal conflicts |
| | Formation of: | |
| | (a) affiliative bonds with close friends | |
| | (b) reproductive bonds with romantic partners | |
| | Affectional bonds tested as reciprocal attachments | |
| | New attachment bonds result in transformation of attachment hierarchy | Reliance on peers as safe haven or secure base |
| | | Reorganization of the attachment hierarchy |
| Adulthood | Formation of caregiving bond with offspring | Caregiving sensitivity and responsiveness |

bond, including desired closeness and separation distress, and be preferred and sought out in emergency situations where help is needed.

Bowlby's emphasis on the highly selective nature of attachment bonds provides an additional criterion for distinguishing attachment from other types of affectional bonds. He indicated that individuals would direct their attachment behaviors "towards one or a few specific individuals, usually in a clear order of preference" (Bowlby, 1979, p. 130). These preferred individuals are "usually conceived of as stronger and/or wiser." The idea that preferences for attachment figures are hierarchically ordered suggests that one individual would be consistently preferred over a second attachment figure in contexts in which both are accessible. This ordering of preferences accounts for how infants and young children organize their relationships with multiple caregivers, with one person serving as the primary or principal attachment figure and the other serving as a secondary or subsidiary figure. Although the young child would show clear preference for the primary figure when both figures were present, the child would be able to gain security from the secondary figure when the primary figure was not accessible.

The concept of an attachment hierarchy takes on new significance in adolescence as youth begin to form affectional bonds with friends and romantic partners (Kobak, Rosenthal, Zajac, & Madsen, 2007). With puberty and the emergence of the sexual system, adolescents experience powerful new motivations for attraction to romantic partners and the eventual formation of affectional bonds with peers. Although many romantic attractions are relatively short-lived and do not meet criteria for a long-enduring affectional bond, they may increase adolescents' reliance on close friendships that are more stable and more likely to meet criteria for affectional bonds. During this time of relationship experimentation and transition, attachment bonds with adult caregivers continue to serve as a source of protection and support, with evidence that open communication between parents and adolescents, along with continued caregiver monitoring of adolescents' activities, reduces risk for a variety of problem behaviors (Kerr & Stattin, 2000).

Adolescence is a period marked by continued reliance on long-enduring bonds with adult caregivers and by the initiation of new bonds with sexual partners. Yet there is substantial variability in the *timing* of bond formation and the transition into adult roles. Becoming a parent and assuming a caregiving role is a critical life transition from the standpoint of attachment theory and creates a context in which adolescents approach sexual partners and the formation of a romantic attachment bond. The concept of "age expectancies" from life course theory suggests that individuals' sense of the timing of these transitions is shaped by contextual factors such as ethnicity and social class (Elder, 1998). Life course theory also attends to historical changes reflected in cohort effects. Although most adolescents anticipate that marriage will precede childbearing, the growing number of children born to single and unwed mothers is likely to alter these expectations over time. These historical changes have far-reaching implications for how the transition to parenthood is managed for adolescent mothers. Insofar as reproduction occurs without the support of an adult pair bond with the biological father, mothers will need alternative sources in their hierarchy of attachment figures to support prenatal and postnatal care for the next generation (Crosnoe & Elder, 2002).

As indicated in Table 6.2, the relationship/lifespan view of adolescent attachment requires assessments of security within caregiver-adolescent dyads as well as ways of assessing affectional bonds with friends and sexual partners and the testing of these partners as attachment figures. Measures of adolescents' attachment hierarchies (Rosenthal & Kobak, 2010) and observations of how attachment dyads negotiate goal-conflicts (Lyons-Ruth, Hennighausen, & Holmes, 2005) offer two promising ways of generating new attachment measures that capture developmental changes in adolescents' attachment relationships. By developing theoretically guided measures of adolescent attachment processes, the dynamic interplay between states of mind as an aspect of adolescent personality and attachment security as a quality of current attachment relationships can be evaluated.

## REEVALUATING ADOLESCENT STATES OF MIND

Adolescent states of mind have proved remarkably successful in accounting for broad patterns of adolescent adaptation (Allen, Porter, McFarland, McElhaney, & Marsh, 2007; Allen, 2008). However, there is growing evidence that adolescents' states of mind are still developing and are subject to socio-cultural influences. In their meta-analysis of 10,000 AAIs, Bakermans-Kranenburg & van IJzendoorn (2009) compared the distribution of adolescent classifications to a reference group of mothers of young infants. Overall, adolescents and low-SES participants were less likely to be classified as autonomous/secure and more likely to be classified as dismissing than the reference group of middle-income mothers with young infants. Findings from the MPCLS further illustrate and specify the role of development and later experience in influencing states of mind. Using repeated AAI administrations, initially at age 19 and again seven years later at age 26, the Minnesota study showed a marked shift from dismissing to more autonomous states of mind (Sroufe et al., 2005). Furthermore, romantic relationships characterized by cooperation and successful negotiation of conflict predicted a change from insecure to secure states of mind between ages 19 and 26 for male adolescents.

Our longitudinal study of economically disadvantaged families revealed a similar pattern of AAI classifications when adolescents interviewed at age 15 (Kobak, Zajac, & Smith, 2009) were compared with their adult caregivers (Zajac & Kobak, 2009). The majority of adolescents (60%) were classified as dismissing compared with only 33% of their adult caregivers. Much of this difference was accounted for by higher proportions of autonomous/secure states of mind among caregivers (41%) compared to adolescents (24%). However, adult caregivers also received more preoccupied and atypical classifications (26%) than adolescents (17%). The consistently higher rates of adolescents classified as dismissing suggest that states of mind are still developing during adolescence and that the tendency is to move from dismissing to more autonomous states of mind over this period. The developmental transitions that include leaving home, establishing a pair bond, and caring for a young infant are likely to influence young parents' ability to "freely evaluate" their relationships with their own parents (Sroufe et al., 2005).

## Attachment Security, Caregiver-Adolescent Communication, and Adolescent States of Mind

The relationship/lifespan framework views adolescents' capacity to freely evaluate relationships with parents as developing in the context of secure attachment relationships. From this perspective, states of mind as strategies for regulating emotion and attention can be distinguished from the adolescent's current expectancies for a caregiver's availability. Adolescents who maintain secure relationships are more likely to engage in cooperative discourse in the AAI. In many respects, adolescents' current attachment security provides them with a base to explore attachment-related topics flexibly in the AAI. This suggests that the AAI provides a cognitive test of the secure base phenomena observed in younger children, insofar as confidence in the caregiver provides the child with the "epistemic space" to explore or evaluate attachment-related topics (Allen, 2008; Kobak & Cole, 1994; Main, 1990). In this sense, confident expectations in the availability of an attachment figure provides a context for the emergence of an autonomous state of mind.

Adolescents' confidence in their caregiver's availability should also facilitate their willingness to engage in direct, open, and flexible communication during discussions of goal conflicts. Not only should attachment security foster a more direct and open presentation of the adolescent's viewpoint, but the epistemic space provided by a secure relationship should also facilitate the adolescent's ability to take the caregiver's concerns into account to negotiate and maintain cooperative discourse. Presumably, the same expectancies that facilitate the ability to "freely evaluate" attachment topics in the AAI should also facilitate cooperative and open communication about goal conflicts with the caregiver. This claim is supported by both cross-sectional and longitudinal studies of caregiver-adolescent communication and states of mind (Allen & Hauser, 1996; Kobak et al., 1993). Using data from the MPCLS, Roisman and colleagues found that secure states of mind at age 19 were predicted by balanced and cooperative caregiver-teen interactions at age 13 (Roisman, Madsen, Hennighausen, Sroufe, & Collins, 2001). Observational assessments of caregiver-adolescent discussions of goal conflicts have consistently been associated with states of mind in the AAI (Allen & Hauser, 1996, Allen et al., 2003; Kobak et al., 1993).

Caregiver states of mind may also influence the security of the caregiver-adolescent relationship. Caregiver states of mind are presumed to be relatively stable aspects of adult personality. As a result, they are likely to index an important aspect of adolescents' current and past caregiving environment. In adolescence, autonomous states of mind should facilitate caregivers' ability to support adolescents voicing their own concerns while maintaining the position of an older and wiser attachment figure that intervenes judiciously if the adolescent gets in trouble. Two studies suggest small to modest effects of caregiver states of mind on daughters' (Benoit & Parker, 1994) or adolescents' states of mind (Allen et al., 2003). In a study of younger children, Cowan et al. (2009) demonstrated links between mothers' and fathers' AAI classifications, parenting behaviors, and subsequent child adaptation. In this study of the context of two-parent intact families, other aspects of the family system add to the effect of caregiver states of mind, including representations and observations of the marriage relationships.

If expectancies for caregiver's availability both define and organize a secure attachment relationship, it becomes important to measure these expectancies. Ainsworth showed that expectancies for caregiver availability measured in the Strange Situation were built from prior interactions. Subsequent efforts to measure expectancies in older children have relied primarily on analysis of narratives about attachment experiences. Main and Goldwyn's (1998) AAI inferred experience scales share much in common with these narrative methods. These scales assess the degree to which mothers and fathers were "loving" based on raters' analyses of autobiographical memories generated during the AAI. Memories of mother or father response in situations that typically activate the attachment system are presumably guided by current expectancies for mother or father availability. As a result, inferred experiences judged as more "loving" can be considered an index of attachment security in a particular attachment relationship (consistent with the relationship/lifespan model). By contrast, states-of-mind scales rate the overall level of discourse coherence in the AAI and more generally support the notion of a general strategy or rules for processing attachment information. These strategies are thought to operate outside of awareness and would generalize across attachment relationships as a relatively stable aspect of personality (consistent with the personality/early experience model).

Main and Goldwyn's (1998) system for classifying AAI transcripts assigns the inferred experience scales a secondary role to states-of-mind scales. This approach highlights the core innovation of the AAI with its focus on interview process and protects the AAI from being misinterpreted as a veridical measure of childhood experiences. By focusing on the underlying strategies that organize attention deployment to interview topics, the states-of-mind scales code the subject's ability to maintain cooperative discourse during the interview (Hesse, 2008). Consequently, discourse coherence is the basis for assigning a classification for autonomous/secure states of mind, while violations of coherence maxims lead to a classification of dismissing or preoccupied state of mind. Scales involving not remembering and idealization of parents results in a dismissing classification, while scales involving loss of discourse context through angry involvement or passive speech result in preoccupied classifications. Other types of lapses in monitoring of discourse, such as fearful preoccupation with trauma or unresolved loss or abuse, result in atypical or unresolved classifications. Finally, adequate levels of coherence, but notably low ratings on scales evaluating parents' loving or availability, characterize this earned-secure group. This infrequently assigned sub-category illustrates the priority given to states-of-mind scales over inferred experience scales in assigning classifications.

The categorical system for describing states of mind has played a critical role in defining attachment-related aspects of personality in adolescent and adult attachment research (Bakermans-Kranenburg & van IJzendoorn, 2009). Yet, the categorical system fails to capture more nuanced distinctions between the inferred experience and states-of-mind scales. During the past decade, investigators have explored new ways of analyzing Main and Goldwyn's rating system. Several questions have begun to be addressed. First, are states of mind best understood as categories or dimensions, or to put it another way, are there dimensions that can account for the states-of-mind categories? Second, the distinction between two types of autonomous states of mind: "earned- versus continuous-secure" has been subject to closer examination. Finally, on the basis of these findings, new questions can be posed about the degree that states-of-mind scales are independent of inferred-experience scales. This last question is critical to the interpretation of how states of mind are linked to attachment security in current relationships and to adaptation and psychopathology. Because a substantial level of co-variation exists between states of mind and inferred experience with parents, the relative contributions of these two components to adaptation remains uncertain. Drawing on our analyses of states of mind and inferred-experience factors derived from the AAI Q-sort, we will illustrate these issues and suggest hypotheses for future studies.

## Dimensions Versus Categories

The relative merits of dimensional versus categorical assessments have been subject to controversy within the attachment field. In the early 1990s, Kobak developed an AAI Q-set to allow raters greater flexibility in describing AAI transcripts and improve interrater reliability by aggregating Q-sorts across multiple raters (Kobak et al., 1993). The Q-sort items were primarily derived from the Main and Goldwyn (1998) coding system and consisted of approximately 60 items that evaluated discourse coherence or states of mind and 40 items evaluating inferred experiences with mothers and fathers (Kobak, 1989). Following standardization of the AAI classification system in the mid-1990s, the Q-set was assumed to only be valid in labs where at least one of the raters had received training and passed Main's reliability testing protocol. After reading an interview, two independent raters provide a Q-sort description, and these Q-descriptions are correlated and composited to increase reliability. In cases where the first two descriptions fail to achieve adequate reliability, a third independent rater is required.

By correlating descriptions of transcripts with prototypes for attachment categories, the Q-sort system yields ratings of two dimensions: secure/anxious states of mind and deactivating/hyperactivating states of mind. These dimensions capture variability not only between dismissing and preoccupied states of mind (i.e., insecure subjects with deactivating or hyperactivating strategies, respectively), but also within the autonomous subjects who may have deactivating or hyperactivating tendencies (Kobak et al., 1993). These two dimensions have been used productively in several studies and have been shown to capture dimensions of the AAI classification system (Fortuna & Roisman, 2008; Roisman, 2006). In addition, the Q-sorts of transcripts have been correlated with autonomous, dismissing, and preoccupied prototypes to yield dimensional scores for the three major states-of-mind classifications. Although this productive strategy has also been used in several studies, the high negative correlation between dismissing and secure prototypes has limited investigators to consider these dimensions as simultaneous predictors of outcomes (Allen, 2008).

Roisman, Fraley, and Belsky (2007) took a psychometric approach to the dimensional versus categorical question in an analysis of the Main and Goldwyn's states-of-mind scales. This analysis had the advantage of working with adult transcripts and with a set of scales that included those used to assign subjects to the category of unresolved for loss or abuse. Using scale scores from more than 500 subjects from three previously reported studies, Roisman and colleagues initially reduced the states-of-mind scales with a principal component analysis that yields two components. The first component included scales that differentiated autonomous/secure from dismissing subjects and included the mother and father idealization scales, coherence of mind, lack of memory, and metacognitive monitoring. The second component consisted of scales that identify preoccupied and unresolved states of mind. It included mother anger, unresolved abuse, father anger, passivity, unresolved loss, fear of loss, and overall derogation. On the basis of these dismissing/secure and preoccupied/unresolved dimensions, the authors conducted a MAXCOV analysis (Meehl, 1973) to determine if the states-of-mind dimensions were more compatible with a categorical or dimensional model. Whereas these analyses produced results that supported a continuous model for the dismissing/secure dimension, similar analyses of the preoccupied/unresolved dimension could not rule out either a categorical or dimensional model.

In order to determine whether the AAI Q-sort yields dimensions that parallel those in the analysis of the states-of-mind scales, we conducted a principal components analysis (PCA) using a promax rotation of the 100 Q-sort items in our sample of 199 economically disadvantaged adolescents. We did not limit this analysis to only states-of-mind items, but we were interested in the degree to which states of mind and inferred experience produced distinct components. The analyses produced five components with eigenvalues greater than 1. The fifth component consisted of three items that evaluated inferences about the degree to which participants view the marital relationship between mother and father as satisfactory or conflicted. Items from this fifth component will not be presented.

The PCA produced four primary components, two of which consisted of states-of-mind items and two that consisted of inferred experience with mother and father. The component loadings of the items are shown in Table 6.3. The first component contained items intended to distinguish autonomous and dismissing states of mind. This dimension parallels the secure/dismissing dimension in the meta-analysis of the states-of-mind scales. The third component consists primarily of states-of-mind items used to describe preoccupied states of mind. This reduction of the states-of-mind items to two dimensions closely parallels the secure/dismissing and preoccupied dimensions reported in the PCA of Main and Goldwyn's states-of-mind scales by Roisman et al. (2007). In addition, the PCA revealed that the Q-sort items designed to capture inferred experiences with mothers and fathers formed distinct dimensions, indicating that expectancies for mother or father availability are relationship-specific and not a generalized aspect of adolescent personality (for additional convergent evidence based on the AAI Q-sort, see Haydon, Roisman, & Burt, in press).

## Earned Versus Continuous Security in the AAI

The emphasis given to states of mind over the inferred-experience scales is best illustrated by the subgroup of subjects who are classified with autonomous states of mind but who fail to generate memories of being loved by their mothers and fathers. In contrast to continuous-secure participants who receive midpoint or above ratings on the coherence scales and who receive ratings midpoint or above on scales for loving mothers or fathers, earned-secure subjects receive adequate coherence ratings but poor ratings for loving with one or both parents. This group appears to have established an autonomous state of mind despite markedly negative expectancies for mother and/or father availability or responsiveness.

**Table 6.3    Principal component analysis of adult attachment interview Q-sort items**

| | Factor | | | |
|---|---|---|---|---|
| | 1 | 2 | 3 | 4 |
| 10. Subject recalls specific childhood memories of distress (subject avoids recalling distressing events). | .96 | .05 | .17 | .04 |
| 1. Parental descriptions are stereotyped (parental descriptions are based upon first-hand experience). | −.93 | −.14 | .03 | −.14 |
| 71. Relies on others in frustrated or dissatisfied way (demeans or plays down the need to rely on others). | .90 | .05 | −.35 | .04 |
| 64. Acknowledges setbacks that have been overcome (denies any setbacks, negative effects, or hurt from parents). | .90 | .12 | .07 | .09 |
| 19. Responses are superficial and require further probes (talks easily and in depth at appropriate times). | −.89 | −.13 | −.12 | .02 |
| 74. Memories of childhood are recalled during interview (makes little effort to search for memories relevant to interview topics). | .89 | .03 | .08 | −.07 |
| 57. Is detached or uninfluenced by childhood experiences (has integrated childhood experiences into a well-developed understanding of self). | −.89 | .06 | .00 | .05 |
| 91. Subject reports negative experience that is not accompanied by feelings of hurt or distress (negative experiences are "felt" or openly acknowledged). | −.87 | .10 | −.21 | .03 |
| 11. Parental faults or limitations are depicted directly (negative aspects of relationships with parents emerge indirectly). | .88 | .13 | −.06 | .15 |
| 61. Presents self as invulnerable (acknowledges vulnerability and need to rely on others). | −.88 | .10 | −.13 | .05 |
| 3. Is dissatisfied with parental availability (plays down the significance of parental availability). | .88 | .04 | .13 | −.02 |
| 73. Adjectives supported by vague or shallow memories (adjectives supported by detailed episodic memories). | −.87 | −.08 | .03 | .04 |
| 56. Parental shortcomings are implied but not directly acknowledged (parental shortcomings are acknowledged without anger). | −.86 | −.13 | .17 | −.09 |
| 46. Subject persistently does not remember (recalls specific events with ease). | −.84 | −.03 | −.22 | .05 |

*(Continued)*

**Table 6.3    (Continued)**

|  | Factor | | | |
|---|---|---|---|---|
|  | 1 | 2 | 3 | 4 |
| 66. Provides only minimal responses (responds at length and has to be interrupted or refocused by interviewer). | **−.80** | −.05 | −.65 | .11 |
| 39. Subject values attachment (devalues attachment relationships). | **.80** | −.12 | −.04 | −.06 |
| 38. Has accepted parental practices with no reevaluation or reappraisal (shows some reevaluation and reappraisal of parental practices). | **−.79** | −.17 | .10 | −.16 |
| 93. Depicts parents as perfect or wonderful without convincing reader (describes convincing positive features of parents). | **−.78** | .04 | .14 | −.08 |
| 72. Integrates specific memories with more general abstractions (focuses excessively on specific experiences or general abstractions). | **.77** | .07 | −.35 | .08 |
| 13. Mother called attention to her own needs and concerns (mother was responsive to subject's needs and concerns). | .01 | **.86** | −.02 | −.04 |
| 95. Mother enjoyed parenting (was a martyr, complainer, or burdened by parenting). | .04 | **−.86** | .01 | .02 |
| 40. Mother pushed subject toward precocious independence (mother was available when subject encountered setbacks). | −.07 | **.84** | −.07 | .06 |
| 49. Mother was too busy or preoccupied to pay attention to subject (was regularly involved with subject). | −.07 | **.84** | −.17 | −.07 |
| 5. Relationship with mother was relaxed and open (subject was tense with mother). | .13 | **−.81** | .04 | .01 |
| 41. Mother was patient and tolerant (mother was angry, irritable, or harsh). | .02 | **−.81** | .03 | .04 |
| 59. Mother was strict or rigid, intimidated subject (mother established appropriate maturity expectations). | .12 | **.81** | −.02 | .05 |
| 85. Mother was psychologically unavailable (mother was psychologically available). | −.32 | **.80** | −.11 | −.11 |
| 23. Mother relied on subject for affection and support (mother was affectionate and supportive toward subject). | .17 | **.77** | −.09 | .12 |

| | | | | |
|---|---|---|---|---|
| 31. Mother was a competent and supportive confidant (mother was unwilling or unable to listen to child's problems). | .30 | −.73 | .00 | .12 |
| 86. Mother was generally forgiving of mistakes and limitations (mother was critical and perfectionistic). | .12 | −.72 | −.01 | .02 |
| 45. Is currently preoccupied with negative experiences with parents (has resolved negative feelings toward parents). | .12 | −.17 | .92 | −.04 |
| 55. Is confused and overwhelmed with information about parents (information about parents is adequate and well-organized). | .08 | .09 | .87 | .05 |
| 8. Responses maintain focus on interview questions (responses include sudden "intrusions" or topic shifts). | −.12 | −.08 | −.86 | −.06 |
| 48. Vacillates between positive and negative attitudes toward parents (has integrated positive and negative experiences). | −.22 | −.04 | .85 | −.05 |
| 20. Is conflicted or confused about parents (provides a consistent account of relationships with parents). | −.05 | .10 | .82 | −.07 |
| 30. Responds in excessive detail about attachment relationships (responds with appropriate detail to interview topics). | −.04 | −.01 | .82 | .01 |
| 92. Is caught up with analyzing parental shortcomings (thinking has led to acceptance of self and parents). | −.02 | −.12 | .08 | .06 |
| 75. Loses topic during interview, failing to complete thoughts (responses convey complete thoughts). | .29 | .18 | .74 | .11 |
| 83. Responds in a clear, well-organized fashion (fails to grasp and passively struggles with interview questions). | .13 | −.14 | −.64 | −.10 |
| 79. Father enjoyed parenting (was a martyr, complainer, or burdened by parenting). | −.04 | −.03 | .03 | −.86 |
| 51. Father was too busy or preoccupied to pay attention to subject (was regularly involved with subject). | .07 | −.07 | −.11 | .84 |
| 87. Father was psychologically unavailable (father was psychologically available). | −.20 | −.14 | −.03 | .82 |
| 15. Father called attention to his own needs and concerns (father was responsive to subject's needs and concerns). | −.05 | −.11 | −.02 | .80 |

(Continued)

**Table 6.3    (Continued)**

|  | Factor | | | |
|---|---|---|---|---|
|  | 1 | 2 | 3 | 4 |
| 24. Relationship with father was relaxed and open (subject was tense with father). | −.01 | .14 | −.10 | **−.80** |
| 7. Father relied on subject for affection and support (father was affectionate and supportive toward subject). | −.04 | .12 | −.09 | **.77** |
| 32. Father was a competent and supportive confidant (father was unwilling or unable to listen to child's problems). | .27 | .10 | −.03 | **−.76** |
| 18. Currently maintains a close relationship with father (is emotionally cut-off from father). | .17 | −.01 | .05 | **−.75** |
| 42. Father pushed subject toward precocious independence (father was available when subject encountered setbacks). | −.09 | .09 | .03 | **.75** |
| 22. Felt much closer to mother than father as a child (felt much closer to father than to mother). | −.04 | −.51 | −.05 | **.72** |

Initial studies of the earned-secure group struggled with cutoff criteria for identifying this subgroup. In the first study of earned security, any participant who received less than a 5 or midpoint rating on either the loving-mother or loving-father scales was counted as earned-secure (Pearson, Cohn, Cowan, & Cowan, 1994; Roisman, Padron, Sroufe, & Egeland, 2002). More restrictive criteria proposed by Main and Goldwyn (1998) requires scores of less than 2.5 on a loving scale, a cut-off that effectively eliminates earned-secure subjects from adolescent or young adult samples (Hesse, 2008). Using the more liberal cutpoint of 5 on either loving scale, Roisman et al. (2002) found that the earned-secure group assessed at age 19 had a consistent history of more internalizing and depressive symptoms than did their continuous-secure counterparts. Furthermore, these symptoms dated back to maternal reports of the subject's internalizing symptoms in kindergarten/first grade. In contrast to the symptom ratings, observations of parenting quality at 24 months and again at age 13 indicated that earned-secures had a higher quality of care than their insecure counterparts. Thus, Roisman and colleagues (2002) emphasized the limits of the inferred-experience scales as "veridical" reports of past experience.

In a subsequent study, Roisman, Fortuna, and Holland (2006) tested the effects of happy and sad moods on inferred-experience and coherence scales using a mood-induction procedure. The effects of the mood manipulation were tested after dividing the sample into secure and insecure groups using the coherence scale. The sad versus happy moods strongly influenced inferred-experience ratings in predicted directions only among those in the autonomous or coherent group. Among these autonomous subjects, sad mood lowered ratings of inferred experience with mothers and fathers in ways that suggested the earned-secure group could be the product of negative mood. As in the previous studies, depressive symptoms before the mood manipulation significantly differentiated the earned-secure from the continuous-secure subjects. Coherence ratings were not affected by the mood manipulation in either group or the full sample.

The studies of earned-security have several important implications for future research. One implication is that the criteria for earned-security are subject to variable and somewhat arbitrary decision rules. These range from strict criteria that are unlikely to be observed in adolescent or young adult samples to the much looser criteria used to generate groups in the Pearson and Roisman studies. Furthermore, there appears to be no evidence for treating earned-secures as a distinct category or taxon (Roisman et al., 2007). These studies also provide some evidence that states of mind rated from discourse coherence are a more stable aspect of personality than the inferred-experience scales. Whereas the discourse coherence scale was systematically associated with earlier measures of caregiving quality, the inferred-experience scales were not. Furthermore, inferred-experience scales appear to be more sensitive to current mood states and depressive symptoms, but only for autonomous and not for dismissing or preoccupied subjects. Thus, it seems appropriate to conclude that the inferred-experience scales come closer to assessing current experience, whereas ratings of discourse coherence capture a more enduring or stable aspect of personality.

The exclusive focus on earned-secure subjects neglects the more common group of continuous-secure subjects who have more positive inferred experiences of mother or father availability. The degree of covariation between the inferred-experience and states-of-mind scales can be quite substantial and is rarely reported in AAI studies. In our analyses of adolescent transcripts, the inferred-experience and states-of-mind components show substantial covariaton: inferred experience with mother and father correlated with the dismissing/secure state of mind ($-.46$, $p < .001$, and $-.29$, $p < .001$), respectively, and with the preoccupied dimension ($-.55$, $p < .001$, and $-.31$, $p < .001$), respectively. The size of these correlations may be larger in samples of adolescents, as they have not yet moved away from home and their states of mind are still more influenced by their *current* relationships with parents with whom they reside. Similar findings from the Roisman studies illustrate the covariation of inferred experience with parents and states of mind.

The linkage between inferred experience and states of mind is an integral part of the AAI classification system. Main and Goldwyn's (1998) classification guidelines indicate ratings of inferred experience with parents that are at or above the midpoint on the loving-parent scales are a sufficient though not a necessary condition for classifying a transcript as autonomous/secure. Even earned-secure subjects have higher ratings of loving mothers than did subjects with nonautonomous states of mind (Roisman et al., 2006). Although these inferred experiences are not likely to provide a veridical developmental history, they may provide an index of current expectancies about mother and father availability derived from the quality of autobiographical memories produced during the interview. By bringing the relationship between these scales and states of mind to the foreground, the studies of earned-security point to new questions about the validity of the inferred-experience scales and the contribution of current attachment relationships to emerging states of mind.

## Evaluating the Validity of Inferred-Experience Scales

The primary focus on states of mind in the AAI classification system has led to a relative neglect of the inferred-experience scales. Our PCA of adolescent Q-items suggest that raters trained in the Main and Goldwyn system clearly differentiate between inferred-experience and states-of-mind scales in their ratings of AAI transcripts. The canonical approach of combining these ratings into a singular state of mind captures a view of attachment as a personality construct. However, this approach is less sensitive to the continuing interplay between expectancies for caregiver availability and the caregiving environment as parents continue to serve as attachment figures to their adolescent children. If the inferred-experience scales are more sensitive to the quality of current attachment relationships with mothers and fathers, they may contribute to a better understanding of the contribution of the security of adolescent-caregiver relationships to current and future adaptation.

Ratings of inferred experience in the AAI share important similarities with representational measures of attachment used in childhood (see Solomon & George, 2008). These childhood measures are generally based on narratives generated by either projective or interview techniques. Security in most of these assessments is based on raters' inferences about underlying expectancies for mother or father availability from narratives of situations that typically activate the attachment system. Following the AAI's emphasis on discourse coherence and states of mind, the developers of the Child Attachment Interview (CAI) coding system focused on coherence of narratives generated by children. However, in discussing their coding system, Shmueli-Goetz and colleagues (2008) noted the potential value of incorporating inferred experiences into their coding system. They suggested that the child's representations of caregiver "responses to the child's expressed attachment needs" are likely to be useful in understanding the *current* quality or security of the child-caregiver attachment relationship. Such a focus may be more likely to differentiate the child's current expectancies for mother and father availability and more clearly differentiate the constructs of attachment security as relationship-specific expectancies for caregiver availability from states of mind as a more general strategy for monitoring attachment-related discourse.

If inferred experiences provide a closer depiction of subjects' current expectancies for caregivers' availability, they should guide adolescents' behavior during interactions that potentially test the adolescent's confidence in the caregiver's availability. These expectancies should also be sensitive to sociocultural factors that affect the family context and caregiver availability. For instance, expectancies for father availability would be influenced by family structure and would likely occur at lower frequency in single-parent mother-headed families. Stressful life events, such as residential instability, job loss, or illness, could reduce the extent to which the caregiver is available to the adolescents. In two-parent families, the quality of the marital relationship may influence both mother and father availability and adolescents' expectancies. In general, we would anticipate that inferred-experience ratings would be more sensitive to changes or fluctuations in the adolescents' relationships with mothers and fathers than states of mind.

A largely unanswered question is the direction of influence between inferred experience and states of mind. On the one hand, a relationship model would suggest that autonomous states of mind, or the capacity to flexibly deploy attention in the AAI, must be supported by attachment security in relationships with mothers or fathers. On the other hand, a personality model would suggest that the self-regulatory strategies emerging in early relationships provide the child with the skills for maintaining a secure partnership with parents that increase their expectancies for caregiver availability. Ultimately, consideration of inferred experiences as a component of adolescent attachment organization will depend on reliable measures of inferred experience, research designs that test the stability of inferred experience of states of mind, and, most importantly, independent measures of attachment processes in caregiver-adolescent and peer attachment relationships. Such an approach would make it possible to validate the states-of-mind construct within a broader network of constructs suggested by attachment theory.

## A FRAMEWORK FOR PSYCHOPATHOLOGY AND INTERVENTION

Studies of the AAI and psychopathology have explored the notion that different types of insecure states of mind would account for different forms of psychopathology. There was some initial support for the hypothesis that dismissing states of mind would be associated with externalizing disorders whereas preoccupied states of mind would account for internalizing difficulties (Cole-Detke & Kobak, 1996; Dozier, Stovall, & Albus, 1999; Rosenstein & Horowitz, 1996). However, during the past decade, adolescent AAI and psychopathology studies have suggested that links between preoccupied states of mind demonstrate the most substantial associations with a range of disorders, and these associations become stronger in the presence of other risk factors (Allen, 2008; Bakermans-Kranenburg & Van IJzendoorn, 2009; Kobak, Cassidy, Lyons-Ruth, & Ziv, 2006; Kobak, Zajac, & Smith, 2009).

Atypical or disorganized states of mind frequently co-occur with preoccupied states of mind. These atypical states of mind (e.g., unresolved loss or abuse, fearful preoccupation with trauma, cannot classify) have been associated with adults' risk for psychopathology (Allen & Hauser, 1996; Zajac & Kobak, 2009) but are not frequently assessed in studies of adolescents. There are two potential impediments to assessing unresolved and fearfully preoccupied states in adolescent samples. First, as was evident in our sample, adolescents have relatively low base rates of unresolved loss and trauma compared with their adult caregivers. This was often the result of adolescents reporting less exposure to loss or trauma. Adolescents by virtue of their age simply had less exposure to loss compared to their caregivers. In addition, as part of informed consent, adolescents were told that incidents involving suspected abuse could result in the need to report their caregivers to Child Protective Services. This creates an obvious disincentive for disclosing abuse during the interview. The second impediment to studying disorganized attachment in adolescent samples is restricted to studies using the AAI Q-sort to code interviews, because this system is not designed to capture atypical or unresolved classifications.

In our economically disadvantaged sample, coders who had passed reliability certification with Mary Main rated transcripts using the AAI Q-sort as well as Main and Goldwyn's classifications. Despite the limitations inherent in coding disorganization in adolescents' AAIs, approximately 11% of the participants were assigned to an atypical classification (i.e., unresolved, fearfully preoccupied, or cannot classify).

This atypical group was compared with the three major classifications using the two AAI states-of-mind dimensions (secure/dismissing, preoccupied). As expected, the secure/dismissing dimension strongly differentiated between dismissing and all other categories, with the preoccupied and atypical subjects falling between dismissing and secure subjects. In Figure 6.1, the preoccupied dimension distinguished the preoccupied and atypical subjects from dismissing and secure subjects. However, this dimension did not differentiate preoccupied from atypical subjects. Furthermore, both preoccupied and atypical adolescents showed similarly elevated levels of aggressive and sexual risk-taking behaviors across three assessments between ages 13 and 17. Atypical and preoccupied subjects were also largely indistinguishable in terms of psychopathology. When atypical and preoccupied adolescents were combined, they had substantially elevated levels of externalizing and risk behavior compared to both autonomous and dismissing adolescents (see Figures 6.2 through 6.4). This pattern was consistent across both caregiver-reported and self-reported symptoms. Dismissing adolescents generally did not self-report higher levels of externalizing behaviors (Figure 6.2), although their caregivers' reports indicated slightly elevated externalizing behavior compared to caregivers' reports of autonomous adolescents (Figure 6.3). Dismissing adolescents also reported more sexual risk-taking behavior than autonomous adolescents at the age 15 and 17 assessments (Figure 6. 4).

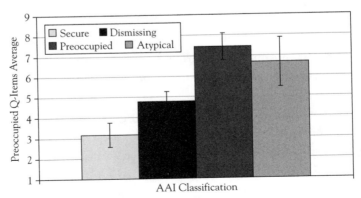

**Figure 6.1**  Dimensional assessment of preoccupied states of mind among AAI classifications

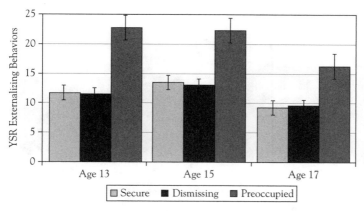

**Figure 6.2**    Self-reported externalizing problems among secure, dismissing, and preoccupied adolescents at ages 13, 15, and 17

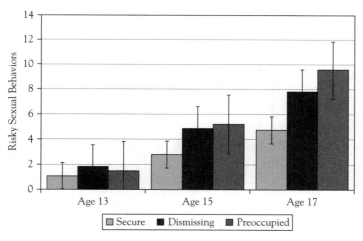

**Figure 6.3**    Risky sexual behaviors among secure, dismissing, and preoccupied adolescents at ages 13, 15, and 17

Preoccupied or atypical adolescents were more vulnerable to psychopathology than those who were classified as dismissing. From a theoretical perspective, this pattern is consistent with the view that preoccupied states of mind involve lapses in organized coping. These lapses, in turn, increase risk for impulsive and hostile behavior. It remains uncertain whether preoccupied states of mind can be viewed as a conditional strategy. Ambivalent/resistant infants are presumed to have adopted a strategy that

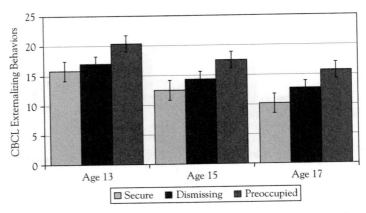

**Figure 6.4**    Caregiver-reported externalizing problems among secure, dismissing, and preoccupied adolescents at ages 13, 15, and 17

helps them to maintain a bond with an inconsistent or unavailable caregiver. Yet the sort of angry or passive lapses that characterize preoccupation in the AAI are likely to leave adolescents vulnerable to a range of interpersonal difficulties. The relationship/lifespan framework directs attention to questions about how these states of mind are implicated in adolescents' expectancies for their relationships with family and peers.

Clues to preoccupied adolescents' expectancies for their caregivers are evident in the association between the states-of-mind and inferred-experiences components derived from the AAI Q-set. Many of the preoccupied/atypical adolescents reported major disruptions or disturbances in their relationships with an adult caregiver. Their lack of confidence in caregiver availability may add to the self-regulatory problems associated with preoccupation to reduce adolescents' access to the support and guidance of an adult caregiver. To better understand the relations between preoccupied states of mind and psychopathology, the link between states of mind as a marker of self-regulatory aspects of personality and adaptation in close relationships with family and peers need to be considered. The relationship/lifespan model points to the continuing importance of current caregiver availability, caregiver-adolescent communication, and the adolescents' interpersonal skills in forming and maintaining relationships with peers, friends, and sexual partners as important mechanisms that may link states of mind to adolescents' psychological disorders.

# Attachment Security, States of Mind, and Risky Behavior in Peer Contexts

The security of the adolescent-caregiver bond may extend beyond the family to patterns of adaptation and maladaptation in peer contexts. The relationship/lifespan framework views adolescence as a period in which youth test close friends or romantic partners as potential attachment figures. However, adolescents' increased engagement with peers increases risky behavior (e.g., delinquency, substance use, unprotected sex; Steinberg, 1990). These risky behaviors, in turn, have long-term effects on adolescents' pathways into adulthood. For instance, sexual risk-taking behavior may result in unplanned pregnancy and child bearing in a way that fundamentally alters adolescents' future relationships (Elder, 1998). The consequences of risky sexual behavior fall disproportionally on female adolescents from low-income backgrounds in the forms of unintended pregnancy and childbearing with poor prospects for long-term support from the biological father. The stresses associated with disrupted romantic bonds and the demands of pregnancy and childcare leave adolescents more vulnerable to mood and anxiety disorders. Similarly, impulsive, delinquent, and substance-abuse behaviors that occur when adolescents affiliate with deviant peers increase the likelihood of involvement with the criminal justice system. This type of risk falls disproportionally on male adolescents from economically disadvantaged families, jeopardizing their ability to transition into the job market, find stable employment, and form stable romantic relationships.

Attachment bonds with adult caregivers remain important during this period, insofar as they offer the perspective of an older and wiser individual who has unique information about the transition into adult roles involving education, work, and childbearing. When communication in these relationships is open and constructive, adolescent-caregiver bonds can reduce adolescents' susceptibility to risky behaviors in peer contexts. Alternatively, when adolescents lacks access to and support from an adult caregiver, they are likely to be more vulnerable to the type of peer relationships that encourage risky behavior. Adolescents' selection of friends and sexual partners, their ability to assert themselves in peer contexts, and the extent to which they test a friend or romantic partner as an attachment figure are all factors that are closely linked to risky behavior and maladaptation. Furthermore, in the absence of support from an adult caregiver, adolescents may prematurely turn to a peer as a source of protection or guidance. Although testing bonds with friends or romantic partners as possible attachments becomes an important task in late adolescence, the continuing availability of an adult caregiver allows this to be a gradual process. Early reliance on sexual partners as attachment figures can leave the adolescent vulnerable to difficult relationship breakups and depressive symptoms (Welsh, Grello, & Harper, 2003). In considering the balance between reliance on peers and adults as attachment figures, assessments of adolescents' attachment preferences can be useful for planning treatment and assessing treatment outcomes (Rosenthal & Kobak, 2010). The way in which adolescents balance their reliance on caregivers and peers as attachment figures has important implications for maladaptive behaviors that increase risk for psychological disorders.

## Implications for Attachment-Based Interventions with Adolescents

The personality and relationship models point to different but complementary targets for clinical intervention. The personality/early experience model focuses primarily on intrapersonal dynamics that include states of mind with respect to attachment and tends to privilege individual treatment modalities. From this perspective, interventions are designed to increase the adolescents' ability to organize painful aspects of experience with attachment figures into more secure or coherent narratives. The adolescent's relationship with the therapist provides a critical mechanism that supports the adolescent's ability to access attachment-related memories and to organize them into a narrative marked by increased perspective taking and acceptance of the caregiver's limitations. These more coherent or autonomous narratives should help adolescents to acknowledge their need to rely upon others and increase their own capacity for empathy. This focus on intra-personal dynamics may be conceived as an effort to alter states of mind and there is some evidence that treatment strategy and outcomes should be adjusted accordingly for individuals with dismissing as opposed to preoccupied/unresolved states of mind (Slade, 2008).

The relationship/lifespan model suggests that the overall goal for treating adolescent psychopathology is increasing security in the caregiver-adolescent dyad. The focus on improving communication brings both intrapersonal and interpersonal aspects of attachment security into play. In working to improve the adolescent and caregiver's ability to cooperatively negotiate goal conflicts, family oriented therapists encounter intrapersonal dynamics that restrict open communication. For instance, adolescents who have developed dismissing states of mind will avoid vulnerable feelings and tend to disengage or become defensive in conflict discussions. These defensive dynamics, in turn, challenge caregivers' ability to respond or empathize with the adolescent. As a result, caregiver behavior often confirms and validates the adolescents' insecurity and distrust in the relationship. Similar self-perpetuating patterns may be evident in caregivers' interactions with preoccupied/unresolved adolescents. If the lapses into dysfunctional anger or passivity during the AAI generalize to the adolescent's interactions with the caregiver, then the caregiver will have more difficulty supporting the adolescent's viewpoint or working toward cooperative negotiation of goal conflicts.

A focus on increasing security in the caregiver-adolescent dyad may also need to consider the caregivers' state of mind. Caregivers with dismissing or preoccupied states of mind may have difficulty understanding or interpreting the adolescents' need for support and understanding that in turn influences the adolescents' expectancies and ability to engage in exchanges marked by direct communication and negotiation of goal conflicts. Evidence for intergenerational transmission of caregiver's states of mind to their children has been most extensively investigated during infancy. However, our own work suggests that caregiver states of mind continue to influence children's adaptation through middle childhood and early adolescence (Zajac & Kobak, 2009). This factor needs to be more extensively investigated in interpersonal and family treatments of adolescents' psychopathology. An attachment-based parenting intervention that produced both short-term and long-term reduction in adolescent externalizing behaviors illustrates the potential value of working directly with parents (Moretti & Obsuth, 2009).

Incorporating intrapersonal and interpersonal processes in clinical interventions illustrates the complementary nature of the personality/

early experience and the relationship/lifespan models. Change in the individual adolescent is likely to be most enduring if it is accompanied by change in the security of the attachment bond with the caregiver. Addressing the transaction between expectancies/states of mind and adolescent-caregiver communication requires assessing (a) the adolescent's expectancies and state of mind, (b) the quality of the caregiver-adolescent relationship, and (c) the caregiver's ability to attend to, monitor, and support the adolescent. As the adolescent develops more confident expectations for caregiver availability, they are likely to develop more adaptive self-regulation. This, in turn, should facilitate more direct and open communication with the caregiver during discussions of goal-conflicts. Presumably, more direct communication by the adolescent would facilitate more supportive and attuned responses from the caregiver.

The challenge for developing attachment-based interventions is in addressing the complex transaction between personality and relationship processes. Multi-modal approaches that combine individual sessions with adolescents, individual sessions with their caregivers, and dyadic sessions designed to increase cooperation negotiation of goal-conflicts would seem to offer the most promising approach to producing enduring change. Such an approach should assess the adolescent's expectancies and seek to increase his or her confidence in caregiver availability as part of the treatment process (Diamond, Reis, Diamond, Siqueland, & Isaacs, 2002). The potential value of targeting adolescent expectancies as a change mechanism is also suggested by the studies of earned-security. These studies indicate that depression tends to bias subjects toward more negative expectancies for caregiver availability. These perceptions may not be accurate reflections of the caregiver's availability but they may prevent the adolescent from seeking the support and gaining security from the relationship. Addressing these biases in individual treatment may reduce the adolescent's isolation and distrust. Alternatively, in many cases, the adolescent's expectancies for their caregiver may be tolerably accurate reflections of their relationship experience. The challenge in these cases is to provide the adolescent and caregiver with successful experiences negotiating important topics in ways that restore confidence and trust in the relationship.

# SUMMARY

Despite nearly two decades of research on this topic, much remains to be learned about adolescent states of mind and their implications for psychopathology. The MPCLS provides a prototype for assessing developing patterns of maladaptation as mechanisms linking attachment to psychopathology. Bowlby and Ainsworth's relationship/lifespan view points to the continuing need to assess adolescent and adult attachments as factors that influence adaptive and maladaptive trajectories. It is likely that new insights can be gained by examining how the security of caregiver-adolescent relationships influences (a) adolescents' reorganization of preferences for attachment figures and (b) their transition into adult roles that include the formation of reciprocal attachment bonds, mating, reproduction, and caring for offspring. Bowlby and Ainsworth's theory offers substantial guidance for expanding the network of attachment-related constructs that are needed to understand adolescent and adult attachment relationships. Expectancies for caregiver availability, communication in goal-corrected partnerships, affectional bonds, and hierarchical ordering of preferences for attachment figures are part of the nomological network needed for construct validation. By embedding states of mind in a broader network of attachment constructs, mechanisms linking attachment processes to psychopathology and clinical intervention can be better specified and investigated.

# REFERENCES

Ainsworth, M. S. (1989). Attachments beyond infancy. *American Psychologist, 44*, 709–716.

Ainsworth, M. (1990). Some considerations regarding theory and assessment relevant to attachments beyond infancy. In M. Greenberg, D. Cicchetti, & E. M. Cummings (Eds.), *Attachment during the preschool years: Theory, research, and intervention* (pp. 463–489). Chicago, IL: University of Chicago Press.

Ainsworth, M. D., Blehar, M., Waters, E., & Wall, S. (1978). *Patterns of attachment: A psychological study of the Strange Situation*. Hillsdale, NJ: Erlbaum.

Allen, J. P. (2008). The attachment system in adolescence. In J. Cassidy and P. R. Shaver (Eds.), *Handbook of attachment: Theory, research, and clinical applications* (2nd ed., pp. 419–435). New York, NY: Guilford Press.

Allen, J. P., & Hauser, S. T. (1996). Autonomy and relatedness in adolescent-family interactions as predictors of young adults' states of mind regarding attachment. *Development and Psychopathology, 8*, 793–809.

Allen, J., McElhaney, K., Land, D., Kuperminc, G., Moore, C., O'Beirne-Kelly, H., et al. (2003). A secure base in adolescence: Markers of attachment security in the mother-adolescent relationship. *Child Development*, 292–307.

Allen, J., Porter, M., McFarland, C., McElhaney, K., & Marsh, P. (2007). The relation of attachment security to adolescents, paternal and peer relationships, depression, and externalizing behavior. *Child Development, 78*(4), 1222.

Bakermans-Kranenburg, M., & van IJzendoorn, M. (2009). The first 10,000 adult attachment interviews: Distributions of adult attachment representations in clinical and non-clinical groups. *Attachment & Human Development, 11*(3), 223–263.

Belsky, J., & Cassidy, J. (1994). Attachment: Theory and evidence. In M. Rutter & D. F. Hay (Eds.), *Development through life: A handbook for clinicians* (pp. 373–402). Oxford, England: Blackwell.

Belsky, J., & Fearon, R. M. (2002a). Infant-mother attachment security, contextual risk, and early development: A moderational analysis. *Development and Psychopathology, 14*(2), 293–310.

Belsky, J., & Fearon, R. M. (2002b). Early attachment security, subsequent maternal sensitivity, and later child development: Does continuity in development depend upon continuity of caregiving? *Attachment & Human Development, 4*(3), 361–387.

Benoit, D., & Parker, K. (1994). Stability and transmission of attachment across three generations. *Child Development, 65*, 1444–1456.

Bowlby, J. (1973). *Attachment and loss: Vol. 2. Separation.* New York, NY: Basic Books.

Bowlby, J. (1979). *The making and breaking of affectional bonds.* London, England: Tavistock.

Bumpass, L. L., & Lu, H. H. (2000). Trends in cohabitation and implications for children's family contexts. *Population Studies, 54*, 29–41.

Cassidy, J., & Kobak, R. (1988). Avoidance and its relation to other defensive processes. In J. Belsky & T. Nezworski (Eds.), *Clinical implications of attachment* (pp. 300–323). Hillsdale, NJ: Erlbaum.

Cherlin, A. J. (2004). The deinstitutionalization of American marriage. *Journal of Marriage and Family*, 66, 848–861.

Cole-Detke, H., & Kobak, R. (1996). Attachment processes in eating disorder and depression. *Journal of Consulting and Clinical Psychology*, 64, 282–290.

Cowan, P., & Cowan, C. (2007). Attachment theory: Seven unresolved issues and questions for future research. *Research in Human Development*, 4(3–4), 181–201.

Cowan, P., & Cowan, C. (2009). Couple relationships: A missing link between adult attachment and children's outcomes. *Attachment & Human Development*, 11(1), 1.

Cowan, P. A., Cowan, C. P., & Mehta, N. (2009). Adult attachment, couple attachment, and children's adaptation to school: An integrated attachment template and family risk model. *Attachment & Human Development*, 11(1), 29–46.

Crosnoe, R., & Elder, G. (2002). Life course transitions, the generational stake, and grandparent-grandchild relationships. *Journal of Marriage and the Family*, 64, 1089–1096.

Diamond, G. S., Reis, B. F., Diamond, G. M., Siqueland, K., & Isaacs, L. (2002). Attachment-based family therapy for depressed adolescents: A treatment development study. *Journal of the American Academy of Child & Adolescent Psychiatry*, 41(10), 1190–1196.

Dozier, M., Stovall, K. C., & Albus, K. E. (1999). Attachment and psychopathology in adulthood. In J. Cassidy and P. R. Shaver (Eds.), *Handbook of attachment: Theory, research, and clinical applications* (pp. 497–519). New York, NY: Guilford Press.

Elder, G. (1998). The life course as developmental theory. *Child Development*, 69, 1–12.

Fortuna, K., & Roisman, G. (2008). Insecurity, stress, and symptoms of psychopathology: Contrasting results from self-reports versus interviews of adult attachment. *Attachment & Human Development*, 10(1), 11.

Fox, N., Kimmerly, N., & Schafer, W. (1991). Attachment to mother/attachment to father: A meta-analysis. *Child Development*, 62(1), 210–225.

Fraley, R. (2002). Attachment stability from infancy to adulthood: Meta-analysis and dynamic modeling of developmental mechanisms. *Personality and Social Psychology Review*, 6(2), 123–151.

Furman, W., & Simon, V. (2004). Concordance in attachment states of mind and styles with respect to fathers and mothers. *Developmental Psychology*, 40, 1239–1247.

George, C., Kaplan, N., & Main, M. (1996). Adult Attachment Interview. Unpublished manuscript, University of California at Berkeley.

Haydon, K. C., Roisman, G. I., & Burt, K. B. (in press). In search of security: The latent structure of the Adult Attachment Interview revisited. *Development and Psychopathology*.

Hazan, C., & Shaver, P. R. (1987). Romantic love conceptualized as an attachment process. *Journal of Personality and Social Psychology, 52*, 511–524.

Hesse, E. (2008). The Adult Attachment Interview: Protocol, method of analysis, and empirical studies. In J. Cassidy and P. R. Shaver (Eds.), *Handbook of attachment: Theory, research, and clinical applications* (2nd ed., pp. 552–598). New York, NY: Guilford Press.

Kerr, M., & Stattin, H. (2000). What parents know, how they know it, and several forms of adolescent adjustment: Further support for a reinterpretation of monitoring. *Developmental Psychology, 36*, 366–380.

Kobak, R. R. (1989). *The Attachment Interview Q-Set.* Unpublished manuscript. Newark: University of Delaware.

Kobak, R., Cassidy, J., Lyons-Ruth, K., & Ziv, Y. (2006). Attachment, stress and psychopathology: A developmental pathways model. In D. Cicchetti & D. J. Cohen (Eds.), *Handbook of developmental psychopathology* (pp. 333–369). Cambridge, England: Cambridge University Press.

Kobak, R. & Duemmler, S. (1994). Attachment and conversation: A discourse analysis of goal-corrected partnerships. In D. Perlman and K. Bartholomew (Eds.). *Advances in the study of personal relationships, Vol. 5* (pp. 121–149), London: Jessica Kingsley Publishers.

Kobak, R., & Cole, H. (1994). Attachment and meta-monitoring: Implications for adolescent autonomy and psychopathology. In D. Cicchetti & S. L. Toth (Eds.), *Disorders and dysfunctions of the self* (pp. 267–297). Rochester, NY: University of Rochester Press.

Kobak, R., Cole, H., Fleming, W., Ferenz-Gillies, R., & Gamble, W. (1993). Attachment and emotion regulation during mother-teen problem-solving: A control theory analysis. *Child Development, 64*, 231–245.

Kobak, R., & Madsen, S. (2008). Disruptions in attachment bonds: Implications for theory, research, and clinical intervention. In J. Cassidy and P. R. Shaver (Eds.), *Handbook of attachment: Theory, research, and clinical applications* (2nd ed., pp. 23–47). New York, NY: Guilford Press.

Kobak, R., Rosenthal, N., Zajac, K., & Madsen, S. (2007). Adolescent attachment hierarchies and the search for an adult pair-bond. *New Directions for Child and Adolescent Development, 2007*, 57–72.

Kobak, R., Zajac, K., & Smith, C. H. (2009). Preoccupied states of mind and trajectories of hostile-impulsive behavior: Implications for the development of personality disorders. *Development and Psychopathology, 21*, 839–851.

Lyons-Ruth, K., Hennighausen, K., & Holmes, B. (2005). *Goal-corrected partnership in adolescence coding system (GPACS): Coding manual.* Version 2. Unpublished document. Department of Psychiatry, Harvard Medical School, Cambridge, MA.

Main, M. (1990). Cross-cultural studies of attachment organization: Recent studies, changing methodologies, and the concept of conditional strategies. *Human Development, 33,* 48–61.

Main, M., & Goldwyn, R. (1998). Adult attachment rating and classification systems. Unpublished manuscript. University of California at Berkeley.

Main, M., Kaplan, N., & Cassidy, J. (1985). Security in infancy, childhood, and adulthood: A move to the level of representation. *Monographs of the Society for Research in Child Development, 50,* 66–104.

Main, M., & Weston, D. R. (1981). The quality of the toddler's relationship to mother and to father: Related to conflict behavior and the readiness to establish new relationships. *Child Development, 52,* 932–940.

Matas, L., Arend, R. A., & Sroufe, L. A. (1978). Continuity of adaptation in the second year: The relationship between quality of attachment and later competence. *Child Development, 49,* 547–556.

Meehl, P. E. (1973). MAXCOV-HITMAX: A taxonomic search method for loose genetic syndromes. *Psychodiagnosis: Selected papers* (pp. 200–224). Minneapolis: University of Minnesota Press.

Moretti, M., & Obsuth, I. (2009). Effectiveness of an attachment-focused manualized intervention for parents of teens at risk for aggressive behaviour: The Connect Program. *Journal of Adolescence, 32,* 1347–1357.

Pearson, J. L., Cohn, D. A., Cowan, P. A., & Cowan, C. P. (1994). Earned- and continuous-security in adult attachment: Relation to depressive symptomatology and parenting style. *Development and Psychopathology, 6,* 359–373.

Roisman, G. I. (2006). The role of adult attachment security in non-romantic, non-attachment-related first interactions between same-sex strangers. *Attachment & Human Development, 8*(4), 341–352.

Roisman, G., Fortuna, K., & Holland, A. (2006). An experimental manipulation of retrospectively defined earned and continuous attachment security. *Child Development, 77*(1), 59–71.

Roisman, G. I., Fraley, R. C., & Belsky, J. (2007). A taxometric study of the adult attachment interview. *Developmental Psychology, 43*(3), 675–686.

Roisman, G. I., & Haydon, K.C. (2011). Earned-security in retrospect: Emerging insights from longitudinal, experimental, and taxometric investigations. In D. Cicchetti & G. I. Roisman (Eds.), *The origins and organization of adaptation and maladaptation: Minnesota symposia on child psychology* (Vol. 36). Hoboken, NJ: Wiley.

Roisman, G. I., Holland, A., Fortuna, K., Fraley, R. C., Clausell, E., & Clarke, A. (2007). The adult attachment interview and self-reports of attachment style: An empirical rapprochement. *Journal of Personality and Social Psychology, 92*(4), 678–697.

Roisman G., Madsen, S. D., Hennighausen, K. H., Sroufe, L. A., & Collins, A. W. (2001). The coherence of dyadic behavior across parent–child and romantic relationships as mediated by the internalized representation of experience. *Attachment & Human Development, 3,* 156–172.

Roisman, G., Padron, E., Sroufe, L. A., & Egeland, B. (2002). Earned-secure attachment status in retrospect and prospect. *Child Development,* 1204–1219.

Rosenstein, D. S., & Horowitz, H. A. (1996). Adolescent attachment and psychopathology. *Journal of Consulting & Clinical Psychology, 64,* 244–253.

Rosenthal, N. L., & Kobak, R. (2010). Assessing adolescents' attachment hierarchies: Differences across developmental periods and associations with individual adaptation. *Journal of Research on Adolescence, 20,* 678–706.

Shaver, P. R., & Mikulincer, M. (2007). Adult attachment strategies and the regulation of emotion. In J. J. Gross (Ed.), *Handbook of emotion regulation* (pp. 446–465). New York, NY: Guilford Press.

Shmueli-Goetz, Y., Target, M., Fonagy, P., & Datta, A. (2008). The child attachment interview: A psychometric study of reliability and discriminant validity. *Developmental Psychology, 44*(4), 939–956.

Slade, A. (2008). The implications of attachment theory and research for adult psychotherapy. In J. Cassidy and P. R. Shaver (Eds.), *Handbook of attachment: Theory, research, and clinical applications* (2nd ed., pp. 762–782). New York, NY: Guilford Press.

Solomon, J., & George, C. (2008). The measurement of attachment security and related constructs in infancy and early childhood. In J. Cassidy and P. R. Shaver (Eds.), *Handbook of attachment: Theory, research, and clinical applications* (2nd ed., pp. 383–416). New York, NY: Guilford Press.

Sroufe, L. (1985). Attachment classification from the perspective of infant-caregiver relationships and infant temperament. *Child Development, 56*(1), 1–14.

Sroufe, L. A., & Fleeson, J. (1986). Attachment and the construction of relationships. In W. Hartup & Z. Rubin (Eds.), *Relationships and development* (pp. 51–72). Oxford: Oxford University Press.

Sroufe, L. A. (1996). *Emotional development: The organization of emotional life in the early years*. New York, NY: Cambridge.

Sroufe, L. A. (1997). Psychopathology as an outcome of development. *Development and Psychopathology, 9*(2), 251–268.

Sroufe, L. A., Carlson, E., Egeland, B., & Collins, A. (2005). *The development of the person: The Minnesota study of risk and adaptation from birth to adulthood*. New York, NY: Guilford Press.

Sroufe, L. A., Carlson, E. A., Levy, A., & Egeland, B. (1999). Implications of attachment theory for developmental psychopathology. *Development and Psychopathology, 11*(1), 1–13.

Steinberg, L. (1990). Autonomy, conflict, and harmony in the family. In S. S. Feldman & G. R. Elliott (Eds.), *At the threshold: The developing adolescent* (pp. 255–276). Cambridge, MA: Harvard University Press.

Weinfield, N., Sroufe, L. A., & Egeland, B. (2000). Attachment from infancy to early adulthood in a high-risk sample: Continuity, discontinuity, and their correlates. *Child Development*, 695–702.

Welsh, D. P., Grello, C. M., & Harper, M. S. (2003). When love hurts: Depression and adolescent romantic relationships. In P. Florsheim (Ed.), *Adolescent romantic relations and sexual behavior: Theory, research, and practical implications.* (pp. 185–211). Mahwah, NJ: Erlbaum.

Wynne, L. (1984). The epigenesis of relational systems: A model for understanding family development. *Family Process, 23*: 297–318.

Zajac, K., & Kobak, R. (2009). Caregiver unresolved loss and abuse and child behavior problems: Intergenerational effects in a high-risk sample. *Development and Psychopathology, 21*, 173–187.

# A Developmental Approach to Clinical Research, Classification, and Practice

Tuppett M. Yates, Keith B. Burt, and Michael F. Troy

Psychopathology *is* an outcome of development (Sroufe, 1997). Yet development received scant attention in clinical psychiatry and remained wanting for empirical documentation well into the 1970s. In this chapter, we take stock of how a developmental perspective *has* informed our understanding of psychopathology over the past three decades and identify key areas in which a developmental framework *should* inform future investigations and applications. Illustrating core developmental principles through the complementary lenses of clinical research, classification, and practice, we generate specific recommendations and highlight caveats for concern as we work to implement a developmental framework in clinical science and practice.

Acknowledgments: Preparation of this chapter was supported by a grant from the National Science Foundation (#0951775) awarded to the first author. The authors wish to acknowledge the enduring legacy of Byron Egeland and Alan Sroufe, whose mentorship has shaped our own developmental trajectories and resulting scholarship in countless ways.

## A DEVELOPMENTAL VIEW OF DISORDER

A developmental view of disorder carries markedly different implications for research, classification, and practice than classical psychiatric paradigms, which are grounded in a tacit assumption that psychopathology is a circumscribed, static entity that follows from a unitary, endogenous pathogen. Although contemporary incarnations of this disease or medical model include contextual factors as potential influences on disorder, organism and context remain largely distinct with relatively independent contributions to adaptive functioning. The assumptions of the medical model have guided processes of scientific exploration and justification in the study of psychopathology in both explicit and implicit ways (Lazare, 1973). When challenged to operationally define the medical model, the physician Ray E. Helfer, then editor of *Child Abuse and Neglect*, wrote:

> Maybe the medical model refers to something I'm not doing, but should;
> or even worse, something I do, but shouldn't. Lately, I've come to think
> this has something to do with process; not something I do or don't do,
> rather how I do or don't do something. Maybe it's even related to how
> I think and solve problems (1985, p. 299).

Having shaped how we think about and engage with the problems of psychopathology for the better part of the last two centuries, classical psychiatric tenets remain active (and problematic) in contemporary clinical science.

In this chapter, we argue that a developmental view of psychopathology can be similarly influential, and it will be intellectually and practically productive as we look ahead to the future of clinical research, classification, and practice. We begin by summarizing the core tenets of a developmental perspective on disorder as illustrated by exemplary investigations from the Minnesota Parent-Child Longitudinal Study (MPCLS). Originating in the mid-1970s, the MPCLS has been a hotbed for developmentally informed thinking and research on the origins and consequences of psychopathology (see Sroufe, Egeland, Carlson, & Collins, 2005 for a comprehensive review of the MPCLS' origins and contributions). This widespread impact is all the more striking given the

MPCLS' initial and explicitly developmental emphasis on the causes and consequences of child maltreatment (Egeland & Brunnquell, 1979). Prescient in its design, the developmentally informed and anchored observations of 267 low-income mothers and their firstborn children from before birth through adulthood fueled a veritable revolution in how we approach the study and practice of clinical science; clinical science, that is, as argued here, fundamentally a science of development. Guided by the empirical insights of the MPCLS, we build on this shared conceptual foundation to consider contemporary applications of developmental principles in clinical research, classification, and practice before concluding with a summary of the promise and pitfalls ahead as we strive to apply these principles in the future.

## The Organization of (Mal)adaptation

A developmental-organismic perspective converges on a picture of disorder as a developmental construction, rather than as an outgrowth of pathological induction (Sroufe, 1989, 1997). In this view, disorder or maladaptation *is* adaptation. Whether positive or negative, adaptations arise through successive reorganizations within and among the biological, cognitive, social, emotional, *and* behavioral systems of the individual (Cicchetti & Schneider-Rosen, 1986; see also Werner, 1957; Werner & Kaplan, 1964). Thus, adaptation resides neither in the individual nor in the context, but rather in the dynamic, transactional relation between them (Gottlieb & Halpern, 2002). Organism and context are in constant contact, and both are transformed as a consequence (Sameroff & Chandler, 1975).

Transactions across multiple systems, and the adaptations they engender, are patterned across time such that prior adaptive organizations are incorporated into more recently acquired adaptations (Sroufe, 1979; Werner, 1957). Thus, current adaptation reflects the combined influence of both contemporaneous experience and the individual's prior developmental history to that point. Early experience has special significance because it provides the foundation on which all subsequent adaptations are constructed (Sroufe, Egeland, & Kreutzer, 1990). Like the foundation of a building on which a range of structures may be built, early experience does not determine a specific course of adaptive functioning, but rather constrains its form in a probabilistic fashion.

Adaptation *is* organization; it is the organization within and among multiple levels of developmental influence, including nature, nurture, and development itself. The quality of this adaptive organization underlies individuals' capacity to use resources within and outside the self to negotiate age-salient developmental issues (Waters & Sroufe, 1983). Although the evaluative referents for adaptation necessarily change over time, *competence* always refers to an organization that enables the individual to effectively negotiate current or future developmental issues, and *maladaptation* refers to an organization that compromises this capacity. The crux of the developmental position is that both competence and maladaptation arise from the same transactional and cumulative processes over time. Thus, studies of positive adaptation and of pathology are mutually informing and defining (Cicchetti, 1990; Sroufe, 1990).

Competence begets competence and maladaptation begets maladaptation because *both* are developmentally grounded in prior experience. Although there is a bias toward developmental continuity because of the probabilistic patterning of adaptations over time and the continuity of many environments, there remains a capacity for change. Indeed, this capacity for change justifies clinical intervention efforts. Moreover, when change does occur, it is assumed to be lawful and comprehensible. Development is complex, yet coherent. By emphasizing the underlying function of adaptive organizations and the probabilistic relations between them, rather than their manifest form, a developmental perspective renders nonisomorphic antecedents of disorder and complex routes to disorder comprehensible (Sroufe & Rutter, 1984; Sroufe & Waters, 1977). In so doing, a developmental view dramatically shifts the kinds of questions researchers pose about human adaptation and the interpretation of their answers.

## A DEVELOPMENTAL VIEW OF CLINICAL RESEARCH

A developmental view of psychopathology shifts the empirical emphasis away from the search for static behavioral isomorphisms of disorder that typifies traditional psychiatric approaches and toward an exploration of patterns of change and continuity in the function of adaptive organizations over time. A developmental analysis examines networks of developmental influence that are probabilistically associated with the initiation, maintenance, or redirection of pathological pathways. Because disorder reflects dynamic transactions across biological, psychological, environmental, *and* historical influences, understanding disorder *requires* a developmental view. In the following sections, we draw on select examples to illustrate core tenets of a developmental perspective and their applications in clinical research.

## Early Experience is Special: A Developmental View of the Dissociative Disorders

All adaptation, including maladaptation, is grounded in prior experience. Yet the meaning of early experience may change as a function of time, context, and/or subsequent events. Just as experience influences current adaptation, current adaptation (and the experience it engenders) may alter the influence of history. A developmental analysis of disorder extends beyond an appreciation for nature and nurture to incorporate the individual's developmental history as a powerful and heretofore underappreciated developmental force. In so doing, however, this perspective also acknowledges that the influence of history may be transformed as a function of more recent experience. Thus, a developmental analysis yields a dynamic, yet developmentally anchored, view of psychopathology.

The MPCLS has documented the unique importance of early experience in development across a range of both positive and problematic outcomes (Egeland, Carlson, & Sroufe, 1993; Sroufe et al., 1990), including dissociation (Ogawa, Sroufe, Weinfield, Carlson, & Egeland, 1997). The dissociative disorders encompass a class of maladaptive organizations wherein there is a fundamental disconnect among memory, identity, emotion, and cognition that interferes with the negotiation of age-salient issues (Braun, 1988; Carlson, Yates, & Sroufe, 2009; Putnam, 1997). Dissociation was among the first pathological conditions to benefit from a developmental awareness in the writings of Breuer, Freud, Janet, and others who recognized the salience of early (traumatic) experience in the elaboration of dissociative processes (Breuer & Freud, 1895/1955; Freud, 1926/1959; Janet, 1889). Yet a comprehensive developmental analysis advances beyond these linear predictions to examine the processes by which early experience contributes to pathological dissociation in a probabilistic, rather than deterministic, fashion (Carlson, Yates et al., 2009; Fink, 1988; Putnam, 1997).

MPCLS scholars were among the first to demonstrate prospective associations between early experiences of trauma and dissociative symptomatology across the preschool, elementary, adolescent, and young adult years (Ogawa et al., 1997). Moreover, mother-infant attachment organization explained additional interindividual variation in dissociative outcomes, revealing the unique influence of early experience on dissociative pathways. These findings paved the way for a comprehensive developmental analysis of dissociation that explained why, when, and for whom these relations would hold (Carlson, Yates et al., 2009).

Early experiences of overwhelming arousal capitalize on young children's natural predilection toward fragmented thinking and representation (Fischer & Ayoub, 1994; Fischer & Pipp, 1984). At a time when children naturally parse their experiential world into good/bad and me/not-me, traumatic experience may canalize normative dissociative tendencies into a fundamentally fragmented sense of self (Cicchetti, 1991; Cole & Putnam, 1992; Harter, 1999; Putnam, 1991). Particularly in the context of the early caregiving milieu, trauma may thwart the development of integrated, coherent cognitive-affective representations of self, other, and self-with-other, which typify organized attachment patterns, be they secure or insecure. In the context of repeated experiences of "fright without solution," wherein the child is simultaneously drawn to and repelled from a threatening caregiver, for example, individual systems of perceiving, thinking, and feeling may progress toward greater complexity in the absence of complementary integration, and dissociative pathology will ensue (Carlson, Yates et al., 2009; Hesse & Main, 2000).

As suggested by Liotti (1992; 1999), and empirically validated by the MPCLS (Carlson, 1998; Ogawa et al., 1997), disorganized attachment may confer a specific vulnerability to pathological dissociation in later development by instantiating a protodissociative pattern that will undergo further differentiation and consolidation in the context of ongoing or subsequent trauma. Thus, contemporaneous traumatic events can change the developmental significance of prior experience by crystallizing early dissociative tendencies into pathology. A history of disorganized attachment influences how the individual experiences and adapts to later trauma and, in turn, subsequent experiences of trauma strengthen the influence of disorganized attachment on later maladaptation. A developmental analysis acknowledges and explains the mobility of developmental influence through which early experience can affect later adjustment, and later adaptation can feedback to alter the subsequent influence (and meaning) of early experience. In this view, opportunities for developmental influence are both omnipresent and coherent, and early experience is special but not unilaterally causal.

The MPCLS studies of dissociation illustrate the patterning of development over time through successive organizations in which "history influences what is experienced, and experience alters history" (Sroufe et al., 2005, p. 229). A developmental approach to clinical research encourages explicit consideration of the cumulative yet dynamic meaning of experience. Furthermore, a developmental lens views the meaning of experience (both past and present) in the context of the entire developmental picture. By attending to the unique significance of early experience, a developmental analysis affords the opportunity to identify meaningful patterns of developmental deviation in advance of clinically significant syndromes, which provides invaluable guidance for targeted intervention and prevention efforts (Sroufe, 1989).

## Development is Multiply Determined: A Developmental View of ADHD

A developmental view is a probabilistic, systems view; it is not a causal view in which circumscribed pathogens linearly predict static disorders. Adaptations, including psychopathology, are supported by a network of developmental influences, both past and present (Sroufe, 1997). Thus, a developmental perspective on disorder shifts the focus of empirical attention away from the search for singular pathogens to the elucidation of developmental networks of historical and current influences that are probabilistically associated with the initiation and maintenance of (mal)adaptive pathways. By attending to transactions within and between levels of analysis, within and between historical and contemporaneous developmental influences, and within and between the person and multiple contexts, the MPCLS has consistently demonstrated that psychopathology "is a dynamic, not static phenomenon in which combinations of constraints on and inputs to adaptation vary over time" (Egeland, Pianta, & Ogawa, 1996, p. 747).

At a time when biological essentialism was the preeminent causal theory of attention deficit hyperactivity disorder (ADHD; e.g., Wender, 1971), MPCLS researchers documented the unique significance of relational factors in the initiation and maintenance of ADHD symptoms. Building on a solid understanding of the normative developmental processes that underlie typical arousal regulation, Jacobvitz and Sroufe (1987) demonstrated the unique contributions of intrusive and overly stimulating parenting behaviors in early childhood to hyperactivity and distractibility in later childhood. Importantly, these investigators pursued this analysis with the explicit aim of exploring both caregiving (i.e., experiential) and child (i.e., organic) contributions to the development of ADHD. Observations of maternal intrusiveness and stimulation were rated during the age-normative tasks of feeding, free play, and guided instruction at 6, 24, and 42 months of age, respectively. In addition, infant measures of temperament, attention, and reactivity were examined as putative predictors of the distractibility and hyperactivity that typify an adaptive organization consistent with ADHD in later childhood. Results indicated that caregiving behaviors were more strongly related to later ADHD symptoms than were biological developmental markers. Moreover, in cases where biological markers, such as motor maturity, did predict ADHD symptoms, the predictive contribution of caregiving variables was not significant, suggesting the presence of multiple and distinct pathways to disorder.

In its attention to, and incorporation of, age-appropriate transitions in salient contexts and developmental issues, this investigation was explicitly developmental in form. Moreover, by acknowledging and evaluating multiple sources of developmental influence, the MPCLS provided a complex and nuanced picture of the etiology of ADHD. This work demonstrates the unique information afforded by developmental investigations that recognize the potential for complementary, rather than competitive, origins of disorder. This study opened a range of avenues for future exploration, including the possibility that children may exhibit comparable levels of attentional dysfunction following distinct developmental trajectories with differentially firm roots in constitutional and/or caregiving factors (i.e., equifinality; Cicchetti & Rogosch, 1996).

Within a developmental-organismic view, disorder is conceptualized as a dynamic developmental process, not a static condition the child *has*; it describes adaptation, but does not explain it. This developmental premise stands in stark contrast to classical tautologies, which presume that a child has certain problems because s/he has a specific disorder, and, in turn, diagnose a child as having the disorder because s/he exhibits those problems. A thoroughgoing developmental analysis would no sooner conclude that a child is disruptive and distractible *because* s/he has ADHD, than it would justify a diagnosis of ADHD on the basis of these same behaviors. A developmental perspective on disorder explicitly attends to both developmental history and current experience across multiple levels of analysis and influence. In this view, a child disrupts other students in class because her/his prior development hindered the acquisition of normative capacities for arousal modulation *and* her/his current environment challenges these capacities in the absence of adequate supports (Sroufe et al., 2005). As demonstrated by Jacobvitz and Sroufe (1987), a developmental analysis of ADHD begins with the assumption that attentional functioning is itself a multiply determined developmental construction, just as the MPCLS's developmental analysis of dissociation began with the recognition that an integrated and coherent self is a developmental construction. In a developmental framework, diagnosis is the start of the analysis, not the end.

## Disorder is Adaptive: A Developmental View of Nonsuicidal Self-Injury

As noted previously, disorder is adaptation; it follows from the same succession of organizational differentiation and hierarchical integration that typifies positive development. A developmental analysis begins with the assumption that disorder is a reflection of the individual's best efforts to cope with contemporaneous challenges in the context of historical, current, and multilevel influences. As observed by Sameroff (1989), "illnesses are indeed achievements that result from the active strivings of each individual to reach an adaptive relation to his or her environment" (p. 63). Thus, in seeking to understand psychopathology, a developmental analysis does not begin with the question, "what is wrong with this person?," nor does it seek to identify the environmental contingencies that reinforce her/his maladaptive behavior. Rather, a developmental analysis starts with the clinically paradoxical, but developmentally sensible questions, "How is this adaptive organization functional?" and "What are the normative developmental processes that preclude most people from coming up with this particular solution to the challenge of development?" These questions follow from the underlying developmental premise that disorder is adaptive. Yet the quality of this organization and its consequent utility for negotiating developmental challenges vary as a function of both historic and contemporaneous resources to which the person may avail her/himself in the service of adaptation.

A developmental view of disturbance as adaptation remains intellectually productive in the face of even the most extreme developmental deviations, such as nonsuicidal self-injury (NSSI; e.g., cutting, burning). Empirical and applied efforts have shifted from the search for static behavioral isomorphisms of NSSI in early development (e.g., infant head banging; Green, 1978) and the marginalizing treatment of persons who self-injure in practice, toward an appreciation of NSSI as a powerful tool for regulating overwhelming affects and relationships when the normative representational and regulatory capacities that render NSSI unnecessary for most people have been undermined (Yates, 2004, 2009). Mounting evidence supports the role of NSSI as a compensatory adaptive strategy in the context of prior and/or concurrent vulnerability. Offering the first longitudinal analysis of the development of NSSI, the MPCLS demonstrated prospective relations between child maltreatment and NSSI in young adulthood (Yates, Carlson, & Egeland, 2008). Moreover, observed pathways between maltreatment and recurrent NSSI were partially explained by trauma-induced deficits in emotion processing and cognitive-affective integration (e.g., somatization, dissociation). When asked about motivations for engaging in NSSI, participants consistently identified NSSI as a powerful compensatory strategy in posttraumatic adaptation, permitting them to cope with overwhelming affect and arousal in lieu of normative symbolic and integrative regulatory capacities (Nock & Prinstein, 2004; Yates et al., 2008). Thus, even in cases of self-injury, the undergirding developmental force is one of survival and adaptive striving. In this way, a developmental analysis brings the person who injures out of the isolation of the "disturbed" individual and into the company and humanity of the "adapting" individual who is negotiating the challenges of development within the confines of available resources, be they regulatory, relational, or material. In this view, NSSI, and psychopathology in general, is a maladaptive means to reach an adaptive end.

## Summarizing a Developmental View of Clinical Research

As demonstrated in the MPCLS's studies of dissociation, ADHD, and NSSI, as well as in a host of other domains, including the behavioral and affective disorders (e.g., Aguilar, Sroufe, Egeland, & Carlson, 2000; Bosquet & Egeland, 2006; Duggal, Carlson, Sroufe, & Egeland, 2001), Byron Egeland, Alan Sroufe, and their collaborators have broadened the domain of developmental psychology to include psychopathology. Employing normative developmental patterns and processes to understand developmental exceptions and deviations, the MPCLS is a testament to the intellectual and applied productivity of developmentally informed research on maladaptation. A developmental perspective on clinical research recognizes that disorder is uniquely influenced by early experience, is an outgrowth of multiple developmental influences, and, perhaps most importantly, is a form of adaptation. Therefore, a productive clinical science is fundamentally a science of development—one in which clinical classification and practice take on new meaning.

# A DEVELOPMENTAL VIEW OF CLINICAL CLASSIFICATION

On the heels of the American Psychiatric Association's (APA) publication of the third edition of the *Diagnostic and Statistical Manual of Mental Disorders* (DSM-III) in 1980, which introduced a new category of "disorders usually first diagnosed in infancy, childhood, or adolescence," Sroufe and Rutter (1984) observed that "current diagnostic classification schemes pay scant attention to development" (p. 24). Writing at the same time, Garber (1984) argued that the absence of a reliable and valid system for classifying emotional and behavioral disorders of childhood significantly hampers efforts to apply a developmental framework to the study of psychopathology. She further noted that, "despite arguments to the contrary (e.g., Santostefano, 1971), the developmental model is not by definition antagonistic to nosology" (p. 31). In fact, a developmental perspective is necessary to construct a reliable and valid system for classifying emotional and behavioral disorders in childhood, adolescence, and adulthood. Thus, clinical classification and developmental science are inextricably linked. In this section, we evaluate contemporary approaches to developmental classification in the DSM, identify core features of a developmental perspective that can and should inform our approaches to classification, and highlight promising instances of developmentally informed classification in research on pediatric behavior problems and, to a somewhat lesser degree, personality disorders.

## DSM-5 and (the Myth of) Developmental Classification

As we review the latest iteration of the APA's DSM-IV-TR (2000) and anticipate the release of the DSM-5, we find developmental principles still fighting for footing in contemporary classification approaches. Even when issues of development have received explicit nosological consideration, it has merely reified rather than rectified the shortcomings of contemporary classification. For example, reviewing the addition of the attachment disorders to the DSM-IV, Sroufe (1997) observed that mainstream psychiatry missed a real chance to introduce a developmental approach to disorder by labeling particular attachment variations as "disorder" and isolating them to a classification of their own, rather than recognizing that attachment is a significant initiating organization for many different kinds of psychopathology. Although both the attachment disorders and the earlier introduction of posttraumatic stress disorder in the DSM-III (1980) represent a modicum of progress because they acknowledge extraorganismic etiologic factors, contemporary approaches to classification have not yet fully integrated a developmental perspective on disorder.

Looking ahead to the DSM-5, developmental issues pertaining to pathways, age-salient referents, and multilevel analyses have been prominent in discussions of the DSM revision. In their contribution to the planning paper, *A Research Agenda for DSM-V* (Kupfer, First, & Regier, 2002), Pine and colleagues (2002) proposed several research directives related to development and classification, including, among other things, integrating neuroscience and genetics into the classification system, devoting greater attention to issues of culture and context in youth, and fostering additional connections with normative developmental research on processes such as attention, memory, and emotion regulation. In delineating directions for future research, Pine and colleagues focus both on the general multiaxial diagnostic system of the DSM and on issues that are more central to particular diagnoses. For example, they suggest that the current DSM grouping of ADHD symptoms into three distinct categories, leading to a single dichotomous diagnostic decision, may not be fully consistent with modern research on the substrates of attention, which highlights clinically meaningful distinctions among different types of attentional processes (e.g., set shifting versus orienting) and integrative constructs that are largely absent from the DSM (e.g., executive function; Nigg, Hinshaw, & Huang-Pollock, 2006; Pennington & Ozonoff, 1996).

Although the commentary of Pine and colleagues (2002) was a laudable attempt by researchers close to the DSM planning process to inject a truly developmental perspective into the classification system, their calls for action have been muted by the pragmatic constraints of implementation. Developmental issues seem to have receded from the picture as the field moves toward specific classification and criterion operationalization processes that signal the impending completion of the DSM-5. In a more recent planning document, *Age and Gender Considerations in Psychiatric Diagnosis* (Narrow, First, Sirovatka, & Regier, 2007), a developmental perspective is strikingly absent, despite the obvious relevance of developmental concepts to the material at hand. With very few exceptions (see the discussion of Wakschlag et al., 2007, as follows), the chapters in this planning document focus on the feasibility of applying existing (or slightly modified) DSM criteria to younger and/or older populations than are typically included in clinical research studies. While this may be a legitimate goal, it sidesteps the important issues of multilevel dynamics and normative developmental research raised by Pine and colleagues (2002) in their earlier commentary. In the next section, we identify core implications of a developmental perspective for classification and highlight pediatric behavior problems and personality disorders as promising domains where these ideas may gain prominence in future classification schemes.

## Classifying Disorder as Classifying Development

Dynamic models of disorder necessitate dynamic models of classification. Indeed, efforts to classify disorder may be better conceptualized as efforts to classify development itself. As discussed previously, development is embodied in patterns of adaptive organizations over time, the quality of which is evaluated with respect to the individual's ability to negotiate age-salient issues, and the cause of which stems from a network of developmental influences across multiple levels of analysis, including prior experience.

### Developmental Pathways

Theorists in developmental psychopathology have elaborated the usefulness of developmental pathways—distinct routes by which an individual or group of individuals arrive at a particular (often maladaptive) outcome (Loeber, 1991)—as a metaphor to guide research and practice (Rutter, 1989; Sroufe, 1989). In light of these probabilistic pathways, static classification paradigms run the risk of aggregating meaningfully distinct subgroups of individuals who arrive at a particular adaptive organization via distinct trajectories (i.e., equifinality) and/or who progress from a singular organization to diverse outcomes (i.e., multifinality; Cicchetti & Rogosch, 1996). Recall, for example, the case of ADHD wherein the behavioral picture at age 6 was virtually indistinguishable between youth who seemed to have a more experientially influenced course to disorder and youth with a more organismically rooted pathway to disorder (Jacobvitz & Sroufe, 1987). As yet another example, both insomnia and a lesion in the prefrontal cortex will contribute to deficits in organizing and planning, decreased short-term memory capacity, and problems with impulse control and emotion regulation. Only by attending to the developmental history of the symptomatic organism can we discern the initiating conditions and probabilistic mechanisms underlying psychopathology.

The recognition that heterogeneity is meaningful and that continuity may rest at the level of functional pathways rather than static form has important implications for diagnosis, treatment, and prognosis. For example, this kind of model may justify a classification system based on developmental pathways rather than isolated adaptations (Loeber, 1991; Loeber et al., 1993). To date, pathway approaches to classification have tended to focus on differences in the timing of behavioral symptoms, with perhaps the best-known example being the distinction between early- and late-onset conduct problems (Moffitt, 1993; Patterson, DeBaryshe, & Ramsey, 1989). Moffitt's (1993, 2006) attention to variation in timing complements the long-standing appreciation of variation in form that characterized prior descriptive classifications in the antisocial/conduct domain (e.g., overt versus covert behaviors; Loeber & Schmaling, 1985). Pathway approaches encourage the incorporation of multiple levels of analysis, rather than making distinctions solely on the basis of the form or timing of behavioral symptoms (see Pickles & Hill, 2006, for additional examples of this approach).

MPCLS findings suggest important environmental and contextual differences between children who do and do not manifest early conduct problems. In a study by Aguilar and colleagues (2000), youth who manifested both persistent oppositional behavior in childhood and conduct problems in adolescence experienced higher levels of early psychosocial risk (e.g., low socioeconomic status, single-parent household, high parental life stress) as compared with youth who initiated conduct problems in adolescence. However, only childhood temperamental and neuropsychological variables, not infant temperament, discriminated the two groups. A pathways approach to classification has the potential to reveal meaningful heterogeneity in development and process, which may be occluded by traditional, static classification systems. The pathways metaphor has encouraged empirical efforts, such as those of Aguilar and colleagues (2000), to tease apart different constellations of etiological factors that underlie disorder, particularly given evidence that these patterns may have diagnostic and prognostic significance (e.g., Fowles & Dindo, 2006; Stieben et al., 2007). In addition, increased attention to developmental pathways in future classification efforts may clarify processes underlying apparent comorbidity, given that prior developmental history can influence the interpretation of complex sets of symptoms, including those that transcend different DSM disorders.

Although not explicitly tied to developmental pathways, it is important to acknowledge a modicum of progress toward the goal of integrating pathways concepts into contemporary classification schemes in the hopes that we can continue to build on this effort. For example, one widely accepted set of criteria for diagnostic validation, Cantwell's (1996) updating of the classic Robins and Guze (1970) criteria, emphasizes *natural history* as a potential tool for separating discrete disorders, in addition to psychosocial, demographic, biological, genetic, and family environment factors, as well as clinical descriptors and response to treatment. In practice, however, this appreciation for the informativeness of developmental history is often constrained to the "history of the specific presenting symptoms." Likewise, research on early- and late-onset conduct problems has resulted in a specific age cutoff for conduct disorder symptoms in DSM subtyping that may not best represent the research evidence. Nevertheless, we continue to encourage the evaluation and expansion of this criterion to incorporate a developmental pathways approach in classification.

### Age-Salient Referents

With far too few exceptions, contemporary classification approaches apply uniform criteria sets to the evaluation of functioning across the developmental continuum. However, because the meaning of behavior changes over time, we must evaluate its adaptive significance with respect to age (Sroufe & Rutter, 1984). As discussed earlier, the coherence of development, including that which is disordered, rests at the level of meaning and function, not manifest form (Sameroff & Chandler, 1975; Waddington, 1940). Children possess different cognitive, linguistic, physiological, and emotional resources over time, which may alter the expression of disorder and/or the developmental significance of those expressions (see Loeber & Hay, 1997; Patterson, 1993, for discussions of changes in the expression of conduct problems over time). Returning to the case of ADHD, extant research has been hampered by a faulty assumption that ADHD is expressed in similar behaviors across the developmental course. In this case, the adoption of developmentally inappropriate, static criteria conflated changes in disorder expression with developmental change, leading to erroneous assertions that ADHD symptoms decline with advancing age (Faraone, 2000; Willoughby, 2003). Although age-salient referents may be especially important in the early years when children develop at a relatively rapid pace, they remain relevant throughout development.

On a related theme, growing evidence points to the significance of age of onset in the etiology, phenomenology, and prognosis of specific disorders. In the case of conduct problems, for example, childhood-onset is associated with different correlates and long-term prognosis than adolescent-onset (Aguilar et al., 2000; Moffitt, 1993, 2006). Additional evidence suggests that early-onset conduct problems are associated with higher levels of conduct disorder in family members, suggesting a disproportionate genetic contribution to conduct problems that begin in childhood (Taylor, Iacono, & McGue, 2000). However, as noted in a recent review by Rutter (2005), an alternative explanation for this pattern may be that higher levels of conduct problems in the immediate family contribute to greater levels of environmental adversity, which foster the early initiation of conduct-disordered pathways. Contemporary classification efforts must attend to the multiple implications of age, both with respect to describing disorder in terms of age-salient manifestations and to clarifying the causes and consequences of disorder as a function of differential ages of onset. Together, these efforts will ensure that our classification system accurately accommodates potential shifts in the form or significance of specific maladaptive organizations over time.

## Multilevel Analyses

The application of multilevel analyses to psychiatric classification has garnered much attention in recent years but few concrete proposals. Progress has come through planning documents that emphasize the importance of both broader cultural/societal differences in criteria as well as neurobiological indices relevant to diagnosis (e.g., Pine et al., 2002). Of course, multilevel analyses call for the meaningful combination of data across levels, such as the interaction of genetic and biological markers with behavioral and contextual criteria. However, the use of such markers in formal diagnosis requires adequate sensitivity and specificity, which presupposes a gold standard of validation that may or may not be forthcoming. It is possible that the effective incorporation of neurobiological markers in classification will only proceed alongside a more radical reconceptualization of the nature of disorder.

Moreover, neurophysiological or biochemical correlates of disturbance should be viewed as markers of a developmental process rather than causes per se (Sroufe et al., 2005). As noted previously, a developmental perspective recognizes that there is rarely a cause and an effect, a beginning and an end, because development is always both—the individual is always creating and becoming. Thus, biological markers may be cause or effect and, in a developmental model, are not limited to one or the other such that a particular marker may be a cause for one person and an effect for another. Moreover, a marker may contribute to one pathway for one individual but to a very different trajectory for a different person. For example, Calkins (1994) notes that autonomic and central nervous system reactivity can lead to either aggression or positive social engagement in later childhood, depending on intervening experiences with caregivers. What appears as vulnerability in one context may emerge as strength in another; thus, there is no disturbance, only difference, the adaptive significance of which is multiply determined and necessarily anchored in development.

## Summary

Developmental pathways, age-salient referents, and multilevel analyses are not the only relevant considerations for developmental approaches to clinical classification; however, they are some of the key themes that emerge from broader discussions of developmental psychopathology (Garber, 1984; Rutter & Sroufe, 2000; Sroufe, 1997). Classification researchers must also negotiate historical and professional trends of the DSM system, a detailed review of which is beyond the scope of this chapter. In fact, one might argue that true incorporation of developmental principles into the DSM system is quite difficult, or perhaps impossible. However, there are select cases where we can see the potential for progress and its grounding in developmental science.

## A Developmental Approach to Assessment: Pediatric Behavior Problems

As reviewed previously, disorder is adaptation, and the quality of this adaptation is dependent on environmental, biological, temporal, cultural, and other factors. Behaviors that undermine competence in one setting may engender it in other contexts. The dynamic yet coherent patterning of development over time, age, and context necessarily complicates processes of assessment, diagnosis, and classification. Yet, efforts that incorporate developmental pathways, age-salient referents, and multi-level analyses show promise in the field of pediatric behavior disorders.

The Disruptive Behavior Diagnostic Observation Schedule (DB-DOS; Wakschlag et al., 2005, 2007, 2008) is a structured observation protocol for distinguishing age-normative disruptive behavior from that which indicates a psychopathological process. The DB-DOS represents an advance toward incorporating developmental theory into the formal DSM process. This approach adopts an *explicitly* developmental framework, which was reviewed and elaborated by Wakschlag, Tolan, and Leventhal (2010), to distinguish the usual "terrible twos and threes" from serious oppositional and disruptive behavior problems in early childhood by integrating structured tasks that "press" for problem behaviors, given evidence from the MPCLS that the meaning and interpretation of behavior can vary dramatically across relational contexts (Egeland et al., 1996; Sroufe et al., 2005).

Several of the specific DB-DOS tasks are drawn from normative developmental research designed to assess constructs, such as emotion regulation and impulse control, including tasks closely related to those developed in the early stages of the MPCLS, such as the "tool problems" task in which frustration is elicited through increasingly difficult problem-solving challenges to evaluate children's coping resources in both low- and high-demand settings (Matas, Arend, & Sroufe, 1978). In addition, the DB-DOS extends beyond quantitative assessments, to evaluate *qualitative* distinctions in behavior, such as the difference between negative affect elicited in the context of positive social stimuli versus negative affect elicited in the context of frustration. Finally, this multifaceted assessment tackles one of the most vexing aspects of child assessment—the context-specificity of behavior problems—by observing child behavior in multiple contexts that vary the stressors presented to the child, including parent with child, child with engaged observer, and child with unengaged observer. This type of assessment advance is not without challenges in terms of heightened training and administration resource demands. However, early results suggest that the DB-DOS adds crucial information to the clinical assessment process, with incremental validity over parent and teacher reports of disruptive behavior demonstrated concurrently and at one-year follow-up (Wakschlag et al., 2007, 2008).

The DB-DOS is consistent with the broad developmental classification themes noted earlier. A developmental systems approach underlies the major rationale for the instrument's creation in that only some preschoolers demonstrating high levels of anger, frustration, and aggression are considered disordered. Furthermore, one must observe behavior across contexts to determine this diagnosis, rather than rely solely on aggregated broad informant ratings. Age-salient tasks such as frustration tolerance, set-shifting, and delay of gratification are incorporated explicitly into the DB-DOS modules. Finally, although not designed to cross into the neurobiological level, data from multiple levels of analysis are available from the DB-DOS via coding schemes for parental behavior in the parent-child context, as well as for child behavior across all three contexts. Multifaceted, developmentally informed assessment tools will pave the way for similarly developmental classification approaches in the future. We anticipate that the DB-DOS will be a key contributor to a thoroughgoing integration of a developmental perspective into future classification systems for pediatric behavior problems.

## A Developmental Approach to Classification: Personality Disorders

Building on a strong legacy of research documenting the coherent developmental progression of personality (Block & Block, 1973; Caspi & Roberts, 1999; Sroufe et al., 2005), formal discussions of the developmental nature of personality disturbance have appeared in the recent literature (Cohen, Crawford, Johnson, & Kasen, 2005; Freeman & Reinecke, 2007; Johnson et al., 2005). These discussions have taken various forms, as reflected in the recent special issues of *Development and Psychopathology* (Cicchetti & Crick, 2009a, 2009b), which include articles demonstrating important precursors to DSM-defined personality disorders, describing processes in childhood and adolescence that are dynamically related to personality disturbance more broadly, and/or discussing developmental issues related to the classification of personality disorders. The latter papers include arguments for incorporating mental representations, coping strategies, and narrative identities into adolescent research connecting personality traits and personality disorders (Shiner, 2009), as well as an extensive review of childhood precursors to personality disorder that supports prior calls for a dimensional classification approach (Tackett, Balsis, Oltmanns, & Krueger, 2009). As a whole, this set of papers is extensively informed by MPCLS research and includes a direct report from the MPCLS that documents the mediating role of self-representation in middle childhood in prospective associations between attachment disorganization in infancy and symptoms of borderline personality disorder in adolescence (Carlson, Egeland, & Sroufe, 2009).

Spurred on by burgeoning evidence that personality functioning is best understood with reference to normative developmental patterns, the development and potential adoption of a continuous/dimensional system for the classification of personality disorders on Axis II of the DSM has been a major topic of discussion throughout the ongoing DSM revision process and is a common theme in several of the papers cited earlier.

Commentators have remarked for some time on the difficulties inherent in the existing categorical classification system for Axis II (e.g., Widiger & Kelso, 1982), with particular concerns raised about the arbitrary nature of the broad cluster categories and the challenge of researching conditions with numerous polythetic criteria sets such that individuals formally meeting diagnostic criteria for the same personality disorder may share few or no common symptoms. The transition to a dimensional system for classifying personality disorder has been slowed by a relative lack of consensus in the personality literature on which dimensions would most appropriately characterize the descriptive variation currently captured in Axis II of the DSM. However, that situation may be changing, as adult personality and clinical researchers appear to be converging on candidate dimensional traits that can serve as an alternative classification framework for personality psychopathology (e.g., Widiger, Livesley, & Clark, 2009). Under these systems, individuals would be assessed on a small number of bipolar dimensions that roughly correspond to four of the Big Five (Costa & McCrae, 1992) factors of mainstream personality research (i.e., neuroticism, agreeableness, conscientiousness, and extraversion). Further assessment would emphasize more fine-grained subscales as indicated by the pattern of obtained scores across the broad domains (e.g., Reynolds & Clark, 2001).

Although not explicitly developmental, this type of classification proposal is worthy of discussion for several reasons. To begin with, it is of note that adult personality researchers have succeeded in bringing a dimensional model to near-fruition within the framework of the DSM planning process. This is no small achievement and has only been accomplished with a tremendous amount of persistence. Second, although limited by a focus on trait-like descriptors of behavior, the proposed system describes phenotypic variability with arguably more nuance and detail than the subscales most commonly used in child assessment. Third, the pathological variants of the Big Five studied in adult research evidence a similar hierarchical factor structure in youth. Although care should be taken not to rely on a sole source of measurement (self- or parent-report questionnaire items), this research suggests that it is possible to link models of personality pathology across the lifespan and opens doors for further developmental work (De Clerq, De Fruyt, Van Leeuwen, & Mervielde, 2006). Fourth, and most important, to a large degree, the concepts and measures employed in these recent discussions are the same as those employed in research on normative personality. Thus, these approaches more fully realize the mutually informing nature and desirable integration of normative and clinical functioning.

At the same time, it is important to note that potentially informative personality disorder classification proposals have emerged that more explicitly take into account developmental issues and/or deliberately operate outside of the formal DSM system. One example of the latter is work by Depue (2009) and colleagues (Depue & Lenzenweger, 2005, 2006) on a neurobehavioral dimensional model of personality pathology. By linking personality pathology to the neurobiological bases of anxiety, fear, affiliative reward, and other processes, the authors effectively remap the core divisions among personality constructs in a biologically plausible manner. More specifically, Depue (2009) has proposed that observed personality disturbance is a function of epigenetic influences on core neurobiological personality traits, and emphasizes, consistent with MPCLS findings and philosophy, that early experience may play a particularly important role in the "tuning" of traits such as neuroticism, which may promote risk for later personality disorder. It is important to recognize that progress on this type of neurobiologically plausible model requires one to essentially abandon the DSM Axis II categories, although particular behavioral symptoms grouped in those categories may remain quite relevant. Thus, this supports our prior assertion that the incorporation of neurobiological markers into contemporary classification systems will likely entail a radical reconceptualization of the nature of disorder.

## Summarizing a Developmental View of Clinical Classification

As we look ahead to the future of clinical classification, we do so with cautious optimism. Hopeful steps toward developmental approaches that incorporate adaptive pathways, age-graded criteria, and multilevel approaches to classification are balanced by seemingly intractable constraints of diagnostic tradition and feasibility. Even at its best, classification will remain an imperfect tool that necessarily compromises between the utility of discrete conceptions of adaptation and the complex, dynamic nature of real-world adaptation (Carey, 1990; Rutter & Sroufe, 2000). To the extent that we fail to recognize the limits of diagnostic classification as a descriptive, rather than explanatory tool, we run the risk of unnecessarily removing development from the scope of future clinical research. As much as possible, given practical constraints of funding priorities and macro trends in the field, classification research should proceed along several fronts simultaneously. Ideally, multiple concurrent approaches will yield theoretically informed, competing predictions that will validate, refine, or inform the integration of complementary classification approaches. In so doing, clinical and classification researchers will move toward a utilitarian (rather than deterministic) view of classification that is more akin to the approach used by front-line practitioners.

## A DEVELOPMENTAL VIEW OF CLINICAL PRACTICE

A developmental perspective has dramatically shifted our understanding of psychopathology, both empirically and practically. Yet the integration of knowledge between the empirical and applied worlds is an iterative process, one that can be frustratingly slow for researchers, clinicians, and clients alike. In this section, we present examples of specific assessment and intervention approaches that incorporate core features of a developmental perspective to illustrate how developmental theory can and should inform clinical practice. Coming full circle, we conclude by highlighting the reciprocally informative translation from clinical classification and practice to developmental theory and research.

### A Developmental Approach to Diagnostic Formulation

A developmental approach to diagnostic formulation begins with a presumption of complexity that far surpasses the bounds of a classifying package. In this view, diagnosis is part of the formulation, rather than the whole of it. Dynamic transactions within and across systems underlie both positive and problematic adaptation, simultaneously reflecting and contributing to the complexity of lived experience. A developmental lens brings the complexities of parenting, growing up, relating with others, as well as the problems associated with each, into clear relief. Similarly, a developmental formulation recognizes the challenge of understanding complex problems and of trying to address and talk about those complexities in real time.

Complexity is intrinsic to both development and lived experience. As naive developmental scientists, people generally understand that their difficulties are influenced by prior experience, follow from multiple factors, and largely reflect their best efforts given available resources. Although clients may appreciate many of the principles outlined earlier in this chapter, the developmentally informed clinician can help them organize and talk about their problems, strengths, and relationships, and encourage them to reflect on both their past and their future. Moreover, a developmental framework guides clinicians toward a diagnostic formulation that is reassuring for clients and their families as they feel the complexity they experience reflected and rendered comprehensible.

Clinical classification is a valuable tool for describing problems in development, but the developmental framework facilitates a greater understanding of a particular individual or family. The developmentally informed clinician integrates clients' lived experiences with larger, fundamental principles of development to create a shared formulation that clarifies how strengths and vulnerabilities came to be, and guides the collaborative identification of short-term, focused goals, while retaining a larger vision of the often harder and longer work of improving relationships and behavioral patterns—of changing developmental trajectories.

A developmental diagnostic formulation informs a multidimensional, tailored treatment plan as the clinician can call upon psychotherapy, environmental changes, or trials of medication, as well as their combination and ordering, in a way that logically follows a formulation of the client as embedded within a network of developmental influences across multiple levels of analysis. Developmental concepts such as probabilistic pathways and consequent capacities for multifinality and equifinality, for example, allow us to talk with a concerned parent about how a father who was diagnosed with ADHD may have encountered school difficulties that led him to associate with delinquent peers and precipitated a series of legal difficulties, while a son's developmental trajectory (though starting in a similar place) can be considerably different with appropriate and early intervention. A developmental formulation provides vocabulary and metaphors that encourage clients to appreciate their capacity for change, to believe in the mobility of meaning and function over time and contexts, and to understand the coherence underlying patterns of continuity and change in development. Thus, a developmental formulation paints a hopeful picture in which there is an enduring capacity for change and, even in the midst of extreme maladaptation, a shared humanity in which we are all more alike than we are different.

Recent efforts to codify developmental principles in standardized approaches to diagnostic formulation have yielded mixed results. The Therapeutic Assessment Model (TAM; Finn, 2007; Finn & Tosanger, 1997) advances beyond static labeling to put diagnostic formulation in the service of changing and improving clients' developmental trajectories. This approach emphasizes, in part, the importance of working collaboratively with clients to identify relevant clinical questions and, through a variety of assessment techniques, to incorporate information regarding current and past experience into working hypotheses concerning the origin of clients' difficulties and probable pathways toward positive change. Interestingly, adult clients were the primary focus of initial studies looking at the effectiveness of the TAM (Finn & Tosanger, 1992; Finn, 1996; Finn, 2007). Initial evaluations of the TAM distinguished between the use of assessment data to describe client functioning and the use of such data as tools for creating clinician–client collaboration in practice. For example, Finn and Tosanger (1992) demonstrated that clients who received feedback about personality testing in accordance with the TAM evidenced greater declines in distress and increases in self-esteem than those who were in the feedback-as-usual group.

Recent research and practice using the TAM with child and adolescent populations points to similarly promising results. This research has documented the unique benefits of including family sessions in pediatric assessments to facilitate greater understanding of the family context within which the child's problems persist, ensure a shared understanding of the clinical issues, and enlist the family as an agent of support and change (Tharinger et al., 2008; Tharinger et al., 2009). The TAM has also informed developmentally appropriate assessment feedback techniques for young children through the use of stories and fables (Tharinger et al., 2008). As we observed earlier in the case of (primarily) adult-oriented personality researchers contributing important insights about developmental classification approaches (Reynolds & Clark, 2001; Widiger et al., 2009), so, too, the TAM illustrates the potential contributions of adult practitioners and researchers to our ongoing progress toward developmentally sensitive approaches to diagnostic formulation and intervention. Ongoing reciprocities across levels of analysis (and practice), between child- and adult-focused scholars, and between basic and applied science, are essential to the integration of a comprehensive developmental approach in clinical research, classification, and practice (see the following discussion of transactional research and practice efforts).

Two additional trends in developmentally based assessment are worth mentioning. First, as noted previously in our discussion of the DB-DOS, assessment approaches that focus on direct observation of developmentally relevant symptoms and behaviors in young children are being emphasized. For example, in the Autism Diagnostic Observation Schedule (ADOS; Lord et al., 2000), the clinician engages the child in a series of semistructured interactions designed to elicit behaviors that are associated with autism spectrum disorders, such as eye contact, joint attention, and verbal communication. Second, the application of standardized mental health screening has increased in early development to identify protopathological patterns in settings where screening (and resultant prevention efforts) is likely to be most effective, such as pediatric clinics and schools. The Modified Checklist for Autism in Toddlers (M-CHAT; Robins, Fein, Barton, & Green, 2001) and the Autism Observation Scale for Infants (AOS; Bryson, Zwaigenbaum, McDermott, Rombough, & Brian, 2008) are two early screening tools that have gained widespread use in primary care settings to screen for autism spectrum disorders. Guided by empirical research documenting the disproportionate salience of early adaptational failures in pathological pathways (Egeland et al., 1993; Sroufe et al., 1990), early identification and intervention responsibilities have entered the domains of primary care providers and early educators (see Hagan, Shaw, & Duncan, 2008; Lawrence, Gootman, & Sim, 2009, for reviews of formal recommendations by the Institute of Medicine, the U.S. Preventive Services, and the American Academy of Pediatrics). Both broad-spectrum screening with instruments, such as the Pediatric Symptom Checklist (Hacker, Williams, Myagmarjav, Cabral, & Murphy, 2009; Jellinek et al., 1999), and disorder-specific assessments, such as suicide and depression screening for adolescents (Williams, O'Connor, Eder, & Whitlock, 2009), are increasingly common components of pediatric care, and these tools accurately identify the presence of disorder much earlier than would be the case without systematic screening.

## A Developmental Approach to Clinical Intervention

Previously, we demonstrated that disorder is an outgrowth of adaptive striving (Sameroff, 1989). A corollary to this idea is that, even within periods of broad maladaptation, there remains, at a minimum, some kind of intact system or adaptive developmental strength (Zigler & Glick, 1986). In the case of NSSI, for example, the injurer nevertheless retains the capacity to feel distress and the motivation to manage it. This shift in perspective informs and justifies a strength-based approach to intervention that engages clients' intrinsic motivation to adapt and harnesses their curiosity to explore how they arrived at a particular (mal)adaptive solution. By its nature, this kind of clinical engagement promotes a dynamic way of thinking about the child or family and creates a belief in the possibility for positive change. These ideas inform the practice of developmentally sensitive therapists and are well represented in several therapeutic approaches.

Psychodynamically-Oriented Brief Therapy, which is alternately termed Time-Limited Dynamic Psychotherapy or Brief Therapy, was developed, in part, as the response of some psychodynamic therapists to the constraints of managed care (Binder, 2004; Budman & Gurman, 1988; Davanloo, 2001; Gustafson, 1987; Mann, 1980; Sifneos, 1987; Strupp & Binder, 1984). Forced to distill psychodynamic therapy's most critical elements into a time-efficient and portable package, the developmental nature and focus of this therapeutic approach came into focus in an especially clear way. Core developmental constructs, such as the unique importance of early experience, adaptive pathways across time (and within the therapeutic arc), age-salient challenges, and temporal factors related to change and stability, were brought into clear relief as a function of this distillation. In addition, the therapeutic relationship, which was always central to psychodynamic and object relations therapies, took on renewed import as a key therapeutic variable and an agent of change in its own right (Safran & Muran, 1988).

In recent years, Dialectical Behavior Therapy (DBT; Linehan, 1993) has been adapted for clinical intervention with adolescents who exhibit early symptoms of borderline personality disorder and/or who are at elevated risk for suicidal and self-destructive behavior (Miller, Rathus, & Linehan, 2007). This approach capitalizes on the intensity of personality (re)organization during adolescence and young adulthood as a paradoxical period of both heightened risk for personality pathology and sensitivity to interventions that promote more adaptive developmental trajectories. In its most recent iterations, DBT is increasingly developmental in its explicit recognition that behavior, including self-destructive behaviors, follow from multifaceted pathways that reflect dynamic transactions between biological vulnerabilities and psychosocial risks over time, rather than discrete (and uniformly) pathological disorders (Crowell, Beauchaine, & Linehan, 2009). Through a variety of therapeutic techniques, and against the backdrop of a consistent and supportive therapeutic relationship, DBT attempts to improve individuals' core capacities for self-regulation and engender benign, flexible, and accurate expectations of self, other, and interpersonal relationships.

In early childhood, Parent-Child Interaction Therapy (PCIT; Eyberg, 1988, 2005) constitutes an empirically supported, developmentally informed intervention for children with disruptive behavior problems and their parents. PCIT recognizes that the parent-child relationship provides a powerful context for both understanding and changing behavioral patterns in young children (Egeland, Weinfield, Bosquet, & Cheng, 2000; Stern, 1985). Utilizing a variety of techniques, parent and therapist collaborate to understand the nature and effects of the parent's behavior on the child, to discover and practice new ways of interacting with the child, and to acknowledge both the problematic aspects of the parent's behavior and her/his capacity to modify those behaviors to change the child's behavior and experience of the world. Again, the message of this developmentally informed intervention is both honest and hopeful. Together, the parent and therapist work to create specific improvements in the child's behavior, as well as a broader foundation of security and satisfaction in the parent-child relationship on which the child can organize a more adaptive and competent developmental trajectory. In recent years, PCIT has extended beyond the global domain of pediatric behavior problems to address more circumscribed issues, including separation anxiety disorder (Pincus, Eyberg, & Choate, 2005), positive development in previously maltreated foster children (Timmer, Urquizq, & Zebell, 2005), and children with both behavioral problems and chronic illness (Bagner, Fernandez, & Eyberg, 2004; Bagner et al., 2009). Use of PCIT has also expanded across cultures (McCabe & Yeh, 2009) and continents (Leung, Tsang, Heung, & Yiu, 2009) with promising results.

Throughout this discussion of developmental approaches to clinical intervention, relationships—as the key developmental construct accessed indirectly through the therapeutic relationship or directly through interactions between child and parent—have been the central focus. Consistent with this emphasis, researchers and clinicians have sought to focus intervention efforts on correcting or strengthening the developing attachment relationship itself (Berlin, Ziv, Amaya-Jackson, & Greenberg, 2005; Egeland & Bosquet, 2002). The Child-Parent Psychotherapy (CPP) model developed by Alicia Lieberman (1992) is based on a developmental model that focuses on the organizing and regulating functions of the attachment relationship to reestablish trust and safety at the level of basic physiological and interpersonal functioning (Sroufe & Waters, 1977; Sroufe, Carlson, Levy, & Egeland, 1999). CPP is a well-researched, broadly applied intervention that has been shown to be especially effective in the treatment of traumatized young children (Lieberman, 2005; Lieberman, van Horn, & Ghosh-Ippen, 2005), as well as among toddlers of mothers with major depressive disorder (Toth, Rogosch, Manly, & Cicchetti, 2006), and among maltreated infants (Cicchetti, Rogosch, & Toth, 2006).

Attachment theory has also been used effectively as the basis of a preventive intervention approach for at-risk mother-child dyads in the Steps Toward Effective, Enjoyable Parenting Program model (STEEP; Egeland & Erickson, 2004; Erickson, Korfmacher, & Egeland, 1992). Guided by early findings from the MPCLS, Byron Egeland and colleagues designed the STEEP program to include home visits and group sessions that help parents understand their child's developmental needs and teach effective, sensitive, predictable, and responsive parenting practices that promote a secure attachment relationship. Using a group therapy format, the Circle of Security (COS; Hoffman, Marvin, Cooper, & Powell, 2006; Powell, Cooper, Hoffman, & Marvin, 2009) intervention model emphasizes the explanation of attachment concepts in everyday language to render them accessible to caregivers so as to support dyadic transitions from insecure attachment relationships to secure attachment organizations. Together, results from these developmentally informed intervention programs underscore the key influence of supportive parent-child relationships on adaptive and maladaptive youth outcomes, and emphasize the role of the clinician in guiding families' efforts to build such relationships.

## From Bench to Bedside and Back: Practice and Research in Translation and Reverse-Translation

Thus far, we have focused our discussion on the implications of a developmental frame for practice, but there is much to be learned from efforts to translate applied experience to developmental theory and research. Some have suggested that *transactional* would be a more fitting term than *translational* for capturing the reciprocity between practice and research, and the reality that both are changed as a function of their interaction (Aber, November 2009). As illustrated by the prescient studies of the MPCLS, developmental science can and should inform clinical classification, diagnostic formulation, and intervention across multiple levels by clarifying goals, identifying theoretical variables that can precipitate (or maintain) developmental change, guiding the measurement of key variables, and providing a conceptual framework within which to interpret findings (Yates & Masten, 2004). Perhaps most importantly, a developmental perspective recognizes the descriptive, rather than proscriptive, significance of disorder, thereby encouraging (and informing) efforts to modify patterns of change and continuity (Sroufe, 2007). In turn, interventions that aim to change the course of development provide a powerful arena in which to evaluate hypotheses about risk, protection, and development (Clingempeel & Henggeler, 2002; Howe, Reiss, & Yuh, 2002). Vygotsky (1978) observed that we must study the *process* of change for "it is only in movement that a body shows what it is" (p. 65). Practical applications of developmental principles offer the unique opportunity to observe experience-dependent plasticity in real time and across multiple levels (Cicchetti & Toth, 2009).

Coie and colleagues (1993) suggested that interventions "should be guided initially by developmental theory and yield results that reflexively inform and revise the original theory" (p. 1017). To this end, researchers have become increasingly sensitive to the importance of empirical work for practical innovations and applications (Cicchetti & Toth, 1992, 1999; Cicchetti & Hinshaw, 2002; Gunnar & Cicchetti, 2009; Toth, Manly, & Nilsen, 2008). However, the reverse-translation from practice to research remains variably misguided or altogether absent. All too often, researchers arrive at erroneous conclusions when they assume that the method of treatment (e.g., medication) provides causal information about the etiology of disorder without directly assessing the putative mechanism involved (e.g., biology; see Hinshaw, 2002, for a discussion of the treatment-etiology fallacy; see also Sroufe, 1997). At other times, researchers fail to capitalize on the potential for developmentally informed interventions to support or refine developmental theory in a recursive fashion.

Studies that demonstrate that changes in a hypothesized causal process (e.g., neuroendocrine function) occur as a result of intervention, and are associated with corresponding changes in the outcome of interest (e.g., improved child behavior), offer strong evidence in support of developmental theory (e.g., Dozier, Lindheim, & Ackerman, 2005; Fisher, Gunnar, Chamberlain, & Reid, 2000). To be sure, randomized controlled intervention trials, such as those of Fisher and colleagues (2000), constitute the gold standard for applied work to inform research (and subsequent practice). Yet, there is much to be said for basic application and basic research as important building blocks in the path toward truly transactional studies of development and psychopathology. The explicit goal of translational research is to refine and extend our understanding of human development in ways that further our progress toward real, positive, enduring, and developmentally sensitive change in the lives of children, families, and communities, and efforts to this end may take many forms (see Gunnar & Cicchetti, 2009, for discussion).

## Summarizing a Developmental View of Clinical Practice

This is an exciting and dynamic time in the fields of developmental psychology, child and adolescent clinical psychology, and psychiatry. As we consider how a developmental perspective has enriched our understanding of psychopathology, we must not lose sight of the ultimate goal of these efforts—a truer, more meaningful understanding of disorder, risk, and resilience as it occurs in the lives of real people. A developmental perspective on diagnostic formulation and clinical intervention is not a part of the story; it is not a piece of the diagnosis, or a stage of the treatment, it *is* the clinical practice. For the clinician with firm roots in developmental theory, day-to-day clinical practice is steeped with these constructs in clear and instructive ways that yield probabilistic diagnostic statements and intervention plans that are informed by research and tailored to the individual. Of equal importance, however, a developmental perspective gives us a natural, meaningful vocabulary to talk about continuity and transformation, as well as risk and resilience, with clients and families in ways that are both honest and hopeful.

## THROUGH THE LOOKING GLASS: A DEVELOPMENTAL VIEW INTO THE FUTURE

Upon finding herself lost in Wonderland, Alice queried the Cheshire Cat, "Do you know which way I ought to go from here?" and the cat observed, "That depends a good deal on where you want to get to." Yet, Rutter (1993) has aptly noted that "knowing what end you want to bring about and knowing *how* to achieve that objective are two very different things" (p. 630, emphasis in original). In this chapter, we assert that researchers, practitioners, and clients alike want (and will benefit from) a comprehensive integration of development in research, classification, and practice. To that end, we have endeavored to identify tangible signposts to guide our journey.

Decades have passed since a developmental view of disorder first came into focus, yet it remains vibrant and full of promise today. The future of developmental psychopathology is bright with robust bridges across prior dualisms between typical and atypical development, pathology and competence, and research and practice. Yet there are concerns ahead as well. In this final section, we look to the future to highlight areas for growth and refinement, as well as to anticipate potential areas for caution and concern.

First, we recognize the inherent potential of a lifespan perspective on development (Baltes, Lindenberger, & Staudinger, 2006), while remaining cognizant that the field has not yet realized a lifespan perspective in research and practice. Ten years ago, Rutter and Sroufe (2000) addressed this issue when they lamented the dearth of literature on the transition to adulthood. Since then, we have witnessed significant progress in this domain through the work of the MPCLS, Arnett, and others on the significance of emerging adulthood (e.g., Arnett, 2004; Masten et al., 2004; Roisman, Masten, Coatsworth, & Tellegen, 2004; Schulenberg, Sameroff, & Cicchetti, 2004; Sroufe, 2005). Now, ten years later, we extend Rutter and Sroufe's (2000) concern to encourage greater empirical and applied attention beyond this transition, across the spectrum of adulthood and into old age. As we have seen in the classification and treatment approaches discussed earlier, there is much to be learned from the study of adults and adulthood. In the future, developmental theory must explore what growing up can tell us about growing old, and, of equal importance, what growing old can teach us about growing up. To say that the study of psychopathology should be developmentally informed is not tantamount to saying that all disorder is rooted in childhood (Rutter, 1980). The roots of disorder are in development, development is lifelong, and a developmental approach to psychopathology should be too.

Second, we agree that "there is no aspect, activity, function, or structure of the psyche that is not subject to development" (Spitz, Emde, &

Metcalf, 1970, p. 417). Although we have limited our discussion here to the domain of psychopathology, we encourage future efforts to expand our appreciation for, and application of, developmental principles beyond the domain of psychopathology. As we look to the future, we see the value of increased attention to when and how developmental principles may further our understanding of disorders that are not tradition-ally conceptualized as psychiatric in nature. Applying basic principles of motor development to the case of sudden infant death syndrome (SIDS), for example, Lipsitt (2005) suggests that SIDS may follow from a deviation in what would otherwise be a normative progression toward increasing complexity, toward "a learned, adaptive response that can prevent death from suffocation" (p. 217). He suggests that the paradoxical vulnerability of older infants to SIDS may be explained by a problematic transition from the obligatory reflexes of the newborn period, which includes a respiratory occlusion reflex to prevent suffocation, to the more deliberate, cortically mediated behavior of the older infant. Applying a develop-mental perspective to SIDS, Lipsitt argues that efforts to identify factors that enable most babies to make a seamless transition from the reflexes of infancy to the learned defensive behaviors of later development will be most profitable for efforts to understand, and ultimately prevent, SIDS. Advancing beyond the confines of psychopathology in a different way, the MPCLS has demonstrated the utility of a developmental perspective in studies of positive development in both typical (e.g., Obradović, van Dulmen, Yates, Carlson, & Egeland, 2006; Sroufe et al., 1990; Sroufe, Egeland, & Carlson, 1999; Waters & Sroufe, 1983) and atypical contexts (Egeland et al., 1993; Yates, Egeland, & Sroufe, 2003).

Third, the multicausal nature of development necessitates the incor-poration of multilevel, interdisciplinary research and training. Beyond an appreciation for biological and social and emotional and cognitive facets of development as relevant—but independent—factors, a devel-opmental framework encourages the study of biological with social with emotional with cognitive levels of development. A "relational view of causality" (Gottlieb & Halpern, 2002) acknowledges the explanatory synergy of multilevel analyses. "The minimum unit for developmental analysis must be the developmental system, comprised of both the organism and the set of physical, biological, and social factors [and we would add historical factors] with which it interacts over the course of development" (Gottlieb, Wahlsten, & Lickliter, 1998, p. 260). Thus, students, clinicians, and researchers must possess (at least) a basic level of knowledge about development at each level of analysis, and research must continue to move toward interdisciplinary collabora-tions (Cacioppo, Bernston, Sheridan, & McLintock, 2000; Cicchetti & Dawson, 2002; Masten, 2007).

On a related note, efforts to capture the complexity of develop-ment bring with them unique opportunities and challenges. To be sure, explaining phenomena in terms of endogenous or even circumscribed factors is antithetical to a developmental analysis in which factors take their meaning only in relation to other variables given the absence of causal primacy. However, we must be careful to ensure that, in our recog-nition of multicausality and developmental complexity, we do not arrive at the antithesis of the medical tautology—a science with no begin-ning and no end. There is an inevitable tension between the desire (and need) for parsimonious models of development and the complex reality of the dynamic systems we seek to understand. Yet, in our effort to render developmental complexity comprehensible and, by extension, modifiable, we must take care not to render it meaningless. Following the logic of Occam's razor, we agree that the shortest distance between two points is a line, unless those points are moving, and unless those points are in dynamic transaction with one another. We echo Einstein in his assertion that "everything should be made as simple as possible, but not simpler" (as cited by Calaprice, 2000, p. 314).

Fourth, we must be cognizant that many developmental principles, including those reviewed here, are deceptively simplistic. However, there is a tendency to interpret longitudinal research designs as de facto studies of development. There remains a pressing need for methodo-logical (and statistical) advances that account for dynamic transactions within and across domains, within and over time. The past 30 years have witnessed tremendous advances in our abilities to capture dynamic and transactional developmental processes over time (Granic & Hollenstein, 2003; Sameroff & Mackenzie, 2003), as can be seen in studies of cascading developmental influences across domains (Burt, Obradović, Long, &

Masten, 2008; Masten et al., 2005; Yates, Obradović, & Egeland, 2010), of individual and clustered trajectories of intraindividual change (Nagin, 1999), and of dimensional representations of dyadic relationships (Hollenstein, 2007). These are impressive, albeit imperfect, approximations of developmental dynamics and complexity. Yet, as observed by Turkheimer and Waldron (2000), "the limitations of our existing social scientific methodologies ought not provoke us to wish that human behavior were simpler than we know it to be; instead they should provoke us to search for methodologies that are adequate to the task of understanding the exquisite complexity of human development" (p. 93).

Finally, we must continue to document and disseminate developmental applications in clinical science. Intellectual and conceptual silos still pepper the academic and applied landscapes. Cross-fertilization and interdisciplinary collaborations remain critical to our success in the future. Beyond speaking and writing about development and psychopathology, we must act to bring these principles to light in research, practice, and policy. To that end, we encourage ongoing appreciation for and reflection on the MPCLS as a model for action within and across these contexts.

The future of developmental science is bound to be both generative and challenging. As we reflect on the past 30 years in the field broadly, and specifically on the groundbreaking investigations of the MPCLS, we see tangible progress in clinical research, classification, and practice. Looking ahead to the future, we anticipate ongoing progress in each of these areas and hope that our efforts here contribute to further integration among them.

# REFERENCES

Aber, J. L. (November, 2009). *School-based strategies to prevent violence, trauma, and psychopathology: Can we get there from here?* Paper presented at the Mt. Hope Family Center's 30th Anniversary Symposium: Frontiers in Translational Research on Trauma, Rochester, NY.

Aguilar, B., Sroufe, L. A., Egeland, B., & Carlson, E. A. (2000). Distinguishing the early-onset/persistent and adolescence-onset antisocial behavior types: From birth to 16 years. *Development and Psychopathology, 12,* 109–132.

American Psychiatric Association. (1980). *Diagnostic and statistical manual of mental disorders* (3rd ed.). Washington, DC: American Psychiatric Association.

American Psychiatric Association. (2000). *Diagnostic and statistical manual of mental disorders* (4th text revision ed.). Washington, DC: American Psychiatric Association.

Arnett, J. J. (2004). *Emerging adulthood: The winding road from the late teens through the twenties.* New York, NY: Oxford University Press.

Bagner, D. M., Fernandez, M. A., & Eyberg, S. M. (2004). Parent-child interaction therapy and chronic illness: A case study. *Journal of Clinical Psychology in Medical Settings, 11*(1), 1–6.

Bagner, D. M., Sheinkopf, S. J., Miller-Loncar, C. L., Vohr, B. R., Hinkley, M., Eyberg, S. M., et al. (2009). Parent-child interaction therapy for children born premature: A case study and illustration of vagal tone as a physiological measure of treatment outcome. *Cognitive and Behavioral Practice, 16*(4), 468–477.

Baltes, P. B., Lindenberger, U., & Staudinger, U. M. (2006). Life span theory in developmental psychology. In W. Damon & R. M. Lerner (Eds.), *Handbook of child psychology* (6th ed., Vol. 1, pp. 1029–1143). Hoboken, NJ: Wiley.

Berlin, L. J., Ziv, Y., Amaya-Jackson, L. M., & Greenberg, M. T. (Eds.). (2005). *Enhancing early attachments: Theory, research, intervention, and policy.* New York, NY: Guilford Press.

Binder, J. L. (2004). *Key competencies in brief psychodynamic psychotherapy: Clinical practice beyond the manual.* New York, NY: Guilford Press.

Block, J., & Block, J. H. (1973). *Ego development and the provenance of thought: A longitudinal study of ego and cognitive development in young children.* Berkeley: University of California Press.

Bosquet, M., & Egeland, B. (2006). The development and maintenance of anxiety symptoms from infancy through adolescence in a longitudinal sample. *Development and Psychopathology, 18,* 517–550.

Braun, B. G. (1988). The BASK (behavior, affect, sensation, knowledge) model of dissociation. *Dissociation, 1*(1), 4–23.

Breuer, J., & Freud, S. (1895/1955). Studies on hysteria (J. Strachey, Trans.). In J. Strachey (Ed.), *The standard edition of the complete psychological works of Sigmund Freud* (Vol. 2). London, England: Hogarth Press. (original work published 1893–1895).

Bryson, S. E., Zwaigenbaum, L., McDermott, C., Rombough, V., & Brian, J. (2008). The Autism Observation Scale for Infants: Scale development and reliability data. *Journal of Autism and Developmental Disorders, 38*(4), 731–738.

Budman, S. H., & Gurman, A. S. (1988). *Theory and practice of brief therapy.* New York, NY: Guilford Press.

Burt, K. B., Obradović, J., Long, J. D., & Masten, A. S. (2008). The interplay of social competence and psychopathology over 20 years: Testing transactional and cascade models. *Child Development, 79*(2), 359–374.

Cacioppo, J. T., Bernston, G. G., Sheridan, J. F., & McLintock, M. K. (2000). Multilevel integrative analyses of human behavior: Social neuroscience and the complementing nature of social and biological approaches. *Psychological Bulletin, 126,* 829–843.

Calaprice, A. (Ed.). (2000). *The expanded quotable Einstein.* Princeton, NJ: Princeton University Press.

Calkins, S. (1994). Origins and outcomes of individual differences in emotion regulation. *Monographs for the Society for Research in Child Development, 59,* 53–72.

Cantwell, D. P. (1996). Classification of child and adolescent psychopathology. *Journal of Child Psychology & Psychiatry, 37*(1), 3–12.

Carey, S. (1990). On the relations between the description and explanation of developmental change. In G. Butterworth & P. Bryant (Eds.), *Causes of development* (pp. 135–160). New York, NY: Harvester Wheatsheaf.

Carlson, E. A. (1998). A prospective longitudinal study of attachment disorganization/disorientation. *Child Development, 69*(4), 1107–1128.

Carlson, E. A., Egeland, B., & Sroufe, L. A. (2009). A prospective investigation of the development of borderline personality symptoms. *Development and Psychopathology, 21,* 1311–1344.

Carlson, E. A., Yates, T. M., & Sroufe, L. A. (2009). Dissociation and development of the self. In P. F. Dell, J. O'Neil, & E. Somer (Eds.), *Dissociation and the dissociative disorders: DSM-V and beyond* (pp. 39–52). New York, NY: Routledge.

Caspi, A., & Roberts, B. W. (1999). Personality continuity and change across the life course. In L. A. Pervin & O. P. John (Eds.), *Handbook of personality: Theory and research* (2nd ed., pp. 300–326). New York, NY: Guilford Press.

Cicchetti, D. (1990). Perspectives on the interface between normal and atypical development. *Development and Psychopathology, 2,* 329–333.

Cicchetti, D. (1991). Fractures in the crystal: Developmental psychopathology and the emergence of self. *Developmental Review, 11,* 271–287.

Cicchetti, D., & Crick, N. R. (Eds.). (2009a). *Development and Psychopathology, special issue: Precursors and diverse pathways to personality disorder in children and adolescents—Part 2* (Vol. 21). New York, NY: Cambridge University Press.

Cicchetti, D., & Crick, N. R. (Eds.). (2009b). *Development and Psychopathology, special issue: Precursors and diverse pathways to personality disorder in children and adolescents—Part 1* (Vol. 21). New York, NY: Cambridge University Press.

Cicchetti, D., & Dawson, G. (Eds.). (2002). *Development and Psychopathology, Special issue: Multiple levels of analysis* (Vol. 14). New York, NY: Cambridge University Press.

Cicchetti, D., & Hinshaw, S. P. (2002). Editorial: Prevention and intervention science: Contributions to developmental theory. *Development and Psychopathology, 14,* 667–671.

Cicchetti, D., & Rogosch, F. A. (1996). Equifinality and multifinality in developmental psychopathology. *Development and Psychopathology, 8*(4), 597–600.

Cicchetti, D., Rogosch, F. A., & Toth, S. L. (2006). Fostering secure attachment in infants in maltreating families through preventive interventions. *Development and Psychopathology, 18*(3), 623–649.

Cicchetti, D., & Schneider-Rosen, K. (1986). An organizational approach to childhood depression. In M. Rutter, C. E. Izard, & P. B. Read (Eds.), *Depression in young people: Developmental and clinical perspectives* (pp. 71–134). New York, NY: Guilford Press.

Cicchetti, D., & Toth, S. L. (1992). The role of developmental theory in prevention and intervention. *Development and Psychopathology, 4,* 489–493.

Cicchetti, D., & Toth, S. L. (Eds.). (1999). *Rochester Symposium on Developmental Psychopathology: Developmental approaches to prevention and intervention* (Vol. 9). Rochester, NY: University of Rochester Press.

Cicchetti, D., & Toth, S. L. (2009). The past achievements and future promises of developmental psychopathology: The coming of age of a discipline. *Journal of Child Psychology & Psychiatry, 50*(1–2), 16–25.

Clingempeel, W. G., & Henggeler, S. W. (2002). Randomized clinical trials, developmental theory, and antisocial youth: Guidelines for research. *Development and Psychopathology, 14,* 695–711.

Cohen, P., Crawford, T., Johnson, J. G., & Kasen, S. (2005). The children in the community study of developmental course of personality disorder. *Journal of Personality Disorders, 19*(5), 466–486.

Coie, J. D., Watt, N. F., West, S. G., Hawkins, J. D., Asarnow, J. R., Markman, H. J., et al. (1993). The science of prevention: A conceptual framework and some directions for a national research program. *American Psychologist, 48,* 1013–1022.

Cole, P. M., & Putnam, F. W. (1992). Effects of incest on self and social functioning: A developmental psychopathology perspective. *Journal of Consulting and Clinical Psychology, 60*, 174–184.

Costa, P. T., & McCrae, R. R. (1992). *NEO-PI-R professional manual.* Odessa, FL: Psychological Publishing Resources.

Crowell, S. E., Beauchaine, T. P., & Linehan, M. (2009). A biosocial developmental model of borderline personality: Elaborating and extending Linehan's theory. *Psychological Bulletin, 135*(3), 495–510.

Davanloo, H. (2001). *Intensive short-term dynamic psychotherapy: Selected papers of Habib Davanloo, MD.* Hoboken, NJ: Wiley.

De Clerq, B., De Fruyt, F., Van Leeuwen, K., & Mervielde, I. (2006). The structure of maladaptive personality traits in childhood: A step toward an integrative developmental perspective for DSM-V. *Journal of Abnormal Psychology, 115*, 639–657.

Depue, R. A. (2009). Genetic, environmental, and epigenetic factors in the development of personality disturbance. *Development and Psychopathology, 21*, 1031–1063.

Depue, R. A., & Lenzenweger, M. F. (2005). A neurobehavioral dimensional model of personality disturbance. In J. F. Clarkin & M. F. Lenzenweger (Eds.), *Major theories of personality disorders* (2nd ed., pp. 391–454). New York, NY: Guilford Press.

Depue, R. A., & Lenzenweger, M. F. (2006). Toward a developmental psychopathology of personality disturbance: A neurobehavioral dimensional model. In D. Cicchetti & D. J. Cohen (Eds.), *Handbook of developmental psychopathology* (2nd ed., Vol. 2, pp. 762–796). Hoboken, NJ: Wiley.

Dozier, M., Lindheim, O., & Ackerman, J. P. (2005). Attachment and biobehavioral catch-up: An intervention targeting empirically identified needs in foster infants. In L. J. Berlin, Y. Ziv, L. Amaya-Jackson, & M. T. Greenberg (Eds.), *Enhancing early attachments: Theory, research, intervention, and policy* (pp. 178–194). New York, NY: Guilford Press.

Duggal, S., Carlson, E. A., Sroufe, L. A., & Egeland, B. (2001). Depressive symptomatology in childhood and adolescence. *Development and Psychopathology, 13*, 143–164.

Egeland, B., & Bosquet, M. (2002). Emotion regulation in early childhood: The role of attachment-oriented interventions. In B. S. Zuckerman, A. F. Lieberman, & N. A. Fox (Eds.), *Emotional regulation and developmental health: Infancy and early childhood* (pp. 101–124). Skillman, NJ: Johnson & Johnson Pediatric Institute.

Egeland, B., & Brunnquell, D. (1979). An at-risk approach to the study of child abuse: Some preliminary findings. *Journal of the American Academy of Child Psychiatry, 18*, 219–235.

Egeland, B., Carlson, E., & Sroufe, L. A. (1993). Resilience as process. *Development and Psychopathology, 5*(4), 517–528.

Egeland, B., & Erickson, M. F. (2004). Lessons from STEEP: Linking theory, research, and practice for the well-being of infants and parents. In A. J. Sameroff, S. C. McDonough, & K. L. Rosenblum (Eds.), *Treating parent-infant relationship problems: Strategies for intervention* (pp. 213–242). New York: Guilford.

Egeland, B., Pianta, R., & Ogawa, J. (1996). Early behavior problems: Pathways to mental disorders in adolescence. *Development and Psychopathology, 8*(4), 735–749.

Egeland, B., Weinfield, N. S., Bosquet, M., & Cheng, V. K. (2000). Remembering, repeating, and working through: Lessons from attachment-based interventions. In J. D. Osofsky & H. E. Fitzgerald (Eds.), *Infant mental health in groups at high risk. WAIMH handbook of infant mental health* (Vol. 4, pp. 35–89). Hoboken, NJ: Wiley.

Erickson, M. F., Korfmacher, J., & Egeland, B. (1992). Attachments past and present: Implications for therapeutic intervention with mother-infant dyads. *Development and Psychopathology, 4*(4), 495–507.

Eyberg, S. M. (1988). Parent-child interaction therapy: Integration of traditional and behavioral concerns. *Child & Family Behavior Therapy, 10*, 33–46.

Eyberg, S. M. (2005). Tailoring and adapting parent-child interaction therapy for new populations. *Education and Treatment of Children, 28*, 197–201.

Faraone, S. V. (2000). Attention-deficit hyperactivity disorder in adults: Implications for theories of diagnosis. *Current Directions in Psychological Science, 9*, 33–36.

Fink, D. L. (1988). The core self: A developmental perspective on the dissociative disorders. *Dissociation, 1*, 43–47.

Finn, S. E. (1996). Assessment feedback: Integrating MMPI-2 and Rorschach findings. *Journal of Personality Assessment, 67*, 543–557.

Finn, S. E. (2007). *In our clients' shoes: Theory and techniques of therapeutic assessment.* Mahwah, NJ: Erlbaum.

Finn, S. E., & Tosanger, M. E. (1992). Therapeutic effects of providing MMPI-2 test feedback to college students awaiting therapy. *Psychological Assessment, 4*(3), 278–287.

Finn, S. E., & Tosanger, M. E. (1997). Information-gathering and therapeutic models of assessment: Complementary paradigms. *Psychological Assessment, 9*, 374–385.

Fischer, K. W., & Ayoub, C. (1994). Affective splitting and dissociation in normal and maltreated children: Developmental pathways for self in relationships. In D. Cicchetti & S. L. Toth (Eds.), *Rochester Symposium on Developmental Psychopathology: Disorders and dysfunctions of the self* (Vol. 5, pp. 149–222). Rochester, NY: University of Rochester Press.

Fischer, K. W., & Pipp, S. L. (1984). Development and the structures of unconscious thought. In K. Bowers & D. Meichenbaum (Eds.), *The unconscious reconsidered* (pp. 88–148). New York, NY: Wiley.

Fisher, P. A., Gunnar, M. R., Chamberlain, P., & Reid, J. B. (2000). Preventive intervention for maltreated preschool children: Impact on children's behavior, neuroendocrine activity, and foster parent functioning. *Journal of the American Academy of Child and Adolescent Psychiatry, 39*(11), 1356–1364.

Fowles, D. C., & Dindo, L. (2006). A dual-deficit model of psychopathy. In C. J. Patrick (Ed.), *Handbook of psychopathy* (pp. 14–34). New York, NY: Guilford Press.

Freeman, A., & Reinecke, M. A. (Eds.). (2007). *Personality disorders in childhood and adolescence.* Hoboken, NJ: Wiley.

Freud, S. (1926/1959). Inhibitions, symptoms, and anxiety (J. Strachey, Trans.). In J. Strachey (Ed.), *The standard edition of the complete psychological works of Sigmund Freud.* London, England: W. W. Norton. (Original work published 1926.)

Garber, J. (1984). Classification of childhood psychopathology: A developmental perspective. *Child Development, 55*, 30–48.

Gottlieb, G., & Halpern, C. T. (2002). A relational view of causality in normal and abnormal development. *Development and Psychopathology, 14*, 421–435.

Gottlieb, G., D., Wahlsten, D., & Lickliter, R. (1998). The significance of biology for human development: A developmental psychobiological systems view. In R. Lerner (Ed.), *Handbook of child psychology* (Vol. 1, pp. 233–273). New York, NY: Wiley.

Granic, I., & Hollenstein, T. (2003). Dynamic systems methods for models of developmental psychopathology. *Development and Psychopathology, 15*(3), 641–669.

Green, A. H. (1978). Self-destructive behavior in battered children. *American Journal of Psychiatry, 135*, 579–582.

Gunnar, M. R., & Cicchetti, D. (2009). Meeting the challenge of translational research in child development. In M. R. Gunnar & D. Cicchetti (Eds.),

*Minnesota symposia on child psychology: Meeting the challenge of translational research in child psychology* (Vol. 35, pp. 1–27). Hoboken, NJ: Wiley.

Gustafson, J. P. (1987). *The complex secret of brief psychotherapy.* New York, NY: W.W. Norton.

Hacker, K. A., Williams, S., Myagmarjav, E., Cabral, H., & Murphy, M. (2009). Persistence and change in Pediatric Symptom Checklist scores over 10 to 18 months. *Academic Pediatrics, 9*(4), 270–277.

Hagan, J. F., Shaw, J. S., & Duncan, P. (Eds.). (2008). *Bright futures: Guidelines for health supervision of infants, children, and adolescents* (3rd ed.). Elk Grove Village, IL: American Academy of Pediatrics.

Harter, S. (1999). *The construction of the self: A developmental perspective.* New York, NY: Guilford Press.

Helfer, R. E. (1985). The medical model: In search of a definition. *Child Abuse & Neglect, 9,* 299.

Hesse, E., & Main, M. (2000). Disorganized infant, child, and adult attachment: Collapse in behavioral and attentional strategies. *Journal of the American Psychoanalytic Association, 48*(4), 1097–1127.

Hinshaw, S. P. (2002). Prevention/intervention trials and developmental theory: Commentary on the Fast Track special section. *Journal of Abnormal Child Psychology, 30*(1), 53–59.

Hoffman, K., Marvin, R., Cooper, G., & Powell, B. (2006). Changing toddlers' and preschoolers' attachment classifications: The Circle of Security intervention. *Journal of Consulting and Clinical Psychology, 74*(6), 1017–1026.

Hollenstein, T. (2007). State space grids: Analyzing dynamics across development. *International Journal of Behavioral Development, 31*(3), 384–396.

Howe, G. W., Reiss, D., & Yuh, J. (2002). Can prevention trials test theories of etiology? *Development and Psychopathology, 14,* 673–694.

Jacobvitz, D., & Sroufe, L. A. (1987). The early caregiver-child relationship and Attention-Deficit Disorder with Hyperactivity in kindergarten: A prospective study. *Child Development, 58*(6), 1496–1504.

Janet, P. (1889). *L'automatisme psychologique: Essai de psychologie expérimentale sur les formes inférieures de l'activité humaine.* Paris, France: Felix Alcan.

Jellinek, M. S., Murphy, J. M., Little, M., Pagano, M. E., Comer, D. M., & Kelleher, K. J. (1999). Use of the Pediatric Symptom Checklist to screen for psychosocial problems in pediatric primary care: A national feasibility study. *Archives of Pediatrics & Adolescent Medicine, 153*(3), 254–260.

Johnson, J. G., McGeoch, P. G., Caskey, V. P., Abhary, S. G., Sneed, J. R., & Bornstein, R. F. (2005). The developmental psychopathology of personality disorders. *Development and Psychopathology,* 417–464.

Kupfer, D. J., First, M. B., & Regier, D. A. (Eds.). (2002). *A research agenda for DSM-V*. Washington, DC: American Psychiatric Association.

Lawrence, R. S., Gootman, J. A., & Sim, L. J. (Eds.). (2009). *Adolescent health services: Missing opportunities*. Washington, DC: The National Academies Press.

Lazare, A. (1973). Hidden conceptual models in clinical psychiatry. *New England Journal of Medicine, 288*, 345–350.

Leung, C., Tsang, S., Heung, K., & Yiu, I. (2009). Effectiveness of Parent-Child Interaction Therapy (PCIT) in Hong Kong. *Research on Social Work Practice, 19*(3), 304–313.

Lieberman, A. F. (1992). Infant-parent psychotherapy with toddlers. *Development and Psychopathology, 4*, 559–574.

Lieberman, A. F. (2005). Traumatic stress and quality of attachment: Reality and internalization in disorders of infant mental health. *Infant Mental Health Journal, 25*(4), 336–351.

Lieberman, A. F., van Horn, P., & Ghosh-Ippen, C. (2005). Toward evidence-based treatment: Child-parent psychotherapy with preschoolers exposed to marital violence. *Journal of the American Academy of Child & Adolescent Psychiatry, 44*(12), 1241–1248.

Linehan, M. M. (1993). *Cognitive behavioral treatment of Borderline Personality Disorder*. New York, NY: Guilford Press.

Liotti, G. (1992). Disorganized/disoriented attachment in the etiology of the dissociative disorders. *Dissociation, 4*, 196–204.

Liotti, G. (1999). Disorganization of attachment as a model for understanding dissociative psychopathology. In J. Solomon & C. George (Eds.), *Attachment disorganization* (pp. 39–70). New York, NY: Guilford Press.

Lipsitt, L. P. (2005). Ignoring behavior science: Practice and perils. In D. B. Pillemer & S. H. White (Eds.), *Developmental psychology and social change: Research, history and policy* (pp. 203–221). New York, NY: Cambridge University Press.

Loeber, R. (1991). Questions and advances in the study theory, practice, and analysis of developmental pathways. In D. Cicchetti & S. L. Toth (Eds.), *Rochester symposium on developmental psychopathology* (pp. 97–115). Rochester, NY: Rochester University Press.

Loeber, R., & Hay, D. (1997). Key issues in the development of aggression and violence from childhood to early adulthood. *Annual Review of Psychology, 48*, 371–410.

Loeber, R., & Schmaling, K. B. (1985). Empirical evidence for overt and covert patterns of antisocial conduct problems: A metaanalysis. *Journal of Abnormal Child Psychology, 13*, 337–353.

Loeber, R., Wang, P., Keenan, K., Giroux, B., Stouthamer–Loeber, M., VanKammen, W., et al. (1993). Developmental pathways in disruptive child behaviors. *Development and Psychopathology, 5*, 103–134.

Lord, C., Risi, S., Lambrecht, L., Cook, E. H., Leventhal, B. L., DiLavore, P. C., et al. (2000). Autism Diagnostic Observation Schedule—Generic: A standard measure of social and communication deficits associated with the spectrum of autism. *Journal of Autism and Developmental Disorders, 30*(3), 205–223.

Mann, J. (1980). *Time-limited psychotherapy.* Cambridge, MA: Harvard University Press.

Masten, A. S. (Ed.). (2007). *Minnesota symposia on child psychology, Multilevel dynamics in developmental psychopathology: Pathways to the future* (Vol. 34). New York, NY: Taylor & Francis Group/Lawrence Erlbaum Associates.

Masten, A. S., Burt, K. B., Roisman, G. I., Obradović, J., Long, J. D., & Tellegen, A. (2004). Resources and resilience in the transition to adulthood: Continuity and change. *Development and Psychopathology, 16*, 1071–1094.

Masten, A. S., Roisman, G. I., Long, J. D., Burt, K. B., Obradović, J., Riley, J. R., et al. (2005). Developmental cascades: Linking academic achievement, externalizing and internalizing symptoms over 20 years. *Developmental Psychology, 41*(5), 733–746.

Matas, L., Arend, R. A., & Sroufe, L. A. (1978). Continuity and adaptation in the second year: The relationship between quality of attachment and later competence. *Child Development, 49*, 547–556.

McCabe, K., & Yeh, M. (2009). Parent-child interaction therapy for Mexican Americans: A randomized clinical trial. *Journal of Child & Adolescent Psychology, 38*(5), 753–759.

Miller, A. L., Rathus, J. H., & Linehan, M. M. (2007). *Dialectical behavior therapy with suicidal adolescents.* New York, NY: Guilford Press.

Moffitt, T. E. (1993). Adolescence-limited and life-course-persistent antisocial behavior: A developmental taxonomy. *Psychological Review, 100*(4), 674–701.

Moffitt, T. E. (2006). Life-course-persistent versus adolescence-limited antisocial behavior. In D. Cicchetti & D. J. Cohen (Eds.), *Handbook of developmental psychopathology* (2nd ed., Vol. 3, pp. 570–598). Hoboken, NJ: Wiley.

Nagin, D. S. (1999). Analyzing developmental trajectories: A semiparametric, group-based approach. *Psychological Methods, 4*(2), 1181–1196.

Narrow, W. E., First, M. B., Sirovatka, P., & Regier, D. A. (Eds.). (2007). *Age and gender considerations in psychiatric diagnosis: A research agenda for DSM-V.* Washington, DC: American Psychiatric Publishing.

Nigg, J. T., Hinshaw, S. P., & Huang-Pollock, C. (2006). Disorders of attention and impulse regulation. In D. Cicchetti & D. J. Cohen (Eds.), *Handbook of developmental psychopathology* (2nd ed., Vol. 3, pp. 358–403. Hoboken, NJ: Wiley.

Nock, M. K., & Prinstein, M. J. (2004). A functional approach to the assessment of self-mutilative behavior. *Journal of Consulting and Clinical Psychology, 72*(5), 885–890.

Obradović, J., van Dulmen, M., Yates, T. M., Carlson, E. A., & Egeland, B. (2006). Developmental assessment of competence from early childhood to middle adolescence. *Journal of Adolescence, 29,* 857–889.

Ogawa, J. R., Sroufe, L. A., Weinfield, N. S., Carlson, E. A., & Egeland, B. (1997). Development and the fragmented self: Longitudinal study of dissociative symptomatology in a nonclinical sample. *Development and Psychopathology, 9,* 855–879.

Patterson, G. R. (1993). Orderly change in a stable world: The antisocial trait as chimera. *Journal of Consulting and Clinical Psychology, 61*(6), 911–919.

Patterson, G. R., DeBaryshe, B. D., & Ramsey, E. (1989). A developmental perspective on antisocial behavior. *American Psychologist, 44,* 329–335.

Pennington, B. F., & Ozonoff, S. (1996). Executive functions and developmental psychopathology. *Journal of Child Psychology & Psychiatry & Allied Disciplines, 37*(1), 51–87.

Pickles, A. R., & Hill, J. (2006). Developmental pathways. In D. Cicchetti & D. J. Cohen (Eds.), *Handbook of developmental psychopathology* (2nd ed., Vol. 1, pp. 211–243). Hoboken, NJ: Wiley.

Pincus, D. B., Eyberg, S. M., & Choate, M. L. (2005). Adapting parent-child interaction therapy for young children with separation anxiety disorder. *Education & Treatment of Children, 28*(2), 163–181.

Pine, D. S., Alegria, M., Cook, E. H., Costello, E. J., Dahl, R. E., Koretz, D., et al. (2002). Advances in developmental science and DSM-V. In D. J. Kupfer, M. B. First, & D. A. Regier (Eds.), *A research agenda for DSM-V* (pp. 85–122). Washington, DC: American Psychiatric Association.

Powell, B., Cooper, G., Hoffman, K., & Marvin, S. (2009). The Circle of Security. In C. H. Zeanah (Ed.), *Handbook of infant mental health* (3rd ed., pp. 450–467). New York, NY: Guilford Press.

Putnam, F. W. (1991). Dissociative disorders in children and adolescents: A developmental perspective. *Psychiatric Clinics of North America, 14,* 519–532.

Putnam, F. W. (1997). *Dissociation in children and adolescents: A developmental perspective.* New York, NY: Guilford Press.

Reynolds, S. K., & Clark, L. A. (2001). Predicting dimensions of personality disorder from domains and facets of the Five-Factor Model. *Journal of Personality, 69*, 199–122.

Robins, D., Fein, D., Barton, M., & Green, J. (2001). The Modified Checklist for Autism in Toddlers: An initial study investigating the early detection of autism and pervasive developmental disorders. *Journal of Autism and Developmental Disorders, 31*(2), 131–144.

Robins, E., & Guze, S. B. (1970). Establishment of diagnostic validity in psychiatric illness: Its application to schizophrenia. *American Journal of Psychiatry, 126*, 983–986.

Roisman, G. I., Masten, A. S., Coatsworth, J. D., & Tellegen, A. (2004). Salient and emerging developmental tasks in the transition to adulthood. *Child Development, 75*(1), 123–133.

Rutter, M. (Ed.). (1980). *Scientific foundation of developmental psychiatry*. London, England: Heinemann.

Rutter, M. (1989). Pathways from childhood to adult life. *Journal of Child Psychology & Psychiatry, 30*, 23–51.

Rutter, M. (1993). Resilience: Some conceptual considerations. *Journal of Adolescent Health, 14*, 626–631.

Rutter, M. (2005). Multiple meanings of a developmental perspective on psychopathology. *European Journal of Developmental Psychology, 2*(3), 221–252.

Rutter, M., & Sroufe, L. A. (2000). Developmental psychopathology: Concepts and challenges. *Development and Psychopathology, 12*, 265–296.

Safran, J. D., & Muran, J. C. (Eds.). (1988). *The therapeutic alliance in brief psychotherapy*. Washington, DC: American Psychological Association.

Sameroff, A. J. (1989). Models of developmental regulation: The environtype. In D. Cicchetti (Ed.), *Rochester Symposium on Developmental Psychopathology: The emergence of a discipline* (Vol. 1, pp. 41–68). Hillsdale, NJ: Erlbaum.

Sameroff, A. J., & Chandler, M. J. (1975). Reproductive risk and the continuum of caretaking casualty. In F. D. Horowitz, M. Hetherington, S. Scarr-Salapatek, & G. Siegel (Eds.), *Review of child development research* (Vol. 4, pp. 187–243). Chicago, IL: Chicago University Press.

Sameroff, A. J., & Mackenzie, M. J. (2003). Research strategies for capturing transactional models of development: The limits of the possible. *Development and Psychopathology, 15*, 613–640.

Santostefano, S. (1971). Beyond nosology: Diagnosis from the viewpoint of development. In H. E. Rie (Ed.), *Perspectives in child psychopathology* (pp. 130–177). Chicago, IL: Aldine & Atherton.

Schulenberg, J. E., Sameroff, A., & Cicchetti, D. (Eds.). (2004). *Development and Psychopathology, special issue: Transition from adolescence to adulthood* (Vol. 16). New York, NY: Cambridge University Press.

Shiner, R. L. (2009). The development of personality disorders: Perspectives from normal personality development in childhood and adolescence. *Development and Psychopathology, 21*, 715–734.

Sifneos, P. E. (1987). *Short-term dynamic psychotherapy: Evaluation and technique.* New York, NY: Plenum.

Spitz, R., Emde, R. N., & Metcalf, D. (1970). Further prototypes of ego formation. *Psychoanalytic Study of the Child, 25*, 417–444.

Sroufe, L. A. (1979). The coherence of individual development: Early care, attachment, and subsequent developmental issues. *American Psychologist, 34*(10), 834–841.

Sroufe, L. A. (1989). Pathways to adaptation and maladaptation: Psychopathology as developmental deviation. In D. Cicchetti (Ed.), *Rochester Symposium on Developmental Psychopathology: The emergence of a discipline* (Vol. 1, pp. 13–40). Hillsdale, NJ: Erlbaum.

Sroufe, L. A. (1990). Considering normal and abnormal together: The essence of developmental psychopathology. *Development and Psychopathology, 2*(4), 335–347.

Sroufe, L. A. (1997). Psychopathology as an outcome of development. *Development and Psychopathology, 9*(2), 251–268.

Sroufe, L. A. (2005). Attachment and development: A prospective, longitudinal study from birth to adulthood. *Attachment & Human Development, 7*(4), 349–367.

Sroufe, L. A. (2007). The place of development in developmental psychopathology. In A. S. Masten (Ed.), *Minnesota symposia on child psychology, Multilevel dynamics in developmental psychopathology: Pathways to the future* (Vol. 34, pp. 285–299). New York, NY: Taylor & Francis Group/Lawrence Erlbaum Associates.

Sroufe, L. A., Carlson, E. A., Levy, A. K., & Egeland, B. (1999). Implications of attachment theory for developmental psychopathology. *Development and Psychopathology, 11*(1), 1–13.

Sroufe, L. A., Egeland, B., & Carlson, E. (1999). One social world: The integrated development of parent-child and peer relationships. In W. A. Collins & B. Laursen (Eds.), *The Minnesota Symposia on Child Psychology: Relationships as developmental contexts* (Vol. 30, pp. 241–262). Hillsdale, NJ: Erlbaum.

Sroufe, L. A., Egeland, B., Carlson, E. A., & Collins, W. A. (2005). *The development of the person: The Minnesota study of risk and adaptation from birth to adulthood.* New York, NY: Guilford Press.

Sroufe, L. A., Egeland, B., & Kreutzer, T. (1990). The fate of early experience following developmental change: Longitudinal approaches to individual adaptation in childhood. *Child Development, 61,* 1363–1373.

Sroufe, L. A., & Rutter, M. (1984). The domain of developmental psychopathology. *Child Development, 55,* 17–29.

Sroufe, L. A., & Waters, E. (1977). Attachment as an organizational construct. *Child Development, 48,* 1184–1199.

Stern, D. N. (1985). *The interpersonal world of the infant.* New York, NY: Basic Books.

Stieben, J., Lewis, M. D., Granic, I., Zelazo, P. D., Segalowitz, S., & Pepler, D. (2007). Neurophysiological mechanisms of emotion regulation for subtypes of externalizing children. *Development and Psychopathology, 19,* 455–480.

Strupp, H. A., & Binder, J. L. (1984). *Psychotherapy in a new key: A guide to time-limited dynamic psychotherapy.* New York, NY: Basic Books.

Tackett, J. L., Balsis, S., Oltmanns, T. F., & Krueger, R. F. (2009). A unifying perspective on personality pathology across the life span: Development considerations for the fifth edition of the *Diagnostic and Statistical Manual of Mental Disorders. Development and Psychopathology, 21,* 687–713.

Taylor, J., Iacono, W. G., & McGue, M. (2000). Evidence for a genetic etiology of early onset delinquency. *Journal of Abnormal Psychology, 109,* 634–643.

Tharinger, D. J., Finn, S. E., Gentry, L., Hamilton, A. H., Fowler, M. M., Krumholz, L., et al. (2009). Therapeutic assessment with children: A pilot study of treatment acceptability and outcome. *Journal of Personality Assessment, 91*(3), 238–244.

Tharinger, D. J., Finn, S. E., Hersh, B., Wilkinson, A., Christopher, G., & Tran, A. (2008). Assessment feedback with parents and preadolescent children: A collaborative approach. *Professional Psychology: Research and Practice, 39,* 600–609.

Timmer, S. G., Urquizq, A. J., & Zebell, N. (2005). Parent-child interaction therapy: Application to maltreating parent-child dyads. *Child Abuse & Neglect, 29*(7), 825–842.

Toth, S. L., Rogosch, F. A., Manly, J. T., & Cicchetti, D. (2006). The efficacy of Toddler-Parent Psychotherapy to reorganize attachment in the youth offspring of mothers with major depressive disorder: A randomized preventive trial. *Journal of Consulting and Clinical Psychology, 74*(6), 1006–1016.

Toth, S. L., Manly, J. T., & Nilsen, W. J. (2008). From research to practice: Lessons learned. *Journal of Applied Developmental Psychology, 29*, 317–325.

Turkheimer, E., & Waldron, M. (2000). Nonshared environment: A theoretical, methodological, and quantitative review. *Psychological Bulletin, 126*(1), 78–108.

Vygotsky, L. S. (1978). *Mind in society: The development of higher psychological processes* (M. Cole, V. John-Steiner, S. Scribner, & E. Souberman, Trans.). Cambridge, MA: Harvard University Press.

Waddington, C. H. (1940). *Organizers and genes.* Cambridge, England: Cambridge University Press.

Wakschlag, L. S., Briggs-Gowan, M. J., Carter, A. S., Hill, C., Danis, B., Keenan, K., et al. (2007). A developmental framework for distinguishing disruptive behavior from normative misbehavior in preschool children. *Journal of Child Psychology & Psychiatry, 48*(10), 976–987.

Wakschlag, L. S., Briggs-Gowan, M. J., Hill, C., Danis, B., Leventhal, B. L., Keenan, K., et al. (2008). Observational assessment of preschool disruptive behavior, part II: Validity of the Disruptive Behavior Diagnostic Observation Schedule (DB-DOS). *Journal of the American Academy of Child & Adolescent Psychiatry, 47*(6), 632–641.

Wakschlag, L. S., Leventhal, B. L., Briggs-Gowan, M. J., Danis, B., Keenan, K., Hill, C., et al. (2005). Defining the "disruptive" in preschool behavior: What diagnostic observation can teach us. *Clinical Child and Family Psychology Review, 8*(3), 183–201.

Wakschlag, L. S., Tolan, P. H., & Leventhal, B. L. (2010). 'Ain't misbehavin': Towards a developmentally-specific nosology for preschool disruptive behavior. *Journal of Child Psychology and Psychiatry, 51*, 3–22.

Waters, E., & Sroufe, L. A. (1983). Social competence as a developmental construct. *Developmental Review, 3*, 79–97.

Wender, P. H. (1971). *Minimal brain dysfunction in children.* New York, NY: Wiley.

Werner, H. (1957). The concept of development from a comparative and organismic point of view. In D. B. Harris (Ed.), *The concept of development* (pp. 125–148). Minneapolis: University of Minnesota Press.

Werner, H., & Kaplan, B. (1964). *Symbol formation: An organismic-developmental approach to language and the expression of thought.* New York, NY: Wiley.

Widiger, T. A., & Kelso, K. (1982). Psychodiagnosis of Axis II. *Clinical Psychology Review, 3*, 491–510.

Widiger, T. A., Livesley, W. J., & Clark, L. A. (2009). An integrative dimensional classification of personality disorder. *Psychological Assessment, 21*, 243–255.

Williams, S. B., O'Connor, E. A., Eder, M., & Whitlock, E. P. (2009). Screening for child and adolescent depression in primary care settings: A systematic evidence review for the US Preventive Services Task Force. *Pediatrics, 123*, 716–735.

Willoughby, M. T. (2003). Development course of ADHD symptomatology during the transition from childhood to adolescence: A review with recommendations. *Journal of Child Psychology & Psychiatry, 44*(1), 88–106.

Yates, T. M., Egeland, B., & Sroufe, L. A. (2003). Rethinking resilience: A developmental process perspective. In S. S. Luthar (Ed.), *Resilience and vulnerability: Adaptation in the context of childhood adversities* (pp. 234–256). New York, NY: Cambridge University Press.

Yates, T. M. (2004). The developmental psychopathology of self-injurious behavior: Compensatory regulation in posttraumatic adaptation. *Clinical Psychology Review, 24*(1), 35–74.

Yates, T. M. (2009). Developmental pathways from child maltreatment to non-suicidal self-injury. In M. Nock (Ed.), *Understanding non-suicidal self-injury: Current science and practice* (pp. 117–137). Washington, DC: American Psychological Association.

Yates, T. M., Carlson, E. A., & Egeland, B. (2008). A prospective study of child maltreatment and self-injurious behavior in a community sample. *Development and Psychopathology, 20*, 651–672.

Yates, T. M., & Masten, A. S. (2004). Fostering the future: Resilience theory and the practice of positive psychology. In P. A. Linley & S. Joseph (Eds.), *Positive Psychology in Practice* (pp. 521–539). Hoboken, NJ: Wiley.

Yates, T. M., Obradović, J., & Egeland, B. (2010). Transactional relations across contextual strain, parenting quality and early childhood regulation and adaptation in a high-risk sample. *Development and Psychopathology, 22*, 539–555.

Zigler, E., & Glick, M. (1986). *A developmental approach to adult psychopathology.* New York, NY: Wiley.

# 8

# Frightening Maternal Behavior, Infant Disorganization, and Risks for Psychopathology

Deborah Jacobvitz, Nancy Hazen, Maria Zaccagnino, Serena Messina, and Lauren Beverung

One of the most challenging issues in child psychiatry is to identify qualities of early care that increase the risk of childhood psychopathology. Alan Sroufe and Byron Egeland's seminal studies following children from birth to adulthood were among the first to demonstrate that caregiving patterns are often carried forward across generations, and that quality of early care has lasting effects on children (Sroufe, Egeland, Carlson, & Collins, 2005; Sroufe, Egeland, & Kreutzer, 1990). However, they have also sought to identify and explain exceptions to otherwise expectable continuities. As an example, whereas maltreated mothers often unwittingly repeat negative and even abusive behavior with their children, they are markedly less likely to do so if they have had the benefit of a supportive relationship with a therapist or an alternative attachment figure before the birth of their child (Egeland, Jacobvitz, & Sroufe, 1988).

As Bowlby (1969/1982) made clear through his emphasis on the early origins of an individual's "internal working model," and as Ainsworth (1978) made clear through her empirical work, repeated interactions with the parenting figure can lead children to act as though they are either worthy—or, unfortunately, unworthy of care. It is this experience-based view of themselves, others, and their important relationships that children carry forward into later life (Sroufe, 1983; 1986; Sroufe, Carlson, & Shulman, 1993). This chapter will draw on lessons learned from the Minnesota Parent-Child Longitudinal Study to explore the intergenerational origins and stability of a relatively newly recognized form of early disrupted parental behavior with infants and toddlers—frightened and frightening maternal behavior—and its effects on children during middle childhood.

## BACKGROUND

Drawing on observations of both human and nonhuman primate anthropologists, as well as Mary Ainsworth's observations in Uganda (1967), the London psychiatrist John Bowlby hypothesized that neurologically normal infants are strongly predisposed to become attached to those caregivers with whom they interact (Bowlby, 1969/1982; see Sagi-Schwartz, van IJzendoorn, & Bakersmans-Kranenburg, 2008, for recent confirmations across multiple countries and continents). Furthermore, and now drawing on ideas from evolutionary biology, John Bowlby (1979) suggested that attachment behavior in ground-living primates serves the biological function of protection from predation. Thus, for most ground-living primates, and certainly for human infants, early infant helplessness assures that the caregiver is the infant's source of safety and protection. Hence, the infant's survival depends on forming strategies for gaining access to the caregiver (alternately, hereafter, the attachment figure) when the infant is distressed.

It is thus particularly problematic for infants to be frightened by their own attachment figures, because in this circumstance the infant will be compelled to seek comfort in the face of a competing tendency to escape (Hesse and Main, 2006; Main & Hesse, 1990). Main and Hesse

(1992, 1998, 2005) have identified six forms of parental behavior that may be frightening to an infant who relies on the attachment figure for safety and security. These include not only anomalous forms of threatening behaviors (such as growling, canine display, or stalking behaviors), but also parental entrance into a trancelike state and exhibitions of fear of the infant (e.g., backing away from the infant as though it were dangerous). Disorganized/disoriented behaviors of the type usually observed in infants, timid/deferential and role-inverting behavior, and sexualized behavior are also considered potentially frightening.

The primary purpose of this chapter is to draw on findings from our prospective longitudinal study, inspired by the earlier work of Sroufe and Egeland, to examine the nature of maternal frightening behavior and its consequences for infants. Specifically, we will discuss the antecedents of frightening maternal behavior, showing that there is continuity in frightening maternal behavior from 8 to 24 months, and illustrate the forms that frightening maternal behavior takes with 24-month-old toddlers. In addition, we will describe our findings showing a surprisingly strong relationship between frightening maternal behavior during the first two years of life and the development of emotional and behavioral problems in middle childhood. Finally, we will discuss possible strategies for intervening with mothers who are at risk for engaging in frightening behavior.

## MOTHERS' UNRESOLVED TRAUMA AS AN ANTECEDENT OF MOTHERS' FRIGHTENING BEHAVIOR

Using the Strange Situation procedure to assess the quality of the infant-caregiver attachment relationship, Ainsworth, Blehar, Waters, and Wall (1978) discovered three patterns of infant attachment that corresponded with the quality of care that infants had experienced over the first year of life. As has since been replicated in many studies (De Wolff & Van IJzendoorn, 1997), infants whose mothers responded immediately and sensitively to their distress were found able to seek comfort when they needed it; these infants are considered securely attached. On the other hand, infants whose caregivers were consistently rejecting when they were distressed came to avoid or minimize contact with the caregivers, forming an avoidant attachment relationship (replicated in two further samples by Main & Stadtman, 1981). Finally, those infants whose mothers were unpredictable and inconsistent tended to form a resistant-ambivalent attachment; they both approached and resisted contact from the caregiver when distressed (see Cassidy & Berlin, 1994, for an overview of succeeding studies). What all of these infants have in common is that, even if insecure in their attachments, they are able to form an organized strategy for managing distress (Main & Hesse, 1990), an organization that is particularly visible in the infant's response to Ainsworth's separation-and-reunion Strange Situation procedure, and may well become a more general strategy for managing distress.

Yet, many infants do not form an organized strategy for gaining support when they are distressed. When observed in the Strange Situation, a substantial minority of infants appear disoriented, conflicted, and disorganized when their parents returned after a brief separation (Main & Solomon, 1986, 1990; see Lyons-Ruth and Jacobvitz, 1999, 2008, for an overview). For example, they may seem frightened and apprehensive, start to approach the mother and then collapse huddled face down on the floor, spin around in a circle, or put their hands to their mouth and look down with their shoulders hunched. Others appear disoriented and may freeze all movements and appear to be in a trance. They seem to be experiencing an approach-avoidance conflict, wanting to approach the mother for comfort, but at the same time, fearful of doing so.

Some infants, then, seem unable to form an organized strategy for dealing with distress, and put succinctly, this seems to be because their mothers have difficulty protecting them from their own experiences of disorganizing fear or stress. Thus, Main and Hesse (1990) proposed that mothers who suffer trauma resulting from loss through death or having experienced maltreatment, and who are unable to resolve or fully integrate these traumatic experiences—i.e., mothers assigned to unresolved/disorganized status on the Adult Attachment Interview (Hesse & Main, 2000, 2006)—would not be able to protect their children from showing signs of disorganization and disorientation under stress.

In fact, strong associations have been found between child maltreatment and infant attachment disorganization. Cicchetti and colleagues (Cicchetti & Barnett, 1991; Cicchetti, Rogosch, & Toth, 2006) and Lyons-Ruth and colleagues (Lyons-Ruth & Block, 1996; Lyons-Ruth, Bronfman, & Parsons, 1999) discovered that the great majority of infants in their high-risk samples—children from low socioeconomic samples who experienced maltreatment—were classified as disorganized in the Strange Situation. However, experiencing maltreatment is not the only pathway to disorganized attachment. Mothers who have not resolved early trauma may temporarily become frightened and therefore behave in ways that are likely to frighten their infants. Thus, frightening behavior is believed to mediate the relationship between mothers' unresolved trauma, as identified in transcripts of the Adult Attachment Interview (AAI; George, Kaplan, & Main, 1984, 1985, 1996, protocol; Main, Goldwyn, & Hesse, 1984–2003, scoring system) and infant attachment disorganization (Hesse & Main, 2006; Main & Hesse, 1990).

The AAI attempts to assess an individual's overall state of mind with respect to attachment, i.e., their working model of attachment (Main, Kaplan, & Cassidy, 1985; Main, Hesse, & Goldwyn, 2008; Steele & Steele, 2008). For example, adults are asked to describe their early relationships with their parents and their sense of how these relationships affected their adult personality. They are also asked to describe experiences of loss and abuse and how these experiences might have affected their personality. If the individual remains frightened by these events, both speaking and reasoning processes may be affected, and signs of these effects as seen in the interview transcript lead to designating the speaker as unresolved/disorganized via discussion of these events during the Adult Attachment Interview (Hesse & Main, 2006). Thus, traumatic events may continue to frighten some individuals to the point that their mental processes—and, as we will describe later, their actions—may be affected.

Mothers will, then, be classified as U/d (Unresolved/disorganized) on the AAI if their speech indicates mental disorganization or disorientation regarding the loss of a significant person or experiences of sexual or physical maltreatment. Signs of mental disorganization include lapses in their ability to monitor their discourse during discussions of loss or abuse—for example, falling silent for more than 60 seconds in the middle of discussing a loss and then continuing to speak about another topic. Other indices involve a lapse in the ability to monitor their reasoning, such as a brief slip indicating that they momentarily believe that the lost person is still alive. For example, in response to queries about the death of a boyfriend that occurred 10 years earlier, one mother in our sample who was classified as unresolved for loss said, "I still think he's just kind of gone away, you know, and he's hiding, that's what I think." Another mother who was sexually abused by her father at age 9, when asked how she thinks the experience of abuse will affect how she raises her child, replied "I do worry and get scared sometimes, that, what happens if, if some uncontrollable animal comes out of me, and something happens like that?"

The same process that leads to mothers being categorized as unresolved may cause them to behave in frightening ways with their infant. Unexplained, sudden, and brief disruptions in a person's mental state indicate that individuals have not fully integrated early traumatic experiences. And, if a mother is still frightened/traumatized by her past experiences, reminders of these experiences may trigger frightened responses that she is unaware of.

One effect of experiences of continuing unintegrated fright may be seen in alterations in the parent's physiology. Thus, studies suggest that the persisting effects of a psychological trauma during development, such as loss or abuse, may lead to long-term alterations in regulation of the hypothalamic-pituitary-adrenal (HPA) axis (Pettito, Quade, & Evans, 1992). The HPA axis is activated in response to stress and regulates the release of cortisol and, as is well known, adrenocortisol is often released in the body following a stressful experience. Experiences of loss have been associated with dysregulation of HPA axis activity, mostly in the realm of exaggerated activity (e.g., Meinlschmidt & Heim, 2005; Nicolson, 2004; Pettito et al., 1992; Tyrka et al., 2009). The long-term elevation of the HPA axis caused by stress or trauma may cause hypercortisolism in response to future stressful experiences (Corbin, 2007). Hence, adults who are unresolved with respect to trauma may respond more strongly to mild stress because of dysregulation of the HPA axis. It may be, then, that adults who suffer from unresolved trauma may have stronger fear responses to memories of negative experiences than other adults, and they may engage in frightening behavior with their infant as a consequence. For example, if, during an interaction with her infant, a mother suddenly recalls how she was abused as a child, she may respond to this memory by entering what appears to be a trancelike state.

In our prospective longitudinal study, we examined the relationship of mothers' unresolved trauma to frightening behavior with their infants, as well as factors that may moderate this relationship (Jacobvitz, Leon, & Hazen, 2006). Our original sample consisted of 125 mothers and children in the Austin, Texas, area. Mothers were recruited primarily from childbirth classes while they were in their third trimester of pregnancy. Although the median family income ranged from $30,000 to $45,000, this was a somewhat diverse sample with respect to socioeconomic background. One-third of the sample was either at or below poverty level when they were recruited, and another one-third was from upper-middle socioeconomic background. About 60% of the couples had at least a bachelor's degree, and 30% had some college or trade/business coursework. Most of the couples were married (94.4%) and Caucasian (80%). About 3% were Hispanic, 3% were African American, and 4% were from mixed racial backgrounds. Expectant parents ranged in age from 16 to 41 years (mean age = 30.5 years).

During their third trimester of pregnancy, the Adult Attachment Interview was conducted with mothers to assess their attachment security and whether they suffer from an unresolved/disorganized mental state (roughly, level of mental disorganization stemming from experiences of loss or abuse). Later, when their babies were 8 months old, mothers were videotaped in their homes playing with, feeding, and changing their babies. We later coded videotapes of mother-infant interaction. Mothers' frightening behavior with their infants was coded on a 9-point Frightening/Frightened/Dissociated (FR) scale using Main and Hesse's (1992) initial version of the Frightening/Frightened mother-infant behavior coding system; some further examples of FR behaviors were identified and added to the coding system. Main and Hesse (1998, 2005) subsequently revised this coding system delineating six FR subscales, including frightened, threatening, and dissociative (the "major" scales, above), but now considering as well timid-deferential/role-inverting, sexualized, and disorganized parental behavior. It is important to note as well that in the majority of instances in order for maternal behaviors to be considered frightening, observations must show that they occur out of context and without warning.

Threatening behaviors may appear primitive, such as attack postures, growls, looming into the child's face, and nonplayful stalking. Threatening maternal behavior can also include abruptly invading into vulnerable parts of their babies' bodies and aggressive verbal behavior. Other examples of threatening frightening behavior include prolonged widening of the eyes so that whites are exposed, making unusual vocalizations, and frightening pursuit of the baby. For instance, one mother in our sample, while playing with her baby, suddenly and without warning totally covered her baby's face with a big stuffed teddy bear. Another mother came suddenly from behind her baby and moved her hands across the baby's face and throat while baring her teeth.

Frightening behavior on the part of the parent may also appear in displays of anomalous fear of the child. These frightened behaviors include mothers suddenly retreating from their babies without apparent reason, abruptly raising their voices as if scared while handling their babies, or becoming startled. For example, while playing with her baby, one mother in our sample flinched for no apparent reason and said to her baby, "You startled me." None of the coders could identify anything that the baby did that would have startled the mother.

In addition, it is considered frightening to an infant to have a parent who is physically present suddenly seem to enter a dissociative, trancelike state or posture. Dissociative behavior can involve becoming inexplicably expressionless or abrupt or showing inexplicable changes in mood. It can also involve anomalous vocalizations—a haunted voice tone or a sudden frightened rise in intonation. For example, one mother in our sample appeared to enter multiple trancelike states, each of which lasted more than 60 seconds. Her face became still—she stared ahead without blinking and with a blank expression—for a total of 5 minutes over the 20-minute feeding session. During one episode, she appeared completely frozen, with her arm suspended in the air and her face inexpressive.

Other FR behaviors include both timid and deferential behavior during approaches to the baby or treating the baby in a sexualized way. For example, one mother in our sample lay next to her baby while feeding her with a bottle and made pelvic thrusts toward her while singing a romantic song that was popular during the mother's childhood.

As expected, we found a robust relationship between mothers' U/d classification and their likelihood of displaying FR behaviors with their 8-month-old infants (Jacobvitz et al., 2006; Jacobvitz, Hazen, & Riggs, 1997). Thus, for our sample of 112 dyads, mothers classified as Unresolved/disorganized scored significantly higher on the 9-point scale for FR maternal behavior compared to mothers who were not Unresolved/disorganized (t = 5.11, p < .0001, d = 1.01). This relationship held even when U/d loss and U/d abuse were examined separately; that is, mothers with unresolved trauma were more likely than other mothers to show FR behaviors with their infants, whether the trauma they had experienced was loss or abuse.

We also examined the discriminant validity of FR behavior and maternal sensitivity. Numerous studies have found that mothers classified as having a secure state of mind in the AAI are more likely to show sensitive caregiving with their infants (van IJzendoorn, 1995). It could be argued that FR behavior is just a type of maternal insensitivity, and therefore that mothers classified as U/d are simply less likely to be sensitive rather than more likely to be frightening. Although we found some overlap between FR behavior and sensitivity in the form of a modest negative correlation (r (119) = −.24, p < .01), we also found that maternal U/d classification was not related to maternal sensitivity (and in contrast, maternal insecure classification *was* related to lower sensitivity; see Jacobvitz et al., 2006). In fact, several mothers classified as U/d were very sensitive with their infants apart from occasional lapses in which they displayed sudden, inexplicable frightening behaviors.

Similar to findings reported by Schuengel, Bakermans-Kranenburg, and van IJzendoorn (1999), we found that U/d mothers with a secondary classification of secure showed lower levels of FR behavior than those with a secondary classification of insecure, although their usage of FR behavior was higher than that of mothers who were not unresolved (Jacobvitz et al., 2006). Thus, secondary secure status may be an important moderating factor that buffers the negative effects of unresolved loss or abuse on maternal caregiving.

Another moderating factor may be the type of trauma that was experienced. In our study, we found that loss of a parent before age 16 was a particularly robust predictor of maternal FR behavior; in fact, loss of a parent predicted FR behavior independent of U/d status (Jacobvitz et al., 2006). Thus, mothers' loss of a parent, their primary source of security during childhood, may be particularly likely to create long-lasting anxiety and fear, which may manifest itself as FR behavior during caregiving.

## FRIGHTENING MATERNAL BEHAVIOR AS AN ANTECEDENT OF INFANT ATTACHMENT DISORGANIZATION

Because the infant is not aware of the mother's traumatic memories or hypersensitivity to stress, sudden (seemingly unprovoked) behavior is frightening to the infant. As noted earlier, a primary attachment figure who behaves in frightening ways with the infant becomes simultaneously a source of comfort and a source of distress for the infant (Main & Hesse, 1990). In consequence, the infant experiences competing tendencies to approach and flee from the caregiver. The resulting infant reaction is an approach-avoidance conflict: the need to seek proximity to the caregiver in times of fear, while the caregiver is simultaneously the source of that fear, will predictably result in a collapse of behavioral strategies and the display of disorganized behavior. Maternal FR behavior has been associated with infant attachment disorganization in the United States (e.g., Abrams, Rifkin, & Hesse, 2006), the Netherlands (Schuengel et al., 1999), and Africa (True, Pasani, & Oumar, 2001). Our own data taken from our Austin longitudinal sample also reveal that maternal FR behavior is significantly correlated with attachment disorganization at 12 to 15 months (r = .27, p < .05).

Lyons-Ruth and her colleagues (Lyons-Ruth, Bronfman, & Parsons, 1999; Lyons-Ruth, Bronfman, & Atwood, 1999) have suggested that, in addition to maternal FR behavior, mothers' atypical behaviors, including contradictory and disrupted forms of affective communication, may lead to fear in the infant and consequently to disorganized attachment. They developed a coding scheme, AMBIANCE (Atypical Maternal Behavior Instrument for Assessment and Classification), to assess disruptions in mother-child interactions, including affective errors (e.g., asking the child to approach and then failing to respond, or failing to comfort the child when the child is distressed) and extreme emotional unavailability (e.g., holding the child at a distance from her body) (Lyons-Ruth, Bronfman, & Parsons, 1999; Lyons-Ruth, Bronfman, & Atwood, 1999). This coding system also includes the FR behaviors identified by Main and Hesse (1992). Several studies have found significant associations between higher scores on AMBIANCE and infant attachment disorganization from both middle and lower socioeconomic backgrounds (Forbes, Evans, Moran, & Pederson, 2007; Goldberg, Benoit, Blokland, & Madigan, 2003; Grienenberger, Kelly, & Slade, 2005; Lyons-Ruth, Bronfman, & Parsons, 1999; Madigan, Moran, & Pederson, 2006; Madigan, Moran, Schuengel, Pederson, & Otten, 2007).

However, not all of the children who experienced FR or atypical maternal behavior became disorganized, and not all infants categorized as disorganized experienced FR or atypical maternal behavior. Because FR maternal behavior is brief and infrequent, it is possible that we did not observe some of the mothers in our study long enough at eight months to see them display FR behavior. It is also possible that failure to find links between FR or atypical behavior and attachment disorganization for some children in our study was a result of errors in measurement at 12 to 15 months. Indices of attachment disorganization are brief, and some children who are disorganized in other contexts may simply not have displayed disorganized behavior during the Strange Situation. However, there may also be multiple pathways to infant attachment disorganization.

One alternative pathway to attachment disorganization may simply be the absence of a consistent primary caregiver. For example, in our sample, infants who experienced more than 60 hours of nonmaternal care per week were significantly more likely to be classified as disorganized than those who experienced less than 60 hours of nonmaternal care per week (Allen, Hazen, & Jacobvitz, 2005; Hazen, Allen, & Jacobvitz, in preparation). The mothers of these children (11 of the 104 mothers in our sample who had Strange Situation and caregiving arrangement data available) were not more likely to be unresolved for trauma or to show frightening behavior with their infants, nor were they more likely to be insensitive, hostile, interfering, or disengaged with their infants. They simply were not around their infants most of the time. Yet, seven of these mothers (64%) had infants who were classified as disorganized, and interestingly, by 24 months, the mothers of these seven children were more likely to show anomalous/frightening behavior to their children compared with all other mothers. This finding also held for all 11 of the infants who experienced more than 60 hours of nonmaternal care per week, including the four who were not disorganized as infants. Thus, infants may need at least a minimal amount of interaction with a consistent caregiver to form an organized strategy for obtaining comfort in times of need.

Another pathway to disorganization, or at least unorganized behavior in the Strange Situation, may be institutional care. A study conducted in Greece compared 86 infants reared in residential group care with 41 infants raised with their mothers at home. Whereas 66% of the infants raised in residential group care were classified as disorganized, 25% of the infants raised at home were disorganized (Vorria et al., 2003). Similar results were obtained in a study of infants in Romania. Compared to 22% of the 50 infants who had never been institutionalized, 65% of the 95 infants reared in institutions were classified as disorganized (Zeanah, Smyke, Koga, Carlson, & the Bucharest Early Intervention Project Core Group, 2005).

Some researchers have wondered whether child factors might also contribute to attachment disorganization. Thus, several researchers have investigated whether some children are genetically more vulnerable than others to form a disorganized attachment. A study of 157 twin pairs found no evidence that genetic factors determined attachment disorganization, which instead was found associated with nonshared environment (Bokhorst et al., 2003). An initial study with Hungarian infants reported that 71% of the disorganized infants had the 7-repeat dopamine D4 receptor (DRD4) gene polymorphism, compared with only 29% of the nondisorganized children (Lakatos et al., 2000). Using the same sample, these researchers found that children carrying both the 7-repeat allele of the DRD4 gene and the 52IT allele versus those who did not carry either of these alleles were 10 times more likely to be classified as disorganized (Lakatos et al., 2002). However, the two studies that attempted to replicate finding a direct link between the 7-repeat allele of the DRD4 gene and attachment disorganization failed to do so. There was no association between the 7-repeat allele of the DRD4 gene and attachment disorganization either in twins (Bakermans-Kranenburg & van IJzendoorn, 2004) or singletons (van IJzendoorn & Bakermans-Kranenburg, 2006).

Van IJzendoorn and Bakermans-Kranenburg (2006) utilized the concept of "differential sensitivity to the environment" and provided evidence for a gene-environment interaction in their sample. In contrast to infants who lacked the DRD4-7-repeat allele, infants who had the DRD4-7-repeat polymorphism were significantly more likely to become disorganized if their mothers were classified as unresolved with respect to loss on the AAI. Thus, infant genetics may moderate the relationship between mothers' unresolved loss and attachment disorganization, rather than being an alternate pathway to disorganization. Clearly, it will be important to further investigate this link. For example, are babies with the 7-repeat allele of the DRD4 gene more susceptible to the negative effects of experiencing frightening maternal behavior, and perhaps to other factors related to becoming disorganized?

The amount of stress that mothers and infants experience may be another important factor that moderates the relationship between unresolved trauma and frightening behavior. Put another way, high levels of stress could increase the risk that mothers who are unresolved behave in ways that frighten their infants. In our study, when we asked mothers to participate in tasks requiring interaction with their baby, we chose tasks that would produce mild stress. During the 30 minutes we observed mothers, they did display frightening behavior. Recognizing the potential role of stress in producing frightening behavior, Forbes, et al. (2007) created an even more stressful paradigm termed the "interesting-but-Scary paradigm": following the Strange Situation procedure, they asked mothers to interact with their infants in a room with no toys. The procedure lasted only 8 minutes and successfully evoked frightening maternal behavior, specifically in the mothers of disorganized infants.

In light of the potential for stress to evoke frightening maternal behavior, it is not surprising that high socioeconomic risk has been linked with disorganized attachment. A recent meta-analysis conducted with 55 studies of 4,792 children, including 59 samples of non-maltreated high-risk children and 10 samples of maltreated children found that children from non-maltreated high-risk backgrounds who experienced at least five socioeconomic risk factors were at a higher risk for attachment disorganization than were the other children in the nonmaltreated sample (Cyr, Euser, Bakermans-Kranenburg, & van IJzendoorn, 2010). Moreover, children who were maltreated were significantly more likely to be classified as disorganized than were those who were not maltreated. Yet, children exposed to five socioeconomic risks were just as likely to be disorganized as those who experienced maltreatment (Cyr et al., 2010). The socioeconomic risks examined included (1) low income; (2) maternal substance abuse, including children who were prenatally exposed to alcohol/drug abuse and children with a parent currently using alcohol/drugs; (3) ethnic minority group; (4) single parenthood; (5) adolescent mother; and (6) low education.

One possible inference we might draw from these findings is that mothers who are unresolved with respect to loss and abuse may be more likely to engage in frightening behavior more frequently if they are experiencing the high levels of stress that typically accompany poverty, are engaged in substance abuse, and/or are single and do not have either emotional or instrumental support from a partner. Socioeconomic risk factors may also moderate the extent to which frightening maternal behavior leads to infant disorganization. That is, socioeconomic risk and other types of stressful environmental influences may make infants more susceptible to frightening maternal behavior. It will be important to investigate whether the level of stress experienced by the mother and infant moderates the negative effects of socioeconomic risk on attachment disorganization.

## DOES FRIGHTENING MATERNAL BEHAVIOR MEDIATE THE LINK BETWEEN MOTHER'S UNRESOLVED STATUS AND INFANT ATTACHMENT DISORGANIZATION?

Robust relations between maternal unresolved trauma and infant disorganized attachment have been found in several studies (e.g., Benoit & Parker, 1994; Main & Hesse, 1990; Steele, Steele, & Fonagy, 1996; van IJzendoorn, 1995; and Ward & Carlson, 1995). The issue then is whether—as Main and Hesse had hypothesized—FR maternal behavior mediates the link between mothers' unresolved status and infant disorganization. Mothers whose AAI transcripts lead to their placement in the unresolved category on the AAI are always also assigned a secondary classification, either secure or one of two forms of insecurity (dismissing or preoccupied). Schuengel and his colleagues (1999) reported that FR maternal behavior, coded using Main and Hesse's (1992) system, mediated the relationship between unresolved loss and attachment disorganization, but only for mothers classified as unresolved / insecure. In their middle-class sample, Goldberg et al. (2003) found the expected significant associations between mothers' U/d status and atypical maternal behavior (using AMBIANCE ratings of atypical maternal behavior, which include Main and Hesse's "FR" behaviors) and between atypical maternal behavior and attachment disorganization. However, atypical maternal behavior did not mediate the relationship between mothers' U/d status and atypical behavior. In contrast, in their at-risk sample of adolescent mothers from low socioeconomic backgrounds, Madigan et al. (2006) provide evidence that atypical maternal behavior mediated the relationship between mothers' U/d status and infant attachment disorganization. Their meta-analysis of seven studies including FR and AMBIANCE found a strong partial mediation of .42.

In our sample, however, we found full support for Main and Hesse's (1990) hypothesis that maternal FR behavior mediates the link between maternal U/d attachment and infant disorganization. Using Baron and Kenny's test of mediation (Baron & Kenny, 1986), we found that maternal unresolved trauma, assessed prenatally using the AAI, was significantly correlated with FR maternal behavior at 8 months ($r = .47$, $p < .001$) and with infant attachment disorganization at 12 to 15 months ($r = .37$, $p < .01$). FR maternal behavior was also significantly correlated with attachment disorganization at 12 to 15 months ($r = .27$, $p < .05$). When we conducted a regression, entering both unresolved trauma and FR maternal behavior as the independent variables and infant disorganization as the dependent variable, the relationship between unresolved trauma and attachment disorganization was no longer significant, providing evidence that FR maternal behavior at 8 months mediated the association between unresolved trauma in mothers and infant attachment disorganization.

## STABILITY OF FRIGHTENING MATERNAL BEHAVIOR OVER TIME

If maternal FR behavior predicts psychopathological outcomes for children who experience it, then it is important to know whether experiencing FR maternal behavior during the first year of life has an enduring effect on the child even if it decreases or disappears at a later time, or if FR behavior on the part of the caregiver is stable over time, continuing to impair the child's functioning. In either case, but perhaps even more so if FR behavior continues over time, children who experience FR maternal behavior may have difficulty regulating their emotion and impulses, resulting in elevated levels of anxiety.

Drawing on Alan Sroufe's ideas about continuity and change in development over time (Sroufe, 1979; Sroufe & Jacobvitz, 1989), we hypothesized that, to some extent, the appearance that FR behavior takes is likely to transform in response to the increasing developmental capacities of the child. Children's emerging symbolic abilities create the opportunity for new and more complex patterns of interaction with their caregivers. Sroufe and colleagues (2005) faced the challenge of identifying developmentally equivalent assessments of competence at different ages. Sroufe and Waters (1977) ascertained that although children's behavior may change over time, there is likely continuity in the underlying meaning of their behavior. For example, competence during infancy is based on the infant's ability to gain access to the caregiver when needed, whereas competence during preschool and kindergarten is additionally related to the child's ability to make friends (Waters & Sroufe, 1983). Due to the development of children's language and interest in pretend play during the toddler and preschool years, FR behavior on the part of the caregiver may become more verbal and may often occur in the context of pretend play. Therefore, we expected that mothers who engaged in FR behavior at 8 months would also do so at 24 months, but the FR behaviors would begin to take new forms in line with developmental change in the child.

When the children in our sample were 24 months old, mothers were videotaped playing with them in a laboratory playroom for 20 minutes, followed by a 10-minute period in which they were to ask their toddler to clean up the toys. Videotapes of these interactions were coded for instances of mothers' nonverbal FR behaviors but added frightening *speech contents* that were observable in the context of play. These included catastrophizing on the part of the mother as an aspect of frightening behavior, and voicelessness and whispering as disoriented behavior.

Main and Hesse (1990) had anecdotally recounted incidents of frightening speech to young children as "You'll kill that little (stuffed) bear if you do that" as well as "Gonna have an accident! Everybody's gonna get killed" said with a frightened intake of breath as a child pushed a toy car across the floor (p. 176). We used speech of this kind in extending our Frightening subscale. We also drew on speech indices taken from Kaplan's work with the Separation Anxiety Test as administered to six-year-olds (Kaplan, 1987; Main, Hesse, & Kaplan, 2005), where she had found indices of fear in the speech of children who had been disorganized with the mother in infancy. Kaplan had found that children who were previously classified as disorganized were more likely to exhibit verbal forms of implicitly frightened or frightening behavior. Implicit indices of fear included extreme voicelessness or whispering throughout the procedure, whereas explicit indices included catastrophic fantasies. For example, in the SAT, children were shown a picture in which the parents go out for the evening, leaving the child at home. They were then asked, "How do you think the little boy or girl in the picture feels?" Six-year-olds with a history of attachment disorganization tended to describe frightening situations—for example, they might suggest that the parent might be seriously hurt or killed or that the child might kill himself or herself. Kaplan (1987) explained that "the early interactive experiences between infants and their attachment figures might be eventually internalized as mental representations which guide their interpretation of attachment-related events in later life" (p. 113).

We included as frightening behavior most of the elements seen in the mothers of 8-month-olds, such as growling or sudden and jerky movements that are out of context and unexpected (Main & Hesse, 1992). As in our observations of 8-month-olds, we also observed maternal attack postures and sudden changes of voice pitch. A new example of directly frightening behavior that we noted was a witchlike voice.

The Frightened subscale (Main & Hesse, 1992) is intended to be applied to instances when a mother appears to fear her own child. We observed this in our sample when a mother had a sudden drop in her voice tone, spoke with a haunted voice suggestive of fright on greeting the child, or appeared inexplicably frightened by something the child was doing. One mother helped her child sit a doll on a tricycle, and when the doll fell on the floor, the mother screamed in a very high-pitched and scared voice: "Oh no! Poor doll!" as if something bad was really happening. Our Frightened subscale also included mothers who introduced catastrophic themes into the play session. For instance, one mother was pretending with her child that a doll was extremely sick and in a lot of pain and that the child had to heal the doll. The mother said in a very anxious voice: "She (the doll) needs to go the hospital. . . . Are they coming? Are they coming? Are they coming?" Whenever the child got involved in another activity, the mother would bring the child's attention back to the "sick" doll, saying: "The doll needs oxygen. . . . Give her oxygen" and then addressing the doll: "Breathe little girl . . . breathe. . . ." This went on throughout the entire play session. At the end of the session, the mother went back to the doll, saying that she was very sick, that her eyes were closed and that she needed help, otherwise she was going to die. When it was time to clean up, the mother asked the child to put away the doll, but the visibly frightened child would not touch or go near the doll.

We also coded disoriented and dissociated behavior. Dissociated behavior was observed when mothers began their play by interacting normally with their children but suddenly and without warning seemed to enter a trancelike state during which they did not seem aware of where they were or what they were doing. Another mother in our study was playing with her child when suddenly her face appeared expressionless. Her child called her many times, but the mother remained motionless. When she finally did answer 60 seconds later, she appeared as if she had been abruptly awakened.

Indices of dissociative, disorganized, and disoriented behaviors in mothers of toddlers involved a rapid shift between opposite and incongruent behaviors, an element in Main and Solomon's (1990) system for coding disorganized and disoriented behaviors in infants. For example, one of our mothers started laughing with the child but then suddenly became very hostile to her. Finally, we also considered instances when the mother—in an anomalous, not simply rejecting or dismissing manner—laughed at her child's distress or in response to the child hurting him- or herself, and did so while displaying indices of a disorganized or dissociative state. For instance, one of the children in our sample became frightened of some toy x-rays in the doctor play area and said that they were "monsters." His mother kept repeating the word "monsters" and laughing at the child. The cadence of the laugh involved sudden shifts in high and low tones, creating an eerie effect, and indicating the likely presence of a dissociative state.

In the analysis of our 24-month data we combined the Main and Hesse (1992) *timid/deferential/role/inverting* and *sexualized behavior* subscales into a single scale. This scale included diverse contents. For example, we noted if a mother treated the child as a comfort-providing attachment figure, an inherently disorganizing condition as discussed extensively by

Hesse and Main (see especially Hesse & Main, 2006, p. 324). Sexualized behavior was observed when mothers, for example, touched and kissed their children inappropriately. For instance, as her daughter was showing her some toy tools, one mother began caressing the child's face and neck and asked the child to give her a kiss. The child bent over the mother and gave her a quick kiss on her cheek; the mother told her to kiss her better and took her daughter's face in her hands while giving the child a prolonged kiss on her mouth. These sexualized behaviors have also been observed during the same 24-month mother-toddler task in the Minnesota Study (Waters & Sroufe, 1983).

A composite rating of our four subscales for identifying FR behavior at 24 months was used to assign an overall score on a comprehensive FR behavior scale ranging from 1 to 9. As expected, we found that mothers' FR behavior at 8 months was correlated with their FR behavior at 24 months (Jacobvitz, Zaccagnino, Mock, & Hazen, 2009). In addition, as was the case for mothers' FR behavior at 8 months, mothers' FR behavior at 24 months was also predicted by mothers' U/d classification on the AAI (assessed prenatally) and by infant disorganized attachment (assessed at 12 and 15 months). Thus, our findings suggest that there is continuity from maternal unresolved trauma, assessed even before the baby is born, to maternal FR behavior with the infant at 8 months, infant attachment disorganization at 12 to 15 months, and mothers showing FR behaviors with their toddlers at 24 months. However, although an increasing number of studies have found that infant attachment disorganization forecasts negative and even pathological outcomes for children, we know very little about the long-term implications for children of having early experiences with mothers who show frightening and anomalous behavior.

## PREDICTING CHILDHOOD PSYCHOPATHOLOGY FROM EARLY EXPERIENCES OF FRIGHTENING AND ANOMALOUS MATERNAL BEHAVIOR

The negative effects of attachment disorganization on children's social, cognitive, and behavioral development are well documented (see Lyons-Ruth & Jacobvitz, 2008, for a comprehensive review). Research has shown that children who were disorganized in infancy, compared to those who were not disorganized, more often suffer from externalizing problems at age 5 (Hubbs-Tait, Osofsky, Hann, & McDonald Culp, 1994) and 7 (Lyons-Ruth, Easterbrooks, & Cibelli, 1997), and especially, aggressive behavior (Lyons-Ruth, Alpern, & Repacholi, 1993; Shaw, Owens, Vondra, Keenan, & Winslow, 1997). In addition, a recent meta-analysis of 34 samples, combining studies that assessed attachment disorganization during infancy and/or D-controlling behavior at age 6, indicate that attachment disorganization/D-controlling is associated with externalizing symptoms during middle childhood (Fearon, Bakermans-Kranenburg, van IJzendoorn, Lapsley, & Roisman, 2010).

Impressive longitudinal data from the Minnesota Study indicates that infants classified as disorganized (vs. not disorganized) also suffered from dissociation, internalizing disorders, and poorer overall emotional health in grades 1, 2, and 3. Relatedly, Kaplan (1987; Main, Hesse, & Kaplan 2005) had also found that early attachment disorganization during infancy forecasts elevated levels of fear (e.g., catastrophic fantasies) on the Separation Anxiety Test at age 6. Following children from birth to adolescence, findings from the Minnesota Study also reveal that infant attachment disorganization predicts higher levels of psychopathology in general at 17 ½ (Carlson, 1998). It also predicts dissociative symptoms at ages 17 ½ (Carlson, 1998) and 19 (Ogawa, Sroufe, Weinfield, Carlson, & Egeland, 1997). Interestingly, however, only disorganized children who also experienced abuse reported dissociative symptoms at age 19 (Ogawa et al., 1997). This finding is somewhat consistent with a recent study linking attachment disorganization during infancy with symptoms of post-traumatic stress at age 8.5 years (MacDonald et al., 2008). Further research is needed to clarify why some disorganized children develop externalizing problems whereas others have internalizing problems.

Less is known, however, about the developmental outcomes for infants and children who have experienced frightening or other forms of anomalous maternal behavior. Because experiencing frightening maternal behavior during infancy forecasts attachment disorganization, frightening maternal behavior may explain at least a good part of the association between attachment disorganization and psychopathological outcomes. We therefore expected that elevated levels of FR behavior at 8 and 24 months would increase children's vulnerability to developing emotional and behavioral problems.

Because frightening and anomalous behavior is often brief, two assessments may provide a more reliable estimate of children's experiences than relying solely on 8 or 24 months alone. Thus, we created a composite of the 8- and 24-month assessments by using the highest score on either the 8-month FR scale or the 24-month FR scale as the final scale score (a practice employed by E. Carlson with respect to infant disorganization scores in the Minnesota sample at 12 and 18 months; see Carlson, 1998). We then placed children into one of two groups: those who experienced FR maternal behavior at 8 or 24 months, hereafter referred to as the FRinfancy/24-month group, versus those who did not experience FR maternal behavior (the not-FRinfancy/24-month group). Children in the FRinfancy/24-month group (N = 35) had mothers who received scores above 4.5 on either the FR behavior scale at 8 months or at 24 months, or else at both time periods. Children in the not-FRinfancy/24-month group (N = 82) had mothers who were assigned scores between 1 and 4.5 at both 8 and 24 months.

When the children in our sample were 7 years old, their teachers completed Teacher Report Forms of the Child Behavior Checklist (CBCL-TRF; Achenbach & Edelbrock, 1983) to assess the children's emotional and behavioral functioning. We examined the Internalizing Problems and Externalizing Problems scales of the CBCL-TRF, as well as all of the DSM-IV oriented scales. Complete data were available for 69 children, because only children whose teachers had them in class for at least 3 months were asked to complete the CBCL-TRF. Children in the FRinfancy/24-month group were rated significantly higher on Internalizing, Externalizing, DSM-IV Affective Problems, DSM-IV Anxiety Problems, DSM-IV Somatic Problems, and DSM-IV ADHD Problems, than were children in the not-FRinfancy/24-month group. There was no significant difference between the two groups on DSM-IV Conduct Problems.

Middle-childhood psychopathology was remarkably well predicted from early maternal Frightening behavior. For example, the differences in scores for DSM-IV Affective Problems—which include items such as sleep problems, crying, apathy, feelings of worthlessness/guilt, and harms self—for seven-year-olds whose mothers had (or had not) shown Frightening behaviors in our 8-month or 24-month observations were significant at the .000 level. The corresponding effect size for this difference was large (d = 97, equivalent to r = .44). The effect sizes for Internalizing Problems, Externalizing Problems, and DSM-IV Anxiety Problems were also large or near to large, while the effect size for DSM-IV Somatic Problems was medium. FR maternal behavior did not, however, predict DSM-IV Conduct Problems (Jacobvitz et al., 2009; Jacobvitz, Zaccagnino, & Hazen, in preparation).

The processes by which experiencing frightening and/or anomalous maternal behavior during the first two years of life increase the risk of psychopathology during middle childhood warrants further investigation. One reason that experiencing frightening maternal behavior might place children at risk for later psychopathology is that it is alarming for children to be frightened by their primary attachment figure (Hesse & Main, 2006). These children cannot seek comfort from a caregiver who is threatening, dissociating, or frightened of the child. Children who experienced FR behavior and/or become disorganized likely have difficulty regulating their impulses and emotion, placing them at risk for the several types of disorders found in our Austin sample. Two different studies found that disorganized children display higher levels of cortisol than secure children following a short separation from their caregivers, thus suggesting that they experience higher levels of ongoing stress (Hertsgaard, Gunnar, Erikson, & Nachmias, 1995), and indeed that no behavioral strategy presently provides a "solution" (Spangler & Grossmann, 1993).

## IMPLICATIONS FOR CLINICAL INTERVENTION

Our data, along with other empirical studies in the field, suggests that frightening maternal behavior places children at risk for later psychopathology. When developing preventive interventions to reduce the likelihood that mothers will engage in FR, atypical or anomalous behavior is of critical importance. Studying the effectiveness of such programs is not only important for preventing the deleterious consequences of experiencing anomalous maternal behavior, but also could contribute to understanding developmental processes (Cicchetti, Rogosch, & Toth, 2006). Specifically, if reducing the incidence of U/d in mothers and/or maternal frightening behavior alters the child's developmental course, including lessening the likelihood that attachment disorganization and psychopathological outcomes occur, then U/d and maternal frightening behavior can be considered causal factors. On the other hand, if reducing U/d and/or maternal frightening behavior does not affect the child's developmental course, then U/d and/or maternal frightening behavior might be considered markers of atypical development (Cicchetti et al., 2006).

Over the past decade, the development of interventions programs designed to promote attachment security have proliferated. Some of these programs have been successful in reducing the incidence of attachment disorganization (Cicchetti et al., 2006; Dozier et al., 2006; Heinicke et al., 2000; Hoffman, Marvin, Cooper, & Powell, 2006; Juffer, Bakermans-Kranenburg, & van IJzendoorn, 2005; Sajaniemi et al., 2001; Toth, Rogosch, Manly, & Cicchetti, 2006). Findings from a meta-analysis with 842 participants across 15 preventive interventions (Bakermans-Kranenburg, van IJzendoorn, & Juffer, 2005) indicate that the programs that were more successful in reducing attachment disorganization began when the infant was older than 6 months, and the intervention used trained therapists rather than laypersons (e.g., experienced mothers) or written materials. Moreover, these programs were not short-term—most involved weekly visits with the mother for at least 12 months. However, few studies have examined whether changes in mothers' unresolved status occur and, if so, whether these changes are associated with changes in mothers' propensity to engage in frightening behavior.

One program, however, included an intervention designed specifically to reduce the incidence of frightening and atypical maternal behavior. Similar to other attachment-based intervention programs, the Attachment and Biobehavioral Catch-Up program focuses on improving the caregivers' ability to detect, interpret, and sensitively respond to their infants' signals of distress and to follow the children's lead in order to improve neurobehavioral functioning (Dozier, Dozier, & Manni, 2002). This program is unique in several respects. First, one aim is to reduce frightening behavior by helping unresolved foster parents behave in nonthreatening ways toward their foster children. Parent trainers encourage foster parents to behave in a way that is predictable, even if their natural tendency is to play too roughly or to interact in a way that is threatening or scary. Moreover, issues of having been frightened as a child are addressed very specifically. Finally, this program recognizes that adults classified as unresolved have more difficulty than other adults developing trusting relationships with therapists and committing to the treatment program (Korfmacher, Adam, Ogawa, & Egeland, 1997). Hence, an extra effort was made to help unresolved foster parents form trusting relationships with the parent trainers.

Heinicke and his colleagues also developed an impressive intervention aimed at enhancing maternal sensitivity and infant attachment security. This intervention with 70 mothers was comprehensive; mothers were visited in their homes weekly for the first year (beginning toward the end of pregnancy) and biweekly the second year with telephone and follow-up contacts in the third and fourth year (Heinicke et al., 2000; Heinicke, Fineman, Ponce, & Guthrie, 2001). The authors explain that the primary goal of the intervention was "to offer the mother the experience of a stable, trustworthy relationship that conveys understanding of her situation and that promotes her sense of self-efficacy through a variety of specific interventions (p. 138)." This intervention focused on three goals: (1) enhancing the mother's communication and personal adaptation, (2) alternate approaches to her relationship to her child, and (3) direct affirmation and support. The first two domains were addressed by the intervenor listening to the mother, expressing empathy, and helping the mother to focus her concerns. The intervention was successful in promoting infant attachment security and reducing attachment disorganization.

Two studies reporting a reduction in attachment disorganization following participation in an intervention program are notable because they not only used randomized preventive intervention trials but also included a normal community control group (Cicchetti et al., 2006; Toth et al., 2006). Cicchetti et al. assigned 137 infants from maltreating low-income families and assigned mother-infant dyads to one of three groups: (1) a mother-infant psychodynamic psychotherapy group focused on helping the mother gain insight into herself and how she relates to her child; (2) a psychoeduational parenting intervention; or (3) a community standard control group. A fourth group of infants from nonmaltreating families and their mothers (N = 52) were included as an additional low-income normative comparison. It is notable that there were significantly more disorganized infants in the maltreatment sample (89.9%) compared to the nonmaltreating group (43%). Post-intervention results revealed significantly higher rates of attachment disorganization in the community control group compared to the intervention groups, indicating that both the infant-parent psychotherapy program and the psychoeducational parenting intervention were effective in reducing the incidence of attachment disorganization.

A critical question, then, is why the interventions were effective in reducing attachment disorganization. The psychodynamic psychotherapy intervention implemented by Cicchetti and colleagues (2006) is based on the idea that the infant evokes emotions and memories associated with the quality of care the mother experienced during childhood. The mother may then project onto her child her conflicted feelings, resulting in distorted perceptions of the infant and insensitive and misattuned behavior. Perhaps, raising the mother's awareness of the potential negative effects of an abusive past on her behavior allowed her to more closely monitor her own caregiving behavior, reducing the likelihood that she would dissociate, or become threatening and frightening with her child.

Most attachment interventions, to date, emphasize the importance of developing a trusting relationship between the therapist and mother. A core feature of psychodynamic psychotherapy is to provide mothers with "respect, empathic concern, and unfailing positive regard" (pp. 629–630,

Cicchetti et al., 2006). Similarly, Heinicke and colleagues (2000) demonstrated empirically that reducing a mother's self-doubt and strengthening her relationship to her partner predicted improvements in her infant's attachment security. Perhaps, these interventions fostered a more secure state of mind, allowing mothers to resolve their trauma or at least reduced the mothers' level of stress and anxiety. As noted earlier, unresolved mothers with a secondary secure attachment in our sample were less likely to engage in FR behavior with their infant than those assigned a secondary insecure attachment classification, as were unresolved mothers in a Dutch sample (Schuengel et al., 1999).

To prevent the intergenerational transmission of attachment disorganization, interventions aimed at helping children cope with the death of one or both parents should be developed. In our sample, mothers who lost a parent when they were younger than 16 (vs. those who did not) were at greater risk for engaging in FR behavior (Jacobvitz, Hazen, & Riggs, 1997; Jacobvitz et al., 2006). When parental loss occurs, the surviving parent or relative may have difficulty accepting the loss and unwittingly discourage the child from experiencing or expressing fears associated with the death. Moreover, adults sometimes tell the child that the parent has "gone away," which implies that the parent can come back (Bowlby, 1980). Bowlby emphasizes the importance of making sure that children understand the permanence of the loss, allowing them to reorganize and cope with the reality of losing their parent.

It is also important to develop interventions to help children to cope with a mother who is still frightened by her past. To this end, studies are needed to determine whether some FR behaviors are more damaging to children in the long-term than others. Abrams et al. (2006) found strong evidence that dissociative and threatening maternal behaviors were more strongly linked to attachment disorganization than were other forms of FR behavior. Dissociative maternal behavior is likely terrifying to the child because it is the only FR behavior in which, by definition, the child has no access to the mother (Hesse & Main, 2006). With a larger sample that has more instances of frightening maternal behavior, the developmental outcomes of each type of frightening behavior at 8 and 24 months can be analyzed separately. It is also important to discover whether different subtypes of frightening behavior at 8 and 24 months have distinct outcomes.

## FUTURE DIRECTIONS

The processes underlying pathways from unresolved trauma to frightening maternal behavior and from frightening maternal behavior to attachment disorganization and psychopathology warrant further investigation Unresolved trauma in the mother increases the likelihood that mothers will engage in frightening behavior with their children, but not all mothers who were unresolved engaged in frightening behavior. Similarly, exposure to frightening, atypical, or otherwise anomalous maternal behavior in the early years increases the likelihood that children will develop psychopathological symptoms, but this does not happen for all children. It will thus be particularly important in future research to investigate the role of factors that moderate these pathways by making mothers more or less susceptible to displaying frightening behavior and by making children more or less susceptible to the potentially negative effects of exposure to maternal frightening behavior. In this chapter, we have identified environmental stress and child gender as two factors that should be further investigated as possible moderators.

In research conducted to date, socioeconomic risk factors have been linked to an increased risk of infant attachment disorganization (Cyr et al., 2010), but the processes that underlie this relationship are as yet unknown. Does increased socioeconomic risk increase the likelihood that, for example, infants will be exposed to excessively many, excessively long, and perhaps unpredictable separations, which Main and Solomon (1990, p. 126) had presumed could be an alternative pathway to "unclassifiable," meaning "disorganized," attachment status? Or, may it primarily (or additionally) increase the likelihood that mothers who have experienced unresolved trauma will show frightening behavior? Or does it, perhaps via infant physiology, increase an infant's susceptibility to the negative effects of maternal frightening behavior—acting via some other pathway entirely?

In addition to investigating factors that may explain how socioeconomic factors moderate pathways from maternal frightening behavior to child outcomes, future research should examine the relative impact of different sources of socioeconomic stress (e.g., low income, substance abuse, ethnic minority status, single parenthood, adolescent mother, low education), as well as investigating other sources of environmental stress (e.g., marital conflict, illness, life transitions that may affect the extent to which unresolved mothers engage in frightening behavior or children's susceptibility to the effects of maternal frightening behavior.

Just as there are multiple pathways to infant disorganization, so too can infant disorganization lead to divergent outcomes. Data from our study indicate that child gender may be an important factor that leads to such divergent outcomes. Overall, we found that maternal FR behavior was much more likely to predict symptoms of anxiety, depression, and internalizing problems than externalizing symptoms such as aggression or conduct problems. We also found that disorganized attachment predicted *only* affective disorders, not externalizing problems. This is in contrast to several other studies that have found strong links between disorganized attachment in infancy and later externalizing symptoms (van IJzendoorn, Schuengel, & Bakermans-Kranenburg, 1999; Fearon et al., 2010). We found, however, that disorganized attachment interacted with gender to predict teacher ratings of children's externalizing symptoms at age 7 (Hazen, Jacobvitz, Higgins, Allen, & Jin, in press). That is, boys who had been disorganized as infants had markedly higher ratings on externalizing symptoms than all other children. In fact, 46% of boys classified as disorganized had ratings for externalizing symptoms that were in the clinical or borderline-clinical range, compared with 15% of boys who were not disorganized. In contrast, girls who were disorganized as infants actually had *lower* ratings for externalizing symptoms than did children who were not disorganized; their mean rating was close to zero.

It may be that children who were disorganized as infants show exaggerated gender-role stereotypes later in childhood, such that boys may exhibit extreme forms of acting out, and girls may act overly compliant and anxious to please. These behavior patterns may parallel controlling-punitive and controlling-caregiving patterns that children who were disorganized as infants have been found to develop around age 6 (Main et al., 2005). Controlling-punitive children use hostile, power-assertive tactics to gain their caregiver's attention, whereas controlling-caregiving children suppress their own negative affect and act cheerfully overbright and solicitous to the caregiver. One could examine empirically whether punitive strategies are increasingly more likely to be adopted by boys and caregiving strategies by girls, and whether such strategies generalize to relationships with peers and teachers, leading eventually to increased externalizing symptoms in boys and internalizing symptoms in girls.

Disorganized boys and girls were both high in depressive symptoms. It may be that FR behavior at 8 and 24 months leads to internalizing problems and depressive symptoms. After all, fear of the caregiver, who is supposed to be the child's source of comfort, is assumed to be the driving force behind disorganized attachment patterns, and the source of the disorganized child's feeling that his or her emotional needs cannot be met.

Similarly, research should further investigate the role of child gender as a moderator in predicting child outcomes related to maternal frightening behavior, and infant disorganization is also important to study, given our findings that early attachment disorganization predicts externalizing problems for boys but not for girls (Hazen et al., in press). Perhaps girls and boys have biologically based differential responses to maternal frightening behavior, as suggested by David and Lyons-Ruth (2005), who found that as maternal behavior becomes more frightening, infant girls are more likely to approach their mothers (or "tend and befriend") than are infant boys, who are more likely to show classic "fight or flight" responses to frightening situations. They present evidence indicating that hormones that facilitate mother-infant attachment, particularly oxytocin, are implicated in the female tendency to tend and befriend. Alternatively, as suggested earlier, boys may be more likely than girls to show externalizing symptoms in response to maternal frightening behavior resulting from sex-typed socialization practices that promote the development of self-assertive, competitive, and dominant behaviors in sons and compliant, relationship-enhancing behavior in daughters (Leaper, 1992).

For purposes of intervention, researchers should further investigate ways to effectively reduce frightening, atypical, and anomalous maternal behavior. Interventions have been developed that have successfully reduced the incidence of infant disorganization relative to control groups that did not experience these interventions. These programs assist mothers in recognizing the negative effects of an abusive past and help them gain confidence in themselves and form trusting relationships with others. It is important for future research to delve into the reasons behind the success of these interventions. Did they reduce the incidence of frightening behavior displayed by mothers and, if so, why? Did they reduce stress for these mothers, helping them resolve their early traumas, or help them become more conscious of their parenting so they were less likely to lapse into dissociated states leading to the display of frightening behaviors? Furthermore, future research should investigate the long-term outcomes for each of these particular intervention strategies. Did the programs successfully alter the children's developmental course? More specific information about how particular types of intervention work and their effects on children's development over time is critical, both for understanding developmental processes and for preventing the onset of debilitating emotional and behavior problems during childhood.

# REFERENCES

Abrams, K., Rifkin, A., & Hesse, E. (2006). Examining the role of parental frightened/frightening subtypes in predicting disorganized attachment within a brief observational procedure. *Development and Psychopathology, 18*, 344–362.

Achenbach, T. M., & Edelbrock, C. (1983). *Manual for the child behavior checklist and revised child behavior profile.* Burlington, VT: Queen City Printer.

Ainsworth, M. D. S. (1967). *Infancy in Uganda: Infant care and the growth of attachment.* Baltimore, MD: Johns Hopkins University Press.

Ainsworth, M. D. S., Blehar, M. C., Waters, E., & Wall, S. (1978). *Patterns of attachment: A psychological study of the strange situation.* Hillsdale, NJ: Erlbaum.

Allen, S., Hazen, N., & Jacobvitz, D. (2005 April). Extensive nonparental childcare during the first year: Links with attachment disorganization. Paper presented at the biennial meeting of the Society for Research in Child Development, Atlanta, GA.

Bakermans-Kranenburg, M. J., & van IJzendoorn, M. H. (2004). No association of dopamine D4 receptor (DRD4) and -521 C/T promoter polymorphisms with infant disorganization. *Attachment and Human Development, 6*, 211–218.

Bakermans-Kranenburg, M. J., van IJzendoorn, M. H., & Juffer, F. (2005). Disorganized infant attachment and preventive interventions: A review and meta-analysis. *Infant Mental Health Journal, 26*, 191–216.

Baron, R. M., & Kenny, D. A. (1986). The moderator-mediator variable distinction in social psychological research: Conceptual, strategic and statistical considerations. *Journal of Personality and Social Psychology, 51*, 1173–1182.

Benoit, D., & Parker, K. C. H. (1994). Stability and transmission of attachment across three generations. *Child Development, 65*, 1444–1456.

Bokhorst, C. L., Bakermans-Kranenburg, M. J., Fearon, P., van IJzendoorn, M. H., Fonagy, P., & Schuengel, C. (2003). The importance of shared environment in mother-infant attachment security: A behavioral genetic study. *Child Development, 74*, 1769–1982.

Bowlby, J. (1969/1982). *Attachment and loss: Vol. 1. Attachment.* New York, NY: Basic Books.

Bowlby, J. (1979). *The making and breaking of affectional bonds.* London, England: Tavistock.

Bowlby, J. (1980). *Attachment and loss: Vol. 3. Loss: Sadness and depression.* New York, NY: Basic Books.

Carlson, E. A. (1998). A perspective longitudinal study of attachment disorganization/disorientation. *Child Development, 69*, 1107–1128.

Cassidy, J., & Berlin, L. J. (1994). The insecure/ambivalent pattern of attachment: Theory and research. *Child Development, 65*, 971–991.

Cicchetti, D., & Barnett, D. (1991). Attachment organization in maltreated preschoolers. *Development and Psychopathology, 3*, 397–411.

Cicchetti, D., Rogosch, F. A., & Toth, S. L. (2006). Fostering secure attachment in infants in maltreating families through preventive interventions. *Development and Psychopathology, 18*, 623–649.

Corbin, J. R. (2007). Reactive attachment disorder: A biopsychosocial disturbance of attachment. *Child & Adolescence Social Work Journal, 24*, 539–552.

Cyr, C., Euser, E. M., Bakermans-Kranenburg, M. J., & van IJzendoorn, M. H. (2010). Attachment security and disorganization in maltreating and high-risk families: A series of meta-analyses. *Development and Psychopathology, 22*, 87–108.

David, D. H., & Lyons-Ruth, K. (2005). Differential attachment responses of male and female infants to frightening maternal behavior: Tend or befriend versus fight or flight. *Infant Mental Health, 26*, 1–18.

De Wolff, M. S., & van IJzendoorn, M. H. (1997). Sensitivity and attachment: A meta-analysis on parental antecedents of infant attachment. *Child Development, 68*, 571–591.

Dozier, M., Dozier, D., & Manni, M. (2002). Attachment and biobehavioral catch-up: The ABC's of helping infants in foster care cope with early adversity. *Zero to Three Bulletin, 22*, 7–13.

Dozier, M., Peloso, E., Lindhelm, O., Gordon, M. K., Manni, M., Sepulveda, S., Ackerman, J., Bernier, A., & Levine, S. (2006). Developing evidence based interventions for foster children: An example of randomized clinical trial with infants and toddlers. *Journal of Social Issues, 62*, 767–785.

Egeland, B., Jacobvitz, D., & Sroufe, L. A. (1988). Breaking the cycle of abuse: Implications for prediction and intervention. In K. D. Browne, C. Davies, and P. Stratton (Eds.), *Early prediction and prevention of child abuse*. New York, NY: John Wiley & Sons.

Fearon, R. M. P., Bakermans-Kranenburg, M. J., van IJzendoorn, M. H., Lapsley, A., & Roisman, G. I. (2010). The significance of insecure attachment and disorganization in the development of children's externalizing behavior: A meta-analytic study. *Child Development, 81*, 435–456.

Forbes, L., Evans, E., Moran, G., & Pederson, D. (2007). Change in atypical maternal behavior predicts change in attachment disorganization from 12 to 24 months in a high-risk sample. *Child Development, 78*, 995–971.

George, C., Kaplan, N., & Main, M. (1984). Adult Attachment Interview protocol. Unpublished manuscript, University of California at Berkeley.

George, C., Kaplan, N., & Main, M. (1985). Adult Attachment Interview protocol (2nd ed.). Unpublished manuscript, University of California at Berkeley.

George, C., Kaplan, N., & Main, M. (1996). Adult Attachment Interview protocol (3rd ed.). Unpublished manuscript, University of California at Berkeley.

Goldberg, S., Benoit, D., Blokland, K., & Madigan, S. (2003). Atypical maternal behavior, maternal representations, and infant disorganization attachment. *Development and Psychopathology, 12*, 1–21.

Grienenberger, J., Kelly, K., & Slade, A. (2005). Maternal reflective functioning, mother-infant affective communication, and infant attachment: Exploring the link between mental states and observed caregiving behavior in the intergenerational transmission of attachment. *Attachment and Human Development, 7,* 229–311.

Hazen, N., Allen, S., & Jacobvitz, D (in preparation). Extensive nonmaternal childcare during the first year: Associations with attachment disorganization and emotional and behavior problems during middle childhood.

Hazen, N., Jacobvitz, D., Higgins, K., Allen, S., & Jin, M. K. (in press). Pathways from disorganized attachment to later social-emotional problems: The role of gender and parent-child interaction patterns. In J. Soloman & C. George (Eds.), *Disorganization of attachment and caregiving: Research and clinical advances.* New York, NY: Guilford Press.

Heinicke, C. M., Fineman, N. R., Ruth, G., Recchia, S. L., Guthrie, D., & Rodning, C. (2000). Relationship-based intervention with at-risk mothers: Outcome in the first year of life. *Infant Mental Health Journal, 20*(4), 349–374.

Heinicke, C. M. Fineman, N. R., Ponce, V. A., & Guthrie, D. (2001). Relationship-based intervention with at-risk mothers: Outcome in the second year of life. *Infant Mental Health Journal, 20*(4), 431–462.

Hertsgaard, L., Gunnar, M., Erikson, M. F., & Nachmias, M. (1995). Adreno-cortical response to the Strange Situation in infants with disorganized/disoriented attachment relationships. *Child Development, 66,* 1100–1106.

Hesse, E., & Main, M. (2000). Disorganized infant, child and adult attachment: Collapse in behavioral and attentional strategies. *Journal of the American Psychoanalytic Association, 48* (4), 1097–1127.

Hesse, E., & Main, M. (2006). Frightened, threatening, and dissociative parental behavior in low-risk samples: Description, discussion and interpretations. *Development and Psychopathology, 18,* 309–343.

Hoffman, K. T., Marvin, R. S., Cooper, G., & Powell, B. (2006). Changing toddlers' and preschoolers' attachment classifications: The Circle of Security intervention. *Journal of Consulting and Clinical Psychology, 74,* 1017–1026.

Hubbs-Tait, L., Osofsky, J. D., Hann, D. M., & McDonald Culp, A. (1994). Predicting behavior problems and social competence in children of adolescent mothers. *Family Relations, 43,* 439–446.

Jacobvitz, D., Hazen, N., & Riggs, S. (1997, April). Disorganized mental processes in mothers, frightening/frightened caregiving and disoriented/disorganized behvior in infancy. Paper presented at the biennial meeting for the Society for Research in Child Development, Washington, DC.

Jacobvitz, D., Leon, K., & Hazen, N. (2006). Does expectant mothers' unresolved trauma predict frightening/frightened maternal behavior?: Risk and protective factors. *Development and Psychopathology, 18,* 363–379.

Jacobvitz, D., Zaccagnino, M., Mock, L., & Hazen, N. (2009, April). Intergenerational transmission of attachment disorganization: The role of anomalous maternal behavior. Paper presented at the biennial meeting of the Society for Research in Child Development, Denver, CO.

Jacobvitz, D., Zaccagnino , M., & Hazen, N. (in preparation). Frightening and anomalous maternal behavior at 8 and 24 months: Associations with psychopathological outcomes at 7 years. The University of Texas at Austin.

Juffer, F., Bakermans-Kranenburg, M. J., & van IJzendoorn, M. H. (2005). The importance of parenting in the development of disorganized attachment: Evidence from a preventive intervention study in adoptive families. *Journal of Child Psychology and Psychiatry*, 46, 263–274.

Kaplan, N. (1987). Individual differences in 6-year-olds' thoughts about separation: Predicted from attachment to mother at age 1. Unpublished doctoral dissertation, University of California at Berkeley.

Korfmacher, J., Adam, E., Ogawa, J., & Egeland, B. (1997). Adult attachment: Implications for the therapeutic process in a home visitation intervention. *Applied Developmental Science*, 1, 43–52.

Lakatos, K., Nemoda, Z., Toth, I., Ney, K., Sasvari-Szekely, M., & Gervai, J. (2002). Further evidence for the role of the dopamine receptor (DRD4) gene in attachment disorganization: Interaction of the exon III 48-bp repeat and the -521 C/T promoter polymorphisms. *Molecular Psychiatry*, 7, 27–31.

Lakatos, K., Toth, I., Nemoda, Z., Ney, K., Sasvari-Szekely, M., & Gervai, J. (2000). Dopamine D4 receptor (DRD4) gene polymorphism is associated with attachment disorganization in infants. *Molecular Psychiatry*, 5, 633–637.

Leaper, C. (1992). Parenting girls and boys. In Bornstein, M. H. (Ed.), *Handbook of parenting*. (2nd ed., Vol. 2, pp. 189–225). NJ: Erlbaum.

Lyons-Ruth, K., Alpern, L., & Repacholi, B. (1993). Disorganized infant attachment classification and maternal psychosocial problems as predictors of hostile-aggressive behavior in the preschool classroom. *Child Development*, 64, 572–585.

Lyons-Ruth, K., & Block, D. (1996). The disturbed caregiving system: Relations among childhood trauma, maternal caregiving, and infant affect and attachment. *Infant Mental Health Journal*, 17, 257–275.

Lyons-Ruth, K., Bronfman, E., & Atwood, G. (1999). A relational diathesis model of hostile-helpless states of mind: Expressions in mother-infant interaction. In J. Solomon & C. George (Eds.), *Attachment disorganization* (pp. 33–69). New York, NY: Guilford Press.

Lyons-Ruth, K., Bronfman, E., & Parsons, E. (1999). Maternal frightened, frightening, or atypical behavior and disorganized infant attachment patterns. In J. I. Vondra & D. Barnett (Eds.), Atypical patterns of infant attachment: Theory, research, and current directions. Monographs of the Society for Research in Child Development, 64 (3, Serial No. 258), 67–96.

Lyons-Ruth, K., Easterbrooks, M. A., & Cibelli, C. D. (1997). Infant attachment strategies, infant mental lag, and maternal depressive symptoms: Predictors of internalizing and externalizing problems at age 7. Developmental Psychology, 33, 681–692.

Lyons-Ruth, K., & Jacobvitz, D. (1999). Attachment disorganization: Unresolved loss, relational violence, and lapses in behavioral and attentional strategies. In J. Cassidy & P. Shaver (Eds.), Handbook of attachment: Theory, research, and clinical applications (pp. 530–554). New York, NY: Guilford Press.

Lyons-Ruth, K., & Jacobvitz, D. (2008). Disorganized attachment: Genetic factors, parenting contexts, and developmental transformation from infancy to adulthood. In J. Cassidy & P. Shaver (Eds.), Handbook of attachment: Theory, research, and clinical applications (2nd ed., pp. 666–697). New York, NY: Guilford Press.

Macdonald, H. Z., Beeghly, M., Grant-Knight, W., Augustyn, M., Woods, R. W., Cabral, H., Rose-Jacobs, R., Saxe, G. N, & Frank, D. A. (2008). Longitudinal association between infant disorganized attachment and childhood posttraumatic stress symptoms. Development and Psychopathology, 20, 1351–1351.

Madigan, S., Moran, G., & Pederson, D. (2006). Unresolved states of mind, disorganized attachment relationships, and disrupted interactions of adolescent mothers and their infants, Developmental Psychology, 42, 293–304.

Madigan, S., Moran, G., Schuengel, C., Pederson, D., & Otten, R. (2007). Unresolved maternal attachment representations, disrupted maternal behavior and disorganized attachment in infancy: links to toddler behavior problems. Journal of Child Psychology & Psychiatry, 48, 1042–1050.

Main, M., Goldwyn, R., & Hesse, E. (1984-2003). Adult Attachment Scoring and Classification System. Unpublished manuscript, University of California, Berkeley.

Main, M., & Hesse, E. (1990). Parents' unresolved traumatic experiences are related to infant disorganized attachment status: Is frightened and/or frightening parental behavior the linking mechanism? In M. T. Greenberg, D. Cicchetti, & E. M. Cummings (Eds.), Attachment in the preschool *years: Theory, research and intervention* (pp. 161–182). Chicago, IL: University of Chicago Press.

Main, M., & Hesse, E. (1992). Frightening, threatening, dissociative, timid-deferential, sexualized and disorganized parental behavior: A coding system for frightened/frightening (FR) parent-infant interactions. Unpublished manuscript, University of California at Berkeley.

Main, M., & Hesse, E. (1998, 2005). Frightened, threatening, dissociative, timid-deferential, sexualized, and disorganized parental behavior: A coding system for parent-infant interactions. Unpublished manuscript, University of California, Berkeley.

Main, M., Kaplan, N., & Cassidy, J. (1985). Security in infancy, childhood, and adulthood: A move to the level of representation. In J. Bretherton & E. Waters (Eds.), Growing points of attachment theory and research. *Monographs of the Society for Research in Child Development, 50* (1–2, Serial No. 209), 66–104.

Main, M., Hesse, E., & Kaplan, N. (2005). Predictability of attachment behavior and representational processes at 1, 6, and 18 years of age: The Berkeley longitudinal study. In K. E. Grossmann, K. Grossmann, & E. Waters (Eds.), *Attachment from infancy to adulthood* (pp. 245–304). New York, NY: Guilford Press.

Main, M., Hesse, E., & Goldwyn, R. (2008). Studying differences in language usage in recounting attachment history: An introduction to the AAI. In H. Steele & M. Steele (Eds.), *Clinical applications of the Adult Attachment Interview* (pp. 31–68). New York, NY: Guilford Press.

Main, M., & Solomon, J. (1986). Discovery of an insecure-disorganized/disoriented pattern. In T. B. Brazelton & M. Yogman (Eds.), *Affective development in infancy.* Norwood, NJ: Ablex.

Main, M., & Solomon, J. (1990). Procedures for identifying infants as disorganized/disoriented during the Ainswoth strange situation. In M. T. Greenberg, D. Cicchetti, & E. M. Cummings (Eds.), *Attachment beyond the preschool years: Theory, research, and intervention* (pp. 121–169). Chicago, IL: University of Chicago Press.

Main, M., & Stadtman, J. (1981). Infant response to rejection of physical contact by the mother. *Journal of the American Academy of Child Psychiatry, 20,* 292–307.

Meinlschmidt, G., & Heim, C. (2005). Decreased cortisol awakening response after early loss experience. *Psychoneuroendocrinology, 30*(6), 568–576.

Nicolson, N. (2004). Childhood parental loss and cortisol levels in adult men. *Psychoneuroendocrinology, 29*(8), 1012–1018.

Ogawa, J. R., Sroufe, L. A., Weinfield, N. S., Carlson, E. A., & Egeland, B. (1997). Development and the fragmented self: Longitudinal study of dissociative symptomatology in a nonclinical sample. *Development and Psychopathology, 9*, 855–879.

Petitto, J. M., Quade, D., & Evans, D. L. (1992). Relationship of object loss during development to hypothalamo-pituitary-adrenal axis function during major affective illness later in life. *Psychiatry Research, 44*, 227–236.

Sagi-Schwartz, A., van IJzendoorn, M. H., & Bakermans-Kranenburg, M. J. (2008). Does intergenerational transmission of trauma skip a generation? No meta-analytic evidence for tertiary traumatization with third generation of Holocaust survivors. *Attachment & Human Development, 10*, 105–121.

Sajaniemi, N., Mäkelä, J., Salokorpi, T., von Wendt, L., Hämäläinen, T., & Hakamies-Blomqvist, L. (2001). Cognitive performance and attachment patterns at four years of age in extremely low birth weight infants after early intervention. *European Child and Adolescent Psychiatry, 10*(2), 122–129.

Schuengel, C., Bakermans-Kranenburg, M. J., & van IJzendoorn, M. H. (1999). Frightening maternal behavior linking unresolved loss and disorganized infant attachment. *Journal of Consulting and Clinical Psychology, 67*, 54–63.

Shaw, D. S., Owens, E. B., Vondra, J. I., Keenan, K., & Winslow, E. B. (1996). Early risk factors and pathways in the development of early disruptive behavior problems. *Development and Psychopathology, 8*, 679–699.

Spangler, G., & Grossmann, K. E. (1993). Biobehavioral organization in securely and insecurely attached infants. *Child Development, 64*, 1439–1450.

Sroufe, L. A. (1979). The coherence of individual development. *American Psychologist, 34*, 834–841.

Sroufe, L. A. (1983). Infant-caregiver attachment and patterns of adaptation in preschool: The roots of maladaptation and competence. In M. Perlmutter (Ed.), *Minnesota Symposium in Child Psychology* (Vol. 16): *Development and policy concerning children with special needs* (pp. 41–83). Hillsdale, NJ: Erlbaum.

Sroufe, L. A. (1986). Bowlby's contribution to psychoanalytic theory and developmental psychopathology. *Journal of Child Psychology and Psychiatry, 27*, 841–849.

Sroufe, L. A. (1996). *Emotional development: The organization of emotional life in early years.* New York, NY: Cambridge University Press.

Sroufe, L. A., Carlson, E., & Shulman, S. (1993). Individuals in relationships: Development from infancy through adolescence. In D. C. Funder, R. Parke,

C. Tomlinson, L. Keesey, & K. Widaman (Eds.), *Studying lives through time: Approaches to personality and development* (pp. 315–342). Washington, DC: American Psychological Association.

Sroufe, L. A., Egeland, B., Carlson, E., & Collins, W. A. (2005). *The development of the person: The Minnesota study of risk and adaptation from birth to adulthood.* New York, NY: Guilford Press.

Sroufe, L. A., Egeland, B., & Kreutzer, T. (1990). The fate of early experience following developmental change: Longitudinal approaches to individual adaptation in childhood. *Child Development, 61,* 1363–1373.

Sroufe, L. A., & Jacobvitz, D. (1989). Diverging pathways, developmental transformations, multiple etiologies, and the problem of continuity in development. *Human Development, 32,* 196–204.

Sroufe, L. A., & Waters, E. (1977). Attachment as an organizational construct. *Child Development, 48,* 1184–1199.

Steele, H., Steele, M., & Fonagy, P. (1996). Associations among attachment classifications of mothers, fathers, and their infants: Evidence for a relationship-specific perspective. *Child Development, 67,* 541–555.

Steele, H., & Steele, M. (2008). *Clinical Applications of the Adult Attachment Interview.* New York, NY: Guildford Press.

Toth, S. L., Rogosch, F. A., Manly, J. T., & Cicchetti, D. (2006). The efficacy of toddler-parent psychotherapy to reorganize attachment in the young offspring of mothers with major depressive disorder: A randomized clinical trial. *Journal of Consulting and Clinical Psychology, 74,* 1006–1016.

True, M., Pasani, L., & Oumar, F. (2001). Infant-mother interactions among the Dogon of Mali. *Child Development, 72,* 1451–1466.

Tyrka, A. R., Price, L. H., Gelernter, J., Schepker, C., Anderson, G. M., & Carpenter, L. L. (2009). Interaction of childhood maltreatment with the corticotropin-releasing hormone receptor gene: Effects on hypothalamic-pituitary-adrenal axis reactivity. *Biological Psychiatry,66,* 681–685.

van IJzendoorn, M. H. (1995). Adult attachment representations, parental responsiveness, and infant attachment: A meta-analysis on the predictive validity of the Adult Attachment Interview. *Psychological Bulletin, 117,* 387–403.

van IJzendoorn, M. H., & Bakermans-Kranenburg, M. J. (2006). DRD4-7-repeat polymorphism moderates the association between maternal unresolved loss or trauma and infant disorganization. *Attachment and Human Development, 8,* 291–307.

van IJzendoorn, M. H., & Sagi-Schwartz, A. (2008).

van IJzendoorn, M. H., Schuengel, C., & Bakermans-Kranenburg, M. J. (1999). Disorganized attachment in early childhood: Meta-analysis of precursors, concomitants, and sequelae. *Development and Psychopathology, 11*, 225–249.

Vorria, P., Papaligoura, Z., Dunn, J., van IJzendoorn, M. H., Steele, H., Kontopoulou, A., & Sarafidou, Y. (2003). Early experiences and attachment relationships of Greek infants raised in residential group care. *Journal of Child Psychology and Psychiatry, 44*, 1208–1220.

Ward, M. J., & Carlson, E. A. (1995). Associations among Adult Attachment representations, maternal sensitivity, and infant-mother attachment in a sample of adolescent mothers. *Child Development, 66*, 69–79.

Waters, E., & Sroufe, L.A. (1983). Social competence as a developmental construct. *Developmental Review, 3*, 79–97.

Zeanah, C. Smyke, A. T., Koga, S. F., Carlson, E., & the Bucharest Early Intervention Project Core Group. (2005). Attachment in institutionalized and community children in Romania. *Child Development, 76*, 1015–1028.

# From Research to Practice

*Developmental Contributions to the Field
of Prevention Science*

Sheree L. Toth, Robert C. Pianta,
and Martha Farrell Erickson

Prevention science is focused on intervening in the course of development in order to reduce or eliminate some form of maladaptation or psychopathology. In the United States alone, more than 25% of adults suffer from a diagnosable mental disorder annually (Kessler et al., 2005), approximately 12% of children have a psychiatric disorder (Costello, Egger, & Angold, 2005), and in some cities, more than 60% of youth leave school and drop out before graduation (National Center for Education Statistics [NCES], 2008). Given the prevalence of mental disorders and the personal and financial burdens associated with their treatment (World Health Organization, 2001; National Institute of Mental Health, 2008), it is far more effective to prevent the emergence of mental disorders and other costly outcomes than to offer treatment once a disorder has developed. As one example from education, the costs related to special education for students with attention, learning, or emotional/behavioral disorders are in the range of two to three times that of a student not receiving those services (Layzer & Price, 2008). In order to provide effective prevention initiatives, a solid theoretical foundation on human development and an understanding of both typical and atypical development is necessary (Ialongo et al., 2006).

In this chapter, we describe the utility of a developmental psychopathology framework for informing the design and evaluation of prevention efforts. Although typically the focus has been on the potential of theory for informing prevention, we also discuss the contributions of prevention trials for informing developmental theory. Prevention initiatives that have incorporated aspects of attachment theory and that have been provided to diverse populations and in varied settings, including community clinics, homes, child care centers, and schools, are then presented. The importance of conducting translational research is highlighted, and strategies for addressing barriers to dissemination and increasing the exportation of evidence-based models of prevention from academic arenas to community settings are discussed.

## A DEVELOPMENTAL PSYCHOPATHOLOGY PERSPECTIVE ON PREVENTION

From its inception, the discipline of developmental psychopathology has been committed to bridging scientific research and its application to practice (Cicchetti, 1984; Cicchetti & Toth, 2006). Given its focus on the interplay between normal and abnormal development, developmental psychopathology is uniquely positioned to provide a strong theoretical foundation for prevention science. Building on an organizational perspective (Sroufe & Waters, 1977; Werner & Kaplan, 1963), development is conceived as involving a series of qualitative reorganizations within and among multiple domains of biological and psychological functioning (Cicchetti, 1993; Cicchetti & Sroufe, 1978; Sroufe & Rutter, 1984). Over the course of development, the individual is confronted with a series of stage-salient developmental tasks. These include physiological homeostasis, differentiation and regulation of affect, development of a secure attachment relationship, emergence of an autonomous self, increasing representational capacity, development of effective peer relationships, and adaptation to school. Although successful resolution of earlier stage-salient issues probabilistically increases the likelihood that subsequent issues will be resolved effectively, suggesting coherence in development (Sroufe, 1979), there is both continuity and discontinuity in the course of development depending on individual and contextual experiences. Empirical evidence for these theoretical propositions is strong (Egeland & Farber, 1984; Sroufe, Egeland, Carlson, & Collins, 2005a).

Although the overarching goal of prevention science is to modify the developmental course for individuals who are at risk for maladaptation in order to foster positive outcomes or reduce future problems (Durlak, 1997), prevention trials also possess implications for developmental theory. In essence, understanding processes that can right the course of development can inform our understanding of how various risk and protective factors operate in normal development (Cicchetti & Hinshaw, 2002; Cicchetti & Toth, 1991, 1992; Kellam & Rebok, 1992). Ideally, then, although developmental theory provides the foundation for practice, prevention practice should link directly back to developmental theory (Ialongo et al., 2006). To be more specific, every prevention trial could be designed to test a theoretical model about development.

The Minnesota Parent-Child Longitudinal Study (MPCLS) is an exemplar of the circular feedback that can occur between theory and practice. In this pioneering research initiative, the investigative team sought to demonstrate that the course of development unfolds in a lawful manner and that it is influenced significantly by early relationships with caregivers. Contrary to popular thinking in the early 1970s, Alan Sroufe, Byron Egeland, and their colleagues and students hypothesized that the course of development was not deterministically ordained solely by genetic or temperamental factors, but rather that it was substantially influenced by early social experiences with primary caregivers (Egeland & Sroufe, 1981; Sroufe et al., 2005a). Based on more than three decades of research during which the investigative team followed 180 children who had been born into poverty, several important conclusions were drawn (Sroufe et al., 2005a). These include that:

- Care provided during the early years of life is most important to the developing child.
- Individuals are affected by their cumulative experience, and even when dramatic changes occur, early experience is not erased.

- Resilience and certain types of psychopathology are developmental constructs and not inherent, inborn characteristics.
- Dichotomies such as temperament *or* experience are generally false.
- Change and continuity in development are both coherent and lawful.
- The individual must be understood within a transactional model that examines the person in conjunction with the supports and challenges with which they are confronted.

Some of these tenets flow directly into informing prevention efforts. Perhaps foremost, the importance of intervening early in the developmental process, before the emergence of diagnosable mental disorders, and the fundamental importance of relationships with adults, are highlighted. In this regard, the child's progression through a series of stage-salient issues and the opportunity to intervene to prevent early failure and a subsequent negative hierarchical organization of development is critical. The fact that early experience cannot be erased, even when circumstances change dramatically, possesses important implications for work with children who are at risk for maladaptation. Moreover, the unique and perhaps singular formative role for children's near- and longer-term health in many domains, of attachment relationships with caregivers, provided the field of prevention science with a focus for prevention trials and theories concerning the mechanisms of effects.

For example, this position is dramatically demonstrated when considering how best to address the needs of children in the foster care system. Even though the early traumas that culminated in removal may have ended, the scars may carry over into new environments and, unless they are addressed in the context of attachment-related processes, foster parents are likely to become overwhelmed and children may continue to be retraumatized as they experience repeated failed placements. A key aspect of this perspective is that during early childhood, disturbances need to be viewed as a relationship disturbance and not as a problem residing within the child (Sameroff & Emde, 1989; Sroufe, 1989). Finally, the dynamic nature of development and the effect of both intrinsic and extrinsic influences on the developing individual must be factored into prevention strategies. Although a child may appear to be resilient at a given point in time, developmental transitions and the associated challenges may present new vulnerabilities (Toth & Cicchetti, 1999). Importantly, however, such transitions also may offer windows of opportunity to provide interventions that may deflect the child from a potentially negative pathway onto a more positive course.

In accord with lessons learned from the MPCLS (Egeland & Erickson, 2004) and a developmental psychopathology perspective on development, several attachment-theory-informed interventions have been provided to, and evaluated with, at-risk infants, toddlers, preschoolers, and school-age children. These include Steps Toward Effective Enjoyable Parenting (STEEP™), Child-Parent Psychotherapy (CPP), and the MyTeachingPartner (MTP) initiatives to intervene with preschool teachers.

## THE STEEP™ PROGRAM

The STEEP™ program (Steps Toward Effective, Enjoyable Parenting) was designed to promote healthy parent-child relationships and prevent social-emotional difficulties among children born to first-time parents who are challenged by risk factors that include poverty, lack of education, stressful life circumstances, and social isolation. Attachment theory provided a framework for the program, and research on factors that underlie healthy parent-child relationships (particularly findings from the MPCLS) informed the program's goals, themes, and strategies. First developed in 1986 by Martha Farrell Erickson and Byron Egeland and evaluated in a randomized, controlled study (Egeland and Erickson, 1993, 2004), STEEP™ has been used in varied settings throughout North America, Australia, and Europe and has been adapted for use with several special populations, including indigenous families, women identified as substance abusing during pregnancy, teen parents, mothers who are depressed, families identified as abusive or neglectful, and families of preterm, medically fragile infants.

Participants typically are recruited through obstetric clinics during the second trimester of their pregnancy. Biweekly home visits, tailored to the unique needs, strengths, and interests of each family, begin at the time of enrollment and continue at least until the child's second birthday. Shortly after the babies are born, mothers in the program also begin attending biweekly group sessions with others whose babies are approximately the same age. Reflecting the relationship-based approach that is at the heart of the STEEP™ program, each group is facilitated by the same person who conducts the home visits for that cohort of eight to ten families. Participants indicate that time to build a one-on-one relationship with their STEEP™ facilitator during their pregnancy makes it much easier to join in group activities.

Group sessions in the STEEP™ program begin with parent-child interaction time, involving planned activities structured around the developmental issues typical at that time in the baby's life. However, structure is flexible, allowing opportunities for the facilitator to pick up on here-and-now observations and teachable moments.

Following interaction time and a casual meal, mothers move to another room for mom-talk time while their babies remain in the interaction room for developmentally appropriate activities with childcare staff. Mom-talk time is an opportunity for informal support and semistructured activities that address the parents' own issues, including relationship skills, balancing adult needs and child needs, and examining how one's relationship history influences responses to your child. Although the biweekly group meetings are geared toward mothers and babies, fathers and other family members participate in home-based activities and periodic family events. In some implementations of the STEEP™ program, father groups also are offered.

Building on attachment research that highlights the importance of parental sensitivity and responsiveness to infant cues, STEEP™ aims to support and enhance sensitivity and address the personal and contextual factors that sometimes undermine sensitive care. A centerpiece of the program, with a particular emphasis on promoting sensitivity, is the Seeing Is Believing™ strategy for videorecording parent-infant interaction and engaging parents in a process of self-observation and discovery as they watch the video with their home visitor (Erickson, 2005). (Both mothers and fathers—and sometimes other household members—participate in this activity during home visits.) Through a process of open-ended questions, the STEEP™ facilitator encourages parents to focus on what their baby is telling them and to recognize their own skills in adapting to their baby's needs. Videorecording helps maintain the parent-child relationship as the focus of the intervention, provides a record for monitoring the family's progress, and is a valuable tool when facilitators seek guidance from consultants or supervisors. The recording also is offered as a keepsake for the family—and, according to many parents, it is an incentive for participating in the STEEP™ program.

A baby learns through experience whether parents will offer comfort when he or she cries, take time to play when he or she feels sociable, and provide peace and quiet when he or she would rather sleep than be tickled. However, many factors can underlie a parent's ability to provide and sustain sensitive, responsive care. Although each family has a unique combination of challenges and strengths, research points to certain major factors that commonly underlie sensitivity and responsiveness. The STEEP™ program addresses these factors in both home visits and group interventions:

- **Knowledge and understanding of child development.** Sensitive care is grounded in knowledge about child development and understanding of the developmental meaning of key behaviors such as separation protest or toddler negativism. When parents lack that understanding, they often hold unrealistic expectations and get caught in a cycle of frustration and anger, attributing negative qualities to their child just because he or she is doing what children naturally do.
- **Social support.** For parents to respond sensitively to their children's needs, their own needs must be addressed. Many parents are socially isolated; they lack supportive friends or family members and/or lack the skills or confidence to access supportive resources. Barriers to getting support also may include lack of transportation and money. Sometimes parents are surrounded by family and

friends, but those networks do not support good parenting and the best interest of the child. This is dramatically evident, for example, in families living in a culture of substance abuse. STEEP™ helps parents identify potential sources of support and develop the skills to use support effectively.

- **Looking back, moving forward.** Consistent with attachment theory and research on intergenerational transmission of parenting, an important part of STEEP™ is to help parents reflect on what they learned in their own early relationships and how that influences their responses to their children. Both in home visits and group sessions, STEEP™ creates a supportive environment in which parents reflect on their history, confront painful memories, and identify positive experiences to pass on to their children. Understanding that no one is a perfect parent, the focus is on leaving hurtful patterns behind and mustering all available resources to become a "good enough" parent. As described in the *STEEP™ Facilitators' Guide* (Erickson, Egeland, Simon, & Rose, 2002), group activities give parents permission to begin looking back so they can move forward. Home visits afford an opportunity for more personalized encouragement and support.

Overall, STEEP™ is a relationship-based preventive intervention model, grounded in the belief that relationships change relationships. Attachment theory suggests that the models established early in life are difficult, but not impossible, to change. STEEP™ builds on the belief that, for a person with negative models of self and others, the best pathway for change is a relationship that contradicts those old expectations. For example, if a mother has learned in her childhood that people abandon her when she expresses anger, then the best way to change that belief is to stick with her through thick and thin, working through times of conflict with persistence and a belief that better times are ahead (see Erickson, Korfmacher, & Egeland, 1992, for a thorough discussion). Thus, STEEP™ aims to help parents experience new ways of being in a relationship. Specifically, STEEP™ facilitators strive to (1) be consistent and persistent in following through on what they say they will do with and for a parent; (2) maintain a focus on the parent's strengths (Seeing Is Believing™ provides one valuable tool for doing that); and (3) rather than solving problems *for* the parent, supporting the parent in finding and implementing appropriate solutions. For a parent who learned from the beginning of life that he or she was powerless, it can be a life-changing experience to discover and build the competence to improve one's own life.

## RANDOMIZED CONTROLLED TRIAL OF THE STEEP™ PROGRAM

The first implementation of STEEP™ was subjected to a controlled evaluation, funded by the National Institute of Mental Health and carried out at the University of Minnesota (Egeland & Erickson, 1993). Beginning in 1987, the researchers enrolled 154 pregnant women through obstetric clinics in Minneapolis. Half were randomly assigned to participate in the STEEP™ preventive intervention program and half were randomized to a control group, participating in assessments during pregnancy and when the babies were 13 months, 19 months, and two years of age. All subjects were first-time parents, 17 years of age or older, eligible for Aid to Families with Dependent Children (AFDC) or poor and uninsured, and had no education beyond high school. Most (92%) were single at the time of enrollment, and a majority reported a history of abuse in their own childhood and/or in recent relationships with partners.

Although the evaluation was conducted on the first implementation of the program—without benefit of a pilot project—Project STEEP™ yielded positive findings on the program's efficacy. Compared to the control group, mothers participating in the STEEP™ intervention demonstrated a better understanding of child development, greater sensitivity to their baby's cues, more organized and appropriately stimulating home environments, and better life management skills. Participants also reported fewer symptoms of depression and anxiety, and they had fewer repeat pregnancies within two years of the birth of their baby. Not surprisingly, mothers who participated most fully in the program benefited the most. Interestingly, while stressful life events were related to insensitivity in the control group, this was not true for participants in the intervention. Thus, it appeared that being in the program provided a buffer effect, allowing mothers to sustain sensitive care even when facing challenging life circumstances.

Although the researchers had hoped that the program would show an impact on quality of parent-infant attachment, the study did not yield significant differences between treatment and control subjects in quality of attachment at 13 or 19 months. However, control subjects showed a tendency to move toward more anxious attachments by 19 months, whereas that was not true for the intervention group. The researchers attribute this difference to the complexity of issues the families faced and the fact that parents and facilitators were just reaching a level of trust and beginning to engage in a deeper level of psychological work at the time the program ended. (Note that in the first implementation of STEEP™ the researchers were funded to serve the families only for one year, whereas subsequent adaptations of the program have continued service at least until the child's second birthday.)

## RANDOMIZED CONTROLLED TRIALS OF CHILD-PARENT PSYCHOTHERAPY

### Preventive Interventions for Infants in Maltreating Families

Research with maltreated infants has consistently demonstrated that insecure-disorganized attachments are prevalent and that these babies are likely to unsuccessfully resolve subsequent developmental issues (Cicchetti & Toth, 2005). Therefore, the provision of preventive interventions to promote the attainment of secure attachment organization in infants from maltreating families is essential in order to redirect the developmental course onto a more adaptive pathway.

With support from the National Institute of Mental Health and with the goal of improving attachment security and increasing the occurrence of positive developmental outcomes in infants from maltreating families, two intervention models were implemented at Mt. Hope Family Center,

University of Rochester. The first, Child-Parent Psychotherapy (CPP), consisted of dyadic infant-mother therapy sessions designed to improve infant-mother attachment relationships by altering the influence of negative maternal representational models of attachment on mother-infant relations. The second model, Psychoeducational Parenting Intervention (PPI), focused on providing mothers with didactic training in child development, parenting skills, coping strategies for managing stresses in the immediate environment, and assistance in developing social support networks. Both interventions were home-based in order to assist therapists in gaining a more in-depth understanding of the stressful life contexts of participants, including living in areas with high levels of community violence. Home visitation has been shown to be an effective model for preventing damage to vulnerable children (Shirk, Talmi, & Olds, 2000). In fact, the U.S. Advisory Board on Child Abuse and Neglect (1990) identified home visitation services as the best documented strategy for preventing child maltreatment. Although data on the effectiveness of home visitation for preventing maltreatment have emerged (Olds et al., 1997, 1998), studies on the effectiveness of home visitation services for families where maltreatment has already occurred, as well as assessments of whether home visitation services can alter the future life course development in infants who have been maltreated, had yet to be conducted.

## Child Parent Psychotherapy (CPP) Model

This model of intervention is derived from the work of Fraiberg, Adelson, and Shapiro (1975), and it has been shown to be efficacious in fostering positive development in high-risk, low-income, immigrant families (Lieberman, 1991, 1992; Lieberman & Pawl, 1988), as well as in families where domestic violence is present (Lieberman, Ghosh Ippen, & Van Horn, 2006; Lieberman & Van Horn, 2005). A guiding assumption of CPP is that difficulties in the parent-child relationship are not a function of deficits in parenting knowledge and skill alone. Rather, the problems that maltreating caregivers have in relating sensitively and responsively to their infants stem from insecure internal representational models that evolved in response to the caregiver's own negative experiences in childhood. The infant evokes affects and memories associated with the caregiver's childhood relationship experiences, and unresolved and conflictual feelings can be projected onto the infant, resulting in distorted perceptions of the infant, a lack of attunement, and insensitive care. Consistent with the undergirding assumptions of the STEEP™ program, CPP believes that changes within the relationship matrix—comprised of the caregiver, therapist, and child—are necessary in order to foster positive outcomes.

In CPP, the patient is not the caregiver or the infant, but rather it is the relationship between the caregiver and her baby. Although CPP can be provided to paternal caregivers, custodial family members, or to couples and their offspring, the intervention in the randomized controlled trials (RCTs) reported herein was provided to mother-child dyads. Masters-level therapists met weekly with mothers and their 12-month-old infants during sessions conducted in the home over the course of 1 year. CPP is supportive, nondirective, and nondidactic, and includes developmental guidance based on concerns expressed by mothers. Similar to STEEP™, CPP strives to help caregivers develop their own solutions rather than instructing them on proscribed behaviors. During the sessions, the therapist and the mother engage in joint observation of the infant. The therapist's empathic responsiveness to the mother and the baby allows for expansion of parental understanding and exploration of maternal misperceptions of the infant. Therapists strive to link distorted emotional reactions and perceptions of the infant as they are enacted during mother-infant interaction with associated memories and affects from the mother's prior childhood experiences. Through respect, empathic concern, and unfailing positive regard, the therapeutic relationship provides the mother with a corrective emotional experience, through which the mother is able to differentiate current from past relationships and to form positive internal representations of herself and of herself in relationship to others, particularly her infant. Mothers also are helped to develop more specific models of relationships rather than generalizing past negative relationship experiences to all potential social partners. As a result of this process, mothers are able to expand their responsiveness, sensitivity, and attunement to the infant, fostering security in the mother-child relationship and promoting emerging autonomy in the child.

The following goals were addressed in the CPP intervention:

1. The therapist expanded the mother's empathic responsiveness, sensitivity, and attunement to her infant.
2. The therapist promoted maternal fostering of infant autonomy and positive negotiation of maternal and child goals.
3. Distorted perceptions and reactions to the infant stemming from maternal representational models were altered, and more positive representations of the infant were developed.

## Psychoeducational Parenting Intervention (PPI) Model

In addition to services typically made available to maltreating parents via the Community Standard (CS), weekly home visitation was provided via the PPI model. The PPI model utilized in this investigation focused on two primary goals:

1. Parent education regarding infant development and developmentally appropriate parenting skills was provided in order to increase positive parenting.
2. Support was provided to help women with the development of adequate maternal self-care skills, including assisting mothers with personal needs, fostering adaptive functioning, and improving social supports.

Therapists were trained in the provision of an ecologically informed model of influences on mother and child. This model strives to address how factors at different levels of proximity to the mother and child interact to form a system of influences on functioning. Practically, this results in the simultaneous examination of maternal personal resources, social support, and stresses in the home, family, and community that can affect maternal caregiving. Therapists were employed who were adept at attending to the needs of multiproblem families, were knowledgeable regarding accessing community resources, and had expertise in addressing community violence. Similar to CPP, weekly 60-minute home visits were conducted over a period of 12 months.

The PPI model was a psychoeducationally based model grounded in the present that strived to educate, improve parenting, decrease maternal stress, and increase life satisfaction. The approach is didactic in nature, providing mothers with specific information, facts, procedures, and practices. Within a core agenda of topics on parenting and improved social skills to be addressed, flexibility and latitude in the amount of time spent on various topics was stressed in order to respond to the individual needs of each mother. This flexibility is consistent with that utilized by other home-based interveners working with disadvantaged populations. An initial assessment of client needs within the domains of parenting and maternal self-care was conducted to delineate specific areas most in need of intervention. Thus, although there was a consistent range of issues to be addressed with each mother, the model allowed for special emphasis on areas particularly germane to individual mothers.

Both the CPP and PPI interventions were manualized, with central components and core principles of each approach specified. Therapists participated in individual and group supervision on a weekly basis, and checks on the fidelity of the intervention implementation for each approach were conducted throughout the course of intervention. Extensive outreach was typically necessary to engage mothers in the interventions. The length of the intervention averaged 46 weeks for the CPP group and 49 weeks for the PPI group. Although intervention sessions in the home were scheduled weekly, fewer sessions were conducted as a result of cancellations and missed appointments. On average, 22 sessions were conducted in the CPP group and 25 sessions in the PPI group.

## Design and Recruitment

The baseline (pre-) and post-intervention attachment relationships of mothers and infants in both CPP and PPI interventions were compared with the functioning of mothers and their maltreated infants who received services typically available when a child had been maltreated—the community standard (CS) group. A fourth nonmaltreated comparison (NC) group, comprising infants and mothers who were demographically comparable to the three maltreatment groups, also was recruited. The NC group was included in order to compare normative developmental changes over time in a group of babies who had not experienced maltreatment, but who had similar environmental stressors (e.g., poverty, lack of access to quality child care, community violence) with those who had been identified by the Department of Human Services (DHS) for the occurrence of child abuse and/or neglect within the family. All maltreated infants and their mothers were randomly assigned to the PPI, CPP, or the CS group.

Families were not excluded from study participation because of ethnic or racial considerations, and the racial/ethnic backgrounds of the participants reflected the local demographics of victims of child maltreatment and included high percentages of African American and Latina families. To be randomized to the preventive intervention, mothers and infants could not have any significant cognitive or physical limitations that would hamper their ability to understand and/or participate in the research or the clinical interventions. Despite these exclusionary considerations, the population was not further restricted based on issues such as the presence of domestic violence, parental substance use, or parental psychiatric illness. Therefore, the results of the RCT could be more easily assimilated by front-line professionals in clinic settings, where multiple problems are the norm.

Nonmaltreating (NC) families were chosen randomly from the County's list of recipients of Temporary Assistance to Needy Families (TANF). Because prior experience has revealed that the majority of maltreating families referred to DHS are socioeconomically disadvantaged, utilization of TANF lists provided access to a demographically similar population. Although all families were asked whether they had ever received child protective services, families are not always forthcoming with this information. Therefore, during the initial contact, consent was obtained to verify non-maltreatment status through a partnership with DHS that allowed access to state central registry data.

Reviews of the CPS registry were utilized to confirm that children in the nonmaltreated comparison group did not have histories of maltreatment. Any reports or observations indicative of maltreatment during the course of the study, such as disclosures of maltreatment by the families or observations by project staff of parenting failures severe enough to warrant a CPS report, excluded families from the comparison group. Additionally, the Maternal Maltreatment Classification Interview (MMCI; Cicchetti, Toth, & Manly, 2003) was administered to all mothers as an independent verification of maltreatment status. If a family refused to consent to this procedure, then they were not enrolled in the investigation. Only those families who had never received services through the DHS child protective or preventive units were included in the NC group.

### Intervention Components

Manuals were developed and implemented for each of the two interventions. Because the DHS becomes active via case monitoring, management, or referral when reports of child maltreatment are received, this served as a constant across all conditions. Therefore, all families in which maltreatment had been identified received some services, even if they were not randomized to the theoretically guided intervention conditions.

The provision of intervention to populations struggling with a multitude of stressors requires flexibility and responsivity to the frequent crises and challenges that confront these families. Therefore, although focused intervention models were provided, from an ethical practice standpoint, issues such as domestic violence, inadequate housing, food, or clothing, and substance abuse needed to be addressed as they arose. Treatment models were focused on the improvement of parenting and the elimination of maltreatment and its sequelae, but attention to myriad related issues that were encountered during clinical contacts with this population also were addressed. Therapists in both intervention models not only received extensive training on the respective models of treatment that they were providing, but also on the importance of cultural sensitivity and on how to deal with the extensive needs of these families. Neither treatment model could be effective in the absence of responsivity to the multiple challenges present in maltreating families. The ability to respond to such issues also increases the portability of the models into community clinic settings. Because the interventions were home-based, comfort and skill in navigating inner-city neighborhoods where drug use and violence were normative were necessary.

In the CS condition, the DHS managed cases in accord with their standard approach. Although variability existed, with service provision ranging from no service to referral to existing community clinics, this condition represents the community standard with which the PPI and CPP models were compared. The use of a CS comparison group enabled us to determine the effects of standard practices on child and family functioning, as compared with theoretically informed delivery of services. The approaches that the DHS used with families who have been reported for maltreatment and are participating in the proposed investigation were systematically recorded via a standardized services questionnaire.

## Intervention Outcome

Assessments of the quality of attachment, utilizing the Strange Situation (Ainsworth, Blehar, Waters, & Wall, 1978), were conducted at baseline (infant age of 13 months) and at the conclusion of the intervention (infant age of 26 months) in order to evaluate the efficacy of the interventions. Videotapes of the Strange Situations were coded independently by individuals who were unaware of maltreatment status or intervention treatment conditions.

At baseline, there were no differences among the three maltreatment groups (CPP, PPI, and CS) in the percentage of infants who were securely attached to their mothers. These results attest to the success of the randomization procedure. Notably, 3.6% of the infants in the CPP and 0% of the babies in the PPI and CS groups were securely attached. These findings are consistent with the broader attachment literature that includes the coding of Type D attachments that reveals that a very small percentage of maltreated babies develop secure attachments with their primary caregiver (Cicchetti & Toth, 2005).

Although a significantly greater percentage of infants in the non-maltreated group were securely attached than were infants in any of the three maltreatment groups, the rate of security among the comparisons (33%) underscores that the NC comparisons are a very high-risk group.

The lower than average rate of attachment security found in the NC group (33% versus the typical rate of 50% to 60% in nonrisk samples) is but one illustration of the developmental context of these nonmaltreated babies reared in lower-SES conditions.

In addition, at baseline, the three groups of maltreated infants each displayed extremely high rates of attachment disorganization (86% CPP; 82% PPI; 91% CS). These percentages of disorganized attachment did not significantly differ among the three maltreatment groups. In contrast, the rate of Type D attachment in the NC group was 20%.

Post-intervention attachment findings were compelling. The maltreated infants in the CS group had a 1.9% attachment security rate, a nonsignificant improvement over their 0% baseline rate of security. The maltreated infants in each of the two interventions exhibited large increases in attachment security from baseline to post-intervention (CPP: 3.6% to 60.7%; PPI: 0% to 54.5%). Importantly, both the CPP and PPI interventions were equally successful in modifying attachment insecurity. The percentage of attachment security remained at 39% in the infants in the NC group.

Furthermore, assessments conducted at the conclusion of the intervention revealed that the percentage of Type D attachment had declined from 86% to 32% for the CPP group and from 82% to 46% for the PPI group. Conversely, the infants in the CS group continued to exhibit high rates of disorganization (78%); the percentages of Type D attachment in the NC group at baseline and post-intervention were virtually identical (20% and 19%).

The results of this RCT demonstrate that both an intervention informed by attachment theory (CPP) and an intervention that focuses on improving parenting skills, increasing maternal knowledge of child development, and enhancing the coping and social support skills of maltreating mothers (PPI) were equally successful in altering the predominantly insecure and disorganized attachment organizations of maltreated infants.

Given the demonstrated efficacy of both interventions, it becomes important to consider why these therapeutic models were effective in altering attachment security. Several components of these interventions may have contributed to their success, and it is important to consider them when analyzing the feasibility of exporting these interventions into real-world clinical contexts. First, all therapists received extensive training before implementing the interventions, and they were familiar not only with the intervention modality, but also with the theory from which the interventions were derived. All therapists also had considerable prior experience working with low-income maltreating families. Both models were manualized, weekly individual and group supervision was provided, and therapists' adherence to their respective model was monitored for each case throughout the provision of the intervention. Caseloads were maintained at levels considerably lower than is typical of outpatient mental health settings; therapists were therefore able to devote considerable time to engaging mothers and to conceptualizing treatment plans. The positive outcome of this investigation supports the importance of investing in more costly interventions, including allowing therapists sufficient time for training and supervision.

As predicted by the organizational perspective, the early insecure, generally disorganized attachments displayed by maltreated infants do not doom these youngsters to have poor-quality relationship expectations and negative self-representations throughout development. The success of the interventions, informed by basic research knowledge on the etiology and developmental sequelae of child maltreatment, suggests that attachment organization is modifiable, even if a high percentage of Type D attachment is initially characteristic of the sample. Following the organizational perspective on development, it is expected that these maltreated youngsters, now that they are traversing a more positive trajectory, will be more likely to continue on an adaptive pathway and successfully resolve future salient developmental tasks (compare with Sroufe, Carlson, Levy, & Egeland, 1999). The preventive interventions have demonstrated that behavioral plasticity is possible, at least in the early years of life.

## Preventive Interventions for Maltreated Preschoolers

The preschool years are an especially important time for symbolic and representational development; it is during this period that representational models of the self and of the self in relation to others evolving from the attachment relationship become increasingly structured and organized.

Although developing children are likely to maintain specific models of individual relationships, these models become increasingly integrated into more generalized models of relationships over time (Crittenden, 1990), thereby affecting children's future relationship expectations. Because maltreated children internalize relational features of their caregiving experiences, they are likely to generalize negative representations of the self and the self in relation to others to novel situations and relationship partners (Howes & Segal, 1993; Lynch & Cicchetti, 1991, 1992; Toth & Cicchetti, 1996).

Both cross-sectional and longitudinal research studies demonstrate that maltreatment exerts negative effects on representational development, that these effects become more entrenched as development proceeds, and that the representational themes enacted in children's narratives are reflective of their maltreatment experiences and are related to child behavior problems (see Toth, Cicchetti, Macfie, Maughan, & VanMeenan, 2000). Based on our empirical work, we concluded that the provision of interventions designed to modify maladaptive representational development in maltreated preschoolers were necessary.

In this RCT, participants were again recruited through DHS. Recruitment strategies, determination of child maltreatment, and verification of nonmaltreatment status that were consistent with those utilized in the preventive interventions with maltreated infants described earlier in this chapter were utilized. Maltreating mothers and their preschoolers were randomly assigned to one of three intervention groups: Child Parent Psychotherapy (CPP), Psychoeducational Parenting Intervention (PPI), and Community Standard (CS). The CPP and PPI interventions were manualized and were very similar to those employed in our interventions with maltreated babies delineated earlier, with modifications being made to accommodate the more sophisticated developmental competencies (e.g., language; symbolic and representational abilities) of preschoolers as compared to infants (Toth & Cicchetti, 1999).

### Intervention Outcome

At baseline and at post-intervention, 10 narrative story-stems, selected from the MacArthur Story-Stem Battery (MSSB; Bretherton, Oppenheim,

Buchsbaum, & Emde, 1990), were individually administered to child participants. The narratives utilized depicted moral dilemmas and emotionally charged events in the context of parent-child and family relationships. Narrative story-stems included vignettes designed to elicit children's perceptions of the parent-child relationship, of the self, and of maternal behavior in response to child transgressions, intrafamilial conflicts, and child accidents.

Maternal representations were coded from the children's narratives. These included *positive mother* (the maternal figure is described or portrayed in the narrative as protective, affectionate, providing care, warm, or helpful); *negative mother* (the maternal figure is described or portrayed in the narrative as punitive, harsh, ineffectual, or rejecting); *controlling mother* (the maternal figure is described or portrayed in the narrative as controlling the child's behavior, independent of disciplining actions); *incongruent mother* (the maternal figure is described or portrayed in the narrative as dealing with child-related situations in an opposite or inconsistent manner); and *disciplining mother* (the maternal figure is described or portrayed in the narrative as an authority figure who disciplines the child; inappropriate and harsh forms of punishment were not scored here, but rather were coded as negative mother). A presence/absence method of coding was used to score children's maternal representations.

Self-representation scores were also coded from the children's narratives and were derived from coding any behaviors or references that were made in relation to any child character or when the child participant appeared to be experiencing relevant feelings in response to narrative content. Representational codes of self included *positive self* (a child figure is described or portrayed in the narrative as empathic or helpful, proud, or feeling good about self in any domain); *negative self* (a child figure is described or portrayed in the narrative as aggressive toward self or other, experiencing feelings of shame or self-blame, or feeling bad about self in any domain); and *false self* (a child figure is described or portrayed in the narrative as overly compliant or reports inappropriate positive feelings, for example, in an anger- or fear-producing situation). Consistent with maternal representation coding procedures, a presence/absence method of scoring was used to assess children's self-representations.

In addition to maternal and self-representation codes, a modified version of Bickham and Friese's (1999) global relationship expectation scale was utilized to capture children's expectations of the mother-child relationship. For the current investigation, the scale was modified to assess children's global expectations of the mother-child relationship as portrayed in the children's narratives. In accord with Bickham and Friese's coding procedures, children's expectations of the mother-child relationship were determined by the overall degree of predictability and trustworthiness portrayed between mother and child characters across all 10 narrative administrations. Specifically, the following five relationship dimensions were used to aid in coding children's overall expectation of the mother-child relationship: (1) predictable versus unpredictable, (2) disappointing versus fulfilling, (3) supportive or protective versus threatening, (4) warm or close versus cold or distant, and (5) genuine or trustworthy versus artificial or deceptive. Global mother-child relationship expectation ratings were based on a five-point scale, ranging from very low (participant's narratives describe or portray the mother-child relationship as dissatisfying, unpredictable, and/or dangerous) to very high (participant's narratives describe or portray the mother-child relationship as fulfilling, safe, rewarding, and reliable).

Following the provision of the interventions, preschool-age children in the CPP intervention evidenced a greater decline in maladaptive maternal representations over time than did preschoolers in the PPI and CS interventions. In addition, children who took part in the CPP intervention displayed a greater decrease in negative self-representations than did children in the PPI, CS, and NC groups.

Additionally, the mother-child relationship expectations of children receiving CPP became more positive over the course of the intervention as compared with children in the PPI and NC groups. These results suggest that a model of intervention informed by attachment theory (CPP) is more efficacious at improving representations of self and of caregivers than is a didactic model of intervention (PPI) directed at parenting skills. Because the intervention focused on changing representational models utilizing a narrative story-stem measure, outcomes that might be expected to improve more dramatically in the PPI model (e.g., parenting skills, knowledge of child development) could not be addressed. Consistent with the approach described in our discussion of factors contributing to the success of the mother-infant interventions, we believe that the utilization of skilled and well-trained therapists, adherence to manualized treatment models, and monitoring of the fidelity of the provision of the interventions contributed to the efficacious findings.

These intervention results highlight the potential malleability of representations of the self and of the self in relation to others when an intervention derived from attachment theory is provided. Rather than assuming that "sensitive" periods exist during infancy and that the attachment relationship becomes less amenable to change over the course of development, these findings suggest that, at least during the preschool years, the internalized mother-child relationship remains open to reorganizations.

Given that prior research has discovered that self-determination, positive self-esteem, and other self-system processes are predictors of resilient functioning in maltreated children, the improvements in self-representations found in the children in the CPP intervention are a positive sign that resilient self-strivings may have been initiated in these youngsters (compare with Cicchetti & Rogosch, 1997, 2007). If so, then the developments that occurred in self-system processes may serve a beneficial protective function in future years. Moreover, the positive changes in the maltreated preschoolers who received the CPP intervention may also bode well for these children's future relationships with peers and other relationship partners.

## Developmentally Informed Efficacy Trials in Child Care and Educational Settings

Unfortunately, despite significant investments over the past decade in expansion and improvement of programs, the promise of early education in the United States is not being realized. Too many children, particularly poor children, continue to enter kindergarten far behind their peers (Jacobson-Chernoff, Flanagan, McPhee, & Park, 2007;

Johnson, 2002; National Center for Education Statistics [NCES], 2000). Jacobson-Chernoff et al. (2007) report results from the first follow-up of the nationally representative Early Childhood Longitudinal Study–Birth Cohort (ECLS-B) showing a gap of roughly one standard deviation on school readiness skills for children below the 20th percentile on family socioeconomic status. Because the wide-ranging and diverse set of experiences in preschools are not, in aggregate, producing the level and rate of skills gains required for children to enter school ready (see Howes et al., 2008; Layzer & Price, 2008), simply enrolling more children in more programs will not close the skills gap at school entry. Rather, there is a dire need for research that leads more directly to substantial enhancements of the positive impacts of existing and expanding educational offerings on the very child outcomes on which skills gaps are so evident (see Moorehouse, Webb, Wolf, & Knitzer, 2008); controlled studies of preventive interventions to improve teacher-child interactions and relationships are one point of leverage.

For the early childhood education system to move toward the goal of active and marked advancement of children's skills and competencies, the quality and impacts of programs must be improved via a system of focused professional development through which skill targets for children are aligned with teacher-student interactions that produce gains in these skills, which in turn are aligned with a menu of professional development supports that foster gains in these teacher-child interactions (Howes et al., 2008; Klein & Gomby, 2008; Raver et al., 2008). Thus, improvement of program impacts in early childhood rests on aligning, both conceptually and in terms of empirically demonstrated impacts, (a) a menu of professional development inputs to teachers (preservice or inservice), with (b) processes in classrooms (e.g., teacher-child interactions) that produce (c) skill gains for children in targeted domains (e.g., language and literacy).

Recently, an aligned program of supports to teachers, MyTeaching Partner (MTP; Pianta, Mashburn, Downer, Hamre, & Justice, 2008b) has been developed to focus on improving the quality of teacher-child interactions and relationships, and it has been tested in several RCTs. Following are described the development and evaluation of the MTP system of aligned, focused, and effective professional development for the wide-ranging early childhood workforce. Under the auspices of the National Center for Research on Early Childhood Education (NCRECE), the MTP resources have been evaluated in large-scale trials that focus on improving skill targets in children's early literacy and language development.

## Teacher-Child Interactions as the Core Mechanism for Change

Children spend at least one-quarter of their waking hours in schools, most of it in classrooms, which are one of the most proximal and potentially powerful settings for influencing youth. Within classrooms, children's interactions with teachers either produce or inhibit developmental change to the extent that they engage, meaningfully challenge, and provide social and relational supports. In this sense, these interactions reflect the "carrying capacity" or "affordance value" of the classroom as a setting to promote development. A landmark shift is taking place as we start to reconceptualize the connections between educational settings such as classrooms and developmental processes and outcomes. For example, the National Research Council's 2002 list of setting features that promote positive youth development was a groundbreaking recasting of settings in terms of features that engage developmental mechanisms in adolescence in positive, promotive ways. This recasting of the connection between setting inputs and developmental processes pushes a far more prevention-oriented view, which advances not only the typical program-oriented lens and early detection and delivery systems, but rather presages a radical shift in discourse on setting influences from a focus on amelioration of risk to one that "developmentalizes" an understanding of school settings in terms of assets and provisions that promote and engage competence. This shift is conceptual, design-oriented, and directly informs prevention research.

In this conceptual framework, teacher-child interactions are viewed as mediating the effects of professional development on children's skill gains (see Hamre & Pianta, 2007). The approach taken by the NCRECE in its program of research on professional development rests on evidence from methodologically rigorous studies demonstrating that objectively assessed teacher-child interactions and relationships are active agents of developmental change in preschool classrooms (Domitrovich et al., in press; Mashburn et al., 2008; Ramey & Ramey, 2008; Raver et al., 2008). The NCRECE approach focuses on designing and testing professional development interventions aligned with interactions that change both teachers' classroom behaviors (Pianta et al., 2008b; Raver et al., 2008) and, in classrooms where teachers participate in these supports, children's school readiness (Downer, Pianta, & Fan, 2008; Mashburn et al., 2008; Hamre, Pianta, Downer, & Mashburn, 2008).

Effective teaching in early childhood education requires skillful combinations of explicit instruction, sensitive and warm interactions, responsive feedback, and verbal engagement/stimulation intentionally directed to ensure children's learning while embedding these inter-actions in a classroom environment that is not overly structured or regimented—the very features of adult-child relationships that also account for the quality and impact of attachment relationships with primary caregivers (Burchinal et al., 2000; Hyson & Biggar, 2005; Sroufe et al., 2005b). These constructs are drawn directly from the work of Sroufe and colleagues (2005b) and attachment theory more broadly (Ainsworth et al., 1978). This approach to early childhood teaching is endorsed by those who advocate tougher standards and more instruction and by those who argue for child-centered approaches, and it has strong parallels in the types of instruction and teacher-child interactions that have been shown to contribute to student achievement growth in K–12 studies of teachers' effects on students' achievement gains (see Hart, Stroot, Yinger, & Smith, 2005; National Council on Teacher Quality [NCTQ], 2005). The challenge is how to measure and produce such teaching in large numbers of highly diverse teachers working in diverse early childhood settings.

The NCRECE approach to professional development focuses teachers on learning to skillfully use instructional interactions, implement cur-ricula effectively and intentionally through teacher-child interactions, and provide language-stimulation supports in real-time, dynamic inter-actions that operate at the intersection of children's developing skills and the available instructional materials or activities (e.g., Burchinal et al., 2000; Howes et al., 2008; Hyson & Biggar, 2005; NICHD ECCRN, 2002b). This approach *aligns* (conceptually and empirically) the requisite knowledge of desired skill targets and developmental skill progressions in a particular skill domain (e.g., language development or early literacy) with extensive opportunities for (a) *observation* of high-quality instructional interaction through analysis and viewing of multiple video examples, (b) *skills training* in identifying in/appropriate instructional, linguistic, and social responses to children's cues and how teacher responses can contribute to student literacy and language skill growth, and (c) repeated *opportunities for individualized feedback* and support for high-quality and effectiveness in one's own instruction, implementation, and interactions with children. Conceptually, an aligned system of professional development supports should allow for a direct tracing of the path (and putative effects) of inputs to teachers, to inputs to children, to children's skill gains.

## Teacher-Child Interaction Skills Targets

Teacher training that focuses on interactions and quality of implementation of instructional activities in language and literacy must be based on a way of defining and observing interaction and implementation that has shown strong links to growth in child outcomes, in this case, language and literacy development. In the NCRECE professional development approaches, teachers learn to observe others' effective and ineffective interactions and their own interactions with children and receive feedback and suggestions related to improving quality and effectiveness of interactions. As a result, it is necessary to anchor those professional development supports to a system of observing interactions that have been shown to predict child outcomes in the desired skill targets for children. Because of these needs, the corresponding professional development supports were based on the Classroom Assessment Scoring System, or CLASS (Pianta, La Paro, & Hamre, 2008a). The CLASS was used in more than 700 pre-K classrooms in the 11-state NCEDL/SWEEP pre-K study; it is one of the indices of observed quality of interactions that consistently predicts child outcomes in language and literacy, including growth in receptive vocabulary and alphabet knowledge, with effect sizes ($r$) ranging from .15 to .28 (Howes et al., 2008; Mashburn et al., 2008). The CLASS focuses exclusively on teachers' instructional, language, and social interactions with children (La Paro, Pianta, & Stuhlman, 2004) and in large-scale studies of pre-K through grade 3 classes, higher ratings on CLASS dimensions predict greater gains on standardized assessments of academic achievement and better social adjustment, even adjusting for teacher, program, and family selection factors (Hamre & Pianta, 2005; Howes et al., 2008; Mashburn et al., 2008; NICHD ECCRN, 2002a, 2002b). Because the CLASS validly measures aspects of teachers' instruction and interaction that predict gains in these language and literacy skills during the pre-K years, the NCRECE professional development models rely on the CLASS as one of the central targets for teachers' knowledge and skill training.

The NCRECE program of professional development research has focused on testing the effects of the MyTeachingPartner (MTP) system of professional development supports for fostering teacher-child relationships and teachers' skillful use of instructional interactions and effective implementation of curricula (e.g., Burchinal et al., 2000; Howes et al., 2008; Hyson & Biggar, 2005; NICHD ECCRN, 2002b). These outcomes are achieved through delivery mechanisms that include didactic and skills-focused coursework, web-based video exemplars, and web-mediated consultation.

## Web-Based Video Exemplars as Professional Development Supports

Teachers in the NCRECE professional development studies receive access to the MTP website, which offers three types of resources available to teachers to promote high-quality interactions. First, teachers are provided with detailed descriptions of 10 *dimensions of high-quality teacher-child interactions* that are theoretically derived (Hamre & Pianta, 2007), empirically validated (Hamre, Pianta, Mashburn, & Downer, 2009), and directly associated with children's language, literacy, and social-emotional development (Mashburn et al., 2008; Howes et al., 2008): Positive Climate, Negative Climate, Teacher Sensitivity, Regard for Students'

Perspectives, Behavior Management, Productivity, Instructional Learning Formats, Concept Development, Quality of Feedback, and Language Modeling. In addition to detailed descriptions, the MTP website also includes a *video library* with numerous video examples of teachers demonstrating each dimension within their classrooms, which helps teachers become critical observers of classroom behavior and more attuned to the effects that teachers' behavior have on children.

There is also a *teaching challenges* section in which teachers observe a common challenge faced by a teacher in her preschool classroom, suggest teaching practices that might be useful in each situation, reflect on the teachers' approaches to resolving these challenging situations, and develop strategies that will help with resolution of similarly challenging situations that teachers experience in their classes. These web-based supports and video exemplars can be used in conjunction with the NCRECE course described later or as a stand-alone professional development support accessed by individual teachers or in the context of professional development communities or consultation (described as follows).

## MTP *Consultation*

MTP Consultation provides observationally based, nonevaluative, practice-focused support and feedback for teachers through web-mediated remote consultation, providing individualized support *wherever teachers work*, without consultants having to visit classrooms, thus representing a potential cost savings. The starting point for an MTP Consultation Cycle is the teacher videotaping up to a 60-minute segment of her implementation of a language or literacy instructional activity every two weeks. Their consultant edits that tape into a three-minute video of three smaller segments that focus on indicators of quality teaching identified by the CLASS (Pianta et al., 2003) that is posted with written feedback to a secure website where the segments are viewed and responded to by the teacher, whose comments are automatically sent to the consultant. The teacher and consultant then participate in a regularly scheduled video conference using two-way interactive technologies in real time as they discuss teaching practices face-to-face through a web link.

## The Pre-K Randomized Controlled Trial

An experimental study testing the impacts of the MyTeachingPartner video library and consultation was conducted within pre-K classrooms during 2004–2005 and 2005–2006 in which teachers were randomly assigned to one of three study conditions: one group received a set of language and literacy instructional activities only; the second group received the language and literacy activities and access to the video exemplars on the website; and the third group received the language and literacy activities, access to the website, and participated in MTP consultation. In a series of studies, the effects of the video exemplars and the MTP consultation on teachers' interactions with children and on children's gains in language and literacy skills were evaluated.

Taking full advantage of the RCT study design and two years of intervention implementation, preschoolers' language and literacy outcomes across the three study conditions (Downer et al., 2008) were first evaluated; these conditions include the Consultation and Web-Only groups described previously, as well as a third group that functioned as a comparison group, in which teachers received only curriculum lesson plans (referred to as the Materials group). It was hypothesized that across the treatment conditions the Consultation group would have the greatest effect on children's performance on language and literacy skills at the end of the academic year, while controlling for their performance at the beginning of the year.

For children in classrooms in which the predominant language spoken was English, relative to the Materials condition, the Consultation treatment showed a positive effect on children's literacy outcome measures, after controlling for prior achievement (fall semester measures). The effect (0.10 in the form of standardized regression coefficient, $p \leq .05$) is statistically significant after correcting for the cluster sampling effect and could be characterized as a small effect. On the other hand, the effect of the Web-Only condition in contrast to the Materials condition was very small (0.04) and statistically nonsignificant.

Also using this experimental intent-to-treat approach, the impacts of MTP on children's development of teacher-rated social skills, task-oriented competence, and problem behaviors during pre-K (Hamre et al., 2008) was evaluated. Multilevel modeling was used to estimate mean differences in teachers' ratings of children's end-of-the-year social skills (controlling for beginning-of-the-year social skills, gender, maternal education, and language spoken in the home) between classrooms with teachers participating in the Materials, Web-Only, and Consultation conditions. Results indicated that there were no differences across study conditions related to children's development of problem behaviors during pre-K. However, there were significant differences related to children's development of task-oriented competence and one aspect of social skills—assertiveness. Specifically, children whose teachers participated in the Web-Only and Consultation conditions demonstrated higher levels of task orientation and assertiveness compared to children whose teachers participated in the Materials condition. Moreover, teachers receiving the Consultation supports reported significantly greater increases in the quality of their relationships with children in their classrooms.

In a series of quasi-experimental treatment-on-the-treated analyses, the effects on child outcomes were examined exclusively for teachers in the Consultation and Web-Only conditions (Mashburn et al., 2008). During the intervention, the Web and Consultation teachers varied in their use of MTP web-based resources, including the website that features video exemplars of high-quality classroom interactions, and consultation. Therefore, the associations between teachers' exposure to these resources and children's development of language/literacy skills during pre-K were examined. Controlling for relevant covariates (child, teacher, and classroom characteristics), children showed significant gains in directly assessed receptive language skills when their teachers engaged in more hours of Consultation support. These results complement the intent-to-treat findings reported earlier, showing main effects for the Consultation condition on child outcomes (Downer et al., 2008), as well as the findings showing the Consultation condition to be more effective in changing teacher-child interactions presumed to foster school readiness (Pianta et al., 2008b).

Analyses of results from direct assessments of children's language and early literacy skills show that when teachers receive consultation focused on their interactive behaviors with children (e.g., dimensions of sensitivity, positive emotional climate, feedback, language stimulation), they significantly improve the quality of their interactions with children, which in turn are associated with *gains* in direct assessments of children's performance in language and literacy. Shifts in the quality of teachers' interactive behaviors as a consequence of engagement with professional development supports focused on those behaviors, were associated with gains in children's literacy, language, and social outcomes. In sum, it appeared as if MTP Consultation, derived from an attachment framework applied to education and teacher-child relationships (Pianta, 1999), functioned as a preventive intervention that improved the likelihood of children's early school success.

## Coursework

Building on results and lessons learned from the original MTP evaluation study, NCRECE investigators developed a three-credit course offered in partnership with university-based or community-college programs. The course is an intensive, skill-focused didactic experience in which students (in this case practicing teachers or teachers-in-training) learn how the development of language and literacy skills is linked to features of interactions with adults (using CLASS as the focus) in family and early education settings, and how high-quality implementation of language and literacy curricula and activities leads to skill growth (again using CLASS as the focus). Teachers learn to identify behavioral indicators of high-quality/effective teacher-child interactions and relationships on CLASS dimensions and to identify such indicators in their own teaching. The course draws from the MTP resources, including heavy use of highly specific video examples of actual high-quality implementation. The effects of this course are being evaluated in an RCT with implementation with several hundred early childhood teachers in a half-dozen sites across the country.

Preliminary results from the initial wave of tests of the NCRECE course indicate that the course produces significant improvements in teachers' knowledge of language and literacy skill targets, knowledge of teacher-child interactions linked to gains in these targets, competence in identifying interactive cues and behaviors, and in the independently observed quality of their classroom interactions (Hamre, Pianta, Burchinal, & Downer, 2010).

## FROM RESEARCH TO PRACTICE

In order to foster the health and well-being of young children who are at risk of maladaptation as a function of familial or societal risk factors, it is clear that scientific discoveries such as those reported in this chapter must be translated into practical applications (Insel & Fernald, 2004; Moses, Dorsey, Matheson, & Thier, 2005). In the health sciences, discoveries have typically begun at the "bench" and then progressed to the "bedside." The bench-to-bedside approach to translational research more recently has been viewed as needing to be reciprocal in nature (Cicchetti & Hinshaw, 2002; Ialongo et al., 2006), with scientists developing new tools for utilization in applied contexts and with clinicians sharing observations that can inform basic investigations (Zerhouni, 2005). Increasingly, researchers conducting investigations in academic settings are being asked to consider the practical applications and public policy implications of their work. Although bridging research and practice has been a core tenet of developmental psychopathology since its inception (Cicchetti & Toth, 2006), and certainly significant contributions in this regard emanated from the MPCLS (Sroufe et al., 2005a), too often potentially important policy implications fail to be accessible to those in the public policy worlds (Gunnar & Cicchetti, 2009; Toth, Manly, & Nilsen, 2008). The more recent impetus to conduct translational research in the behavioral sciences has emanated largely from the National Institute of Mental Health (Insel, 2005; Insel & Scolnick, 2006) and was spurred by the recognition of the tremendous individual, social, and economic burden associated with mental illness (National Advisory Mental Health Council, 2000). Hence, the emphasis on translational research by funding agencies is quickly resulting in increased priorities within the academic arena.

The heightened demand for utilization of evidence-based models of prevention and intervention (Weisz & Kazdin, 2010) also is quickening the pace of the dissemination of models that have been shown to be efficacious in academic settings. As one example, the Monroe County Department of Human Services and the United Way of Greater Rochester partnered to issue a Request for Proposals to prevent the occurrence of child maltreatment in families where a mother had her first child before the age of 21 and was currently residing in poverty. These funders not only required that only evidence-based models be utilized, but they also were willing to commit significant funding toward the evaluation of the model. The program developed in response to the RFP "Building Healthy Children" involves a collaboration among community members, including Mt. Hope Family Center, University of Rochester Medical Center Departments of Pediatrics and Social Work, and the Society for the Protection and Care of Children, each of whom possesses expertise in providing evidence based models of intervention. Drawing upon the efficacy results for Child-Parent Psychotherapy, this model was included in the program. The Building Healthy Children model exemplifies the power of building strong community collaborations among academic researchers, community service providers, and government and private funders.

Moreover, at the national level, the Classroom Assessment Scoring System (Pianta et al., 2008a) has just been adopted by Head Start as part of its regular monitoring of programs, with legislative language enabling this scale-up. In partnership with the Center for Advanced Study of Teaching and Learning at the University of Virginia, Head Start has also provided support for careful evaluation of this national scale-up of relationally focused observation and systematic use and evaluation of MTP professional development supports. This partnership builds on the opportunity afforded by policy implementation (i.e., monitoring) to carefully study a key feature of prevention science (scale-up) while also conducting actual intervention studies than can be used to inform further efforts.

Consistent with the focus on providing evidence-based models, recently extensive attention has been given to the importance of utilizing proven-effective manualized curricula or programs as a means of ensuring fidelity and thereby improving impacts on children's skills (e.g., Preschool Curriculum Evaluation Research Consortium; see http://pcer.rti.org). Research on educationally oriented curricula often utilizes measures of procedural fidelity to ensure that they are implemented as intended (e.g., Justice & Ezell, 2002; Lonigan, Anthony, Bloomfield, Dyer, & Samwel, 1999; Reid & Lienemann, 2006; Wasik, Bond, & Hindman, 2006); inclusion of procedural fidelity measures are considered an "essential quality" for intervention research (Gersten et al., 2005). Within practice, procedural fidelity measures are increasingly used to determine whether teachers or mental health providers are using adopted programs as intended, particularly those that are considered to be scientifically based and for which procedural fidelity might be a key moderator of outcomes (see Glenn, 2006).

As important as procedural fidelity is to ensuring that curricula are implemented as intended, it should be distinguished from quality of implementation. Quality of implementation is decidedly more difficult to capture (Sylva et al., 2006) than mere adherence to manualized procedures or scripts, and rather reflects the real-time dynamic and interactive nature of classroom processes or a therapeutic intervention setting: the teacher's or therapist's ability to work flexibly, to individualize to the client or child and respond sensitively to what they bring to the task; that is, to exhibit skilled performance within dynamic interactions in programmatic activities that unfold over time in a given episode or moment. Importantly, whereas measurement of procedural aspects of implementation examines whether therapists or teachers can go through the motions in following step-by-step aspects of an evidence-based curriculum or program, measurement of quality of implementation looks globally at relational processes between teachers or therapists and children across a session to gauge qualities of the systemic nature of interaction and relationships in this setting.

For example, in a recent study of 180 pre-K teachers' implementation of a scripted set of lessons in language and early literacy, teachers exhibited high levels of procedural fidelity to the prescribed language and literacy curriculum following minimal training (Downer, LoCasale-Crouch, Hamre, & Pianta, 2009). Adherence to lesson plans and general guidelines for curriculum implementation exceeded 90% for most aspects of fidelity measured. Although an important sign of teachers' capacity for fidelity, this result must be considered in light of additional findings showing that, in large part, exhibiting fidelity to the curriculum was *not* associated with observed quality of language and literacy instruction when teacher-child interaction during the language or literacy activity was the focus. Fidelity to specific implementation routines (e.g., calling children's attention to the lesson, preparing all materials needed ahead of time) had no predictive value when considering the quality of instruction, a finding that suggests that procedural fidelity with regard to adherence to a curriculum or activity captures only a portion of teachers' interactions and behaviors while implementing that curriculum or specific activity. This is a critical distinction that may account for why treatment effects are often small or moderated by features of the classroom or teacher (Preschool Curriculum Evaluation Research Consortium [PCER], 2008; see http://pcer.rti.org). To state this clearly, demonstrably effective literacy interventions evaluated in clinical trials have *no* effect on child outcomes when the quality and effectiveness of implementation is low (Dickinson & Brady, 2005; Howes et al., 2008). In short, the availability of a demonstrably effective curriculum or program, and even procedural fidelity with respect to delivery of that curriculum or program, are not sufficient to ensure positive outcomes.

## Development of Research Tools for Applied Settings

The exportation of evaluation methods developed in academic research settings into applied settings is particularly challenging. For example, one of the most widely utilized measures for assessing attachment security, the Strange Situation (Ainsworth & Wittig, 1969), requires the conduct of a paradigm that can not easily be implemented in clinic, day care, or school settings. Even if the procedure can be conducted, it requires a high level of training and expertise to determine the attachment classifications. Although efforts have been made to develop questionnaire and Q-sort methods of assessing attachment, even these tend to be unwieldy in real-world contexts. Therefore, the development of measurement strategies that can be utilized in applied settings are particularly noteworthy.

Working in settings serving a young age group, Pianta, Hamre, and others advanced a conceptual and measurement model for early childhood education classroom settings that was driven by a developmentally informed understanding of those settings, with an eye toward enhancing a key provision—the quality of teacher-child interactions. Building on extensive observational work that had been underway in early childhood settings for the past two decades, as well as a very compelling literature demonstrating the value of adult-child interactions for promoting competence in the period between birth to age 8, these investigators embarked on a program of study to conceptualize, measure, and ultimately improve the quality of teacher-child interactions, starting in the preschool and early elementary period. This work resulted in an observational tool for assessing interactions in classrooms, the Classroom Assessment Scoring System (CLASS; Pianta et al., 2008a), an accompanying conceptualization of classrooms, the CLASS framework (Hamre & Pianta, 2005), and an approach to enhancing the quality of teacher-child interactions based on the CLASS observational system, referred to as MyTeachingPartner. Efforts such as these are critical if scientifically based strategies are to become more broadly accessible.

## BARRIERS TO DISSEMINATION OF RESEARCH-BASED INTERVENTIONS

Although it is seemingly straightforward to write about providing attachment-theory-informed interventions with parents, children, and school personnel, there are many barriers to carrying this work out effectively and consistently in real-world contexts. Following are common challenges encountered in disseminating research-based interventions:

- **Founder passion may not carry over when a program is disseminated.** In her landmark books, *Within Our Reach* (1988) and *Common Purpose* (1997), Lisbeth Schorr highlighted this factor in accounting for why several extremely promising programs had fallen by the wayside when they moved into a larger market. Particularly with programs that are developmental and relationship-based, the motivation, inspiration, and commitment of the program developer and leader may account for some of its success. How does one sustain and pass on that special energy as a program moves further afield from its place of origin? The answer probably lies in careful development of systems of training, reflective consultation, and ongoing research and program refinement in response to changing contexts and evolving social forces. But, in many cases, the professionals who are developing research-based interventions—usually in academic settings—may not have the time, the experience, or the community connections to create those systems that facilitate successful dissemination.

- **"Manualizing" a program that addresses the complexities of human thought and behavior is challenging at best and impossible at worst.** Disseminating a program requires careful documentation of key strategies and procedures. But in a developmental, relationship-based program there are countless variations of personality, issues, and circumstances among participants and their families, thus demanding a high level of clinical skill and insight, as well as practical resource management, on the part of the people delivering the program. In communities around the country, service providers come from a wide range of disciplines and levels of education and clinical training. While some may be very skilled at providing expert advice or case management, they may be ill-prepared for dealing with the complex psychological issues that challenge some families. Other service providers may be very psychologically sophisticated and clinically skilled with adults, but they may lack knowledge of community resources or deep understanding of infant development. Developmental, relationship-based work with parents and infants requires multiple types of knowledge and skills, and professional education programs are only beginning to catch up with the need for a different kind of preservice preparation. Furthermore, emerging research points to the personal qualities (and attachment state of mind) of service providers as a critical factor related to participant outcomes. So, how does a program manual adequately address those complexities? For now, the answer to this challenge once again lies in the development of in-service training, supervision, and consultation. Importantly, cross-systems and cross-discipline collaborations offer considerable promise for fostering the dissemination of efficacious programs.

- **Timing of dissemination is important.** Once a prevention model has been shown to be efficacious in RCTs, it remains unclear when it is ready to be released into community settings. Most would agree that in order to be considered evidence-based, an intervention should have been shown to be efficacious in at least two RCTs, with one being conducted by investigators not involved with model development. However, how actively involved should model developers be in controlling access to and further evaluations of the intervention? Currently, there are a range of approaches to this question. For example, the Nurse-Family Partnership (NFP) program (Olds, 2006) has established a national regulatory arm that oversees initiatives to incorporate NFP into community settings. Although this ensures that model fidelity is maintained, strategies such as this may work against being able to seamlessly integrate NFP with other community initiatives and inadvertently create barriers to collaborative endeavors. High costs associated with receiving training on various evidence-based models and financial burdens associated with accessing intervention manuals and related materials also may impede broader dissemination of evidence-based models. Conversely, if model developers do not advocate for standards to ensure appropriate training and maintenance of fidelity, then the intervention may be utilized ineffectively.

- **Community and societal forces may work against careful and effective dissemination.** Several forces may become barriers to wide and continued dissemination of research-based prevention programs. First, a popular desire (among policymakers, funders, and the general public) for the next new thing may erode support for older program models, even those with good evidence to support their effectiveness. Also, economic changes too often lead to watering down of services, thus sacrificing program integrity, as well as shortchanging staff needs for ongoing education and support—the very things necessary to sustain successful program dissemination. In the broad marketplace of ideas, research-based programs often compete with—and may have no special advantage over—program ideas rooted in ideology or popular belief. For example, the past decade saw a national emphasis on marriage-focused interventions with low-income, fragile families, driven primarily by ideology rather than evidence. That is not to say there is no research to support the benefits of marriage—nor is it to say that marriage-focused interventions are necessarily ineffective—only that the initiative was grounded in and fueled by ideology rather than research. Another example of program ideas rooted in beliefs rather than research is the popular education/social-service philosophy that parents automatically know what's best for their children. Although it surely is important to approach parents in a respectful, supportive, nonjudgmental way that takes into account the unique circumstances of their lives, it does not necessarily follow that all parents know what is best for their children. Research shines light on the countless ways in which parenting may be compromised by a lack of understanding of child development, lack of knowledge of demonstrated best practices in parenting, and misguided approaches shaped by the parent's own relationship history. Yet another example of non-research-based approaches competing in the marketplace of parenting ideas is the well-intentioned but misguided attachment parenting movement that prescribes that moms stay home, co-sleep with their babies, and breastfeed if they want to build a good attachment. Although breastfeeding yields many benefits to mother and child, and co-sleeping and staying home with a baby are fine choices for many families, prescribing those as the necessary elements for building a secure attachment is grounded more in philosophy than research.

Once research findings are published, that information is in the public domain to be massaged and applied, for better or worse. What is the responsibility of prevention researchers to become engaged in efforts to ensure the best possible professional application of knowledge generated through their research? What is their responsibility to actively promote what they have learned in the broader marketplace of ideas? And if they accept responsibility for either or both of those tasks, what are the most effective ways to fulfill those responsibilities?

It is clear that individuals conducting prevention research do so based on a commitment to fostering the greater good of society and reducing the burden of mental illness. Thus, in addition to publishing prevention research findings in academic journals, prevention scientists have a responsibility to present their results, in clear and understandable language, to practitioners, consumers, and social policymakers. Although forging and maintaining partnerships is time intensive, prevention scientists need to be actively engaged with practitioners, program administrators, funders, and policymakers. Such involvement not only facilitates the translation of proven prevention strategies to applied settings but also is integral to maintaining the fidelity of proven approaches.

## RECOMMENDATIONS TO FACILITATE THE DISSEMINATION OF DEVELOPMENTALLY INFORMED PREVENTION STRATEGIES INTO APPLIED AND POLICY ARENAS

Although the translation of prevention programs from research to applied settings is the ultimate goal of prevention science, the pathway to attaining this outcome is by no means straightforward or without challenges. Therefore, we proffer some recommendations that we hope will generate further thinking and ultimately facilitate this process.

### Training Providers

There can be no doubt that practitioners in community settings are passionate about providing the best services available to their clients. Unfortunately, rising caseloads associated with fiscal realities often allow insufficient time for practitioners to be aware of, or to learn, newly emerging interventions. Given a choice between meeting with a distressed parent or child or reading a treatment manual, the decision that must be made is clear. In order to foster the incorporation of evidence-based models into practice settings, researchers, practitioners, administrators, and funding bodies must be equally committed to attaining this goal (Kazdin, 2009).

An excellent example of training emanates from work in educational settings. Given a varied and loosely organized and regulated workforce, it is widely held that professional development that is practice-focused and tied to teachers' experiences in program and classroom settings is a key component for improving teachers' and children's outcomes in early childhood education (Bogard & Takanishi, 2005; National Association for the Education of Young Children [NAEYC], 2009; Zaslow & Martinez-Beck, 2005). In fact, public investments in professional development are often seen as the key to improving program quality and impacts; therefore, it is imperative that such investments return gains to teachers and children.

For education to contribute more directly to the advancement of children's skills and competencies, both quality and impacts of programs must be improved through a system of focused and aligned professional development. In fact, it has been shown that when skill targets for children are aligned with teacher-student interactions that produce gains in these skills, and in turn are aligned with a menu of professional development supports that foster gains in these teacher-child interactions, then growth is evident in both teacher skills and child outcomes (e.g., Clements & Sarama, 2008; Klein & Gomby, 2008; Neuman & Cunningham, 2009; Pianta et al., 2008b; Raver et al., 2008). It is clear that effective professional development must be systematic and produce gains for teacher skills and child outcomes, and for that to occur it is necessary to align, both conceptually and in terms of empirically demonstrated impacts, (a) a menu of professional development inputs to teachers (preservice or inservice) with (b) processes in classrooms (e.g., teacher-child interactions) that produce (c) skill gains for children in targeted domains (e.g., language and literacy, math). The evidence supports this argument.

If conceptual and empirical connections can be demonstrated and replicated across professional development inputs, classroom processes, and child outcomes, in certain skill domains and for certain professional development models, then the potential for scaling and building incentive and policy structures around these models becomes an important feature of systemic improvement and policy. The recent development and expansion of Quality Rating and Improvement Systems (QRISs) are one such example of a set of policy initiatives that integrate measurement of inputs and outcomes with incentives and resources for improvement. These systems could, and perhaps should, be a tool for scaling-up and further evaluating the impacts of the type of models of aligned professional development that have been illustrated in this chapter. In fact, to the extent that alignment is a property of professional development that is critical for both impact and evaluation, it is not unreasonable to suggest that alignment be an explicit property of the professional development models adopted within QRISs and in fact of QRISs themselves.

Finally, one might also envision professional preparation and credentialing models based on what we are learning from aligned professional development and its evaluation. To the extent that these models of support and education for teachers can be demonstrated to produce gains in teacher competencies that produce child outcome gains, then it seems critical to build such opportunities for professional preparation back into the pre-service sector and to find methods for credentialing and certifying teachers on the basis of participation in effective professional development and demonstration of competence. In fact, new policy statements related to professional development and career development being suggested by the NAEYC (2009) explicitly identify teachers' performance in classroom settings, specifically their interactions with children, as a dimension of career advancement that should be credentialed and tied to professional development. Such statements by professional organizations reflect an openness to innovation that, paired with demonstrably effective supports for teachers, could pave the way for tremendous positive change in outcomes for teachers and children and exemplify one way that early childhood education leads.

## Interfacing With the Media

In order to disseminate emerging findings on prevention, researchers need to interface with the media. Although some academic researchers are quite effective at interacting with the media, the prospect of being interviewed causes most researchers anxiety. One reason for a reluctance to engage with the media emanates from a basic cultural difference. Academics are "two-handed" thinkers: on the one hand, the research suggests this, but on the other hand. . . . In the media (particularly broadcast), those in charge want certainty, and they want it in as few words as possible. This has become increasingly true in recent years. (Compare and contrast Edward R. Murrow with CNN!)

Another aspect of academic culture is the time to be deliberative. In broadcast media it is a rare luxury to deliberate. For example, a researcher might receive the following request: "The 5 o'clock news needs a comment from an expert. Can we come to your office in 30 minutes?"

Many academics fear being misrepresented. It is intimidating to have your statements edited by someone who doesn't know your subject—like writing an article for *Child Development*, and then having someone from the French department edit and publish it. Many researchers find themselves saying, "But wait, that's not what I meant!"

Those differences will not go away, but they can be bridged through relationship-building. As academicians get to know broadcasters—and as both acknowledge differences in their respective cultures—they can work effectively together. Explicit training for academicians also is helpful and certain strategies are effective when interfacing with the media.

First, it is important to meet the needs of broadcasters rather than approaching them to fulfill the agenda of the researcher (i.e., publicizing one's own research). Academics need to be responsive when media representatives need someone to comment on their story. Whatever the issue at hand, the interview can be used to mention other possible stories and to suggest other researchers to interview. Once a mutually beneficial relationship is forged, it is more likely that journalists will be willing to assist researchers in sharing their findings.

In order to guard against misrepresentation of research findings, it is useful to proactively frame the story when responding to a request for a comment. In concrete terms, developing a few concise talking points and sharing them with the interviewer can be very effective. Preparing an introductory paragraph to engage listeners or viewers also is an excellent strategy and may result in interviewers utilizing the prepared copy.

In order to prepare new researchers, as well as veterans, for increasing the accessibility of their work, explicit training, preservice and in-service, needs to be provided. It is wise to have journalists, broadcasters, and social scientists collaborate to develop effective training, which includes practice in framing news, handling challenging questions, and identifying the news value in stories that may not be news to researchers but will be to the general public and policymakers.

## Partnering With Policymakers, Funders, and Service Providers

Given very different worldviews and priorities, bridging the research, social policy, funding, and service provision arenas may appear to be daunting, particularly to academics who typically have not been trained in navigating these seemingly diverse venues. To begin, it is important to identify commonalities across groups. In the area of prevention, a shared goal may be reducing ills that place both an economic burden and a significant human toll on society. Although a policymaker may have a somewhat different lens than a researcher on why child maltreatment, school failure, or teen pregnancy is problematic, agreeing that these issues need to be addressed provides a starting point for dialogue. Respecting that each partner, regardless of background, brings important expertise to the planning process also does much to forge trust. In order to develop effective partnerships, patience, a commitment of time, and a minimization of individual egos and turf issues are required. If the focus remains on promoting the well-being of vulnerable children and families, then this shared commitment can help avoid disagreements that might ultimately shatter partnerships. Honest conversations about the overarching goals of the partnerships and the capacity to address concerns openly when they arise also are very effective strategies for building and sustaining cross-systems collaborations.

Finally, it is extremely important that all partners be informed of any new developments that might affect the collaboration. For example, if attaining Institutional Review Board approval to conduct a planned service evaluation results in a delay in implementation, then anticipating this possibility and alerting partners in advance will do much to alleviate frustration and feelings of mistrust. Conversely, if administrators are unable to free up time for staff training because of budgetary constraints, then this information also needs to be shared with all partners. Given an increased impetus to make evidence-based models more widely available, it is a particularly opportune time to forge collaborative partnerships across systems.

## SUMMARY

In the 2006, *Handbook of Child Psychology*, Irving Sigel queried, "Do research findings in child development influence relevant practice and is practice influential in planning research?" (p. 1017). After examining 100 years of cumulative child development research, his conclusion was "no"; however, he acknowledged that the somewhat dismal situation had changed in a positive direction in more recent years. The unfortunate schism between research and practice, although narrowing, continues to require concerted efforts on the parts of those residing in both worlds.

The seminal work of Byron Egeland, Alan Sroufe, and their colleagues on the MPCLS illustrates the potential to inform practice that can emanate from research that is conceived within a solid frame of developmental theory. The recognition that development is a moving target that requires repeated assessments across various developmental domains was foundational in informing current perspectives advocating for multiple levels of analysis approaches to understanding both normal and atypical development (Cicchetti & Dawson, 2002). Moreover, the concept of "heterotypic continuity," wherein the method of measuring constructs must necessarily vary as a function of development, flows directly from the assessment strategies employed by the MPCLS. The recognition that understanding developmental trajectories can inform prevention efforts by suggesting targets for intervention before disorders emerge also flows directly from the project. Thus, more than 30 years since its inception, the seeds sown by the MPCLS continue to contribute to knowledge of development and to the incorporation of such knowledge into real-world contexts that can prevent negative outcomes and foster healthy developmental attainments for at-risk children and families.

## REFERENCES

Ainsworth, M. D. S., Blehar, M. C., Waters, E., & Wall, S. (1978). *Patterns of attachment: A psychological study of the Strange Situation.* Hillsdale, NJ: Erlbaum.

Ainsworth, M. D. S., & Wittig, B. A. (1969). Attachment and the exploratory behavior of one-year-olds in a strange situation. In B. M. Foss (Ed.), *Determinants of infant behavior* (Vol. 4, pp. 113–136). London: Methuen.

Bickham, N., & Friese, B. (1999). Child narrative coding system. Unpublished manual. Syracuse, NY: Syracuse University.

Bogard, K., & Takanishi, R. (2005). PK-3: An aligned and coordinated approach to education for children 3 to 8 years old. *SRCD Social Policy Report, 19,* 1–23.

Bretherton, I., Oppenheim, D., Buchsbaum, H., & Emde, R. N. (1990). MacArthur Story Stem Battery. Unpublished manuscript. Madison: University of Wisconsin.

Burchinal, M., Roberts, J., Riggins, R., Zeisel, S., Neebe, E., & Bryant, D. (2000). Relating quality of center-based child care to early cognitive and language development longitudinally. *Child Development, 71,* 339–357.

Cicchetti, D. (1984). The emergence of developmental psychopathology. *Child Development, 55,* 1–7.

Cicchetti, D. (1993). Developmental psychopathology: Reactions, reflections, projections. *Developmental Review, 13,* 471–502.

Cicchetti, D., & Dawson, G. (Eds.). (2002). Editorial: Multiple levels of analysis. *Development and Psychopathology, 14,* 417–420.

Cicchetti, D., & Hinshaw, S. P. (2002). Editorial: Prevention and intervention science: Contributions for developmental theory. *Development and Psychopathology, 14,* 667–671.

Cicchetti, D., & Rogosch, F. A. (1997). The role of self-organization in the promotion of resilience in maltreated children. *Development and Psychopathology, 9,* 799–817.

Cicchetti, D., & Rogosch, F. A. (2007). Personality, adrenal steroid hormones, and resilience in maltreated children: A multi-level perspective. *Development and Psychopathology, 19,* 787–809.

Cicchetti, D., & Sroufe, A. (1978). An organizational view of affect: Illustration from the study of Down's syndrome infants. In M. Lewis & L. A. Rosenblum (Eds.), *The development of affect* (pp. 309–350). New York, NY: Plenum.

Cicchetti, D., & Toth, S. L. (1991). The making of a developmental psychopathologist. In J. Cantor, C. Spiker, & L. Lipsitt (Eds.), *Child behavior and development: Training for diversity* (pp. 34–72). Norwood, NJ: Ablex.

Cicchetti, D., & Toth, S. L. (1992). The role of developmental theory in prevention and intervention. *Development and Psychopathology, 4,* 489–493.

Cicchetti, D., & Toth, S. L. (2005). Child maltreatment. *Annual Review of Clinical Psychology, 1,* 409–438.

Cicchetti, D., & Toth, S. L. (2006). Developmental psychopathology and preventive intervention. In A. Renninger & I. Sigel (Eds.), *Handbook of child psychology* (pp. 497–547). Hoboken, NJ: Wiley.

Cicchetti, D., Toth, S. L., & Manly, J. T. (2003). Maternal maltreatment interview. Unpublished manuscript. Rochester, NY.

Clements, D. H., & Sarama, J. (2008). Experimental evaluation of the effects of a research-based preschool mathematics curriculum. *American Educational Research Journal, 45*(2), 443–494.

Costello, J., Egger, H., & Angold, A. (2005). 10-year research update review: The epidemiology of child and adolescent psychiatric disorders: I. Methods and public health burden. *Journal of the American Academy of Child and Adolescent Psychiatry, 44*(10), 972–986.

Crittenden, P. M. (1990). Internal representational models of attachment relationships. *Infant Mental Health Journal, 11,* 259–277.

Dickinson, D. K., & Brady, J. (2005). Toward effective support for language and literacy through professional development: A decade of experiences and data. In M. Zaslow & I. Martinez-Beck (Eds.), *Critical issues in early childhood professional development* (pp. 141–170). Baltimore, MD: Brookes.

Domitrovich, C., Gest, S., Gill, S., Bierman, K., Welsh, J., & Jones, D. (in press). Fostering high-quality teaching in Head Start classrooms: Experimental evaluation of an integrated curriculum. *American Educational Research Journal.*

Downer, J., LoCasale-Crouch, J., Hamre, B., & Pianta, R. (2009). Teacher characteristics associated with responsiveness and exposure to consultation and on-line professional development resources. *Early Education and Development, 20*(3), 431–455.

Downer, J., Pianta, R., & Fan, X. (2008). Effects of web-mediated teacher professional development on children's language and literacy development. Manuscript submitted for publication.

Durlak, J. (1997). *Successful prevention programs for children and adolescents.* New York, NY: Plenum Press.

Egeland, B., & Erickson, M. F. (1993). *Final report: An evaluation of STEEP™, a program for high-risk mothers (grant no. MH41879).* Rockville, MD: National Institute of Mental Health, Department of Health and Human Services.

Egeland, B., & Erickson, M. F. (2004). Lessons From STEEP: Thinking theory, research, and practice for the well-being of infants and parents. In A. Sameroff, S. McDonough, & K. Rosenbloom (Eds.), *Treating parent-infant relationship problems* (pp. 213–242). New York, NY: Guilford Press.

Egeland, B., & Farber, E. (1984). Infant-mother attachment: Factors related to its development and changes over time. *Child Development, 55,* 753–771.

Egeland, B., & Sroufe, L. A (1981). Developmental sequelae of maltreatment in infancy. In R. Rizley & D. Cicchetti (Eds.), *Developmental perspectives on child maltreatment* (pp. 77–92). San Francisco, CA: Jossey-Bass.

Erickson, M. F. (2005). Using direct observation in prevention and intervention services in infant and preschool mental health: Training and practice issues. In K. M. Finello (Ed.), *The handbook of training and practice in infant and preschool mental health* (pp. 31–50). San Francisco, CA: Jossey-Bass.

Erickson, M. F., Egeland, B., Simon, J., & Rose, T. (2002). *Steps toward effective, enjoyable parenting (STEEP™): Facilitators' guide.* Minneapolis: Irving B. Harris Training Center for Infant and Toddler Development, University of Minnesota.

Erickson, M. F., Korfmacher, J., & Egeland, B. (1992). Attachments past and present: Implications for therapeutic intervention with mother-infancy dyads. *Development and Psychopathology, 4,* 495–507.

Fraiberg, S., Adelson, E., & Shapiro, V. (1975). Ghosts in the nursery: A psychoanalytic approach to impaired infant-mother relationships. *Journal of the American Academy of Child Psychiatry, 14,* 387–421.

Gersten, R., Fuchs, L., Compton, D., Coyne, M., Greenwood, C., & Innocenti, M. (2005). Quality indicators for group experimental and quasi-experimental research in special education. *Exceptional Children, 71*(2), 149–164.

Glenn, D. (2006). Weighing the "scale-up" study. *The Chronicle of Higher Education, 52*(45), A12.

Gunnar, M. R., & Cicchetti, D. (2009). Meeting the challenge of translational research in child psychology. In D. Cicchetti & M. R. Gunnar (Eds.), *Minnesota Symposia on Child Psychology: Meeting the challenge of translational research in child psychology* (Vol. 35, pp. 1–27). Hoboken, NJ: Wiley.

Hamre, B. K., & Pianta, R. C. (2005). Can instructional and emotional support in the first grade classroom make a difference for children at risk of school failure? *Child Development, 76*(5), 949–967.

Hamre, B. K., & Pianta, R. C. (2007). Learning opportunities in preschool and early elementary classrooms. In R. Pianta, M. Cox, & K. Snow (Eds.), *School readiness & the transition to kindergarten in the era of accountability* (pp. 49–84). Baltimore, MD: Brookes.

Hamre, B. K., Pianta, R.C., Burchinal, M., & Downer, J. T. (2010, March). *A course on supporting early language and literacy development through effective teacher-child interactions: Effects on teacher beliefs, knowledge and practice.* Paper presented at the Annual Meeting of the Society for Research on Educational Effectiveness, Washington, DC.

Hamre, B. K., Pianta, R. C., Downer, J. T., & Mashburn, A. J. (2008). Effects of web-mediated teacher professional development on children's social skills. Manuscript submitted for publication.

Hamre, B. K., Pianta, R. C., Mashburn, A. J., & Downer, J. T. (2009, March 6). *Building a science of classrooms: Application of the CLASS framework in over 4,000 U.S. early childhood and elementary classrooms.* Retrieved from http://www.fcd-us.org/user_doc/BuildingAScienceofclassroomspiantaHamre.pdf.

Hart, P., Stroot, S., Yinger, R., & Smith, S. (2005). *Meeting the teacher education accountability challenge: A focus on novice and experienced teacher studies.* Mount Vernon, OH: Teacher Quality Partnership.

Howes, C., Burchinal, M., Pianta, R., Bryant, D., Early, D., Clifford, R., & Barbarin, O. (2008). Ready to learn? Children's pre-academic achievement in pre-kindergarten programs. *Early Childhood Research Quarterly, 23,* 27–50.

Howes, C., & Segal, J. (1993). Children's relationships with alternative caregivers: The special case of maltreated children removed from their homes. *Journal of Applied Developmental Psychology, 14,* 71–81.

Hyson, M., & Biggar, H. (2005). NAEYC's standards for early childhood professional preparation: Getting from here to there. In M. Zaslow & I. Martinez-Beck (Ed.), *Critical issues in early childhood professional development* (pp. 283–308). Baltimore, MD: Brookes.

Ialongo, N., Rogosch, F. A., Cicchetti, D., Toth, S. L. Buckley, J., Petras, H., & Neiderhiser, J. (2006). A developmental psychopathology approach to the prevention of mental health disorders. In D. Cicchetti & D. Cohen (Eds.), *Developmental psychopathology* (pp. 968–1018). Hoboken, NJ: Wiley.

Insel, T. R. (2005). Developmental psychobiology for public health: A bridge for translational research. *Developmental Psychobiology, 47*(3), 209–216.

Insel, T. R., & Fernald, R. D. (2004). How the brain processes social information: Searching for the social brain. *Annual Review of Neuroscience, 27,* 697–722.

Insel, T. R., & Scolnick, E. M. (2006). Cure therapeutics and strategic prevention: Raising the bar for mental health research. *Molecular Psychiatry, 11,* 11–17.

Jacobson-Chernoff, J., Flanagan, K. D., McPhee, C., & Park, J. (2007). *Preschool: First findings from the third follow-up of the Early Childhood Longitudinal Study, Birth Cohort (ECLS-B).* (NCES 2008-024). Washington, DC: National Center for Education Statistics.

Johnson, R. S. (2002). *Using data to close the achievement gap: How to measure equity in our schools.* Thousand Oaks, CA: Corwin Press.

Justice, L. M., & Ezell, H. K. (2002). Use of storybook reading to increase print awareness in at-risk children. *American Journal of Speech-Language Pathology, 85*(5), 388–396.

Kazdin, A. E. (2009). Bridging science and practice to improve patient care. *American Psychologist, 64*(4), 276–279.

Kellam, S. G., & Rebok, G. W. (1992). Building developmental and etiological theory through epidemiologically based preventive intervention trials. In J. McCord & R. E. Tremblay (Eds.), *Preventing antisocial behavior: Interventions from birth through adolescence* (pp. 162–195). New York, NY: Guilford Press.

Kessler, R. C., Berglund, P., Demler, O., Jin, R., Merikangas, K. R., & Walters, E. E. (2005). Lifetime prevalence and age-of-onset distributions of DSM-IV disorders in the National Comorbidity Survey replication: Erratum. *Archives of General Psychiatry, 62*(7), 768.

Klein, L., & Gomby, D. S. (2008). *A synthesis of federally funded studies on school readiness: What are we learning about professional development?* Washington, DC: U.S. Department of Health and Human Services.

La Paro, K., Pianta, R., & Stuhlman, M. (2004). The classroom assessment scoring system: Findings from the prekindergarten year. *The Elementary School Journal, 104,* 409–426.

Layzer, J., & Price, C. (2008, October). *Closing the gap in the school readiness of low-income children.* Washington, DC: U.S. Department of Health and Human Services.

Lieberman, A. F. (1991). Attachment theory and infant-parent psychotherapy: Some conceptual, clinical, and research considerations. In D. Cicchetti & S. L. Toth (Eds.), *Rochester symposium on developmental psychopathology: Models and integrations* (Vol. 3, pp. 261–287). Rochester, NY: University of Rochester Press.

Lieberman, A. F. (1992). Infant-parent psychotherapy with toddlers. *Development and Psychopathology, 4,* 559–574.

Lieberman, A. F., & Pawl, J. H. (1988). Clinical applications of attachment theory. In J. Belsky & T. Nezworski (Eds.), *Clinical implications of attachment* (pp. 325–351). Hillsdale, NJ: Erlbaum.

Lieberman, A. F., & Van Horn, P. (2005). Don't hit my mommy! A Manual for Child-Parent Psychotherapy with Young Witnesses of Family Violence. Washington, DC: Zero to Three Press.

Lieberman, A. F., Ghosh Ippen, C., & Van Horn, P. (2006). Child-parent psychotherapy: 6-month follow-up of a randomized control trial. *Journal of the American Academy of Child & Adolescent Psychiatry, 45,* 913–918.

Lonigan, C. J., Anthony, J. L., Bloomfield, B. G., Dyer, S. M., & Samwel, C. S. (1999). Effects of two shared-reading interventions on emergent literacy skills of at-risk preschoolers. *Journal of Early Intervention, 22,* 306–322.

Lynch, M., & Cicchetti, D. (1991). Patterns of relatedness in maltreated and nonmaltreated children: Connections among multiple representational models. *Development and Psychopathology, 3,* 207–226.

Lynch, M., & Cicchetti, D. (1992). Maltreated children's reports of relatedness to their teachers. *New Directions for Child Development, 57,* 81–107.

Mashburn, A. J., Pianta, R. C., Hamre, B. K., Downer, J. T., Barbarin, O., Bryant, D., Burchinal, M., . . . & Howes, C. (2008). Measures of classroom quality in prekindergarten and children's development of academic, language, and social skills. *Child Development, 79*(3), 732–749.

Moorehouse, M., Webb, M. B., Wolf, A., & Knitzer, J. (2008). Welcoming and opening remarks. *A working meeting on recent school readiness research: Guiding synthesis of early childhood research.* Washington, DC: ASPE, OPRE, Abt, and NCCP.

Moses, H., Dorsey, E. R., Matheson, D. H., & Thier, S. O. (2005). Financial anatomy of biomedical research. JAMA, *294*(11), 1333–1342. PMID 16174691.

National Advisory Mental Health Council. (2000, June). *Insurance parity for mental health: Cost, access, and quality.* Rockland, MD: U.S. Department of Health and Human Services.

National Association for the Education of Young Children. (2009). *Early childhood inclusion.* A joint position statement of the Division for Early Childhood (DEC) and the National Association for the Education of Young Children (NAEYC). Washington, DC: NAEYC.

National Center for Education Statistics [NCES]. (2000). *America's kindergartners.* Washington, DC: U.S. Department of Education.

National Center for Education Statistics [NCES]. (2008). *The condition of education 2008 in brief*. Washington, DC: U.S. Department of Education.

National Council on Teacher Quality [NCTQ]. (2005). *Increasing the odds: How good policies can yield better teachers*. Washington, DC: NCTQ.

National Institute of Mental Health. (2008). Mental disorders cost society billions in unearned income. Retrieved from http://www.nih.gov/news/health/may2008/nimh-07.html.

Neuman, S. B., & Cunningham, L. (2009). The impact of professional development and coaching on early language and literacy instructional practices. *American Educational Research Journal, 46*(2), 532–566.

NICHD Early Child Care Research Network. (2002a). Child-care structure>process>outcome: Direct and indirect effects of child-care quality on young children's development. *Psychological Science, 13*, 199–206.

NICHD Early Child Care Research Network. (2002b). The relation of global first-grade classroom environment to structural classroom features and teacher and student behaviors. *The Elementary School Journal, 102*(5), 367–387.

Olds, D. L. (2006). The nurse-family partnership: An evidence-based preventive intervention. *Infant Mental Health Journal, 27*(1), 5–25.

Olds, D., Eckenrode, J., Henderson, C., Kitzman, H., Powers, J., Cole, R., & Sidora, K. (1997). Long-term effects of home visitation on maternal life course and child abuse and neglect: Fifteen-year follow-up of a randomized trial. *Journal of the American Medical Association, 278*, 637–643.

Olds, D. L., Henderson, C., Kitzman, H., Eckenrode, J., Cole, R., & Tatelbaum, R. (1998). The promise of home visitation: Results of two randomized trials. *Journal of Community Psychology, 26*, 5–21.

Pianta, R. C. (1999). *Enhancing relationships between children and teachers*. Washington, DC: American Psychological Association.

Pianta, R. C., Kinzie, M., Justice, L., Pullen, P., Fan, X., & Lloyd, J. (2003). *Web training: Pre-K teachers, literacy, and relationships. Effectiveness of early childhood program, curricula, and interventions*. Washington, DC: National Institute of Child Health and Human Development.

Pianta, R. C., La Paro, K. M., & Hamre, B. K. (2008a). *Classroom Assessment Scoring System™: Manual K-3*. Baltimore, MD: Brookes.

Pianta, R., Mashburn, A., Downer, J., Hamre, B., & Justice, L. (2008b). Effects of web-mediated professional development resources on teacher-child interactions in pre-kindergarten classrooms. *Early Childhood Research Quarterly, 23*(4), 431–451.

Preschool Curriculum Evaluation Research Consortium [PCER]. (2008). *Effects of preschool curriculum programs on school readiness (NCER 2008–2009)*.

Washington, DC: National Center for Education Research, Institute of Education Sciences, U.S. Department of Education.

Ramey, S. L., & Ramey, C. T. (2008). The effects of curriculum and coaching supports on classrooms and literacy skills of prekindergarten/Head Start students in Montgomery County Public Schools. Unpublished manuscript. Washington, DC: Georgetown University Center on Health and Education.

Raver, C. C., Jones, A. S., Li-Grining, C. P., Metzger, M., Smallwood, K., & Sardin, L. (2008). Improving preschool classroom processes: Preliminary findings from a randomized trial implemented in Head Start settings. *Early Childhood Research Quarterly, 23*(1), 10–26.

Reid, R., & Lienemann, T. (2006). *Strategy instruction for students with learning disabilities*. New York, NY: Guilford Press.

Sameroff, A. J., & Emde, R.N. (Eds.). (1989). *Relationship disturbances in early childhood*. New York, NY: Basic Books.

Schorr, L. B. & Schorr, D. (1988). *Within our reach: Breaking the cycle of disadvantage*. Garden City, NY: Anchor Press/Doubleday.

Schorr, L. B. (1997). *Common purpose: Strengthening families and neighborhoods to rebuild America*. New York: Anchor Books/Doubleday.

Shirk, S. R., Talmi, A., & Olds, D. (2000). A developmental psychopathology perspective on child and adolescent treatment policy. *Development and Psychopathology, 12*, 835–855.

Sigel, I. (2006). Research to practice redefined. In I. Siegel & A. Renninger (Eds.), *Handbook of child psychology*. Hoboken, NJ: Wiley.

Sroufe, L. A. (1979). The coherence of individual development: Early care, attachment, and subsequent developmental issues. *American Psychologist, 34*(10), 834–841.

Sroufe, L. A. (1989). Relationships, self, and individual adaptation. In A. Sameroff & R. N. Emde (Eds.), *Relationship disturbances in early childhood* (pp. 70–94). New York, NY: Basic Books.

Sroufe, L. A., Carlson, E. A., Levy, A. K., & Egeland, B. (1999). Implications of attachment theory for developmental psychopathology. *Development and Psychopathology, 11*, 1–13.

Sroufe, L. A., Egeland, B., Carlson, E., & Collins, W. A. (2005a). *The development of the person: The Minnesota study of risk and adaptation from birth to adulthood*. New York, NY: Guilford Press.

Sroufe, L. A., Egeland, B., Carlson, E., & Collins, W. A. (2005b). Placing early attachment experiences in developmental context: The Minnesota Longitudinal Study. In K. E. Grossmann, K. Grossmann, & E. Waters (Eds.),

*Attachment from infancy to adulthood: The major longitudinal studies* (pp. 48–70). New York, NY: Guilford Press.

Sroufe, L. A., & Rutter, M. (1984). The domain of developmental psychopathology. *Child Development, 55*, 17–29.

Sroufe, L. A., & Waters, E. (1977) Attachment as an organizational construct. *Child Development, 48*(4), 1184–1199.

Sylva, K., Siraj-Blatchford, I., Taggart, B., Sammons, P., Melhuish, E., Elliot, K., & Totsika, V. (2006). Capturing quality in early childhood through environmental rating scales. *Early Childhood Research Quarterly, 21*, 76–92.

Toth, S. L., & Cicchetti, D. (1996). Patterns of relatedness and depressive symptomatology in maltreated children. *Journal of Consulting and Clinical Psychology, 64*, 32–41.

Toth, S. L., & Cicchetti, D. (1999). Developmental psychopathology and child psychotherapy. In S. Russ and T. Ollendick (Eds.), *Handbook of psychotherapies with children and families*. New York, NY: Plenum Press.

Toth, S. L., Cicchetti, D., Macfie, J., Maughan, A., & VanMeenan, K. (2000). Narrative representations of caregivers and self in maltreated preschoolers. *Attachment and Human Development, 2*, 271–305.

Toth, S. L., Manly, J. T., & Nilsen, W. (2008). From research to practice: Lessons learned. *Journal of Applied Developmental Psychology, 29*, 317–325.

U.S. Advisory Board on Child Abuse and Neglect (1990). *Child abuse and neglect: Critical first steps in response to a national emergency*. (No. 017-092-00104-5). Washington, DC: U.S. Government Printing Office.

Wasik, B. A., Bond, M. A., & Hindman, A. (2006). The effects of a language and literacy intervention on Head Start children and teachers. *Journal of Educational Psychology, 98*, 63–74.

Weisz, J. R., & Kazdin, A. E. (Eds.). (2010). *Evidence-based psychotherapies for children and adolescents*. New York, NY: Guilford Press.

Werner, H., & Kaplan, B. (1963). *Symbol formation*. New York, NY: John Wiley & Sons.

World Health Report. (2001). *Mental Health: New understanding, new hope*. Geneva, Switzerland: World Health Organization.

Zaslow, M., & Martinez-Beck, I. (Eds.). (2005). *Critical issues in early childhood professional development*. Baltimore, MD: Brookes.

Zerhouni, E. A. (2005). U.S. biomedical research: Basic, translational, and clinical sciences. *The Journal of the American Medical Association, 294*(11), 1352–1358.

# Beyond Adversity, Vulnerability, and Resilience

## Individual Differences in Developmental Plasticity

JAY BELSKY AND MICHAEL PLUESS

Notions of risk and protection, so central to thinking about resilience (Cicchetti, 1993; Cicchetti & Garmezy, 1993; Luthar, 2006) and developmental psychopathology more generally, have always been at the heart of the Minnesota Parent-Child Longitudinal Study (MPCLS). Even though many regard the MPCLS as principally—or at least originally—addressing the legacy of early attachment and thus continuity in development, neither Bowlby or Ainsworth nor Sroufe or Egeland ever embraced the simplistic—and strawman—conception of development sometimes attributed to them. Any considered reading of these scholars makes clear that they never contended that much, if not all, of psychological and behavioral development is shaped, veritably exclusively, by the nature of the child's tie to his or her mother, thus making security of attachment early in life the factor that most strongly influences, if not determines, how the future will turn out for a given child.

The fundamental reason why it has never been tenable to attribute such a simplistic, deterministic view of development to attachment theory and thus attachment theorists is because the notion of developmental pathway, influenced by what happens early in life, but also by what happens later in life, was and always has been *central* to attachment theory and thinking. Just because the theory stipulates that as the child develops he becomes an ever more active agent in shaping an early-established developmental trajectory—by selecting, constructing, and interpreting future experience—does not imply that such trajectories are set in stone, impervious to later experiences. In other words, development in middle childhood, adolescence, and even adulthood is not preordained by what the child encounters early in life.

In point of fact, the minute one embraces, as attachment theory and thinking most surely does, a probabilistic rather than deterministic view of early experience and of early development and of the role these forces play in the life course, notions of risk and protection become inevitable intellectual constructs, whether so named or not (Sroufe, 1988; Yates, Egeland, & Sroufe, 2003). An early experience, such as insensitive mothering, or early developmental standing, such as insecure attachment, can pose risks for future well-being, via a variety of complex mechanisms and processes, and thus function, empirically as well as conceptually, as risk factors. In consequence, a child who experiences insensitive care or who is insecure can be regarded as at increased risk for certain unfavorable developmental outcomes. But the fact that the risk is probabilistic, contingent on a host of other factors and processes, means that protective factors are basic conceptual components of attachment theory and thinking, too.

The fact that attachment theory and thinking has always embraced, implicitly if not explicitly, concepts of risk and protection turns out to be not the only reason why the MPCLS has been steeped in risk, protection, and, derivatively, resilience thinking from its inception. Even if not well-appreciated by many who regard the MPCLS primarily as a study of the legacy of early experience and perhaps especially of attachment security, the MPCLS still did not begin as a developmental inquiry designed to test propositions derived from attachment theory pertaining to continuity and discontinuity in development with a focus on developmental tasks and diverse developmental pathways. Instead, and before attachment theory and thinking so creatively influenced Byron Egeland and provided a basis for the incredibly fruitful collaboration with Alan Sroufe that this volume celebrates (Sroufe, Egeland, Carlson, & Collins, 2005), that which was to become the MPCLS began as a groundbreaking investigation of the causes and consequences of child abuse and neglect (Egeland & Brunnquell, 1979; Egeland, Breitenbucher, & Rosenberg, 1980).

Because Egeland was so far ahead of his time when he launched his study of 267 low-income pregnant women at elevated risk for maltreating their offspring, he appreciated that child maltreatment was not caused by any single factor or even domain of factors, as prevailing theories of the time emphasizing psychiatric problems in parents or sociological conditions of families stipulated (Belsky, 1978). Rather, Egeland understood that child abuse and neglect were multiply-determined phenomena, and thus that no singular causes were to be found. To illuminate its etiology, therefore, multiple factors needed to be considered and ultimately measured, which is exactly what Egeland proceeded to do. In fact, well before Garbarino (1977) or Belsky (1980) delineated the ecology of child maltreatment, applying Bronfenbrenner's (1979) emerging framework to this arena of inquiry, or Cicchetti and Rizley (1981) discussed potentiating and ameliorating influences, Egeland appreciated that cutting-edge research on child maltreatment required consideration of factors that increased the risk of maltreatment, like a mother's own childhood history of abuse, as well as ones that attenuated or protected against such risks, such as the availability of social support.

Given, then, that risk and protective thinking was central to the MPCLS as a result of its dual origins in attachment theory and an ecological perspective on child maltreatment, it stands to reason that so was the notion of resilience or the view that risks to well-being did not have to be realized—that is, did not have to compromise development—particularly when compensatory or protective factors existed to mitigate such risk. Development was thus always regarded as a dynamic, unfolding, probabilistic process insofar as the MPCLS is concerned, with developmental history influencing later functioning, sometimes for better and sometimes for worse, but also sometimes not at all. Only by considering the past and the present, as well as the attributes of the individual at any point in time, did the founding fathers of the MPCLS consider it possible to explain current development, much less predict future functioning.

However long these now widely embraced conceptual truisms have been central to the thinking of Sroufe and Egeland, and however much this chapter introduction, like the volume itself, is intended to herald the insights, accomplishments, and contributions of this remarkable investigatory team, our purpose here is not simply to praise these influential scholars and their indisputable contributions to the field of human development. Rather, it is to stand on their shoulders and see ahead, to at least one place where we think our field needs to go. Toward this end, and working from an evolutionary-biological perspective, we raise some questions about how many researchers in the field, including perhaps those we honor, have conceptualized rearing influences on development.

Central to the argument we advance is that some untoward consequences have resulted from so much attention being devoted to the study of adversity, vulnerability, and resilience, in the MPCLS and elsewhere, which is not to say that Egeland and Sroufe's work has been guided exclusively by pathological considerations. Most notably, we advance the still-speculative, evolution-inspired proposition that there may not just be individuals who, for organismic reasons, are more vulnerable to or protected from adversity, thereby and respectively succumbing to it or proving resilient, but that these same individuals may well respond similarly to enriching developmental experiences (Belsky, 1997b, 2005; Belsky, Bakermans-Kranenburg, & van IJzendoorn, 2007; Belsky & Pluess, 2009b). That is, those putatively "vulnerable" as a result of some individual attribute, whether it be a phenotypic characteristic (e.g., difficult temperament), an endophenotype (e.g., physiological reactivity), or a genotype (e.g., short alleles in the case 5-HTTLPR), may not only disproportionately succumb to the negative effects of adversity, thus meriting the label "vulnerable" (for organismic reasons), but also disproportionately benefit from the positive effects of supportive and nurturing rearing environments. (According to Gottesman and Gould [2003], an endophenotype is a measurable component along the pathway between genotype and phenotype.) Relatedly, those who prove resilient in the face of adversity for reasons having to do with their own phenotypic, endophenotypic, or genetic characteristics may prove more or less unaffected by putatively enriching developmental experiences. In other words—and recasting much of the study of adversity, vulnerability, and resilience, or at least that part of it that focuses on the role of organismic characteristics in determining resilience—it will be the central premise of this chapter that children vary in their *developmental plasticity*.

To further develop the argument just advanced, the next section delineates the theoretical basis for hypothesizing that children should vary in their susceptibility to environmental influences, most especially rearing-related ones. After outlining the evolutionary logic of our argument, evidence is reviewed, most of it rather recent, indicating that the very organismic characteristics that seem to make children vulnerable (or resilient) to adversity also make them disproportionately susceptible (or not) to the beneficial effects of supportive and nurturing rearing environments. Even though much of the presentation implies that such variation in susceptibility to rearing is a function of nature rather than nurture, in our concluding section we challenge this view, making it clear that this important issue of the origins of developmental plasticity remains very much open, theoretically and empirically.

In this chapter, we concentrate on three characteristics of individuals that have traditionally—or recently—been regarded as "risk factors," making them developmentally vulnerable in the face of adversity: having a difficult or highly negatively emotional temperament, being physiologically reactive, and carrying a short allele on the serotonin transporter gene *5-HTTPLR*. Elsewhere, we consider a broader array of phenotypic, endophenotypic, and genetic plasticity markers and thus moderators of environmental influences (Belsky & Pluess, 2009a).

## THEORETICAL FOUNDATION

The view that children should vary in their susceptibility to rearing is founded on evolutionary logic that regards the dispersion of genes in future generations as the ultimate biological imperative and thus goal of all living things. From the perspective of modern evolutionary biology, natural selection does not just shape living things to survive—which was the basis of Bowlby's (1969) original argument for why attachment behavior evolved—but to reproduce. Importantly, such reproduction can be direct, as when one produces immediate descendants (i.e., children, grandchildren), but also indirect, as when one's kin—such as brother, sister, niece, or nephew—reproduce and, in so doing, pass on genes that they share, in varying proportions, with the individual in question. *Reproductive fitness* refers to the dispersion of one's genes in future generations, and *inclusive fitness* calls attention to the fact that one's genetic material is distributed both directly and indirectly. With this foundation established, we turn to our theoretical argument.

Because the future is and always has been inherently uncertain, ancestral parents, just like parents today, could not have known (consciously or unconsciously) what child-rearing practices would prove most successful in promoting the reproductive fitness of offspring—and thus their own inclusive fitness. As a result, and as a fitness-optimizing strategy involving the hedging of bets, natural selection would have shaped parents to bear children varying in developmental plasticity (Belsky, 2005). This way, if an effect of parenting proved counterproductive in fitness terms, those children not affected by parenting would not have incurred the cost of developing in ways that ultimately proved "misguided" when it came to passing on genes to future generations. Importantly, in light of inclusive-fitness considerations, these less-malleable children's "resistance" to parental influence would have benefited not only themselves directly but their more-malleable sibs as well—but indirectly, given that sibs, like parents and children, have 50% of their genes in common. By the same token, had parenting influenced children in ways that enhanced fitness, then not only would more plastic or malleable offspring have benefited directly by virtue of parental influence, but so, too, would their parents and even their less-malleable sibs who did not benefit from the parenting they received, again for inclusive-fitness reasons (i.e., shared genes).

This line of evolutionary argument leads directly to the expectation that children should vary in their susceptibility to parental rearing and perhaps to environmental influences more generally. As it turns out, a long line of developmental inquiry informed by a "transactional" perspective (Sameroff, 1983) has been based, more or less, on this unstated assumption. Central to this perspective is the dual-risk model of problematic functioning on which studies of resilience are founded, a perspective that shares much with classical diathesis-stress models of psychopathology (Gottesman & Shields, 1967; Monroe & Simons, 1991; Zuckerman, 1999): Children who are *vulnerable* for reasons pertaining to their biology, temperament, genetics, or some other organismic reason (e.g., prematurity) will most likely manifest compromised development when exposed to some contextual adversity (e.g., hostile parenting, poverty).

Central to this chapter is the view that the widely embraced dual-risk transactional model of development—which has much in common with thinking about resilience (for review, see Luthar, 2006)—may seriously distort the nature of developmental plasticity. This is because it is based on developmental psychology's disproportionate focus on the *adverse* effects of *negative* experiences on *problems* in development and, thereby, the identification of children who, for organismic reasons, are particularly "vulnerable" to contextual risks or "protected" from them. What the aforementioned evolutionary analysis presupposes, in contrast, is that the children who are putatively "vulnerable" to adversity vis-à-vis problems in development may be equally and disproportionately susceptible to the developmentally *beneficial* effects of *supportive* rearing environments. Thus, and more so than other children, they are especially "plastic" or malleable (Belsky, 1997b; Boyce & Ellis, 2005), affected by developmental experiences for better *and* for worse (Belsky et al., 2007).

The conceptual contrast under consideration is nicely illustrated by the results of two recent studies. In one with findings in line with traditional, dual-risk/diathesis-stress transactional models, Boyce et al. (2006) found that low levels of father involvement (i.e., risk #1) among 9-year-olds predicted poorer mental health, but only in the case of children who were disinhibited two years earlier (i.e., risk #2), not those who were inhibited (see Figure 10.1). In a study focused on quality of child care and presenting rather contrasting results, Pluess and Belsky (2009)

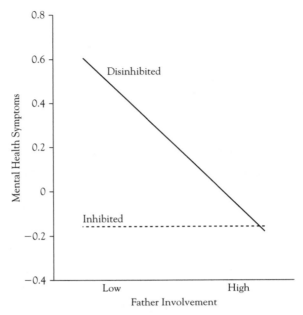

**Figure 10.1**   Example for Dual-Risk/Diathesis-Stress: Parenting (father involvement) by child temperament (inhibition/disinhibition) interaction predicting mental health symptoms at 9 years

(Redrawn from Boyce et al., 2006.)

reported that the developmental benefits of high-quality child care *and* the costs of low-quality care vis-à-vis behavior problems just before school entry accrued exclusively to children who as infants were highly negatively emotional (see Figure 10.2). Thus, whereas the first study cited chronicled the disproportionate *vulnerability* (to adversity) of disinhibited children, the second underscored the disproportionate *plasticity* (for better *and* for worse) of highly negatively emotional infants.

Beyond the research on children, adolescents, and adults to be considered in the next section of this chapter highlighting individual differences in plasticity like those seemingly discerned by Pluess and Belsky (2009), of note is that cross-species evidence indicates that plasticity is heritable (Bashey, 2006; Pigliucci, 2007) and may function as a selectable character in and of itself (Sinn, Gosling, & Moltschaniwskyj, 2007). One wild bird population shows evidence that selection favoring individuals who are highly plastic with regard to the timing of reproduction

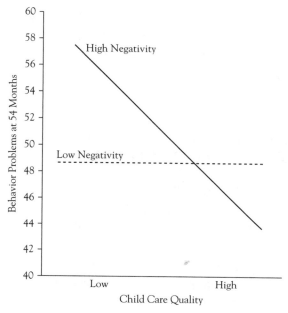

**Figure 10.2**    Example for Differential Susceptibility: Child care quality by child temperament interaction predicting teacher-reported behavior problems at 54 months

(Pluess & Belsky, 2009)

has intensified over the past three decades, perhaps in response to climate change, causing a mismatch between the breeding times of the birds and their caterpillar prey (Nussey, Postma, Gienapp, & Visser, 2005). Moreover, a recent simulation study seeking to determine whether plasticity could evolve, with some individuals being more responsive to environmental conditions than others, has yielded evidence in favor of this possibility (Wolf, van Doorn, & Weissing, 2008).

Also noteworthy is Suomi's (2006) insightful observation that a single genetic difference distinguishes the two species of primates that fill multiple niches around the world from all others that inhabit singular and rather narrow ones—the presence of the *5-HTTLPR* short allele. This leads him to regard humans and macaques as "weed species." Given evidence to be reviewed as follows that this gene does not just increase vulnerability to contextual risk but also appears to be associated with a disproportionately positive response to supportive rearing conditions, one cannot but wonder whether this allele is better conceptualized as a "plasticity gene" (Belsky et al., 2009; Belsky & Pluess, 2009b) rather than, as has routinely been the case in studies of psychopathology based on diathesis-stress thinking, a "vulnerability gene" (Burmeister, McInnis, & Zollner, 2008; Rutter, 2006).

## EVIDENCE OF INDIVIDUAL DIFFERENCES IN DEVELOPMENTAL PLASTICITY

Belsky et al. (2007) recently delineated a series of empirical requirements—or steps—for convincingly establishing evidence of differential susceptibility to environmental influence (i.e., individual differences in plasticity). The first concerns the application of conventional statistical criteria for evaluating genuine moderation of a putative environmental influence by an organismic plasticity or susceptibility factor (Dearing & Hamilton, 2006), with some emphasis on excluding interactions with regression lines that do not cross (sometimes referred to as *removable interactions*). The next steps distinguish differential susceptibility from person–environment correlations that may reflect evocative effects of person characteristics on environmental experiences and from dual-risk/ diathesis-stress models. If the susceptibility factor and the outcome are related, then dual risk (or gain, when positive factors are involved) is suggested (see Figure 10.1). For example, early negativity would lead to externalizing behavior, but even more so when combined with negative parenting. The specificity of the differential-susceptibility effect is demonstrated if the model is not replicated when other susceptibility factors (i.e., moderators) and outcomes are used (Caspi & Moffitt, 2006; Rutter, 2006). Differential susceptibility is thus demonstrated when the moderation reflects a crossover interaction (as in Figure 10.2) that covers both the positive and the negative aspects of the environment (i.e., susceptibility instead of dual risk). The slope for the susceptible subgroup should be significantly different from zero and at the same time significantly steeper than the slope for the non- (or less-) susceptible subgroup.

In the remainder of the chapter, we review evidence of differential susceptibility to environmental influence involving (1) difficult temperament/

negative emotionality, (2) physiological reactivity, and (3) the serotonin transporter gene *5-HTTPLR*, which is consistent with the view that individuals differ in their plasticity, with some being more affected than others by experiential influences—and in a for-better-*and*-for-worse manner. This review should not be considered exhaustive; nor should it be regarded as implying that evidence of differential susceptibility outweighs evidence of diathesis-stress/dual-risk, either in the literature as a whole or even in all of the studies cited. To make the case, as we exclusively seek to, that differential susceptibility *appears* operative in human development and functioning, but that individual differences in plasticity have been largely overlooked—in favor of prevailing views that some individuals are simply more vulnerable to adversity than others—it is our contention that this compilation of findings from diverse areas of inquiry is exactly what is appropriate at the present time.

Perhaps because so much of the work to be cited is new—and often conducted with a dual-risk/diathesis-stress frame of reference in mind—it is actually rare for investigations to address all or even most of the statistical criteria highlighted by Belsky et al. (2007) for providing convincing evidence of differential susceptibility to environmental influence. When and where they do, this will be noted, especially with respect to whether the susceptibility factor in question, be it phenotypic, endophenotypic, or genetic, proved independent of (i.e., unrelated to) the environmental predictor *and* psychological/behavioral outcome(s) being investigated. These latter criteria are considered especially important, because the absence of such direct statistical links rules out evocative- and dual-risk interpretations of the significant crossover interactions that will be the exclusive focus of the remainder of this chapter. Because all of the findings to be cited are based on such interactions between a putative susceptibility factor and an environmental measure, there is no need to call attention to such beyond this comment here.

What should also be made clear is that investigators detecting interactions follow them up analytically in two basic ways in the research to be considered; and in neither case is sufficient information routinely provided to determine whether all of the criteria listed earlier for inferring differential susceptibility are met. Whereas some investigations adopt a grouping approach for dealing with the interacting predictor variables, plotting or tabling subgroup means (see Figure 10.1), others calculate and contrast slopes reflecting the differential predictive relation between the continuously measured environmental predictor and outcome for groups that differ on the moderating susceptibility factor (see Figure 10.2). Only rarely is it reported whether such slopes differ significantly from each other, as would be preferable when the moderator does not have a natural breakpoint but is a continuous dimension (and as would not be required when the moderator is naturally binary). Perhaps analogously, only rarely is it reported, when subclass means are plotted, exactly which means differ significantly from which others.

For these reasons, we adopt here a liberal standard of evidence once a significant crossover interaction has been detected when it comes to regarding results as evidence of differential susceptibility to environmental influences. Specifically, and with regard to subgroup means, if one subgroup shows both the highest *and* lowest mean of all susceptibility-factor-defined subgroups (e.g., short vs. long *5-HTTLPR* allele) on an outcome with regard to the environmental effect in question, this is interpreted as in line with the for-better-and-for-worse, differential-susceptibility patterning of results. Similarly, but with regard to slopes, whenever they indicate that one subgroup defined on the basis of the susceptibility factor in question would score highest *and* lowest given the environmental influence under investigation (i.e., steepest slope), this, too, is interpreted as evidence of differential susceptibility. All of the findings to be presented meet these criteria—unless otherwise stipulated.

To be crystal clear, what follows is a purposefully selective review of evidence that is, at the least, not inconsistent with a differential susceptibility perspective, which should by no means be read to imply that it confirms such a viewpoint. To repeat, few studies meet all criteria for testing differential susceptibility. Extremely few come close to measuring both positive and negative poles of the environment; instead, most of the relevant psychiatric genetic studies in particular assess only adverse environments and their absence, and thus not the presence of environmental supports. Relatedly, many of these and other studies fail to assess competent functioning, focusing instead on disturbance or just its absence. Also missing from virtually all studies is any effort to determine whether detected interactions reflect certain individuals functioning both more poorly under conditions of adversity *and* better than others under conditions of support—resulting form their personal characteristics, be they phenotypic, endophenotypic, or genetic in nature. At best, only the former possibility is directly evaluated following detection of significant person-X-context interaction, something no doubt caused by the role that diathesis-stress thinking has played in shaping virtually all of the work to be cited. Also needing to be appreciated is that sample sizes in the studies cited are often small, thereby raising questions about the replicability of the statistical interactions discerned.

Finally, and perhaps most imporantly, this selected review purposefully does not focus on studies that are inconsistent with differential susceptibility for two reasons. First, as hopefully just made clear, many studies are not ideally designed to determine whether individuals with certain (phenotypic, endophenotypic, or genetic) characteristics both differentially succumb to adversity and benefit from environmental enrichment. Second, and perhaps more importantly, this presentation is not intended to compellingly make the case for differential susceptibility so much as advance the hypothesis of differential susceptibility. More than anything else, then, the goal is to highlight many results in the literature that appear consistent with it, not that confirm it and thus disconfirm diathesis-stress models of environmental action. It will take much more carefully conducted work to test whether that is the case—or to identify when it is and when it is not. Although it would be good to be in a position, theoretically, to stipulate when one model of environmental action is more likely to fit the data than another, it remains difficult to stipulate that at the current time.

## Negative Emotionality and Difficult Temperament as Phenotypic Plasticity Markers

Some of the earliest and most suggestive evidence of differential susceptibility to environmental influences emerged in research on temperament-X-parenting interaction (Belsky, 1997a), a long-standing focus of inquiry, typically conducted from a dual-risk/diathesis-stress perspective (Rothbart & Bates, 2006). Belsky's (2005) review of relevant research revealed that predictive links (i.e., variation accounted for) between rearing experience and a variety of behavioral outcomes often were consistently greater for a subgroup of children characterized by a temperamental propensity for high negative affectivity, whether operationalized in terms of difficult temperament, irritability, fearfulness, or inhibition. Cross-sectional and longitudinal studies by Kochanska (1993), Belsky, Hsieh, and Crnic (1998), and Feldman, Greenbaum, and Yirmiya (1999) showed, for example, that diverse measures of rearing of infants and toddlers (e.g., discipline, interactional synchrony, positive and negative parenting) accounted for substantially more variance in self-control, externalizing problems, and/or inhibition in the case of more negatively emotional infants/toddlers than other children.

In considering such correlational findings, Belsky (2005) noted how reminiscent they were of those emanating from Suomi's (1997) experimental studies with rhesus macaques selectively bred to vary in their fearfulness and proclivity to become anxious. When highly anxious (so-called "uptight") monkeys and their far less anxious counterparts were cross-fostered to highly skilled or average foster mothers, dramatic (for-better-*and*-for-worse) rearing effects emerged, but only in the case of the highly anxious monkeys. Whereas uptight infants foster-reared to average mothers exhibited expected deficits in early exploration patterns and exaggerated biobehavioral responses to minor environmental perturbations, these same highly reactive infants actually appeared to be behaviorally precocious when cross-fostered to especially nurturant females. These latter infants physically separated from their mother at an earlier point in development, locomoted and explored their environment more, and displayed less behavioral disturbance during weaning than not only the highly reactive infants cross-fostered to average mothers but even the average infants reared by either type of foster mother.

Moreover, when these selectively bred and differentially foster-reared monkeys were moved into larger social groups at 6 months of age, the uptight monkeys reared by particularly competent foster mothers proved especially adept at recruiting and retaining other group members as allies in response to agonistic encounters and, perhaps as a consequence, subsequently rose to and maintained top positions in the group's dominance hierarchy. In contrast, temperamentally similar, highly reactive individuals cross-fostered to control mothers tended to drop to and remain at the bottom of the same dominance hierarchy. Importantly, no such longer-term rearing effects were evident among the average infants. In other words, the range of reaction of the uptight monkeys in response to these contrasting rearing conditions greatly exceeded that of their average-reactive counter-parts subjected to the same variation in rearing regimens.

Even though most of the research on children reviewed by Belsky (2005) showed, following documentation of significant temperament-X-parenting interactions, that *greater variance* in a variety of developmental outcomes could be explained by rearing experiences in the case of more negatively emotional children, statistical analyses in the studies reviewed often did not afford determination of whether, as in the Suomi (1997) work, this result was a function of a for-better-*and*-for-worse parenting effect. In consequence, it remained unclear whether individual differences in plasticity—or just vulnerability—were responsible for the repeatedly detected finding that more variance was explained in one group's functioning than in another's by the environmental factor investigated. Fortunately, a growing number of studies provide substantial empirical evidence that rearing and other environmental effects do not just account for more variance in the functioning of more negatively emotional children—or even that such individuals are more vulnerable to negative experiences as the dual-risk/diathesis-stress model would suggest—but that they are differentially susceptible to environmental experiences in a for-better-*and*-for-worse manner. Van Aken, Junger, Verhoeven, van Aken, and Dekovic (2007) found, for example, that 16- to 19-month-old boys ($n = 115$) with difficult temperament showed the smallest increase six months later in externalizing problems scores when reared by highly sensitive mothers who only infrequently used negative control, but they showed the largest increase when highly insensitive mothers relied heavily on negative control. These striking parenting effects simply did not obtain in the case of other children.

In a series of investigations, Kochanska, Aksan, and Joy (2007) sought to determine whether child temperament moderated parenting effects on positive developmental outcomes. In one study, children's fearfulness, maternal power assertion, and mother-child positive relations were assessed behaviorally when children were 22 and 33 months old, and children's moral self was measured using a puppet interview at 56 months ($n = 74$). Although no parenting effects emerged in the case of children who, as toddlers, scored low in fear, those who were highly fearful evinced a greater moral sense if their mothers (at 22 months only) relied little on power assertion to regulate their behavior, but they had a limited one if their mothers relied heavily on power to control earlier child behavior. The fact that child fearfulness was significantly and negatively related to maternal power assertion raises some questions about how much confidence to place in this study when it comes to inferring individual differences in plasticity. In circumstances such as these, in which the putative susceptibility factor is related to the environmental factor, thereby raising the prospect of evocative person effects, a better approach would be to statistically partial the effect of the susceptibility factor from the environmental one before testing interactions between the two; this would eliminate the potential evocative effect that confounds interpretation of differential susceptibility.

In a second study ($n = 100$ families), this time focused on father's reliance on power assertion (15 months), children's fearfulness (7 and 15 months) and their rule-compatible conduct (38 months), Kochanska et al. (2007) once again documented evidence of for-better-*and*-for-worse parenting effects: Whereas high versus low power assertiveness made no apparent difference for children scoring low in fearfulness (at 7 and 15 months), children who had been highly fearful infants proved less obedient than all others when fathers' power assertion was high, yet more obedient than all others when fathers' power assertion was low. And this time child fearfulness was not associated with paternal power assertion or rule-compatible conduct, hence fulfilling important criteria for inferring differential susceptibility.

Drawing on data of the large-scale longitudinal NICHD study of Early Child Care and Youth Development (NICHD Early Child Care Research Network [ECCRN], 2005) and focusing on maternally reported difficult temperament at 1 and 6 months of age (composited), Bradley and Corwyn (2008) also discerned evidence of differential susceptibility when it came to evaluating effects of observed and reported maternal sensitivity, harshness, and productive activity (composited and averaged across measurements at 6, 15, 24, 36, 54 months, and first grade) on teacher-reported behavior problems in first grade ($n = 929$): Children with more difficult temperaments had more behavior problems in first grade than all other children if they experienced low-quality parenting, but they had fewer problems than all other children if they experienced high-quality parenting; the anticipated effect of parenting quality was weaker in the case for children with intermediate levels of difficult temperament and weaker still in the case of children scoring very low on difficult temperament (i.e., easy temperament), thereby revealing a possible plasticity gradient (Belsky, 2000). (See also Warren & Simmens, 2005, for similar results using the same data.) The fact that simple slopes between parenting and behavior problems were significant for children with difficult temperament ($> 1$ SD from the mean of temperament) but not for children with easy temperaments ($< 1$ SD from the mean) means that this study provided strong evidence of differential susceptibility given the Belsky et al. (2007) criteria.

Dopkins-Stright, Cranley-Gallagher, and Kelley (2008) were able to extend findings of differential susceptibility to positive developmental outcomes, also drawing on data from the NICHD study of Early Child Care (NICHD Early Child Care Research Network [ECCRN], 2005). Once again a temperament-X-parenting interaction emerged, this time between difficult temperament (at 6 months) and parenting style (composited across 6, 15, 24, 36, and 54 months) in predicting teacher-rated academic competence, social skills, teacher-child relationships, and peer status at first grade. Predictive power proved greater for infants with more difficult temperaments than for infants with less difficult temperaments. Although all interactions were of a crossover nature and in line with a for-better-*and*-for-worse parenting effect for only some children, not all criteria for differential susceptibility were met; of special significance, as already noted, is that the temperament susceptibility factor predicted the parenting predictor (as well as at least one outcome measured).

Pluess and Belsky (2010) overcame this problem in their longer-term analysis of differential susceptibility using the same NICHD Study data.

After finding that parenting quality before school entry predicted reading, math, picture vocabulary, social competence, and academic work habits in the fifth grade more strongly for children with difficult temperament than for those with easy temperaments—and in a for-better-*and*-for-worse manner—they reran their analysis using the method proposed earlier for discounting discerned evocative effects of a putative susceptibility factor (i.e., temperament) on the environmental predictor (i.e., parenting quality). When the composite measure reflecting quality of parenting across the infant, toddler, and preschool years was statistically adjusted to control for the effect of 6-month, mother-reported difficult temperament, differential-susceptibility findings remained virtually unchanged.

## Beyond Parenting: Child Care Quality

All of the rearing data considered up to this point pertains to parenting, but with so many children being routinely cared for by alternative caregivers in child care settings, the question arises as to whether quality of child care differentially affects children's development as a function of their temperament. Some research clearly suggests this to be the case. In perhaps the earliest pertinent study, Volling and Feagans (1995) detected a relevant and thus noteworthy interaction between children's social fear (i.e., negative emotionality?), as rated by mothers, and the observed quality of center-based child care in the prediction of observed nonsocial activity (i.e., solitary play, onlooker behavior) a year later when children were 14 to 48 months of age ($n = 36$). The highly fearful children manifest both the most and least nonsocial activity, depending on the quality of child care, whereas no such environmental effect emerged in the case of the low-fear children.

Given Volling and Feagan's (1995) small sample size, perhaps more convincing evidence that differential susceptibility characterizes some effects of child care comes from a recent analysis of data from the aforementioned NICHD Study of Early Child Care and Youth Development, which investigated both negative and positive developmental outcomes (Pluess & Belsky, 2009). In this work on samples ranging from 761 to 915 children, the observed quality of care (averaged across measurements at 6, 15, 24, 36, and 54 months) differentially predicted behavior problems (see Figure 10.2) and social competence rated by caregivers in the year before school entry and by kindergarten teachers. Children with difficult temperament (rated at 6 months) not only had more behavior problems when reared in low-quality environments and fewer problems when quality was high compared to children with easy temperaments, but the regression lines (i.e., slopes) proved significant only for the children who scored high on difficult temperament as infants. The same was true when the outcome to be explained was social competence. The fact that temperament proved to be unrelated to both child care quality and the dependent measures means that these results meet important statistical criteria for inferring evidence of differential susceptibility. This was also the case when Pluess and Belsky (2010) extended their research to determine if, after imputing missing data and thereby increasing their sample size to 1,364, differential susceptibility to the effects of good- and poor-quality child care in the first 4.5 years of life extended to teacher-reported behavior problems and teacher-child conflicts when children were 10 to 11 years of age.

## Beyond Field Studies: Experimental Evidence

In view of the fact that all research considered up to this point, with the exception of Suomi's (1997) primate studies, can be regarded as limited because of its correlational (and often cross-sectional) nature, experimental demonstrations of an environmental effect operating on a differential-susceptibility basis must be regarded as especially important. After all, the possibility exists that the relations detected between experience and development in virtually all of the work cited so far could be a function of some unmeasured third variable, most notably, perhaps, genes that both elicit environmental experiences and influence development.

For this reason, special importance should be attributed to the reanalysis of data from the Infant Health and Development Program (1990), a well-known, early intervention that involved the random assignment of poor, low-birth infants and their families to treatment or control condition, putatively generating positive, across-the-board program effects. Blair (2002) tested Belsky's (1997b, 1997a) proposition that an enriched rearing experience (involving educational day care in the second and third year of life, combined with home visiting and parent support over the child's first three years) would differentially impact children with varying temperaments. As predicted, infants who were highly negatively emotional and assigned to the early-intervention group scored substantially lower on externalizing problems at 3 years of age than did similarly tempered infants randomly assigned to the control group, with no such treatment effect in evidence in the case of other infants. Especially intriguing, given the fact that virtually all research considered as yet has focused on differential susceptibility vis-à-vis social and emotional functioning, is that exactly the same results emerged in this research on the Infant Health and Development Project (IHDP) when the outcome in question was severely impaired cognitive functioning. More specifically, highly negative infants assigned to the experimental intervention were five times less likely to score at or below 75 on an IQ test at age 3 than their negatively emotional counterparts assigned to the control condition; no such experimental effect emerged in the case of infants scoring low on negative emotionality.

Noteworthy, too, are two recent studies designed to test Belsky's (1997b) hypothesis that the reason that van den Boom's (1994) experimental enhancement of sensitivity produced such powerful effects on infant attachment security was because she included only highly negatively emotional newborns in her investigation. Velderman, Bakermans-Kranenburg, Juffer, and Van IJzendoorn (2006) observed that their experimental efforts, using video feedback to enhance maternal sensitivity, proved beneficial in terms of promoting infant attachment security exclusively to those infants who scored high on negative reactivity. Only for these infants did experimentally induced increases in sensitivity translate into increased infant-mother attachment security. Somewhat similarly, Cassidy, Woodhouse, Sherman, Stupica, and Lejuez (submitted) found in a randomized control trial that a home-based intervention that included video feedback along with other strategies for enhancing the quality of maternal care increased the probability of security, but only for the especially irritable infants who met the same criteria for irritability that van den Boom (2004) used to select her original sample.

# Why Negative Emotionality/Difficult Temperament?

The repeatedly discerned moderational effect of negative emotionality/difficult temperament raises the question of why this should be the case. This is an especially important issue because even though Belsky (1997b, 2005) theorized that children should vary in their susceptibility to environmental influences (i.e., plasticity), his differential-susceptibility hypothesis did not stipulate that more negatively emotional children or those with difficult temperament would prove especially malleable; this was an empirical observation (Belsky, 2005). As it turns out, several non-mutually-exclusive explanations have been advanced with regard to the issue at hand. Drawing on his primate evidence, Suomi (1995, 1997) suggested that highly fearful/inhibited/"uptight" rhesus macaques spent more time than other young monkeys observing the world around them, thereby learning more than others about how to function effectively in their social environment. Kochanska (1993) drew explicitly on Dienstbier's (1985) thinking on anxiety to account for her results, arguing that more negatively emotional/fearful/inhibited infants have lower thresholds for anxiety, thereby making them more easily aroused by discipline and thus responsive to it. Not unrelatedly, Belsky (2005) contended that a negatively emotional/difficult temperament reflects a highly sensitive nervous system on which experience—of both the positive and negative variety—registers especially strongly (see also Aron & Aron, 1997).

# Physiological Reactivity as an Endophenotypic Plasticity Marker

Boyce and Ellis (2005) have advanced a theory of "biological sensitivity to context," which shares much in common with Belsky's (1997b, 2005) original differential-susceptibility hypothesis, in that it, too, is based on (different) evolutionary reasoning and presumes that some individuals, specifically children, are more susceptible to positive and negative developmental experiences than are others. They theorize that children who are highly physiologically reactive to stress will manifest the most developmental plasticity. Given that many such children probably begin life as highly negative infants or ones with difficult temperaments, it seems likely that many of the very same children that Belsky (1997b, 2005) first called attention to in this regard are being identified by different means. In any event, Boyce and Ellis's (2005) viewpoint highlights the fact that endophenotypic characteristics, not just the behavioral ones considered in the preceding section, might moderate environmental influences, functioning thereby as plasticity markers. In this section, evidence consistent with the claim is considered after first providing a brief summary of the two separate physiological systems with specific functions: the autonomic nervous system and the neuroendocrine system.

The so-called fight-or-flight response to stress is primarily controlled by the autonomic nervous system (ANS), which is further divided into the sympathetic nervous system (SNS) and the parasympathetic nervous system (PNS). The SNS controls those activities that are mobilizing during stress and anxiety (e.g., acceleration of heart rate, increased blood pressure, enhanced blood flow to the skeletal muscles, decreased blood flow to the internal organs and extremities, sweating). Physiologically opposing activities under PNS control serve the basic functions of rest, repair, and relaxation of the body and restoration of energy stores (e.g., decreases in heart rate and blood pressure, stimulation of the digestive system, sexual arousal, sleep). The neuroendocrine response to stress is primarily controlled by the hypothalamus-pituitary-adrenal axis (HPA). Corticotropin-releasing hormone (CRH), which is released from the hypothalamus in response to stress, activates the secretion of adrenocorticotropic hormone (ACTH) from the pituitary gland, which then causes the adrenal cortex to release cortisol into the general bloodstream. Finally, cortisol leads to many diverse physiological and metabolic changes in order to prepare the organism for optimal functioning under stressful conditions (e.g., increase of blood pressure and blood sugar, breakdown of lipids and proteins, mobilization of amino acids, reduction of immune responses).

In the earliest pertinent investigation of physiological reactivity of which we are aware that reports differential-susceptibility-like effects, Gannon, Banks, Shelton, and Luchetta (1989) studied 50 undergraduates on whom a range of SNS markers of physiological reactivity were obtained (before and after a math problems' stress test; plasticity factor). These students also reported on daily hassles (environmental factor), as well as common physical symptoms and depression. Compared to individuals showing low reactivity of blood volume pulse amplitude, highly reactive students reported both few physical symptoms when experiencing few daily hassles and many symptoms when experiencing many hassles. Also consistent with differential-susceptibility thinking, those students showing slow heart rate recovery after the stress test reported fewer depressive symptoms when experiencing fewer daily hassles and more symptoms when experiencing more daily hassles compared to individuals with a fast recovery.

Findings in line with those just presented, but evident at much younger ages, emerged in Boyce and associates' (1995) test of the hypothesis that mean arterial blood pressure reactivity to a stress test at ages 3 to 5 would interact with a composite measure of child care quality (measured across a two-year period) in predicting frequency of respiratory illness during the six months following the physiological-reactivity assessment. Specifically, children with higher blood pressure reactivity exhibited higher rates of respiratory illness than other children when growing up in stressful rearing contexts, yet under low-stress conditions such highly reactive children had a significantly lower incidence of respiratory illnesses than other children.

Reactivity-moderated effects of environmental experiences are also evident when skin conductance level (SCL) reactivity serves as the index of physiological functioning. This is perhaps noteworthy in view of the fact that SCL is controlled solely by the SNS, in contrast to the other cardiovascular-reactivity measures, which are generally innervated and controlled by both SNS and PNS. Thus, El-Sheikh, Keller, and Erath (2007) investigated associations between SCL reactivity (assessed during a star-tracing problem-solving task), marital conflict (parent report), and change (from ages 9 to 11.5 years) in adjustment problems (parent report). Compared to girls with low SCL reactivity, highly reactive girls showed the largest increase in internalizing problems if they were from highly conflicted homes but the smallest increase when marital conflict was low in their families. A significant crossover interaction consistent with differential susceptibility also emerged for boys with respect to change in externalizing problems; rather surprisingly, however, those scoring low in physiological reactivity appeared (exclusively) susceptible to the adverse effect of marital conflict. That SCL reactivity proved unrelated to marital conflict and also did not predict the outcomes included in this work means that the findings, even when perhaps inconsistent with expectations (i.e., boys), met criteria for inferring differential susceptibility (Belsky et al., 2007).

The same research team has also used vagal tone (indexed by respiratory sinus arrhythmia [RSA]) and vagal suppression (during exposure to an audio recording of a male-female verbal conflict) to investigate whether and how PNS measures moderate effects of marital conflict on child adjustment in middle childhood (El-Sheikh, Harger, & Whitson, 2001). Compared to children with high vagal tone (who were not seemingly affected by marital conflict), those scoring low in vagal tone proved less anxious when growing up in families with little marital conflict but more anxious when residing in high-conflict homes. Similar crossover interaction results emerged with respect to vagal suppression, but for boys only. Importantly with respect to inferring differential susceptibility, the PNS moderators of these marital-conflict effects were not related to the predictor variable or the dependent measures.

In a recent cross-sectional study of more than 300 5-year-olds, Obradovic, Bush, Stamperdahl, Adler, and Boyce (2010) report yet more data chronicling the role of RSA in moderating environmental effects, along with some pertaining to cortisol reactivity (both assessed during a stress test). In this research, a composite index of childhood adversity (based on parental reports of financial stress, parenting overload, marital conflict, negative/anger expressiveness, maternal depression, and harsh and restrictive parenting) proved predictive of composite well-being measures (based on parent, teacher, and child self-reports), but more so in the case of children with a more reactive parasympathetic nervous system (in contrast to findings by El-Sheikh and associates [(El-Sheikh et al., 2001; El-Sheikh, Erath, & Keller, 2007). More specifically, children with high RSA reactivity were rated as more prosocial under low-adversity conditions and less prosocial under high-adversity conditions compared to children with low RSA reactivity. Children with high RSA reactivity also scored higher on school engagement under low-adversity conditions and lower under high-adversity conditions compared to children with low RSA reactivity. Importantly, the RSA moderator proved unrelated to the adversity predictor and to the outcomes cited.

Although multiple PNS investigations provide evidence in line with the differential-susceptibility hypothesis, seeming to highlight individual differences in plasticity, not just vulnerability, only two investigations involving the *neuroendocrine system* appear to provide comparable evidence. In the aforementioned work by Obradovic et al. (2010), children with high cortisol reactivity were rated as more prosocial under low adversity and less prosocial under high adversity compared to children with low cortisol reactivity. In a small intervention study involving 22 8- to 13-year-old children with disruptive behavior disorder, van de Wiel, van Goozen, Matthys, Snoek, and van Engeland (2004) observed that those showing greater cortisol reactivity in response to a stressor manifest greater reductions in parent-reported problems following treatment than their less-reactive counterparts.

It is difficult to be sure that this apparent imbalance in evidence across the autonomic nervous system and the neuroendocrine system is caused by the two stress reactivity systems playing fundamentally different roles vis-à-vis environmental influences, or whether one has just received more attention from investigators as a moderator of environmental effects. The latter could be the case, given that most developmentalists measuring cortisol reactivity in studies of environmental effects regard it as a dependent construct, something affected by contextual adversity, rather than as a moderator of environmental influences on development (Gunnar & Quevedo, 2007; Fernald, Burke, & Gunnar, 2008).

## 5-HTTPLR Short Alleles as a Genetic Plasticity Marker

Whereas almost all of the evidence cited so far derives from studies of children, gene-environment interaction (GxE) findings consistent with the differential-susceptibility hypothesis often derive from research with adults; this is especially true of psychiatric research focused on pathological outcomes (e.g., depression, antisocial behavior). The fact that most of this work has been guided by traditional diathesis-stress thinking means that evidence that those carrying a putative "risk allele" actually function better than others when not exposed to the risk condition being studied (e.g., negative life events) is often not even noted by investigators who, instead, exclusively herald evidence consistent with diathesis-stress thinking (Belsky et al., 2009). In what follows, we call attention to GxE findings involving the serotonin transporter gene 5-HTTPLR that appear to reflect differential susceptibility. The primary reason for selecting this gene for consideration in this chapter is that short alleles on this polymorphism have been linked to both negative emotionality (Auerbach, Faroy, Ebstein, Kahana, & Levine, 2001) and physiological reactivity (Gotlib, Joormann, Minor, & Hallmayer, 2008).

The serotonin-transporter-linked polymorphic region (5-HTTLPR) is a degenerate repeat polymorphic region in SLC6A4, the gene that codes for the serotonin transporter. Most research focuses on two variants—those carrying at least one short allele ($s/s$, $s/l$) and those homozygous for the long allele ($l/l$)—though more variants than these have been identified (Nakamura, Ueno, Sano, & Tanabe, 2000). The short allele has generally been associated with reduced expression of the serotonin transporter molecule, which is involved in the reuptake of serotonin from the synaptic cleft, and thus considered to be related to depression, either directly or in the face of adversity.

Caspi and associates (2003) were the first to show that the 5-HTTLPR moderates the effects of stressful life events during early adulthood on depressive symptoms, as well as on the probability of suicide ideation/ attempts and of major depression episodes at age 26 years. Individuals with two $s$ alleles proved most adversely affected, whereas effects on $l/l$ genotypes were weaker or entirely absent. Of special significance given our focus on differential susceptibility is that carriers of the $s/s$ allele scored best on the outcomes just mentioned when stressful life events were absent, though not by very much.

Several research groups have attempted to replicate Caspi et al.'s findings (2003) of increased vulnerability to depression in response to stressful life events for individuals with one or more copies of the $s$ allele, with most succeeding (see the following discussion), even if not all did (Surtees et al., 2006). Going unnoticed in most, even if not all, of this work to be summarized as follows, however, is that those carrying short alleles (*s/s, s/l*) did not just function most poorly when exposed to many stressors, but they also did best—showing the least problems—when encountering few or no stressors. Consider, for example, Taylor and associates' (2006) findings (appreciated by the investigators) showing that young adults homozygous for short alleles (*s/s*) manifested greater depressive symptomatology than individuals with other allelic variants when exposed to early adversity (i.e., problematic child-rearing history), as well as many recent negative life events, consistent with a diathesis-stress framework, yet they had the fewest symptoms when they experienced a supportive early environment or recent positive experiences.

A similar for-better-*and*-for-worse pattern of environmental effects emerged in still other investigations of stressful life events and depression, including one targeting depressed patients, healthy controls, and experiences during the six months before study enrollment (Zalsman et al., 2006), and another of a sizeable community sample (*n* = 567) and life events up to two years before the assessment of depression (Lazary et al., 2008). The same for-better-*and*-for-worse pattern of results are evident—and noted—in Brummett et al.'s (2008) investigation of more than 200 adults (mean age, 58 years) who differed in whether they served as caregiver of a relative with Alzheimer's disease and in Eley et al.'s (2004) research on adolescent girls who were and were not exposed to risky family environments. Although all of the work just cited, with the exception of Caspi et al. (2003), was cross-sectional in design, Wilhelm and associates' (2006) longitudinal data also shows that individuals with the *s/s* genotype had the lowest probability of lifetime major depression if they were exposed to no adverse life events in a five-year study period, but the highest probability when reporting two, three, or more adverse life events compared to other genotypes. Importantly, genotype did not predict exposure to life events or depression.

The effect of *5-HTTLPR* in moderating environmental influences in a manner consistent with differential susceptibility is not restricted to depression and its symptoms but also includes, perhaps unsurprisingly, anxiety and ADHD. Gunthert et al. (2007) documented the former result in a longitudinal study of 350 college students. At study entry and a year later, participants reported anxiety and negative events daily for 30 days. Genotyping distinguished three alleles, but the $L_G$ allele was grouped with s alleles because of its functional equivalence vis-à-vis promoter activity. Individuals who were judged homozygous for short alleles (including $s/L_G$ and $L_G/L_G$) reported more anxiety in the evening when daily-event stress was high compared to individuals with different genotypes, but they also had less anxiety than other genotypes when experiencing little daily-event stress, a pattern consistent across measurement occasions. Once again, the fact that the susceptibility factor did not predict the environmental measure or the outcome is considered important.

In a second study focused on undergraduate students ($n = 247$) and anxiety (Stein, Schork, & Gelernter, 2008), but this time concerned with (retrospectively reported) emotional abuse in childhood, a GxE interaction once more emerged, with genotype importantly proving unrelated to the environmental predictor and the outcome, anxiety sensitivity. The significantly steeper abuse-anxiety slope in the case of students who were homozygous for short alleles relative to those with one or more long alleles indicated that s/s individuals scored highest in anxiety sensitivity when exposed to abuse and lowest when not exposed.

Moving on to consider ADHD (in childhood and adulthood), Retz and associates (2008) focused on the moderated effects of an adverse childhood environment in their study of 184 male delinquents who averaged 34 years of age. Using a retrospective assessment of childhood ADHD, as well as of early adversity, but a clinical interview to assess functioning in adulthood, these investigators detected a crossover interaction with respect to the persistence of ADHD over time (though interpretively important associations between moderator and predictor were not reported). Compared to l/l genotypes, individuals with s alleles had more and less persistent ADHD, depending on whether or not, respectively, they experienced an adverse early environment.

The final differential-susceptibility-relevant finding involving 5-HTTLPR to be reviewed comes from Manuck, Flory, Ferrell, and Muldoon's (2004) test of a GxE interaction involving socioeconomic status in the prediction of central nervous serotonergic responsivity, with a sample of 139 adults ranging in age from 26 to 60. Central serotonergic responsivity was measured indirectly by means of the fenfluramine challenge test. Fenfluramine increases serotonergic neurotransmission by release of serotonin stores and reuptake inhibition. Such stimulation of hypothalamic serotonin receptors promotes as well the pituitary release of the hormone prolactin. This relative release in circulating prolactin concentration provides an index of the serotonergic responsivity in the HPA axis. Consistent with all the findings summarized previously pertaining to depression, anxiety, and persistent ADHD, *s/s* individuals manifest the most and least serotonergic responsivity, depending on whether they were high or low in SES. Moreover, SES proved unrelated to this dependent measure among individuals who are homozygous for the long allele. The fact that genotype predicted neither SES nor the outcome measure is once again noteworthy.

## DISCUSSION

Before drawing any conclusions or making any additional comments, the following critical point must be reiterated. The preceding review was designed to highlight findings published within much larger literatures on mostly parent-X-temperament and gene-X-environment interactions that are fully or partly consistent with the differential-susceptibility hypothesis; that is, that there are individual differences in plasticity, with some individuals being more affected—for better *and* for worse—than others by rearing experiences and, perhaps, environmental circumstances more generally. The first conclusion to draw, then, is that there now exists abundant evidence that, at the least, is not inconsistent with this claim, a claim that is strikingly different from the diathesis-stress view that is central to virtually all parent-X-temperament and gene-X-environment interaction research. These latter viewpoints are so deeply held that even when evidence emerges—in studies designed exclusively to test the proposition that some individuals are more adversely affected by stressors than others—these same putatively vulnerable individuals benefit more than others from supportive conditions, including the absence of the adversity being investigated, the latter fact is simply missed or ignored. We suspect that it is missed rather than ignored given the well-established proclivity of humans to be biased information processors who disproportionately attend to that which is consistent with what they already believe. Having said that, it should be acknowledged that without letting this bias run amuck in the authors' case, this review would not have been possible!

More than anything else, what the findings cited suggest—given the aforementioned limits of virtually all relevant work—is that not just some individuals are more vulnerable to adversity than others, but in some, perhaps many, cases these same putatively vulnerable individuals are actually highly susceptible to the benefits of positive environmental conditions, even when this just means the absence of adversity. Thus, future work needs to consider both sides of the for-better-*and*-for-worse differential-susceptibility equation so that it can be determined whether and when only one side or the other is operative. This will mean focusing not just on adversity and pathological outcomes (and their absence) but also on supportive environmental conditions and positive outcomes. An important unknown in the differential-susceptibility equation is whether some individuals could be especially susceptible to just adversity, some to just environmental support and enrichment, some to both, and some to neither. Of note in this regard is that whereas the English language has terms to characterize those who are highly susceptible to both positive and negative conditions (i.e., plastic/malleable) and highly susceptible to adversity (i.e., vulnerable), it is difficult to find a term that would characterize those who are disproportionately responsive to supportive conditions only—besides lucky!

There are also implications of the work reviewed here and elsewhere (Belsky et al., 2009; Belsky & Pluess, 2009a) for the study of resilience. Often, even if not always, individuals are considered resilient when the presumed adverse effects of some experience, such as exposure to child maltreatment or growing up in poverty, do not occasion. Differential-susceptibility thinking suggests that when such resilience derives from some attribute of the individual—like positive temperament, a sense of humor, or high IQ (e.g., Jaffee, Caspi, Moffitt, Polo-Tomas, & Taylor, 2007; Werner, 1997)—such resilience may actually reflect a lack of developmental plasticity. This implies that if the same individuals who seem resilient in the face of adversity were provided with especially nurturing experiences that they might also prove unaffected by it. Certainly consistent with this view is evidence cited earlier showing that those children who were randomly assigned to the IHDP intervention (Blair, 2002) and whose mothers received video feedback to enhance their sensitive responsiveness (Velderman et al., 2006) but who did not score highly on negative emotionality apparently did not benefit from it. The absence of intervention effects also emerged in the Dutch work on children suffering from disruptive behavior disorder when they manifest low levels of cortisol reactivity (van de Wiel et al., 2004).

One of the most striking features of the work considered in this chapter is how diverse the evidence base is suggesting that individuals differ in their plasticity. That pertaining to environmental factors highlights differential-susceptibility-related effects of parenting, child care quality, early intervention, and life events. That pertaining to outcomes seemingly affected by these diverse environmental influences includes attachment security in infancy, children's disruptive behavior, and depression throughout adulthood. And that pertaining to moderators of diverse environmental effects on these diverse outcomes, so-called susceptibility (not just vulnerability) factors, include phenotypic, endophenotypic, and genetic attributes of individuals.

This latter point raises one of the other unknowns in the differential-susceptibility equation. Is this research being carried out by investigators often working in different fields actually identifying the same more-and-less-susceptible individuals by different means? Consider in this regard that the children who score high in negative emotionality and physiological stress reactivity and who have short alleles on the 5-HTTPLR gene could often actually be one and the same. Not inconsistent with this claim is evidence that the behavioral and physiological factors highlighted as moderators of environmental influences, and thus markers of plasticity—infant negative emotionality (Auerbach et al., 2001; Lesch et al., 1996; Schmidt, Fox, & Hamer, 2007) and HPA reactivity (Gotlib et al., 2008)—are themselves related to the s/s allele of the serotonin transporter promoter polymorphism.

Another issue that merits consideration in future work is whether individual differences in plasticity are best conceptualized in dimensional or typological terms. Adopting evolutionary terminology pertaining to reproductive strategy, we can ask whether there exist "plastic and fixed strategists" who are and are not susceptible to environmental conditions, respectively following conditional and alternative pathways of development (Belsky, 2000), or whether it makes more sense to think in terms of a "plasticity gradient," with individuals varying in degree in terms of susceptibility to environmental influences, along a continuum. Perhaps most consistent with the latter conceptualization is work using many putative plasticity genes to create an index of "cumulative-genetic plasticity." It revealed that the more such alleles an adolescent carried (and thus the higher the score on the composite index), the more parenting predicted—in a for-better-*and*-for-worse manner—adolescent self-control/regulation (in the case of males only) (Belsky & Beaver, in press). Just as important as underscoring the notion of a plasticity gradient, this work highlights the potential benefits of moving beyond single genes in GxE work. One fact that needs to be appreciated is that as investigators move to explore multiple genes, especially in work specifically testing GxE interactions, large sample sizes are required to ensure adequate cell sizes (Cicchetti, Rogosch, & Sturge-Apple, 2007; Kaufman et al., 2006).

Also unknown is whether it makes the most sense to regard more and less plasticity as a global, macro trait-like characteristic of individuals or to regard it in more domain-specific terms? Are some people simply more malleable than others across the board, almost irrespective of the environmental factor and aspect of functioning under consideration, as much of the text more or less implied; or are people a complex mosaic of components that are more and less susceptible to environmental influence and thus more and less malleable themselves? Whereas the latter conceptualization might make more intuitive sense, of interest is a recent computer simulation of whether individual differences in susceptibility to environmental influences could evolve through natural selection that not only indicated that it could, but that it *would* show more of a domain-general, across-the-board character rather than a domain-specific one (Wolf et al., 2008).

A final issue of the many that could be raised for future research pertains to whether plasticity should be regarded as principally born or made (i.e., a function of nature or nurture). Certainly, the GxE evidence calls attention to heritable individual differences in plasticity, as well as to the fact that so-called vulnerability genes or risk alleles might in many cases be better conceptualized as plasticity genes. After all, and with regard to the latter point, why would natural selection, for example, maintain much less favor and select genes that only functioned to foster depression in the face of negative life events or antisocial behavior in the face of child maltreatment? Were these perhaps downside costs of selecting and preserving genes that engendered benefit in the face of sup-portive contextual conditions, or even operated as adaptations when also operating in a diathesis-stress manner, it would seem to make more sense for them to be selected.

But just because GxE studies are replete with evidence, often unno-ticed, of differential-susceptibility findings (Belsky et al., 2009; Belsky & Pluess, 2009a), not just genetic-vulnerability and thus diathesis-stress ones, should not lead to the presumption that plasticity is only born, a function of genotype, never made by experience (Belsky & Pluess, 2009b). Central to Boyce and Ellis's (2005) biological-sensitivity-to-context thesis is the proposition that elevated physiological reactivity, a moderator of for-better-*and*-for-worse environmental effects, is a function of (especially supportive or unsupportive) developmental experience. Notably consistent with this claim is recent research on the putatively adverse effects on the developing child of maternal stress during pregnancy, as so-called fetal programming may shape several of the susceptibility factors mentioned earlier that seem to be markers of differ-ential susceptibility (Pluess & Belsky, submitted). Consider in this regard research showing that (1) maternal stress during pregnancy pre-dicts difficult temperament at 3 months of age (Huizink, de Medina, Mulder, Visser, & Buitelaar, 2002), emotional reactivity to novelty in 4-month-olds (Möhler, Parzer, Brunner, Wiebel, & Resch, 2006), and fearfulness in the second year of life (Bergman, Sarkar, O'Connor, Modi, & Glover, 2007); (2) prenatal maternal depression and elevated cortisol levels in late pregnancy predict negative reactivity at age 2 (Davis et al., 2007); (3) maternal prenatal depression predicts increased cortisol reactivity in 6-month-olds (Brennan et al., 2008), while prenatal anxiety predicts awakening cortisol in 10-year-olds (O'Connor et al., 2005); and (4) across many species, even if not all, prenatal stress predicts increased HPA activity (Breuner, 2008).

On the one hand, such data suggest that very early experience—in the womb—may shape plasticity, not just genetics, as the developmental sequelae just considered are among the very child characteristics found in work cited previously to demarcate heightened susceptibility to environmental influences. Just as importantly, this reinterpretation of putatively negative effects of prenatal stress raises fundamental questions about the problem-focused perspective that pervades virtually all research and theory on prenatal programming: Do prenatal stressors compromise later development, as prevailing thinking presumes, or do these prenatal experiences promote plasticity—and thus the organism's openness to future experiential inputs, be they positive or negative in character? That is, is there fetal programming of postnatal programming (Pluess & Belsky, submitted)? Oberlander et al.'s (2008) recent epigenetic findings showing that maternal depressed mood in pregnancy predicts increased methylation of the human glucocorticoid receptor gene (NR3C1, measured in neonatal cord blood), which forecasts elevated cortisol stress reactivity at age 3 months, illuminates at least one biological mechanism that may be central to such fetal programming of postnatal plasticity. Recall in this regard that cortisol reactivity may well demarcate heightened susceptibility to rearing influences.

Before concluding on the basis of fetal programming research that plasticity is made (i.e., a function of experience) as much as born (i.e., a function of genetics), we should not forget that GxE may characterize the fetal programming process (Gluckman & Hanson, 2005). This raises the final unanswered question regarding differential susceptibility: Are some fetuses more susceptible to fetal programming than others, for genetic reasons? If they are—and as of yet we simply do not know—it would suggest that plasticity is a function not just of nature or nurture, but that postnatal plasticity may be "born to be made" (Belsky & Pluess, 2009b). That is, some individuals may be more likely than others to be affected by experience, most notably perhaps, fetal experience, in ways that subsequently affect whether or the degree to which they will be influenced by the postnatal world they encounter. By incorporating molecular-genetic measurements into fetal-programming studies, it should prove possible to illuminate the issue of GxE interaction in this fast-developing arena of inquiry.

In conclusion, we trust it is clear how the perspective advanced in this chapter builds on the work of the MPCLS and thus derives from our ability to "stand on the shoulders" of Sroufe and Egeland to see farther than we would have otherwise. After all, they have done so much to advance the case for considering multiple features of context in understanding the dynamics of child development, for appreciating that early experience is not determinative but nevertheless probabilistically influential, for chronicling the long-term consequences of early developmental status, most notably secure versus insecure attachment, and thus for appreciating the role of risk and protective factors in shaping vulnerability and resilience. Considering many of these contributions from an evolutionary perspective has alerted us to the possibility that the developmental processes that Sroufe and Egeland and the MPCLS have done so much to illuminate may apply differentially to individuals, especially those who for any of a variety of reasons may be more and less developmentally plastic. To what extent that inference, which takes the form of the differential-susceptibility hypothesis, accurately characterizes human development will only be determined by research more definitive than most of that considered herein.

## ACKNOWLEDGEMENTS

Preparation of the manuscript was supported by a grant of the Swiss National Science Foundation awarded to Michael Pluess (grant PBBS11—120809).

## REFERENCES

Aron, E. N., & Aron, A. (1997). Sensory-processing sensitivity and its relation to introversion and emotionality. *Journal of Personality and Social Psychology*, 73(2), 345–368.

Auerbach, J. G., Faroy, M., Ebstein, R., Kahana, M., & Levine, J. (2001). The association of the dopamine D4 receptor gene (DRD4) and the serotonin transporter promoter gene (5-HTTLPR) with temperament in 12-month-old infants. *Journal of Child Psychology & Psychiatry, 42*(6), 777–783.

Bashey, F. (2006). Cross-generational environmental effects and the evolution of off-spring size in the Trinidadian guppy *Poecilia reticulata*. *Evolution: International Journal of Organic Evolution, 60*(2), 348–361.

Belsky, J. (1978). Three theoretical models of child abuse: A critical analysis. *Journal of Child Abuse and Neglect, 2*, 37–49.

Belsky, J. (1980). Child maltreatment: An ecological integration. *American Psychologist, 35*(4), 320–335.

Belsky, J. (1997a). Theory testing, effect-size evaluation, and differential suscepti-bility to rearing influence: The case of mothering and attachment. *Child Development, 68*(4), 598–600.

Belsky, J. (1997b). Variation in susceptibility to rearing influences: An evolutionary argument. *Psychological Inquiry, 8*, 182–186.

Belsky, J. (2000). Conditional and alternative reproductive strategies: Individual differences in susceptibility to rearing experience. In J. Rodgers, D. Rowe, & W. Miller (Eds.), *Genetic influences on human fertility and sexuality: Theoretical and empirical contributions from the biological and behavioral sciences* (pp. 127–146). Boston, MA: Kluwer.

Belsky, J. (2005). Differential susceptibility to rearing influences: An evolutionary hypothesis and some evidence. In B. Ellis & D. Bjorklund (Eds.), *Origins of the social mind: Evolutionary psychology and child development* (pp. 139–163). New York, NY: Guilford Press.

Belsky, J., Bakermans-Kranenburg, M. J., & van IJzendoorn, M. H. (2007). For better and for worse: Differential susceptibility to environmental influences. *Current Directions in Psychological Science, 16*(6), 300–304.

Belsky, J., & Beaver, K. M. (in press). Cumulative-genetic plasticity, parenting and adolescent self-control/regulation. *Journal of Child Psychology and Psychiatry*.

Belsky, J., Hsieh, K. H., & Crnic, K. (1998). Mothering, fathering, and infant negativity as antecedents of boys' externalizing problems and inhibition at age 3 years: Differential susceptibility to rearing experience? *Development and Psychopathology, 10*(2), 301–319.

Belsky, J., Jonassaint, C., Pluess, M., Stanton, M., Brummett, B., & Williams, R. (2009). Vulnerability genes or plasticity genes? *Molecular Psychiatry, 14*, 746–754.

Belsky, J., & Pluess, M. (2009a). Beyond diathesis-stress: Differential suscepti-bility to environmental influences. *Psychological Bulletin, 135*(6), 885–908.

Belsky, J., & Pluess, M. (2009b). The nature (and nurture?) of plasticity in early human development. *Perspectives on Psychological Science, 4*(4), 345–351.

Bergman, K., Sarkar, P., O'Connor, T. G., Modi, N., & Glover, V. (2007). Maternal stress during pregnancy predicts cognitive ability and fearfulness in infancy. *Journal of the American Academy of Child and Adolescent Psychiatry, 46*(11), 1454–1463.

Blair, C. (2002). Early intervention for low birth weight, preterm infants: The role of negative emotionality in the specification of effects. *Development and Psychopathology, 14*(2), 311–332.

Bowlby, J. (1969). *Attachment and loss: Vol. 1, Attachment.* New York, NY: Basic Books.

Boyce, W. T., Chesney, M., Alkon, A., Tschann, J. M., Adams, S., Chesterman, B., et al. (1995). Psychobiologic reactivity to stress and childhood respiratory illnesses: Results of two prospective studies. *Psychosomatic Medicine, 57*(5), 411–422.

Boyce, W. T., & Ellis, B. J. (2005). Biological sensitivity to context: I. An evolutionary-developmental theory of the origins and functions of stress reactivity. *Development and Psychopathology, 17*(2), 271–301.

Boyce, W. T., Essex, M. J., Alkon, A., Goldsmith, H. H., Kraemer, H. C., & Kupfer, D. J. (2006). Early father involvement moderates biobehavioral susceptibility to mental health problems in middle childhood. *Journal of the American Academy of Child and Adolescent Psychiatry, 45*(12), 1510–1520.

Bradley, R. H., & Corwyn, R. F. (2008). Infant temperament, parenting, and externalizing behavior in first grade: A test of the differential susceptibility hypothesis. *Journal of Child Psychology and Psychiatry and Allied Disciplines, 49*(2), 124–131.

Brennan, P. A., Pargas, R., Walker, E. F., Green, P., Newport, D. J., & Stowe, Z. (2008). Maternal depression and infant cortisol: Influences of timing, comorbidity and treatment. *Journal of Child Psychology and Psychiatry and Allied Disciplines, 49*(10), 1099–1107.

Breuner, C. (2008). Maternal stress, glucocorticoids, and the maternal/fetal match hypothesis. *Hormones and Behavior, 54*(4), 485–487.

Bronfenbrenner, U. (1979). *The ecology of human development.* Cambridge, MA: Harvard University Press.

Brummett, B. H., Boyle, S. H., Siegler, I. C., Kuhn, C. M., Ashley-Koch, A., Jonassaint, C. R., et al. (2008). Effects of environmental stress and gender on associations among symptoms of depression and the serotonin transporter gene linked polymorphic region (5-HTTLPR). *Behavior Genetics, 38*(1), 34–43.

Burmeister, M., McInnis, M. G., & Zollner, S. (2008). Psychiatric genetics: Progress amid controversy. *Nature Reviews. Genetics, 9*(7), 527–540.

Caspi, A., & Moffitt, T. E. (2006). Gene-environment interactions in psychiatry: Joining forces with neuroscience. *Nature Reviews. Neuroscience, 7*(7), 583–590.

Caspi, A., Sugden, K., Moffitt, T. E., Taylor, A., Craig, I. W., Harrington, H., et al. (2003). Influence of life stress on depression: Moderation by a polymorphism in the 5-HTT gene. *Science, 301*(5631), 386–389.

Cassidy, J., Woodhouse, S. S., Sherman, L. J., Stupica, B., & Lejuez, C. W. (submitted). Enhancing infant attachment security: An examination of treatment efficacy and differential susceptibility.

Cicchetti, D. (1993). Developmental psychopathology: Reactions, reflections, projections. *Developmental Review, 13*(4), 471–502.

Cicchetti, D., & Garmezy, N. (1993). Prospects and promises in the study of resilience. *Development and Psychopathology, 5*(4), 497–502.

Cicchetti, D., & Rizley, R. (1981). Developmental perspectives on the etiology, intergenerational transmission, and sequelae of child maltreatment. *New Directions for Child Development, 11*, 31–55.

Cicchetti, D., Rogosch, F. A., & Sturge-Apple, M. L. (2007). Interactions of child maltreatment and serotonin transporter and monoamine oxidase A polymorphisms: Depressive symptomatology among adolescents from low socioeconomic status backgrounds. *Development and Psychopathology, 19*(4), 1161–1180.

Davis, E. P., Glynn, L. M., Schetter, C. D., Hobel, C., Chicz-Demet, A., & Sandman, C. A. (2007). Prenatal exposure to maternal depression and cortisol influences infant temperament. *Journal of the American Academy of Child and Adolescent Psychiatry, 46*(6), 737–746.

Dearing, E., & Hamilton, L. C. (2006). Contemporary advances and classic advice for analyzing mediating and moderating variables. *Monographs of the Society for Research in Child Development, 71*, 88–104.

Dienstbier, R. A. (1985). The role of emotion in moral socialization. In C. E. Izard, J. Kagan, R. B. Zajonc, C. E. Izard, J. Kagan, & R. B. Zajonc (Eds.), *Emotions, cognition, and behavior* (pp. 484–514). New York, NY: Cambridge University Press.

Dopkins Stright, A., Cranley Gallagher, K., & Kelley, K. (2008). Infant temperament moderates relations between maternal parenting in early childhood and children's adjustment in first grade. *Child Development, 79*(1), 186–200.

Egeland, B., Breitenbucher, M., & Rosenberg, D. (1980). Prospective-study of the significance of life stress in the etiology of child-abuse. *Journal of Consulting and Clinical Psychology, 48*(2), 195–205.

Egeland, B., & Brunnquell, D. (1979). At-risk approach to the study of child-abuse: Some preliminary findings. *Journal of the American Academy of Child and Adolescent Psychiatry, 18*(2), 219–235.

Eley, T. C., Sugden, K., Corsico, A., Gregory, A. M., Sham, P., McGuffin, P., et al. (2004). Gene-environment interaction analysis of serotonin system markers with adolescent depression. *Molecular Psychiatry, 9*(10), 908–915.

El-Sheikh, M., Erath, S. A., & Keller, P. S. (2007). Children's sleep and adjustment: The moderating role of vagal regulation. *Journal of Sleep Research, 16*(4), 396–405.

El-Sheikh, M., Harger, J., & Whitson, S. M. (2001). Exposure to interparental conflict and children's adjustment and physical health: The moderating role of vagal tone. *Child Development, 72*(6), 1617–1636.

El-Sheikh, M., Keller, P. S., & Erath, S. A. (2007). Marital conflict and risk for child maladjustment over time: Skin conductance level reactivity as a vulnerability factor. *Journal of Abnormal Child Psychology, 35*(5), 715–727.

Feldman, R., Greenbaum, C. W., & Yirmiya, N. (1999). Mother-infant affect synchrony as an antecedent of the emergence of self-control. *Developmental Psychology, 35*(1), 223–231.

Fernald, L. C., Burke, H. M., & Gunnar, M. R. (2008). Salivary cortisol levels in children of low-income women with high depressive symptomatology. *Development and Psychopathology, 20*(2), 423–436.

Gannon, L., Banks, J., Shelton, D., & Luchetta, T. (1989). The mediating effects of psychophysiological reactivity and recovery on the relationship between environmental stress and illness. *Journal of Psychosomatic Research, 33*(2), 167–175.

Garbarino, J. (1977). Human ecology of child maltreatment: Conceptual-model for research. *Journal of Marriage and the Family, 39*(4), 721–735.

Gluckman, P., & Hanson, M. (2005). *The fetal matrix: Evolution, development and disease.* Cambridge, England: Cambridge University Press.

Gotlib, I. H., Joormann, J., Minor, K. L., & Hallmayer, J. (2008). HPA axis reactivity: A mechanism underlying the associations among 5-HTTLPR, stress, and depression. *Biological Psychiatry, 63*(9), 847–851.

Gottesman, I. I., & Gould, T. D. (2003). The endophenotype concept in psychiatry: Etymology and strategic intentions. *American Journal of Psychiatry, 160*(4), 636–645.

Gottesman, I. I., & Shields, J. (1967). A polygenic theory of schizophrenia. *Proceedings of the National Academy of Sciences of the United States of America, 58*(1), 199–205.

Gunnar, M., & Quevedo, K. (2007). The neurobiology of stress and development. *Annual Review of Psychology, 58,* 145–173.

Gunthert, K. C., Conner, T. S., Armeli, S., Tennen, H., Covault, J., & Kranzler, H. R. (2007). Serotonin transporter gene polymorphism (5-HTTLPR) and anxiety reactivity in daily life: A daily process approach to gene-environment interaction. *Psychosomatic Medicine, 69*(8), 762–768.

Huizink, A. C., de Medina, P. G., Mulder, E. J., Visser, G. H., & Buitelaar, J. K. (2002). Psychological measures of prenatal stress as predictors of infant temperament. *Journal of the American Academy of Child and Adolescent Psychiatry, 41*(9), 1078–1085.

Infant Health and Development Program. (1990). Enhancing the outcomes of low-birth-weight, premature infants. *Journal of the American Medical Association, 263,* 3035–3042.

Jaffee, S. R., Caspi, A., Moffitt, T. E., Polo-Tomas, M., & Taylor, A. (2007). Individual, family, and neighborhood factors distinguish resilient from non-resilient maltreated children: A cumulative stressors model. *Child Abuse & Neglect, 31*(3), 231–253.

Kaufman, J., Yang, B. Z., Douglas-Palumberi, H., Grasso, D., Lipschitz, D., Houshyar, S., et al. (2006). Brain-derived neurotrophic factor-5-HTTLPR gene interactions and environmental modifiers of depression in children. *Biological Psychiatry, 59*(8), 673–680.

Kochanska, G. (1993). Toward a synthesis of parental socialization and child temperament in early development of conscience. *Child Development, 64*(2), 325–347.

Kochanska, G., Aksan, N., & Joy, M. E. (2007). Children's fearfulness as a moderator of parenting in early socialization: Two longitudinal studies. *Developmental Psychology, 43*(1), 222–237.

Lazary, J., Lazary, A., Gonda, X., Benko, A., Molnar, E., Juhasz, G., et al. (2008). New evidence for the association of the serotonin transporter gene (SLC6A4) haplotypes, threatening life events, and depressive phenotype. *Biological Psychiatry, 64*(6), 498–504.

Lesch, K. P., Bengel, D., Heils, A., Sabol, S. Z., Greenberg, B. D., Petri, S., et al. (1996). Association of anxiety-related traits with a polymorphism in the serotonin transporter gene regulatory region. *Science, 274*(5292), 1527–1531.

Luthar, S. S. (2006). Resilience in development: A synthesis of research across five decades. In D. Cicchetti & D. J. Cohen (Eds.), *Developmental psychopathology, Vol 3: Risk, disorder, and adaptation* (2nd ed., pp. 739–795). Hoboken, NJ: Wiley.

Manuck, S. B., Flory, J. D., Ferrell, R. E., & Muldoon, M. F. (2004). Socio-economic status covaries with central nervous system serotonergic responsivity as a function of allelic variation in the serotonin transporter gene-linked polymorphic region. *Psychoneuroendocrinology, 29*(5), 651–668.

Möhler, E., Parzer, P., Brunner, R., Wiebel, A., & Resch, F. (2006). Emotional stress in pregnancy predicts human infant reactivity. *Early Human Development, 82*(11), 731–737.

Monroe, S. M., & Simons, A. D. (1991). Diathesis-stress theories in the context of life stress research: Implications for the depressive disorders. *Psychological Bulletin, 110*(3), 406–425.

Nakamura, M., Ueno, S., Sano, A., & Tanabe, H. (2000). The human serotonin transporter gene linked polymorphism (5-HTTLPR) shows ten novel allelic variants. *Molecular Psychiatry, 5*(1), 32–38.

NICHD Early Child Care Research Network. (2005). *Child care and child development: Results of the NICHD Study of Early Child Care and Youth Development.* New York, NY: Guilford Press.

Nussey, D. H., Postma, E., Gienapp, P., & Visser, M. E. (2005). Selection on heritable phenotypic plasticity in a wild bird population. *Science, 310*(5746), 304–306.

Oberlander, T. F., Weinberg, J., Papsdorf, M., Grunau, R., Misri, S., & Devlin, A. M. (2008). Prenatal exposure to maternal depression, neonatal methylation of human glucocorticoid receptor gene (NR3C1) and infant cortisol stress responses. *Epigenetics, 3*(2), 97–106.

Obradovic, J., Bush, N. R., Stamperdahl, J., Adler, N. E., & Boyce, W. T. (2010). Biological sensitivity to context: The interactive effects of stress reactivity and family adversity on socio-emotional behavior and school readiness. *Child Development, 81*(1), 270–289.

O'Connor, T. G., Ben-Shlomo, Y., Heron, J., Golding, J., Adams, D., & Glover, V. (2005). Prenatal anxiety predicts individual differences in cortisol in pre-adolescent children. *Biological Psychiatry, 58*(3), 211–217.

Pigliucci, M. (2007). Do we need an extended evolutionary synthesis? *Evolution: International Journal of Organic Evolution, 61*(12), 2743–2749.

Pluess, M., & Belsky, J. (2009). Differential susceptibility to rearing experience: The case of childcare. *Journal of Child Psychology and Psychiatry and Allied Disciplines, 50*(4), 396–404.

Pluess, M., & Belsky, J. (2010). Differential susceptibility to parenting and quality child care. *Developmental Psychology, 46*(2).

Pluess, M., & Belsky, J. (submitted). Prenatal programming of postnatal plasticity?

Retz, W., Freitag, C. M., Retz-Junginger, P., Wenzler, D., Schneider, M., Kissling, C., et al. (2008). A functional serotonin transporter promoter gene polymorphism increases ADHD symptoms in delinquents: Interaction with adverse childhood environment. *Psychiatry Research, 158*(2), 123–131.

Rothbart, M. K., & Bates, J. E. (2006). Temperament. In N. Eisenberg, W. Damon, & R. M. Lerner (Eds.), *Handbook of child psychology: Vol. 3, Social, emotional, and personality development* (6th ed., pp. 99–166). Hoboken, NJ: Wiley.

Rutter, M. (2006). *Genes and behavior: Nature-nurture interplay explained.* London, England: Blackwell.

Sameroff, A. J. (1983). Developmental systems: Contexts and evolution. In P. Mussen (Ed.), *Handbook of child psychology* (Vol. 1, pp. 237–294). New York, NY: John Wiley & Sons.

Schmidt, L. A., Fox, N. A., & Hamer, D. H. (2007). Evidence for a gene-gene interaction in predicting children's behavior problems: Association of serotonin transporter short and dopamine receptor D4 long genotypes with internalizing and externalizing behaviors in typically developing 7-year-olds. *Development and Psychopathology, 19*(4), 1105–1116.

Sinn, D. L., Gosling, S. D., & Moltschaniwskyj, N. A. (2007). Development of shy/bold behaviour in squid: Context-specific phenotypes associated with developmental plasticity. *Animal Behaviour, 75*, 433–442.

Sroufe, L. A. (1988). The role of infant-caregiver attachment in development. In J. Belsky & T. Nezworski (Eds.), *Clinical implications of attachment* (pp. 18–38). Hillsdale, NJ: Erlbaum.

Sroufe, L. A., Egeland, B., Carlson, M., & Collins, A. (2005). *The development of the person: The Minnesota study of risk and adaptation from birth to adulthood.* New York, NY: Guilford Press.

Stein, M. B., Schork, N. J., & Gelernter, J. (2008). Gene-by-environment (serotonin transporter and childhood maltreatment) interaction for anxiety sensitivity, an intermediate phenotype for anxiety disorders. *Neuropsychopharmacology, 33*(2), 312–319.

Suomi, S. J. (1995). Influence of attachment theory on ethological studies of biobehavioral development in nonhuman primates. In S. Goldberg, R. Muir, J. Kerr (Eds.), *Attachment theory: Social, developmental, and clinical perspectives.* (pp. 185–201). Hillsdale, NJ: Analytic Press.

Suomi, S. J. (1997). Early determinants of behaviour: Evidence from primate studies. *British Medical Bulletin, 53*(1), 170–184.

Suomi, S. J. (2006). Risk, resilience, and gene x environment interactions in rhesus monkeys. *Annals of the New York Academy of Sciences, 1094,* 52–62.

Surtees, P. G., Wainwright, N. W., Willis-Owen, S. A., Luben, R., Day, N. E., & Flint, J. (2006). Social adversity, the serotonin transporter (5-HTTLPR) polymorphism and major depressive disorder. *Biological Psychiatry, 59*(3), 224–229.

Taylor, S. E., Way, B. M., Welch, W. T., Hilmert, C. J., Lehman, B. J., & Eisenberger, N. I. (2006). Early family environment, current adversity, the serotonin transporter promoter polymorphism, and depressive symptomatology. *Biological Psychiatry, 60*(7), 671–676.

van Aken, C., Junger, M., Verhoeven, M., van Aken, M. A. G., & Dekovic, M. (2007). The interactive effects of temperament and maternal parenting on toddlers' externalizing behaviours. *Infant and Child Development, 16*(5), 553–572.

Van den Boom, D. C. (1994). The influence of temperament and mothering on attachment and exploration: An experimental manipulation of sensitive responsiveness among lower-class mothers with irritable infants. *Child Development, 65*(5), 1457–1477.

van de Wiel, N. M., van Goozen, S. H., Matthys, W., Snoek, H., & van Engeland, H. (2004). Cortisol and treatment effect in children with disruptive behavior disorders: A preliminary study. *Journal of the American Academy of Child and Adolescent Psychiatry, 43*(8), 1011–1018.

Velderman, M. K., Bakermans-Kranenburg, M. J., Juffer, F., & van IJzendoorn, M. H. (2006). Effects of attachment-based interventions on maternal sensitivity and infant attachment: Differential susceptibility of highly reactive infants. *Journal of Family Psychology, 20*(2), 266–274.

Volling, B. L., & Feagans, L. V. (1995). Infant day care and children's social competence. *Infant Behavior & Development, 18*(2), 177–188.

Warren, S. L., & Simmens, S. J. (2005). Predicting toddler anxiety/depressive symptoms: Effects of caregiver sensitivity of temperamentally vulnerable children. *Infant Mental Health Journal, 26*(1), 40–55.

Werner, E. E. (1997). Vulnerable but invincible: High-risk children from birth to adulthood. *Acta Paediatrica Supplement, 422,* 103–105.

Wilhelm, K., Mitchell, P. B., Niven, H., Finch, A., Wedgwood, L., Scimone, A., et al. (2006). Life events, first depression onset and the serotonin transporter gene. *British Journal of Psychiatry, 188,* 210–215.

Wolf, M., van Doorn, G. S., & Weissing, F. J. (2008). Evolutionary emergence of responsive and unresponsive personalities. *Proceedings of the National Academy of Sciences of the United States of America, 105*(41), 15825–15830.

Yates, T. M., Egeland, B., & Sroufe, L. A. (2003). Rethinking resilience: A developmental process perspective. In S. S. Luthar (Ed.), *Resilience and vulnerabilities: Adapation in the context of childhood adversities* (pp. 243–266). New York, NY: Cambridge University Press.

Zalsman, G., Huang, Y. Y., Oquendo, M. A., Burke, A. K., Hu, X. Z., Brent, D. A., et al. (2006). Association of a triallelic serotonin transporter gene promoter region (5-HTTLPR) polymorphism with stressful life events and severity of depression. *American Journal of Psychiatry, 163*(9), 1588–1593.

Zuckerman, M. (1999). *Vulnerability to psychopathology: A biosocial model.* Washington, DC: American Psychological Association.

# 11

# Pathways to Resilient Functioning in Maltreated Children

## From Single-Level to Multilevel Investigations

Dante Cicchetti, Ph.D.

Developmental psychopathologists stress that there is multifinality in developmental processes such that the manner in which individuals respond to and interact with vulnerability and protective factors at each level of the ecology allows for diversity in developmental outcomes (Cicchetti, 1990; Cicchetti & Lynch, 1993; Cicchetti & Rogosch, 1996; Sroufe, 1989). Just as deviations from the average expectable environment potentiate some individuals toward the development of maladaptation, others demonstrate adaptation in the face of the same challenges (Cicchetti & Lynch, 1995; Luthar, 2006; Luthar, Cicchetti, & Becker, 2000; Masten, 2001; Masten, Best, & Garmezy, 1990). Accordingly, it is equally informative to comprehend the mechanisms that promote adaptation among individuals experiencing significant adversity as it is to investigate the developmental trajectories toward maladaptation (Egeland, Carlson, & Sroufe, 1993; Luthar, 2006; Luthar et al., 2000; Masten, 1989, 2007).

Child maltreatment represents an extremely adverse experience. Growing up under conditions of child maltreatment indisputably constitutes a profound immersion in severe stress that challenges and frequently impairs development across diverse domains of psychological and biological functioning (Cicchetti, 1989; Cicchetti & Lynch, 1995; Cicchetti & Toth, 1995, 2005; DeBellis, 2001, 2005; Egeland, 1997; Tarullo & Gunnar, 2006; Trickett & McBride-Chang, 1995). The ecological conditions associated with maltreatment represent a severe deviation from the average expectable environment. Without adequate environmental supports, the probabilistic path of ontogenesis for abused and neglected children is characterized by an increased risk for unsuccessful resolution of the stage-salient issues of development (Cicchetti, 1989; Cicchetti & Toth, 2005; Egeland, 2007; Egeland & Sroufe, 1981; Pianta, Egeland, & Erickson, 1989). Failure of any stage-salient issue increases the probability of the unsuccessful resolution of subsequent developmental challenges (Sroufe, 1979; Sroufe, Egeland, Carlson, & Collins, 2005).

Maltreated children are likely to manifest atypicalities in neurobiological processes, physiological responsiveness, emotion recognition and affect differentiation, emotion regulation, attachment relationships, self-system development, representational processes, social information processing, peer relationships, romantic relationships, adaptation to school, and personality organization (Cicchetti & Valentino, 2006). Thus, maltreated children are likely to develop a profile of relatively enduring vulnerability factors, placing them at great risk for future maladaptation and psychopathology (Cicchetti & Lynch, 1995; Cicchetti & Toth, 2005; DeBellis, 2001, 2005; Egeland, 1997, 2007).

Nonetheless, not all individuals who have been abused and neglected succumb to the extreme adversity in their lives. Investigation of how some maltreated individuals cope adaptively despite experiencing significant stress and trauma offers an opportunity to discover processes at multiple levels of analysis that are likely to be germane to effective coping in the face of adversity, yet less readily detectable under more normative stress exposure (Cicchetti & Gunnar, 2008). Thus, the study of resilience—one of the most intriguing phenomena of human development that is conceptualized as a dynamic developmental process encompassing positive adaptation within the context of significant threat or severe adversity—among maltreated children seeks to understand how the various aspects of children's ecologies eventuate in multiplicity in developmental outcome, adaptive or maladaptive (Cicchetti & Lynch, 1993; Egeland et al., 1993; Luthar et al., 2000). Discovering how maltreated children develop and function adaptively despite experiencing a multitude of stressors offers considerable promise for prevention and intervention and for elucidating developmental theories of coping (Cicchetti, Rogosch, & Toth, 2006; Cicchetti, Toth, & Bush, 1988; Toth & Cicchetti, 1993, 1999).

## GOALS OF THE CHAPTER

Other contributions to this volume have highlighted the major influences that the seminal Minnesota Parent-Child Longitudinal Study (MPCLS) has made to elucidating normative development, including attachment and relationships, as well as atypical developmental processes, psychopathology, and evidence-based preventive interventions across varying contexts. This chapter focuses on the impact that the MPCLS has made to understanding resilience, both conceptually and empirically. After discussing the conceptualization of resilience proffered by Egeland and colleagues (1993), the longitudinal investigation of resilient adaptation in maltreated children conducted by Farber and Egeland (1987) is reviewed, and the effect of this study on the manner in which resilience has come to be viewed is examined.

Next, as an example of the far-reaching impact of the MPCLS, research conducted in the laboratory at Mt. Hope Family Center on the determinants of resilience in maltreated children is reviewed. As a graduate student at the University of Minnesota, I was extremely fortunate to be mentored by both Egeland and Sroufe. These experiences have exerted a profound influence on the odyssey of discovery we have undertaken in investigating the biological and psychological mechanisms whereby some maltreated children achieve resilient functioning. Beginning in 1979, when Ross Rizley and I initiated the Harvard Child Maltreatment Project (Cicchetti & Rizley, 1981), through work conducted at Mt. Hope Family Center with Sheree Toth and Fred Rogosch from 1985 to the present, the theoretical and empirical contributions of the MPCLS (Sroufe et al., 2005) have played a prominent role in guiding our thinking about resilience. In the penultimate section, I discuss how the organizational perspective, the theoretical framework adopted by the MPCLS, naturally led to the field's adoption of a multilevel dynamic systems view of resilience. Finally, the wisdom of incorporating a multiple-levels-of-analysis approach into the evaluation of resilience-promoting preventive interventions is discussed.

## RESILIENCE AS PROCESS

Research conducted on the MPCLS led Egeland and colleagues (1993) to conceptualize resilience as a dynamic, transactional process within an organizational framework of development (Cicchetti & Schneider-Rosen, 1986; Cicchetti & Sroufe, 1978; Sroufe, 1979; Sroufe et al., 2005; Sroufe & Waters, 1976). Research conceived with the organizational developmental framework not only takes into account the interrelations among dynamic systems and the processes characterizing system breakdown, but also is interested in identifying the mechanisms by which compensatory, self-righting tendencies are initiated whenever higher-level monitors detect deviances in a subsystem (Sameroff & Chandler, 1975).

Guided by the organizational perspective, developmental outcomes are conceived as the result of interactions and transactions among genetic, biological, behavioral, socioenvironmental, and cultural factors (Cicchetti & Schneider-Rosen, 1986; Gottlieb, 2007; Sroufe, 1996; Sroufe et al., 2005). From within the organizational framework, the developmental process is characterized by a hierarchical integration of biological and behavioral systems whereby earlier structures become incorporated into later structures, resulting in increasing complexity of developmental forms (Cicchetti & Schneider-Rosen, 1986; Kaplan, 1967; Sroufe, 1979; Werner, 1948; Werner & Kaplan, 1963). Throughout the course of epigenesis, individuals play increasingly active roles in their own development, bringing thoughts, feelings, expectations, and representations that are derived from their history of interpersonal interactions and that influence the manner in which new experiences are interpreted and organized (Egeland et al., 1993; Sroufe & Fleeson, 1986, 1988). Consistent with the organizational perspective on development, early experience is thought to be critically important for shaping the manner in which later experience is organized (Cicchetti & Tucker, 1994; Egeland et al., 1993; Fox & Rutter, 2010; Sroufe, Carlson, Levy, & Egeland, 1999).

Findings from the MPCLS have demonstrated how the organizational framework provides a valuable perspective for examining the relationships among risk and protective mechanisms, prior adaptation, and resilient functioning (Egeland et al., 1993; Sroufe et al., 2005). Accordingly, the construct of resilience must be conceptualized as a dynamic process, not a static or trait-like condition, so that resilience research may elucidate the mechanisms through which individuals are able to initiate or maintain their self-righting tendencies when confronted with extreme stress or adversity (Cicchetti & Rizley, 1981; Luthar et al., 2000; Luthar, 2006). Discovering and comprehending the determinants of resilience will contribute to our understanding of which developmental processes, biological and psychosocial, play critical roles in determining whether adaptation or maladaptation will manifest at each stage of development (Cicchetti & Curtis, 2006; Cicchetti & Tucker, 1994).

## CHILD MALTREATMENT AND RESILIENCE: ILLUSTRATIVE FINDINGS FROM THE MPCLS

In one of the earliest investigations of resilience and child maltreatment, Farber and Egeland (1987) identified 44 children in the MPCLS who had been physically abused, neglected, and/or psychologically maltreated during the infancy through preschool period and followed these youngsters longitudinally through the end of the sixth grade (age 11). They discovered that none of these maltreated children were functioning in a resilient fashion. For example, although more than half of the children were securely attached at 12 months, upon entry into grade school, none of these children were judged to be functioning competently. Although some of these maltreated children possessed good social skills or were performing satisfactory academic work, none of the youngsters were resilient with respect to their overall adaptation (Farber & Egeland, 1987).

A small number of maltreated children exhibited improvements in functioning over the course of infancy through the preschool period. These improvements were associated with (a) placement in a positive foster care situation; (b) the availability of a caring nonparental adult; (c) intensive developmentally appropriate intervention; (d) the father or father-figure not permitted child visitation; and (e) a structured school environment with sensitive, compassionate, and caring teachers (Farber & Egeland, 1987). Despite the improvements the maltreated children displayed across specific domains, the overall adaptive functioning of these children through the preschool years was largely poor. Tellingly, at the conclusion of the sixth-grade assessments, the authors concluded that "all of these children demonstrated clear dysfunction resulting from maltreatment" (Egeland et al., 1993; page 520). Stated differently, not a single maltreated child in the study consistently functioned competently across each developmental period. In contrast to the maltreated children, the nonmaltreated disadvantaged comparisons from low-SES backgrounds showed a far less steep decline in competence across the longitudinal study (Farber & Egeland, 1987).

In keeping with the results obtained by Farber and Egeland (1987), Herrenkohl, Herrenkohl, and Egolf (1994) conducted a longitudinal study of developmental outcomes in maltreated children and found that fewer than 15% of children who had been maltreated before age 6 were identified as resilient. When these maltreated children were assessed again in adolescence, nearly half of the maltreated children who were previously designated as resilient were found to be no longer demonstrating resilient functioning.

Several valuable lessons were learned from the results of the Farber and Egeland (1987) longitudinal study of resilient adaptation in maltreated children that have contributed to the conceptualization of resilience as a dynamic developmental process. Included among these lessons are the importance of regular assessments of stage-salient developmental issues over time and the criticality of using broadband measures of adaptation.

In order to label children as resilient, one must follow them longitudinally and assess a variety of competencies, rather than focusing on an isolated domain. Because resilient children may fluctuate in their functioning over time, longitudinal investigations present the opportunity to discover whether these children demonstrate a recovery of positive function (e.g., Masten et al., 1990). As noted in Egeland et al.'s (1993) seminal paper, resilience is an ongoing, lifespan developmental process. An organizational perspective on resilience elucidates the study of normal and abnormal development. Moreover, the results of studies on resilience in maltreated children can be fruitfully translated into the development and implementation of efficacious prevention and intervention strategies for children who have experienced extreme stress and adversity (Cicchetti & Toth, 2006; Luthar & Cicchetti, 2000).

## STUDIES OF THE DEVELOPMENT OF RESILIENT FUNCTIONING IN MALTREATED CHILDREN

Although the declining quality of adaptation portrayed by Farber and Egeland (1987) and Herrenkohl et al. (1994) painted a bleak picture for the future outcomes of maltreated children, it was clear that much additional research must be conducted before we could confidently render a conclusion regarding maltreated children's prospects for resilient adaptation. It would be surprising if all maltreated children displayed the same developmental profile. Children of different ages, at different developmental periods, from diverse environments, and with varying experience, who are exposed to vastly different forms of maltreatment, are likely to manifest vulnerabilities and competencies in a wide array of age-appropriate ways (Cicchetti & Rizley, 1981).

In our early work at Harvard and our initial work at Mt. Hope Family Center, we focused our research on discovering the developmental sequelae of child maltreatment. Prior research on child maltreatment was replete with flaws in operationalization and method (see Aber & Cicchetti, 1984, for a review); thus, we felt that it was critical to build a firm knowledge base on the effects of maltreatment (see, e.g., Cicchetti & Carlson, 1989) before investigating pathways to resilience.

In the first study on adaptive functioning conducted in our laboratory, Cicchetti, Rogosch, Lynch, and Holt (1993) examined processes leading to resilience in school-age, disadvantaged maltreated ($n = 127$) and nonmaltreated ($n = 79$) children from low-socioeconomic backgrounds in the context of a research summer camp day program. Multiple areas of adaptation (e.g., social adjustment, risk for school difficulty, psychopathology) were assessed from self, peer, and camp counselor perspectives and school records. We developed a composite index of adaptive functioning, and levels of competence were delineated. Personality dimensions (e.g., ego-control and ego-resiliency) and personal resources (e.g., self-esteem and cognitive maturity) were evaluated as mechanisms promoting individual differences in successful adaptation (i.e., resilience).

Maltreated children were found to evidence significantly more maladaptation on several of the measures of adaptive functioning. Specifically, in comparison to their disadvantaged nonmaltreated counterparts, maltreated children were rated by adult camp counselors, who were unaware of maltreatment status and study hypotheses, as more disruptive-aggressive and more withdrawn with peers and were rated as possessing significantly greater internalizing behavior problems. There also were several indices of functioning on which no statistically significant differences were obtained. In particular, the maltreated and nonmaltreated children did not differ on adult counselor ratings of prosocial behavior with peers and externalizing behavior problems, self-reported depressive symptomatology, and the risk indicators for adaptational problems in school. Beyond these similarities and differences between maltreated and nonmaltreated children, our main interest was in investigating patterns of adaptation across multiple areas of functioning.

An examination of the composite index of seven indicators of competent adaptation revealed that maltreated children had fewer areas of adaptive functioning than their nonmaltreated counterparts. Additionally, an inspection of the three categorical levels of competence (i.e., low, medium, high) revealed that whereas the percentage of maltreated and nonmaltreated children at the medium and high levels were the same, there was a much larger representation of maltreated children in the lowest level, where children displayed few or minimal signs of competence.

These results suggest that group contrasts between maltreated and nonmaltreated children, indicating greater dysfunction in the maltreated group, may overlook a sizable number of maltreated children who are doing well—at least as well as socioeconomically comparable nonmaltreated children. The group differences between maltreated and nonmaltreated children may be driven by the greater proportion of a substantial group of abused and neglected children who exhibit impairments in their competence across multiple domains of functioning (Egeland et al., 1993; Farber & Egeland, 1987).

Garmezy (1971, 1974) consistently emphasized that most children maintain the ability to display some resilience strivings in the presence of chronic and serious adversity. An examination of the number and percentage of maltreated and nonmaltreated children who exhibited indicators of competent adaptation sheds positive light on Garmezy's thesis. Fifteen percent of the nonmaltreated children and 22% of the maltreated children displayed no indices of resilient adaptation; similarly, 11% of nonmaltreated and 21% of maltreated exhibited only one index of competent functioning. Interestingly, the majority of both groups of children manifested two or more areas of competent functioning. Thus, congruent with Garmezy's writings, it appears that most of these children continue to have resilient strivings as they actively cope with life's vicissitudes. The complete absence of resilient strivings in some of the maltreated and nonmaltreated children may be of grave concern, because self-righting tendencies are vital characteristics of all living organisms (Sameroff & Chandler, 1975; Waddington, 1957).

An examination of the manner in which personal resources contributed to competent functioning revealed that ego-overcontrol, ego-resiliency, and positive self-esteem were found to account for significant amounts of variance in adaptive functioning for the maltreated children. In contrast, only ego-resiliency and positive self-esteem contributed significant amounts of variance in the prediction of competent adaptation in the nonmaltreated children. Given the predictive role of ego-overcontrol for more adaptive functioning in maltreated children, there is likely to be a greater tendency for successfully adapting maltreated children to be characterized by the resilient overcontrolling type of personality organization (Block & Block, 1980).

Through adopting a more reserved, controlled, and rational way of interacting and relating (i.e., resilient overcontrol), maltreated children may be more attuned to what is necessary for successful adaptation in their adverse home environments. It is conceivable that their more overcontrolled style may protect them from being targets of continued maltreatment incidents. In contrast, the more affectively expressive style of resilient undercontrollers may not be well suited for successful adaptation in maltreating environments, because such styles may provoke attention and reactions from others that could result in greater risk for maltreatment. Because resilience is an ongoing and dynamic developmental process, we knew that it was important to conduct longitudinal studies of maltreated children in order to conclude with confidence that some children are genuinely resilient. Moreover, given the nonstatic nature of the construct, we do not necessarily expect children to function resiliently at all developmental assessment periods. Hence, it is equally important to discover the processes underlying recovery of function as it is to discern the mechanisms that contribute to ongoing resilient adaptation or to a decline from such functioning.

We next conducted a three-year longitudinal investigation of another sample of maltreated ($n = 133$) and nonmaltreated children ($n = 80$) from lower socioeconomic backgrounds again in the context of a research summer day camp (Cicchetti & Rogosch, 1997). Utilizing a measurement battery that was very similar to our earlier study (i.e., Cicchetti et al., 1993), we sought to ascertain if there were different pathways to adaptive functioning in maltreated and nonmaltreated children and to discover whether there were differences between these groups in resilient functioning, recovery of function, or decline in functioning over the three-year period.

Consistent with the literature on the consequences of child abuse and neglect (Cicchetti & Toth, 1995; Cicchetti & Valentino, 2006; Egeland, 2007), maltreated children demonstrated greater dysfunction than nonmaltreated children on six of the seven indicators of adaptive functioning. Moreover, many of these deficits persisted across two or three consecutive years of assessment. Furthermore, across each of the three years, maltreated children exhibited a lower level of competent functioning than did the nonmaltreated children. Additionally, the continuity of maladaptive functioning displayed by maltreated children across the course of this longitudinal study was substantial. Taken together, these findings underscore the deleterious impact that maltreatment experiences exert on competent functioning and attest to the nontransient nature of their influence.

Unlike our earlier study (i.e., Cicchetti et al., 1993), in this investigation we examined the differential impact that maltreatment subtypes exert on adaptive functioning. We found that sexually abused, physically abused, and emotionally maltreated children exhibited lower competence on the adaptive functioning composite constructed from the measurement battery for this study than did either the neglected or the nonmaltreated children, neither of whom differed from one another (Cicchetti & Rogosch, 1997). Conceivably, the active commission of maltreatment acts upon the child (such as the case with sexual and physical abuse and emotional maltreatment) may exert a more deleterious effect on resilient self-strivings than does the omission (i.e., neglect) of attention to the provision of basic needs.

An inspection of placement in the three-year pattern resilience groups revealed that there were a significantly greater percentage of maltreated children (40.6%) than nonmaltreated children (20%) in the low resilient functioning group. Furthermore, 9.8% of the maltreated children compared to only 1.3% of nonmaltreated children displayed zero competence indicators, thereby reflecting an absence of resilient strivings across the three-year period. A recent review of the literature on resilience following child maltreatment obtained findings that dovetail nicely with these results. Specifically, Walsh, Dawson, and Mattingly (2010) found that the presence of competent functioning in one domain (out of three assessed) did not guarantee that maltreated children would manifest competence across other domains. Furthermore, approximately 20% of maltreated children were functioning poorly in all three domains. In addition, there was a higher percentage of nonmaltreated (10%) than maltreated (1.5%) children in the high competence group. Finally, one-third of the nonmaltreated children had ever received membership in the high group, whereas slightly under 10% of the maltreated children had done so.

Of concern to us was the consistently low functioning of the least competent group, comprised predominantly of maltreated children. In particular, we feel that the not-insignificant percentage of maltreated children who exhibited no resilient strivings across the course of the three-year longitudinal study is cause for great concern. Self-righting tendencies are characteristics inherent to all living organisms; thus, the consistent absence of such strivings over time in 10% of the maltreated children is extremely aberrant and alarming.

As was the case in the Cicchetti et al. (1993) study, we examined the factors that contributed to the development of resilient functioning in the groups of disadvantaged maltreated and nonmaltreated children. For the maltreated group of children, the major predictors of resilient functioning were ego-overcontrol, ego-resiliency, and positive self-esteem. In contrast, for the nonmaltreated children, positive relationships with their mother and with camp counselors (not measured in our prior study) and ego-resiliency played prominent roles in the prediction of adaptive functioning. Given the high percentage of insecure and disorganized attachments in maltreated youngsters (Cyr, Euser, Bakermans-Kranenburg, & Van IJzendoorn, 2010), it makes sense that relationship factors would be more vital to the attainment of resilience in disadvantaged nonmaltreated children.

Of note, the predictors of resilient adaptation in the maltreated children in this longitudinal study were identical to those obtained in the cross-sectional study conducted by Cicchetti et al. (1993). Personality characteristics and self-system processes were more important in achieving resilient adaptation in maltreated children. Thus self-reliance and self-confidence, in concert with interpersonal reserve, appear to bode well for the development of resilient adaptation in maltreated children. Moreover, these findings highlight the active role that children play in constructing their own outcomes and in influencing their ultimate adaptation. Considering that personality resources and aspects of self-development were major predictors of resilient adaptation in maltreated children, interventions that focus on the enhancement of self-system processes such as autonomy, mastery, and self-determination may be effective in promoting resilience in maltreated children.

A subsequent investigation in our laboratory was designed to gain an understanding of the processes contributing to resilient functioning in maltreated and nonmaltreated Latino children at high risk for adverse outcomes (Flores, Cicchetti, & Rogosch, 2005). We also strived to ascertain whether cultural factors, in concert with child maltreatment, would contribute any unique predictors of resilient functioning.

Maltreated Latino children were found to evince more difficulty across multiple aspects of functioning than their nonmaltreated Latino peers. Even though both maltreated and nonmaltreated Latino children experienced multiple adversities that placed them at high risk for maladaptive functioning (i.e., living in single-parent homes with multiple children, low SES, dependency on the state for financial support, and minority status), maltreated children evinced more difficulties in several important areas of functioning. In accord with prior investigations of resilience in samples of maltreated children that have been composed predominantly of African American and European American children (Cicchetti & Rogosch, 1997; Cicchetti et al., 1993), maltreated Latino children were rated by both peers and counselors as having more difficulties in interpersonal relations (e.g., exhibiting more aggressive behavior and less prosocial behavior and being more likely to be rated as fighters) than were nonmaltreated Latino children, and they also displayed more symptoms of internalizing and externalizing behavior problems than did nonmaltreated Latino children.

Although prior research in our laboratory identified predictors of resilient adaptation in maltreated children, there was a lack of knowledge regarding whether these same factors would be applicable to Latino children. Considering the evidence that relationships are very highly valued in Latino cultures, we sought to determine whether relationship features would predict resilient adaptation for both maltreated and nonmaltreated Latino children.

In agreement with previous investigations of resilience in heterogeneous samples of maltreated children, maltreated Latino children demonstrated a lower level of resilient functioning than did disadvantaged nonmaltreated Latino children. Ego-resiliency and moderate ego-over-control were associated with higher resilient functioning for both mal-treated and nonmaltreated Latino children. In contrast to our prior studies, ego-resiliency and ego-overcontrol did not differentially predict resilience for maltreated and nonmaltreated children. Congruent with the results of our prior studies, however, the predictive impact of relation-ship variables on resilience was more significant for nonmaltreated than maltreated Latino children (Flores et al., 2005).

Furthermore, more maltreated Latino children evinced low levels of resilient self-strivings than did nonmaltreated Latino children (39.5% maltreated vs. 19.3% nonmaltreated), underscoring the fact that in addition to ethnicity, culture, SES, and other high-risk environmental factors, child maltreatment promotes maladaptive functioning in Latino children. Future research with Latino and other ethnic minority popula-tions must be guided by developmental models that are sensitive to the effects of culture on developmental processes and to culture's unique contributions to how successful adaptation is achieved in the face of adversity (see, for example, the paradigm proposed by Garcia-Coll et al., 1996). Furthermore, interventions that strive to promote resilience in maltreated Latino children should emphasize the importance of fostering supportive relationships with adults and peers outside of the immediate family system.

## MULTILEVEL PERSPECTIVES ON PATHWAYS TO RESILIENT FUNCTIONING

Historically, empirical investigations of resilience predominantly have examined a wide range of psychosocial correlates and determi-nants of the phenomenon (Luthar, 2006; Masten & Obradovic, 2006). Over the past decade, several scientists have urged researchers study-ing pathways to resilient functioning to incorporate neurobiological and molecular genetic assessments into their investigations (Charney, 2004; Cicchetti & Curtis, 2006, 2007; Curtis & Cicchetti, 2003). Technological advances in neuroimaging, electroencephalographic recording, hormonal assays, and molecular genetics have made it more feasible to conduct research on the development of resilience from a multilevel perspective.

In recent years, we have completed two multilevel studies on the determinants of resilience in maltreated children. The transactional, organizational perspective provides an orientation that inherently takes into account multiple levels of analysis and allows for combining biological and psychological mechanisms within the same explanatory framework (Cicchetti & Schneider-Rosen, 1986; Egeland et al., 1993). This perspective does not ascribe ascendancy to any level of analysis over another, and it encourages loosening of conceptual boundaries between nature and nurture and biology and psychology (Cicchetti & Cannon, 1999; Gottlieb, 1992; Thelen & Smith, 1998).

In our laboratory we conducted a multilevel investigation of resilience, emotion regulation, and hemispheric electroencephalogram (EEG) asymmetry in a sample of maltreated and nonmaltreated school-age children. We hypothesized that the positive emotionality and increased emotion regulatory ability associated with resilient functioning would be associated with relatively greater left frontal EEG activity (Davidson, 2000). We also investigated the pathways to resilience for maltreated and nonmaltreated children.

We found that EEG asymmetry across central cortical regions distinguished between children with high and low resilient functioning, such that greater left hemisphere activity characterized those who were adapting resiliently based on our competence composite (Curtis & Cicchetti, 2007). In addition, there was a significant interaction between resilience, maltreatment status, and gender for asymmetry at anterior frontal electrodes, where nonmaltreated resilient females had greater left frontal activity compared to more right frontal activity exhibited by resilient maltreated females. Furthermore, we found that a behavioral measure of emotion regulation significantly contributed to the prediction of resilience in maltreated and nonmaltreated children; however, EEG asymmetry in central cortical regions independently predicted resilience only in the maltreated group.

It is important to view EEG asymmetry not as a mechanism in and of itself, but rather, as a marker of some underlying neural process

(Cacioppo, 2004). In the case of resilience, even without knowing the specific mechanisms underlying their association, it is nevertheless reasonable to view EEG asymmetry as an emotion-based protective factor that interacts with several extraorganismic variables to contribute to adaptive functioning in the context of adversity.

The investigation of a neural-level phenomenon such as hemispheric EEG asymmetry in the context of resilient adaptation reminds us that no one single characteristic will be ascendant in the process of resilience over the course of development. Resilience is a dynamic, interactive process between multiple levels across time, none of which holds primary importance at any given moment (Curtis & Cicchetti, 2003). However, viewed across development, the relative importance of various biological systems for promoting resilience may vary within an individual, and the relative importance of biological and psychological processes, although inevitably interrelated, may also vary across development.

In another multilevel investigation conducted in our laboratory, Cicchetti and Rogosch (2007) examined resilient functioning in maltreated and nonmaltreated low-income children in relation to the regulation of two stress-responsive adrenal steroid hormones, cortisol and dehydroepiandrosterone (DHEA), as well as the personality constructs of ego-resiliency and ego-control. The steroid hormones we chose to investigate as potential predictors of resilience are the two primary adrenocortical products of secretory activity of the hypothalamic-pituitary-adrenal (HPA) axis. The capacity of individuals to elevate cortisol levels in response to exposure to acute trauma is important for survival (Gunnar & Vazquez, 2006; Hart, Gunnar, & Cicchetti, 1996). DHEA influences a diverse array of biological actions, including effects on the immune, cardiovascular, endocrine, metabolic, and central nervous systems (Majewska, 1995).

As in our prior studies on the pathways to resilient adaptation, we utilized a composite measure of resilience that included multimethod, multi-informant assessments of competent peer relations, school success, and low levels of internalizing and externalizing symptomatology. We found that ego-resiliency (i.e., the degree of relative flexibility in regulating affect and behavior to meet situational demands) and ego-control (i.e., the ability to monitor and control impulses and regulate affect), and the adrenal steroid hormones associated with stress (i.e., cortisol and DHEA) made independent and noninteractive contributions to resilience. Although operating at different levels of analysis, behavioral/psychological and biological factors each made unique contributions to resilience. For both maltreated and nonmaltreated children, a more reserved, restrained, and rational style of interacting with peers and adults contributed to these children being more attuned to behave in ways that were critical for adapting successfully to their stress-laden environments.

Prolonged stress, as is often the case in child maltreatment, can lead to allostatic load, characterized by cumulative physiological dysregulation across multiple biological systems, through a cascade of causes and sequelae that can change the brain, organ systems, and the neurochemical balance that undergirds cognition, emotion, mood, personality, and behavior (Lupien et al., 2006). In a seminal article, McEwen and Stellar (1993) proffered the concept of allostatic load to refer to the price the body pays for repeatedly using allostatic responses to adapt to stress; allostatic load is thought to occur when the adaptation to stress necessitates that the responses must be maintained over sustained time periods. As described by Lupien and colleagues (2006), allostasis and allostatic load can be conceived as embodying a general biological principle—namely that the systems that help the body adapt to stress and serve a protective function in the short term also may take part in the development of pathophysiological processes when overused or managed ineffectively.

In our study (Cicchetti & Rogosch, 2007), we found that higher morning cortisol levels were related to lower levels of resilient strivings for the nonmaltreated children. High basal cortisol may indicate that nonmaltreated children are experiencing greater stress exposure and, consequently, are constrained in their ability to adapt competently. Within the group of maltreated children, differences in cortisol regulation were found as a function of the subtype(s) of maltreatment experienced. Physically abused children with high morning cortisol had higher resilient functioning than did physically abused children with lower levels of morning cortisol. The positive role of increased cortisol for physically abused children is divergent from the more general pattern of higher cortisol being related to lower resilient functioning, as we discovered in the nonmaltreated and sexually abused children.

Prior research on neuroendocrine regulation has indicated that physically abused children generally exhibit lower levels of morning cortisol secretion (Cicchetti & Rogosch, 2001). It may be that the subgroup of physically abused children who were able to elevate cortisol to cope with the life stressors was demonstrating a greater striving for resilient adaptation. In contrast, the larger subgroup of physically abused children with lower levels of morning cortisol may have developed hypocortisolism over time in response to chronic stress exposure. As a result, for these children there may be a diminished capacity to mobilize the HPA axis to promote positive adaptation under conditions of ongoing stress. Additionally, Cicchetti and Rogosch (2007) found that the very low level of resilience among sexually abused children with high basal cortisol may be a product of their different traumatic experiences and consequences of chronic excessive vigilance and preoccupation, with commensurate HPA axis hyperarousal.

Finally, we also discovered that maltreated children with high resilient functioning exhibited a unique atypical pattern of a relative DHEA diurnal increase (Cicchetti & Rogosch, 2007). Maltreated children who have the capacity to elevate DHEA over the course of the day may be better equipped to cope with the demands of high chronic exposure to stress and to adapt competently. In contrast, the nonmaltreated children who functioned resiliently did not exhibit the pattern of diurnal DHEA increase; instead, they displayed the lowest levels of DHEA across the day.

In addition, recent years have witnessed a renascence of interest in investigating the interaction between genes and environmental pathogens in the development of psychopathology and resilience (Kim-Cohen & Gold, 2009; Rutter, 2006). From a genetic perspective, resilience can be conceptualized as the extent to which individuals at genetic risk for maladaptation are not affected (Luthar et al., 2000;

Rende & Plomin, 1993). Additionally, genetic contributors to resilient adaptation may protect some individuals in families where there is a high genetic loading for developing maladaptation and mental disorder from succumbing to these deleterious outcomes (Cicchetti & Blender, 2004, 2006; Kim-Cohen & Gold, 2009). Moreover, genes are equally likely to protect against environmental insults for some individuals. Thus, it is apparent that genetic influences on maladaptation and psychopathology operate in a probabilistic and not in a deterministic manner.

In our laboratory, we have begun to investigate the contribution of molecular genetic polymorphisms, in interaction with child maltreatment, to resilient adaptation. In gene-environment interaction (GxE), environmental experiences moderate genetic effects (or vice versa) on normal, psychopathological, and resilient developmental outcomes. For example, genetic effects on functioning outcomes may be observed only under certain environmental contexts or in conjunction with different histories of experience; conversely, experience may only relate to outcomes among individuals with specific genetic characteristics (see Belsky & Pluess, this volume).

Maltreated children are at risk for developing a profile of relatively enduring vulnerability factors that place them at high risk for future maladaptation and psychopathology (Cicchetti & Toth, 1995, 2005). The variability exhibited in children's behavioral responses to the environmental hazard of child maltreatment suggests that this heterogeneity may be within the sphere of genetic influence (Moffitt, Caspi, & Rutter, 2006).

Environmental variables must be precisely defined and clearly specified to permit investigators to discover ways in which genes may moderate environmental variables, or vice versa. The advances that have occurred in the measurement and operationalization of child abuse and neglect (Barnett, Manly, & Cicchetti, 1993; Manly, 2005) have enabled developmentalists to investigate the interaction of genes and maltreating environments in the development of psychopathology and resilience. The experience of child maltreatment has proven to be a strong candidate environmental pathogen that has generated some provocative findings that have contributed to engendering interest in research on GxE (Caspi et al., 2002; Caspi et al., 2003; Cicchetti, Rogosch, Sturge-Apple, & Toth, 2009; for meta-analyses, see Kim-Cohen et al., 2006; Taylor & Kim-Cohen, 2007; Uher & McGuffin, 2008, 2009).

The vast majority of GxE studies that have involved child maltreatment as the environmental pathogen have focused on polymorphisms in the serotonergic system, MAOA and 5-HTT (Kim-Cohen & Gold, 2009). Both MAOA and 5-HTT have been implicated in early brain maturation and the regulation of mood, behavior, and responsiveness to stress.

Most epidemiological cohort studies yield relatively small numbers of maltreated individuals. Similarly, many studies that have specifically recruited maltreated children for GxE interaction research have enrolled small sample sizes. GxE findings that are generated in studies of small samples may bring about spurious results. In contrast, in our laboratory, we examined the interaction between a large sample of maltreated children and polymorphisms of the serotonin transporter (5-HTT) and monoamine oxidase A (MAOA) genes in relation to depressive symptomatology (Cicchetti, Rogosch, & Sturge-Apple, 2007). The serotonin transporter gene (5-HTT), one of the major genes involved with serotonergic transmission, has a functional insertion/deletion polymorphism region, the 5-HTT linked promoter region (5-HTTLPR), which has two allelic forms, the long (l) and the short (s) variants. The l allelic variant has been shown to have two to three times the basal level of transcriptional activity than the s variant (Lesch et al., 1996; Lesch & Hiels, 2000). MAOA is responsible for the degradation of a variety of biogenic amines (e. g., the neurotransmitters dopamine, norepinephrine, and serotonin). A polymorphism in the promoter region of the MAOA gene is known to affect gene expression; the length of this polymorphism (i.e., low vs. high number of tandem repeats) determines the efficiency with which MAOA is transcribed and ultimately produced within individuals (Caspi et al., 2002; Kim-Cohen et al., 2006).

Adolescents (M age = 16.7 years) from low socioeconomic backgrounds with a history of child maltreatment or no such history were administered a semi-structured diagnostic interview for mental disorders; moreover, these adolescents provided buccal cells for genetic analysis. Heightened depressive symptoms were found among extensively maltreated youth (i.e., those who experienced sexual, physical, and emotional abuse, and/or neglect) with low MAOA activity. The finding that maltreated children with low MAOA activity have a greater probability of developing high depressive symptoms suggests that low MAOA is not sufficient to render maltreatment-induced changes in neurotransmitter systems inactive. Among comparably maltreated youths with high MAOA activity, self-coping strategies related to lower depressive symptoms. The finding that self-coping strategies and high MAOA activity were related to lower depressive symptoms calls to mind results from several studies on resilience in maltreated children. Specifically, self-reliance and self-determination were found to be predictors of resilient functioning in maltreated children (Cicchetti & Rogosch, 1997). It is conceivable that the maltreated children with positive self-system characteristics who functioned resiliently may also have possessed polymorphic variants of genes (such as high MAOA activity) that protected against maladaptation.

Sexual abuse and the 5-HTT short/short genotype predicted higher depression, anxiety, and somatic symptoms. This GxE interaction was further moderated by MAOA activity level. Specifically, we found that sexually abused adolescents with one or two copies of the 5-HTT short allele had significantly reduced levels of internalizing symptoms if they also had the high activity version of the MAOA gene (Cicchetti et al., 2007). In addition, the finding that some genotypes conferred protection to a subset of highly vulnerable adolescents provides further evidence that both biological and psychological factors contribute to competent functioning in the face of significant adversity.

Presently, we are conducting several GxE and multigenic (i.e., GxGxE) investigations in our laboratory. One of the most exciting projects has been the collection of DNA in a very high percentage of the individuals who have participated in the MPCLS. At the inception of the Minnesota longitudinal study, it was not possible to examine molecular genetic elements. The technology was not available, and the human genome had not yet been genotyped. Currently, Byron Egeland, Alan Sroufe, Andy Collins, and I are integrating the molecular data with the vast body of laboratory, experimental, observational, and interview data from the MPCLS.

Participants in the ongoing MPCLS, all from disadvantaged poverty backgrounds, some of whom had been maltreated during their early years of life, have been followed longitudinally for more than 32 years. To the best of the author's knowledge, no GxE investigations have been conducted with high-risk individuals who have experienced significant adversity, such as child maltreatment or chronic stress, to test the hypothesis that particular genotypes might increase the likelihood of resilient functioning on stage-salient developmental tasks. It is essential that research on resilient functioning move beyond an absence of psychopathology criterion and also incorporate measures of competence that are likely to be influenced by variation in genetic elements (Kim-Cohen & Gold, 2009). Planned GxE analyses of the genetic and longitudinal behavioral data from the MPCLS will contribute to reducing this significant gap in the literature. Similarly, such information could play a vital role in developing resilience-promoting interventions that target protective and vulnerability forces at multiple levels of influence.

In our laboratory, we also have begun to decipher co-actions across multiple levels of analysis through incorporating genetic and multiple physiological measures in our multilevel research on pathways to resilience in abused and neglected children. For example, in a longitudinal investigation that is currently underway in our laboratory, we are employing a multiple-levels-of-analysis approach to examining the course of trauma-related psychopathology in maltreated children, as well as the multilevel processes that contribute to resilient outcomes. In addition to genotyping relevant candidate genes, we have incorporated multiple measures of neurophysiological (e.g., EEG hemispheric activation asymmetry; event-related potential responses to classes of emotion stimuli; and emotion-potentiated startle), hormonal, neurocognitive, and behavioral functioning.

The field can no longer afford to continue the artificial distinction among genetics, neurobiology, and behavior in research on the determinants of resilience. The pathways to resilience are influenced, in part, by a complex matrix of the individual's level of biological and psychological organization, experience, social context, timing of adverse events and experiences, and developmental history (Sroufe, Egeland, & Kreutzer, 1990). The incorporation of a multilevel perspective into research on resilience still requires adherence to a dynamic, transactional view that acknowledges the importance of context, just as Egeland and Sroufe espoused in 1993 (Egeland et al., 1993). Biological and psychological domains are both essential to include in basic research on resilience and in resilience-promoting interventions. If we are to grasp the true complexity of the construct of resilience, then we must investigate it with a commensurate level of complexity (Cicchetti & Blender, 2006).

## IMPLICATIONS FOR RESILIENCE-PROMOTING INTERVENTIONS

Luthar and Cicchetti (2000) stated that research on the pathways to resilience has considerable potential to guide the development of interventions for facilitating the promotion of resilient functioning in children exposed to significant adversity. Curtis and Cicchetti (2003) asserted that it is now essential for researchers to adopt a multiple-levels-of-analysis perspective in research evaluations aimed at assessing the efficacy of resilience-promoting interventions.

The examination of the biological and psychological changes that occur as a function of resilience-promoting interventions, in concert with the conduct of basic studies of the biological and psychological processes contributing to resilient functioning, will greatly enhance our present knowledge base on the development of resilience and on the recovery of positive function (Curtis & Cicchetti, 2003). Efficacious interventions should change both behavior and physiology through producing alterations in gene expression (transcription) that produce new structural changes in the brain (Kandel, 1999).

At Mt. Hope Family Center, several randomized control trial (RCT) interventions aimed at fostering resilient adaptation in maltreated children have been conducted. The translation of basic research knowledge on the developmental sequelae of child maltreatment and on pathways to resilient functioning in abused and neglected children underscores the importance of broadening such efforts in the future.

Cicchetti, Rogosch, and Toth (2006) conducted an RCT that demonstrated that Child-Parent Psychotherapy (CPP), an attachment-theory-informed intervention, and a didactic parenting intervention that also focused on providing increased supports to mothers, each were effective in altering insecure and disorganized attachments in maltreated infants. At the conclusion of the two 12-month interventions, maltreated infants changed from nearly 0% secure and 90% disorganized attachment organizations at baseline to approximately 60% security and 54% security, respectively, for the CPP and parenting interventions. Likewise, the percentage of disorganized attachment significantly decreased from baseline to post-intervention in the CPP and parenting groups. In contrast, maltreated infants receiving the community standard intervention exhibited stable insecure and disorganized attachments. Notably, the rate of attachment security did not differ among the two intervention groups and a comparison group of nonmaltreated infants (Cicchetti et al., 2006).

Maltreated infants receiving the CPP and parenting interventions also exhibited basal cortisol levels that did not differ from nonmaltreated children. At the 12-month baseline (preintervention), cortisol reactivity among infants in the intervention groups, infants receiving the community standard (i.e., what services are typically provided by human services workers), and nonmaltreated comparisons was the same. These results attest to the success of the randomization process. At the end of the intervention (i.e., at 24 months) and again at the one-year follow-up (i.e., at 36 months), the cortisol reactivity of infants in the intervention groups did not differ from the nonmaltreated comparisons. In contrast, the infants in the community standard group displayed low levels of cortisol, suggestive of hypocortisolism brought about by maltreatment experiences causing prolonged allostatic load (see Cicchetti & Rogosch, 2001; Cicchetti, Rogosch, Toth, & Sturge-Apple, in preparation).

Additionally, we plan to genotype DNA obtained from participants in the two intervention groups and those in the community standard group to ascertain if infants with particular genotypes were more likely than those with other genotypes to be responsive to the interventions.

Included among the genes that we will examine are those that have been associated with disorganized attachment (i.e., DRD4 7 repeat; –521 C/T SNP) and stress regulation (GR; CRHR1).

In another RCT conducted in our laboratory, maltreated preschoolers receiving CPP displayed increases in positive self-representations from pre- (age 3) to post- (age 4) intervention. At post-intervention their representations of self and others in the CPP intervention did not differ from those of preschoolers in the nonmaltreated group. However, neither preschoolers in the parenting intervention nor those in the community standard group exhibited these positive changes in representations (Toth, Maughan, Manly, Spagnola, & Cicchetti, 2002). These intervention results point to the potential malleability of these representations of self and of self in relation to others when an intervention derived from attachment theory is provided. Rather than assuming that sensitive periods exist during infancy and that the attachment relationship becomes less amenable to change over the course of development, our findings suggest that, at least during the preschool years, the internalized mother-child relationship continues to evolve and remains open to reorganizations.

Given that prior research in our laboratory has discovered that self-determination, positive self-esteem, and other self-system processes are predictors of resilient functioning in maltreated children (Cicchetti & Rogosch, 1997, 2007), the improvements in self-representations found in the children in the CPP preschool interventions are a positive sign that resilient self-strivings may have been initiated in these youngsters. If so, then the developments that occurred in self-system processes may serve a beneficial protective function in future years. Moreover, the positive changes in the maltreated preschoolers who received the CPP intervention may also bode well for these children's future relationships with peers and other relationship partners (Sroufe, 1989, 1990; Sroufe et al., 2005).

The finding that developmental plasticity is possible during infancy and that attachment insecurity, including its most disorganized form, and negative representations of self and others, are modifiable in extremely dysfunctional mother-child dyads offers significant hope for thousands of maltreated children and their families. Through fostering these positive developments in both attachment organization and representational models of the self and of attachment figures, costlier interventions such as foster care placement, special education services, residential treatment, and incarceration can be averted.

There is growing evidence that successful intervention modifies not only maladaptive behavior but also the physiological correlates of behavior (Cicchetti & Gunnar, 2008; Kandel, 1979, 1998, 1999). The fact that interventions are able to bring about beneficial effects beyond the early years of life suggests that there is a psychobiology and a neuropsychology of hope and optimism for maltreated children that can minimize or eradicate the adverse effects of their histories. Furthermore, just as knowledge of genetic predisposition to medical illness can result in the modification of behavior to minimize the expression of genes associated with medical illness, so, too, might knowledge of the effect of maltreatment on methylation and gene expression and a related genetic vulnerability to mental illness help individuals alter their life course to inhibit the expression of genes that are associated with maladaptation and psychopathology. Moreover, it is conceivable that successful interventions may activate genes that protect maltreated individuals from pathological outcomes and promote resilient functioning.

A crucial issue that can be informed by research on neuropsychological and psychophysiological functioning in maltreated children is determining whether the timing of interventions matters (Cicchetti, Rogosch, Gunnar, & Toth, 2010). A major implication of a dynamic developmental systems approach is that the implementation of intervention following the experience of trauma should ameliorate the intensity and severity of the response to the trauma, as well as the developmental course (Toth & Cicchetti, 1993, 1999). Such interventions that are closely timed to trauma, maladaptation, and disorder onset also should decrease the probability of developing, in a use-dependent fashion, sensitized neural systems that may cascade across development (Cicchetti, 2002; Rogosch, Oshri, & Cicchetti, 2010). This is not to suggest that if intervention is *not* time-tied to the trauma, then it will ultimately fail. Rather, one may need to ascertain alternative treatment methods that will address the sequelae of the maltreatment experience.

Moreover, if a long-term course of trauma has occurred and a significant period has passed, then it may be counterproductive to continue to revisit the trauma.

## CONCLUSION

Although groups of maltreated children differ from groups of nonmaltreated children on most of the neurobiological and psychological domains investigated thus far, not all individual maltreated children are affected by their experiences in the same manner. Moreover, the neurobiological and psychological functioning of some maltreated children appears not to be negatively affected, or it may reflect an enhanced neural plasticity in resilient individuals (Cicchetti & Curtis, 2006). We do not know whether the biological difficulties exhibited by many maltreated children are permanent or irreversible, or, if reversible, at what point in ontogeny or to what degree.

Additionally, we do not possess the knowledge regarding whether some to-be-identified neural systems may be more plastic than other neural systems that may be more refractory to change or have a more time-limited window when neural plasticity can occur. Thus, a person-oriented approach (Bergman & Magnusson, 1997; von Eye & Bergman, 2003), in which multiple neurobiological and psychological systems are studied within individuals over developmental time, should be implemented in future research on the effects of maltreatment on biological and psychological processes. In this manner, we can acquire vital information on how the neurobiological systems of maltreated children develop at different periods, as well as when such developing neural systems may be most vulnerable or resilient in different profiles of individuals who share similar aspects of neurobiological and psychological functioning and who may range from none or minimal damage to major neurobiological and psychological dysfunction.

Even in instances of long-term damage, the neurobiological and psychological consequences of maltreatment may not prove to be irreversible. Because postnatal brain structuration and neural patterning are thought to occur, in part, through interactions and transactions of the child with his or her environment (Cicchetti, 2002), changes in the internal and external environment may lead to improvement in the ability of the individual to grapple with developmental challenges. Thus, although genetic and historical developmental factors canalize and constrain the adaptive process to some degree (Sroufe et al., 1992), it is conceivable that behavioral and neural plasticity are possible throughout the life course as a result of adaptive neural and psychological self-organization (Cicchetti, 2002; Cicchetti & Tucker, 1994; Curtis & Cicchetti, 2003).

Clearly, this is an exciting period for research on the pathways to resilient functioning in maltreated children. Advances in genomics, epigenetics, brain imaging, and hormonal and immunological assay techniques will help propel increased knowledge about the developmental processes leading to resilience in maltreated children. Such understanding has the potential for the development of novel, perhaps even individualized, resilience-promoting interventions for maltreated children who are not developing well.

Byron Egeland and Alan Sroufe deserve credit for spearheading the initial longitudinal work in this arena for maltreated children. Researchers in developmental psychology, developmental psychopathology, and child maltreatment owe a great debt to these scholars for their pioneering theoretical and empirical work and for their generous spirit in sharing their ideas with the field so openly.

## REFERENCES

Aber, J. L., & Cicchetti, D. (1984). Socioemotional development in maltreated children: An empirical and theoretical analysis. In H. E. Fitzgerald, B. Lester, & M. Yogman (Eds.), *Theory and research in behavioral pediatrics* (Vol. 2, pp. 147–205). New York, NY: Plenum Press.

Barnett, D., Manly, J. T., & Cicchetti, D. (1993). Defining child maltreatment: The interface between policy and research. In D. Cicchetti & S. L. Toth (Eds.), *Child abuse, child development, and social policy* (pp. 7–74). Norwood, NJ: Ablex.

Bergman, L. R., & Magnusson, D. (1997). A person-oriented approach in research on developmental psychopathology. *Development and Psychopathology, 9,* 291–319.

Block, J. H., & Block, J. (1980). The role of ego-control and ego resiliency in the organization of behavior. In W. A. Collins (Ed.), *Minnesota Symposium on Child Psychology* (Vol. 13, pp. 39–101). Hillsdale, NJ: Erlbaum.

Cacioppo, J. T. (2004). Feelings and emotions: roles for electrophysiological markers. *Biological Psychology, 67,* 235–243.

Caspi, A., McClay, J., Moffitt, T., Mill, J., Martin, J., Craig, I. W., et al. (2002). Role of genotype in the cycle of violence in maltreated children. *Science, 297,* 851–854.

Caspi, A., Sugden, K., Moffitt, T. E., Taylor, A., Craig, I. W., Harrington, H. L., . . . & Poulton, R. (2003). Influence of life stress on depression: Moderation by a polymorphism in the 5-HTT gene. *Science, 301,* 386–389.

Charney, D. (2004). Psychobiological mechanisms of resilience and vulnerability: Implications for successful adaptation to extreme stress. *American Journal of Psychiatry, 161,* 195–216.

Cicchetti, D. (Ed.). (1989). *Rochester symposium on developmental psychopathology: The emergence of a discipline* (Vol. 1). Hillsdale, NJ: Erlbaum.

Cicchetti, D. (1990). A historical perspective on the discipline of developmental psychopathology. In J. Rolf, A. Masten, D. Cicchetti, K. Nuechterlein, & S. Weintraub (Eds.), *Risk and protective factors in the development of psychopathology* (pp. 2–28). New York, NY: Cambridge University Press.

Cicchetti, D. (2002). How a child builds a brain: Insights from normality and psychopathology. In W. Hartup & R. Weinberg (Eds.), *Minnesota Symposia on Child Psychology: Child psychology in retrospect and prospect* (Vol. 32, pp. 23–71). Mahwah, NJ: Erlbaum.

Cicchetti, D., & Blender, J. A. (2004). A multiple-levels-of-analysis approach to the study of developmental processes in maltreated children. *Proceedings of the National Academy of Sciences, 101*(50), 17325–17326.

Cicchetti, D., & Blender, J. A. (2006). A multiple-levels-of-analysis perspective on resilience: Implications for the developing brain, neural plasticity, and preventive interventions. *Annals of the New York Academy of Sciences, 1094,* 248–258.

Cicchetti, D., & Cannon, T. D. (1999). Neurodevelopmental processes in the ontogenesis and epigenesis of psychopathology. *Development and Psychopathology, 11,* 375–393.

Cicchetti, D., & Carlson, V. (Eds.). (1989). *Child maltreatment: Theory and research on the causes and consequences of child abuse and neglect.* New York, NY: Cambridge University Press.

Cicchetti, D., & Curtis, W. J. (2006). The developing brain and neural plasticity: Implications for normality, psychopathology, and resilience. In D. Cicchetti & D. Cohen (Eds.), *Developmental psychopathology: Developmental neuroscience* (Vol. 2, 2nd ed., pp. 1–64). Hoboken, NJ: Wiley.

Cicchetti, D., & Curtis, W. J. (Eds.). (2007). A multi-level approach to resilience [Special Issue]. *Development and Psychopathology, 19*, 627–955.

Cicchetti, D., & Gunnar, M. R. (2008). Integrating biological processes into the design and evaluation of preventive interventions. *Development and Psychopathology, 20*, 737–743.

Cicchetti, D., & Lynch, M. (1993). Toward an ecological/transactional model of community violence and child maltreatment: Consequences for children's development. *Psychiatry, 56*, 96–118.

Cicchetti, D., & Lynch, M. (1995). Failures in the expectable environment and their impact on individual development: The case of child maltreatment. In D. Cicchetti & D. J. Cohen (Eds.), *Developmental psychopathology: Risk, disorder, and adaptation* (Vol. 2, pp. 32–71). New York, NY: Wiley.

Cicchetti, D., & Rizley, R. (1981). Developmental perspectives on the etiology, intergenerational transmission and sequelae of child maltreatment. *New Directions for Child Development, 11*, 31–55.

Cicchetti, D., & Rogosch, F. A. (1996). Equifinality and multifinality in developmental psychopathology. *Development and Psychopathology, 8*, 597–600.

Cicchetti, D., & Rogosch, F. A. (1997). The role of self-organization in the promotion of resilience in maltreated children. *Development and Psychopathology, 9*, 799–817.

Cicchetti, D., & Rogosch, F. A. (2001). The impact of child maltreatment and psychopathology upon neuroendocrine functioning. *Development and Psychopathology, 13*, 783–804.

Cicchetti, D., & Rogosch, F. A. (2007). Personality, adrenal steroid hormones, and resilience in maltreated children: A multi-level perspective. *Development and Psychopathology, 19*(3), 787–809.

Cicchetti, D., Rogosch, F. A., Gunnar, M. R., & Toth, S. L. (2010). The differential impacts of early abuse on internalizing problems and diurnal cortisol activity in school-aged children. *Child Development, 81*, 252–269.

Cicchetti, D., Rogosch, F. A., Lynch, M., & Holt, K. (1993). Resilience in maltreated children: Processes leading to adaptive outcome. *Development and Psychopathology, 5*, 629–647.

Cicchetti, D., Rogosch, F. A., & Sturge-Apple, M. L. (2007). Interactions of child maltreatment and 5-HTT and monoamine oxidase A polymorphisms:

Depressive symptomatology among adolescents from low-socioeconomic status backgrounds. *Development and Psychopathology, 19*(4), 1161–1180.

Cicchetti, D., Rogosch, F. A., Sturge-Apple, M., & Toth, S. L. (2009). Interaction of child maltreatment and 5-HTT polymorphisms: Suicidal ideation among children from low SES backgrounds. *Journal of Pediatric Psychology, 35*, 536–546.

Cicchetti, D., Rogosch, F. A., & Toth, S. L. (2006). Fostering secure attachment in infants in maltreating families through preventive interventions. *Development and Psychopathology, 18*(3), 623–650.

Cicchetti, D., Rogosch, F. A., Toth, S. L., & Sturge-Apple, M. (in preparation). Longitudinal effects of early intervention on basal cortisol in maltreated infants and toddlers.

Cicchetti, D., & Schneider-Rosen, K. (1986). An organizational approach to childhood depression. In M. Rutter, C. Izard, & P. Read (Eds.), *Depression in young people, clinical and developmental perspectives* (pp. 71–134). New York, NY: Guilford Press.

Cicchetti, D., & Sroufe, L. A. (1978). An organizational view of affect: Illustration from the study of Down's syndrome infants. In M. Lewis & L. Rosenblum (Eds.), *The development of affect* (pp. 309–350). New York, NY: Plenum Press.

Cicchetti, D., & Toth, S. L. (1995). A developmental psychopathology perspective on child abuse and neglect. *Journal of the American Academy of Child and Adolescent Psychiatry, 34*, 541–565.

Cicchetti, D., & Toth, S. L. (2005). Child maltreatment. *Annual Review of Clinical Psychology, 1*, 409–438.

Cicchetti, D., & Toth, S. L. (2006). A developmental psychopathology perspective on preventive interventions with high risk children and families. In A. Renninger and I. Sigel (Eds.), *Handbook of child psychology* (6th ed., pp. 497–547). Hoboken, NJ: Wiley.

Cicchetti, D., Toth, S. L., & Bush, M. (1988). Developmental psychopathology and incompetence in childhood: Suggestions for intervention. In B. Lahey & A. Kazdin (Eds.), *Advances in clinical child psychology* (pp. 1–71). New York, NY: Plenum Press.

Cicchetti, D., & Tucker, D. (1994). Development and self-regulatory structures of the mind. *Development and Psychopathology, 6*, 533–549.

Cicchetti, D., & Valentino, K. (2006). An ecological transactional perspective on child maltreatment: Failure of the average expectable environment and its influence upon child development. In D. Cicchetti & D. J. Cohen (Eds.), *Developmental psychopathology* (Vol. 3, 2nd ed., pp. 129–201). Hoboken, NJ: Wiley.

Curtis, W. J., & Cicchetti, D. (2003). Moving research on resilience into the 21st century: Theoretical and methodological considerations in examining the biological contributors to resilience. *Development and Psychopathology, 15*, 773–810.

Curtis, W. J., & Cicchetti, D. (2007). Emotion and resilience: A multilevel investigation of hemispheric electroencephalogram activity and emotion regulation in maltreated and nonmaltreated children. *Development and Psychopathology, 19*, 811–840.

Cyr, C., Euser, E. M., Bakermans-Kranenburg, M. J., & Van Ijzendoorn, M. H. (2010). Attachment security and disorganization in maltreating and high-risk families: A series of meta-analyses. *Development and Psychopathology, 22*, 87–108.

Davidson, R. J. (2000). Affective style, psychopathology, and resilience: Brain mechanisms and plasticity. *American Psychologist, 55*, 1196–1214.

DeBellis, M. D. (2001). Developmental traumatology: The psychobiological development of maltreated children and its implications for research, treatment, and policy. *Development and Psychopathology, 13*, 539–564.

DeBellis, M. D. (2005). The psychobiology of neglect. *Child Maltreatment, 10*, 150–172.

Egeland, B. (1997). Mediators of the effects of child maltreatment on developmental adaptation in adolescence. In D. Cicchetti & S. L. Toth (Eds.), *Rochester Symposium on Developmental Psychopathology, Vol. VIII: The effects of trauma on the developmental process* (pp. 403–434). Rochester, NY: University Press.

Egeland, B. (2007). Understanding developmental process and mechanisms of resilience and psychopathology: Implications for policy and practice. In A. Masten (Vol. Ed.), *The Minnesota Symposium on Child Psychology, Vol. 34: Multilevel dynamics in developmental psychopathology: Pathways to the future.* (pp. 83–118). Hillside, NJ: Erlbaum.

Egeland, B., Carlson, E. A., & Sroufe, L. A. (1993). Resilience as process. *Development and Psychopathology, 5*, 517–528.

Egeland, B., & Sroufe, L. A. (1981). Developmental sequelae of maltreatment in infancy. *New Directions for Child Development, 11*, 77–92.

Farber, E., & Egeland, B. (1987). Abused children: Can they be invulnerable? In J. Anthony & B. Cohler (Eds.), *The invulnerable child* (pp. 253–288). New York, NY: Guilford Press.

Flores, E., Cicchetti, D., & Rogosch, F.A. (2005). Predictors of resilience in maltreated and nonmaltreated Latino children. *Developmental Psychology, 41*(2), 338–351.

Fox, N. A., & Rutter, M. (2010). Introduction to the special section on the effects of early experience on development. *Child Development, 81*, 23–27.

Garcia-Coll, C., Crnic, K., Lamberty, G., Wasik, B., Jenkins, R., Garcia, H., & McAdoo, H. (1996). An integrative model for the study of developmental competencies in minority children. *Child Development, 67*, 1891–1914.

Garmezy, N. (1971). Vulnerability research and the issue of primary prevention. *American Journal of Orthopsychiatry, 41*, 101–116.

Garmezy, N. (1974). The study of competence in children at risk for severe psychopathology. In E. J. Anthony & C. Koupernik (Eds.), *The child in his family: Children at psychiatric risk* (Vol. 3, pp. 77–97). New York, NY: Wiley.

Gottlieb, G. (1992). *Individual development and evolution: The genesis of novel behavior.* New York, NY: Oxford University Press.

Gottlieb, G. (2007). Probabilistic epigenesis. *Developmental Science, 10*, 1–11.

Gunnar, M. R., & Vazquez, D. (2006). Stress neurobiology and developmental psychopathology. In D. Cicchetti & D. Cohen (Eds.), *Developmental psychopathology* (Vol. 2, 2nd ed., pp. 533–577). Hoboken, NJ: Wiley.

Hart, J., Gunnar, M., & Cicchetti, D. (1996). Altered neuroendocrine activity in maltreated children related to symptoms of depression. *Development and Psychopathology, 8*, 201–214.

Herrenkohl, E. C., Herrenkohl, R. C., & Egolf, M. (1994). Resilient early school-age children from maltreating homes: Outcomes in late adolescence. *American Journal of Orthopsychiatry, 67*(3), 422–432.

Kandel, E. R. (1979). Psychotherapy and the single synapse. *The New England Journal of Medicine, 301*, 1028–1037.

Kandel, E. R. (1998). A new intellectual framework for psychiatry. *American Journal of Psychiatry, 155*, 475–469.

Kandel, E. R. (1999). Biology and the future of psychoanalysis: A new intellectual framework for psychiatry revisited. *American Journal of Psychiatry, 156*, 505–524.

Kaplan, B. (1967). Meditations on genesis. *Human Development, 10*, 65–87.

Kim-Cohen, J., Caspi, A., Taylor, A., Williams, B., Newcombe, R., Craig, I., & Moffitt, T. E. (2006). MAOA, maltreatment, and gene-environment interaction predicting children's mental health: New evidence and a meta-analysis. *Molecular Psychiatry, 11*, 903–913.

Kim-Cohen, J., & Gold, A. L. (2009). Measured gene-environment interactions and mechanisms promoting resilient development. *Current Directions in Psychological Science, 18*, 138–142.

Lesch, K. P., Bengel, D., Hiels, A., Sabol, S. Z., Greenberg, B. D., Petri, S., et al. (1996). Association of anxiety-related traits with a polymorphism in the serotonin transporter gene regulatory region. *Science, 274,* 1527–1531.

Lesch, K. P., & Hiels, A. (2000). Serotonergic gene transcription control regions: Targets for antidepressant drug development. *International Journal of Neuropsychopharmacology, 3,* 67–79.

Lupien, S. J., Ouellet-Morin, I., Hupbach, A., Tu, M. T., Buss, C., & Walker, D. (2006). Beyond the stress concept: Allostatic load—A developmental biological and cognitive perspective. In D. Cicchetti & D. Cohen (Eds.), *Developmental psychopathology* (Vol. 2, 2nd ed., pp. 578–628). Hoboken, NJ: Wiley.

Luthar, S. S. (2006). Resilience in development: A synthesis of research across five decades. In D. Cicchetti & D. Cohen (Eds.), *Developmental psychopathology* (Vol. 3, 2nd ed., pp. 739–795). Hoboken, NJ: Wiley.

Luthar, S. S., & Cicchetti, D. (2000). The construct of resilience: Implications for intervention and social policy. *Development and Psychopathology, 12,* 857–885.

Luthar, S. S., Cicchetti, D., & Becker, B. (2000). The construct of resilience: A critical evaluation and guidelines for future work. *Child Development, 71,* 543–562.

Majewska, M. (1995). Neuronal actions of dehydroepiandrosterone. In S. Bellino, R. Datynes, P. Hornsby, D. Lavrin, & J. Nestler (Eds.), *Dehydroepiandrosterone (DHEA) and aging* (pp. 111–120). New York, NY: New York Academy of Sciences.

Manly, J. T. (2005). Advances in research definitions of child maltreatment. *Child Abuse & Neglect, 29*(5), 425–439.

Masten, A. S. (1989). Resilience in development: Implications of the study of successful adaptation for developmental psychopathology. In D. Cicchetti (Ed.), *Rochester Symposium on Developmental Psychopathology: The emergence of a discipline* (pp. 261–294). Hillsdale, NJ: Erlbaum.

Masten, A. S. (2001). Ordinary magic: Resilience processes in development. *American Psychologist, 56,* 227–238.

Masten, A. S. (Ed.). (2007). *Multilevel dynamics in developmental psychopathology: Pathways to the future.* Mahwah, NJ: Erlbaum.

Masten, A. S., Best, K., & Garmezy, N. (1990). Resilience and development: Contributions from the study of children who overcome adversity. *Development and Psychopathology, 2,* 425–444.

Masten, A. S., & Obradovic, J. (2006). Competence and resilience in development. *Annals of the New York Academy of Sciences, 1094,* 13–27.

McEwen, B. S., & Stellar, E. (1993). Stress and the individual mechanisms leading to disease. *Archives of Internal Medicine, 153*, 2093–2101.

Moffitt, T. E., Caspi, A., & Rutter, M. (2006). Measured gene-environment interactions in psychopathology: Concepts, research strategies, and implications for research, intervention, and public understanding of genetics. *Perspectives on Psychological Science, 1*, 5–27.

Pianta, R. C., Egeland, B., & Erickson, M. F. (1989). The antecedents of child maltreatment: The results of the Mother-Child Interaction Research Project. In D. Cicchetti & V. Carlson (Eds.), *Child maltreatment: Theory and research on the causes and consequences of child abuse and neglect* (pp. 203–253). Cambridge, MA: Harvard University Press.

Rende, R., & Plomin, R. (1993). Families at risk for psychopathology: Who becomes affected and why? *Development and Psychopathology, 5*, 529–540.

Rogosch, F. A., Oshri, A., & Cicchetti, D. (2010). From child maltreatment to adolescent cannabis abuse and dependence: A developmental cascade model. *Development and Psychopathology, 22*, 883–898.

Rutter, M. (2006). *Genes and behavior: Nature–nurture interplay explained.* Malden, MA: Blackwell.

Sameroff, A. J., & Chandler, M. J. (1975). Reproductive risk and the continuum of caretaking casualty. In F. D. Horowitz (Ed.), *Review of child development research* (pp. 187–244). Chicago, IL: University of Chicago Press.

Sroufe, L. A. (1979). The coherence of individual development. *American Psychologist, 34*, 834–841.

Sroufe, L. A. (1989). Pathways to adaptation and maladaptation: Psychopathology as developmental deviation. In D. Cicchetti (Ed.), *Rochester Symposium on Developmental Psychopathology: The emergence of a discipline* (pp. 13–40). Hillsdale, NJ: Erlbaum.

Sroufe, L. A. (1990). An organizational perspective on the self. In D. Cicchetti & M. Beeghly (Eds.), *The self in transition: Infancy to childhood* (pp. 281–307). Chicago, IL: University of Chicago Press.

Sroufe, L. A. (1996). *Emotional development: The organization of emotional life in the early years.* New York, NY: Cambridge University Press.

Sroufe, L. A., Carlson, E. A., Levy, A. K., & Egeland, B. (1999). Implications of attachment theory for developmental psychopathology. *Development and Psychopathology, 11*, 1–13.

Sroufe, L. A., Egeland, B., Carlson, E., & Collins, W. A. (2005). *The development of the person: The Minnesota study of risk and adaptation from birth to adulthood.* New York, NY: Guilford Press.

Sroufe, L. A., Egeland, B., & Kreutzer, T. (1990). The fate of early experience following developmental change: Longitudinal approaches to individual adaptation in childhood. *Child Development, 61,* 1363–1373.

Sroufe, L. A., & Fleeson, J. (1986). Attachment and the construction of relationships. In W. Hartup & Z. Rubin (Eds.), *Relationships and development* (pp. 51–76). Hillsdale, NJ: Erlbaum.

Sroufe, L. A., & Fleeson, J. (1988). The coherence of family relationships. In R. A. Hinde & J. Stevenson-Hinde (Eds.), *Relationships within families: Mutual influences* (pp. 27–47). Oxford, England: Oxford University Press.

Sroufe, L. A., & Waters, E. (1976). The ontogenesis of smiling and laughter: A perspective on the organization of development in infancy. *Psychological Review, 83,* 173–189.

Tarullo, A. R., & Gunnar, M. R. (2006). Child maltreatment and the developing HPA axis. *Hormones and Behavior, 50,* 632–639.

Taylor, A., & Kim-Cohen, J. (2007). Meta-analysis of gene-environment interactions in developmental psychopathology. *Development and Psychopathology, 19,* 1029–1037.

Thelen, E., & Smith, L. B. (1998). Dynamic systems theories. In W. Damon & R. Lerner (Eds.), *Handbook of child psychology, Vol. 1: Theoretical models of human development* (pp. 563–634). New York, NY: Wiley.

Toth, S. L., & Cicchetti, D. (1993). Child maltreatment: Where do we go from here in our treatment of victims? In D. Cicchetti & S. L. Toth (Eds.), *Child abuse, child development, and social policy* (pp. 399–438). Norwood, NJ: Ablex.

Toth, S. L., & Cicchetti, D. (1999). Developmental psychopathology and child psychotherapy. In S. Russ & T. Ollendick (Eds.), *Handbook of psychotherapies with children and families* (pp. 15–44). New York, NY: Plenum Press.

Toth, S. L., Maughan, A., Manly, J. T., Spagnola, M., & Cicchetti, D. (2002). The relative efficacy of two interventions in altering maltreated preschool children's representational models: Implications for attachment theory. *Development and Psychopathology, 14,* 877–908.

Trickett, P. K., & McBride-Chang, C. (1995). The developmental impact of different types of child abuse and neglect. *Developmental Review, 15,* 311–337.

von Eye, A., & Bergman, L. R. (2003). Research strategies in developmental psychopathology: Dimensional identity and the person-oriented approach. *Development and Psychopathology, 15,* 553–580.

Uher, R., & McGuffin, P. (2008). The moderation by the serotonin transporter gene of environmental adversity in the aetiology of mental illness: Review and methodological analysis. *Molecular Psychiatry, 13,* 131–146.

Uher, R., & McGuffin, P. (2009). The moderation by the serotonin transporter gene of environmental adversity in the etiology of depression: 2009 update. *Molecular Psychiatry, 15,* 18–22.

Waddington, C. H. (1957). *The strategy of genes.* London, England: Allen & Unwin.

Walsh, W. A., Dawson, J., & Mattingly, M. J. (2010). How are we measuring resilience following childhood maltreatment? Is the research adequate and consistent? What is the impact on research, practice, and policy? *Trauma, Violence & Abuse, 11,* 27–41.

Werner, H. (1948). *Comparative psychology of mental development.* New York, NY: International Universities Press.

Werner, H., & Kaplan, B. (1963). *Symbol formation.* New York: Wiley.

# Author Index

461

# Subject Index

DATE DUE